Adam Smith's Pluralism

Adam Smith's Pluralism

Rationality, Education, and the Moral Sentiments

Jack Russell Weinstein

Yale

UNIVERSITY

PRESS

New Haven & London

Published with assistance from the foundation established in memory of
Amasa Stone Mather of the Class of 1907, Yale College.

Yale University Press books may be purchased in quantity for educational, business,
or promotional use. For information, please e-mail sales.press@yale.edu (U.S. office)
or sales@yaleup.co.uk (U.K. office).

Set in Electra type by IDS Infotech Ltd., Chandigarh, India.
Printed in the United States of America.

Library of Congress Cataloging-in-Publication Data
Weinstein, Jack Russell.
Adam Smith's pluralism : rationality, education, and the moral
sentiments / Jack Russell Weinstein.
pages   cm
Includes bibliographical references and index.
ISBN 978-0-300-16253-0 (hardcover : alk. paper)
1. Smith, Adam, 1723–1790. 2. Pluralism. 3. Education—Philosophy. 4. Ethics.
5. Smith, Adam, 1723–1790. The theory of moral sentiments. I. Title.
B1545.Z7W45 2013
192—dc23   2013003570

A catalogue record for this book is available from the British Library.

This paper meets the requirements of ANSI/NISO Z39.48–1992
(Permanence of Paper).

10 9 8 7 6 5 4 3 2 1

For Kim, for . . . everything

so many selves(so many fiends and gods
each greedier than every)is a man
(so easily one in another hides;
yet man can, being all, escape from none)

so huge a tumult is the simplest wish:
so pitiless a massacre the hope
most innocent(so deep's the mind of flesh
and so awake what waking calls asleep)

so never is most lonely man alone
(his briefest breathing lives some planet's year,
his longest life's a heartbeat of some sun;
his least unmotion roams the youngest star)

—how should a fool that calls him 'I' presume
to comprehend not numerable whom?

—e e cummings

Men of principle? Stalin, Hitler, these are men of principle. Give me a man
who wants a little sex and a little money, and we'll be alright.

—Stanley Helms Kelley

Contents

ACKNOWLEDGMENTS

This book took either ten or twenty years to write, depending on how one chooses to count it. In essence, it started with my very first graduate essay: a ten-page exploration written for Charles L. Griswold on a Commodore 128 computer and made physical by a dot-matrix printer with perforated paper. I have been revising that paper, "Can Men Teach Women's Studies?: A Study of Adam Smith's Sympathy," ever since. It became a chapter in my dissertation, a host of conference presentations, the core of my first book, *On Adam Smith*, an article in *Economics and Philosophy*, and finally this book. Needless to say, the piece is now a lot longer than I originally anticipated, but I think I am finally finished.

This project has taken me far from that first seminar. Its final outline took shape not in the hallowed halls of Boston University but during a conversation I had seventeen years later on a Straßenbahn in Vienna, Austria. Yale University Press had offered me a contract, but one of the anonymous reviewers astutely requested a chapter on the normative value of history. I mentioned this to my father (a philosopher as well), who responded, "So, you're going to write on Foucault?" I reflexively said no. I later mentioned it to someone else who asked the same question in exactly the same way. (Sadly, I cannot remember who this was.) I replied in the negative again. But then, while traversing the *Ringstraßsse*, Amelie Okseberg Rorty asked me the same question in the same tone of voice, and I found myself saying I would. If Amelie tells you to do something, you do it.

From years of conversation and public debate with James Otteson, to a discussion with Ian Ross at a metro station in Washington, D.C., to a momentous evening in Istanbul with Vivienne Brown, my work has benefited tremendously from people who have traveled the Smith route before me. Our disagreements taught me a great deal about my interpretive convictions and

xi

revealed much about my theoretical shortcomings. I am grateful to each of my interlocutors from the scholar to the students who first encounter Smith in my class. Whatever criticisms are contained in these pages should in no way suggest anything but the greatest respect for the community of inquiry I am proud to be a member of.

My thanks must begin with Charles Griswold. We were both in our first semester at Boston University, yet he gave me his full attention. I could not have asked for a better teacher, dissertation adviser, and career advocate. I also had the good fortune to work with my second reader, Lawrence Cahoone, who remained involved in my career and life as well. He has modeled for me not only the tireless efforts of a scholar, but also the impeccable behavior of a *mensch*, the latter being much harder in academia. And, if I can skip ahead in chronology, a similar role is played by my colleague at the University of North Dakota Paul Sum. Our continual discussions about Smith, emergent democracies, politics, academic citizenship, and how to be a father are essential to fuel my inquiries and enthusiasm. Larry and Paul, you two would really like each other.

The faculty and staff at the Institüt für die Wissenschaften vom Menschen in Vienna, my home institution away from home, have been essential in the development of this book. Each time I plateau, it is there I go to meditate, write, dialogue, and lunch. This book could not have been completed without such a sophisticated cloister. As a complement, Daniela and Manfred Hoschek and all the patrons of St. Art in Vienna—my other family—help make my time in Vienna poetry instead of work. I miss *Zollergaße* every day.

For two years I was lucky enough to have had a research assistant, Elizabeth M. K. Sund, who will likely have received her doctorate by the time this book comes out. Her assistance was immeasurable. I am grateful for the efforts, most recently, of Samantha Steele, a graduate student in history from the University of Kentucky. She did outstanding work verifying and editing the citations in the final version of the manuscript. If I have succeeded in not embarrassing myself, it is in part because of her keen eye. I have benefited from extended conversations with Kathryn Joyce, who continued her work with me even after she graduated from UND. And I am thankful for all of the students in my Smith-related seminars at the University of North Dakota, the University of Helsinki, and Oklahoma State University. I learned a great deal from our discussions. An additional note of gratitude goes out to Ken Carlson; he knows why.

In addition to all those named above, my work has improved from discussions, assistance, and commentary by Crystal Alberts, James Alvey, Christopher J. Berry, Chris Blakely, Lauren Brubaker, Otávio Bueno, Bruno Chaouat,

Daniel Dahlstrom, Douglas Den Uyl, Jigna Desai, Paul Gaffney, Dogan Göçmen, Knud Haakanssen, Nora Hangel, Ryan Hanley, William Henderson, Lisa Herzog, Heini Hinkkonnen, Ruskin Hunt, Alexandra Hyard, Mark Jendrysik, Clay Jenkinson, Monica Kelley, Stanley Helms Kelley, Charles Leathers, Juhana Lemetti, David M. Levy, Deirdre McClosky, Thomas Moran, David Mowry, Jay Nickson, Sule Ozler, J. G. A Pocock, Patrick Raines, Douglas Rasmussen, Lori Robison, Heather Salazar, Eric Schliesser, James Schmidt, Amartya Sen, Sandra Sherman, Douglas Skopp, Charles Taylor, Pedro Teixeira, Gloria Vivenza, Rebecca Weaver-Hightower, Terry Winant, the anonymous referees who have commented on my work throughout the process, and William Frucht at Yale University Press for his patience and support. My most sincere apologies to anyone I have neglected to thank.

Portions of this book were developed when I was a visiting professor, resident, or fellow at the Department of Philosophy at Oklahoma State University (where I was both the Norris Scholar and philosopher-in-residence); the State University of New York, Plattsburgh (as a guest of the Honors Program and the Institute for Ethics in Public Life); the Department of Moral and Social Philosophy at the University of Helsinki (twice); the Centre for the Study of Scottish Philosophy at the Princeton Theological Seminary; the Center for the History of Political Economy at Duke University (as a participant in the National Endowment for the Humanities Institute on the Teaching of the History of Political Economy); as a Larry Remele Memorial Fellow through the North Dakota Humanities Council, North Dakota; and as a guest of the faculty of education at the University of Oulu.

This book was made possible because of a summer stipend from the National Endowment for the Humanities and two seminars funded by the Liberty Fund. I am also grateful for a sabbatical leave and numerous other grants from my own institution, the University of North Dakota.

While there are too many conferences to mention, I have been invited to present numerous portions of this book at colloquia at: Department of Philosophy, University of Miami; Department of Philosophy, Oklahoma State University; Department of Philosophy, University of Minnesota, Duluth; Fargo History Conference; Department of Philosophy, University of Uppsala, Sweden; The Center for the Study of Scottish Philosophy, Princeton Theological Seminary; The American Democracy Project at the State University of New York, Plattsburgh; Department of Philosophy and Religion, Montclair State University; Institute for the Advancement of Philosophy with Children, Montclair State University; Minot State University; Department of Philosophy/Centre for Ethics, Tartu University, Estonia; Department of Moral and Social Philosophy, University of Helsinki, Finland; Department of Philosophy, St. Johns University, Jamaica, New York; Department of Ethnic Studies, University of Vermont; and the Department of Philosophy, University of South Carolina. A very early version of my work on Smith and MacIntyre was presented as a plenary session at the 31st Conference on Value Inquiry. The first draft of the chapters on Smith's philosophy of history was presented as a plenary discussion at the International Conference on Political Economy, Kocaeli University, Derbent, Turkey. And the first complete articulation of my chapters on Smith's rationality was presented as the Keynote Address of the Phi Sigma Tau Undergraduate Philosophy Conference at the University of North Dakota.

Early versions of the chapters and smaller sections of this book have appeared in the *Adam Smith Review*; the *British Journal for the History of Philosophy*, *Economics and Philosophy*; *Inquiry: Critical Thinking Across the Disciplines*; *Journal for Eighteenth-Century Studies*; *Kontroversen, Zeitschrift für Philosophie, Wissenschaft und Gesselschaft*; *Mind*; *Proceedings of the Sixth Conference of the International Society for the Study of Argumentation*; *Proceedings of the Fifth Conference of the International Society for the Study of Argumentation*; *Studies in Philosophy and Education*; *Research in the History of Economic Thought and Methodology*; and the *William Mitchell Law Review*.

Finally, it is one of the great ironies of academic publications that family, the people who are the most necessary, are thanked last rather than first. I would not have completed this book without the support of those who put up with its very long impact on their lives. My parents, Mark Weinstein and Joyce Ellen Weinstein, offered encouragement in their own idiosyncratic ways. My in-laws, Wanda and Bill Donehower, have been overly tolerant of the many vacations during which I wrote instead of socialized. And Gail Sherman continues to challenge me personally and intellectually, even at the closing of our third decade of friendship.

Mingus, my friend, my fur-st born, losing you was losing a part of my soul. You taught me much more than why WN I.ii.2 is incorrect. Adina, you follow a dog only in this paragraph. You are the reason I believe in progress. And, finally, to my wife, Kim, whose mark is on every page of my work, I humbly dedicate this book to you and hope that it is worthy of your aspirations for me. Let's hope the next one won't be so stressful.

A note about the text: I have retained the original spelling in all my citations, as is standard practice in Smith studies. I have also retained the original gendered language even though I find it objectionable. In contrast, I have made every attempt to be gender neutral in my own writing. If at any point my words suggest otherwise, I apologize for the mistake. Finally, I have retained the phrase 'slave owner' in my own narrative even though I find it misleading and prefer the more accurate term 'enslaver.' The use of 'slave owner' contributes legitimacy to the false and horrific notion that one could ever own another human being. Unfortunately, one cannot fight every battle, and this book is complicated enough as it is. I recognize that this is a flimsy excuse for contributing to a moral fiction, but it is the best I can do at the moment.

ABBREVIATIONS

Works by Adam Smith

Corr.	*Correspondence of Adam Smith*. Edited by E. C. Mossner and I. S. Ross. Indianapolis: Liberty Press, 1987.
Edinburgh	"A Letter to the Authors of the *Edinburgh Review*," in *EPS*.
EPS	*Essays on Philosophical Subjects*. Edited by W. P. D. Wightman and J. C. Bryce. Indianapolis: Liberty Press, 1982.
ES	"Of the External Senses," from *EPS*.
FFL	"Considerations Concerning the First Formation of Languages," in *LRBL*.
HA	"The Principles Which Lead and Direct Philosophical Enquires Illustrated by the History of Astronomy," from *EPS*.
IA	"Of the Nature of that Imitation which takes place in what are called The Imitative Arts," from *EPS*.
LJ	*Lectures on Jurisprudence*. Edited by R. L. Meek and D. D. Raphael. Indianapolis: Liberty Press, 1982.
LJ(A)	*Lecture on Jurisprudence*, dated 1762–63, from *LJ*.
LJ(B)	*Lecture on Jurisprudence*, dated 1766, from *LJ*.
Logic	"The Principles which lead and direct Philosophical Enquiries Illustrated by the History of the Ancient Logics and Metaphysics," from *EPS*.
LRBL	*The Lectures on Rhetoric and Belles Lettres*. Edited by J. C. Bryce. Indianapolis: Liberty Press, 1985.
Physics	"The Principles Which Lead and Direct Philosophical Enquires Illustrated by the History of Ancient Physics," from *EPS*.
TMS	*Theory of Moral Sentiments*. Edited by A. L. Macfie and D. D. Raphael. Indianapolis: Liberty Press, 1982.

WN   *An Inquiry into the Nature and Causes of the Wealth of Nations.* 2 vols. Edited by R. H. Campbell and A. S. Skinner. Indianapolis: Liberty Press, 1976.

Works by Others

Char   Anthony Ashley Cooper, Third Earl of Shaftesbury, *Characteristicks of Men, Manners, Opinions, Times.* Indianapolis: Liberty Press, 2001.

Fable   Bernard Mandeville, *Fable of the Bees: Private Vices, Publick Benefits.* Indianapolis: Liberty Press, 1988.

Female   "The Female Tattler," in *By A Society of Ladies: Essays in the Female Tatler.* Edited by M. M. Goldsmith. Bristol: Thoemmes Press, 1999.

Inquiry   Francis Hutcheson, *An Inquiry into the Original of Our Ideas of Beauty and Virtue.* Charlottesville: Ibis Publishing, 1986.

Treatise   David Hume, *A Treatise of Human Nature.* Edited by David Fate Norton and Mary J. Norton. Oxford: Oxford University Press, 2000.

INTRODUCTION

When Adam Smith was three years old he was kidnapped by Gypsies. As a biographical event this is interesting. As a metaphor it is synecdochic. In this particular allegory the past holds the future hostage, the emotional takes control of the rational, the capitalist gets commodified, and the thief violates fair exchange.

There is no way to know how much truth there is to the story. There are several accounts of young Adam's recovery and two traditions regarding where the kidnapping took place.[1] More insidiously, stigmatization of the Roma permeated Europe. The myth of child stealing was pervasive, and anti-Rom sentiment drove nations and individuals to despicable acts. For example, during the reign of Henry VII it became a capital offence to be a Rom. In the Netherlands and elsewhere it became fashionable to organize Gypsy hunts. And, "in Hungary, Germany, Spain, and England, Gypsy children as young as 2 or 4 were taken by force and given to non-Gypsies to rear."[2] All of this is exacerbated by the fact that Great Britain had no laws outlawing child theft before 1814, and Roma were a good scapegoat to cover more commercial motivations.[3] Smith's abduction fits all these narratives well.

My interest in Adam Smith's alleged kidnapping lies not in what actually happened but in what it symbolizes. However unfair it may be, the Roma came to represent a pagan culture of mysterious sexuality, dishonorable practices, and uncontrolled emotion. They were perceived as untrustworthy and uncivilized, nomadic and tribal, a remnant of a time long past. Their image represented what Europe wanted not to be and what it was most afraid of acknowledging. As a tale about a philosopher whose central moral prescription involves entering into the perspective of those about whom one knows little, it is unfortunate that this popular legend is likely influenced by prejudice and ignorance. However, given

Smith's theory of the imagined impartial spectator—his theory of conscience describing how moral actors create more objective alter egos—it is certainly appropriate that the story associates the other with that which is within ourselves.

Smith's work is widely misunderstood. His theories are said to justify purely unfettered markets, libertarian governments, interactions solely for the purpose of satisfaction, and atomistic cosmopolitanism. Much that the Roma were supposed to be—emotional, group-centered, and traditional—was surgically removed from the Adam Smith of popular culture and superficial scholarship. These accounts all miss the point. In an age of reason and enlightenment, Smith offered a social theory that glorified the role of emotion. Amidst his theory of market exchange, Smith issued a clarion call for personal relationships. While his fellow philosophers sought access to the universal, Smith developed methods to enter into the particular. Very little of this is acknowledged by anyone but the Smith scholar.

This book is in part about the Smith that so often gets forgotten: the systematic philosopher whose first loyalties were to his theory of moral sentiments; the bachelor-teacher who had a love for young learners and a lifelong commitment to discovering how human behavior is governed by natural laws; the devoted fellow of the Scottish Enlightenment who was cautious about making local political claims but who, paradoxically, was fearless enough to engage, in his words, in a "very violent attack . . . upon the whole commercial system of Great Britain" (*Corr.* 208).

METHODOLOGICAL ASSUMPTIONS: A SYSTEMATIC APPROACH

In this book I argue that Smith presents an account of pluralism that prefigures our more modern theories of diversity; I do so by prioritizing *The Theory of Moral Sentiments* over his other work. In the current context, prioritize means that one ought to read *TMS* as the first chapter in a larger work, as if it contains the "legend" to Smith's systematic map. This is a theory of reading, an interpretive methodology before it is a statement of conceptual priority. It argues that *The Wealth of Nations* ought to be considered an elaboration of Smith's moral philosophy and that *TMS* is not simply a prolegomena to a political economy. I do not mean to suggest that WN cannot stand alone in certain respects. It is a powerful work in philosophy, history, and economics; many of its conclusions require no more elaboration than what is contained within its volumes. However, in terms of understanding Smith's pluralism and insofar as WN is a component of Smith's general system, its metaphors, methods, approach, and categories should not trump *TMS*. Smith's moral psychology is not a system of economics, but his account of universal opulence and natural liberty are themselves components of a much more elaborate moral system.

My interpretation emphasizes that there is enough continuity between Smith's books, lecture notes, essays, and fragments to see how each of these fits with the others. Of course, his two published books retain authority over the rest, and the later editions trump the earlier ones⁴—when there is a contradiction between the texts, I give priority to the works Smith himself endorsed. But this is surprisingly rare, and when his other writing is useful, I call upon it as evidence.

Because I assume the coherence of Smith's project, I reject the interpretive difficulty known as the Adam Smith Problem. The original formulation, a nineteenth-century pseudo-problem, argues against the compatibility of *TMS* and *WN*, suggesting that the former is built upon altruism while the latter is built on self-interest. This challenge is prima facie incoherent: sympathy is not altruism, and Smith never asserts that self-interest governs every human action. Even when his own index suggests that he might propose such a principle— Smith includes an entry that reads "*Self-love* the governing principle in the intercourse of human society" (*WN*, Index of Subjects)—he points only to the famous but complicated discussion referencing the butcher and the baker that includes the sentence, "But man has almost constant occasion for the help of his brethren, and it is in vain for him to expect it from their benevolence *only*" (*WN* I.ii.2, emphasis added). Here, Smith tells us that we cannot expect *only* benevolence from others, but *some* benevolence is certainly implied. As we shall see, Smith qualifies his call for the recognition of self-interest with the realization that other motives—multiple motives—complement self-love. He derives this position from rejecting some parts of Mandeville's *Fable of the Bees* and tempering others, or so I argue.

Smith himself would likely find the Adam Smith Problem baffling. He wrote *WN* while he revised *TMS*, and he advertised the later book in many editions of *TMS*. He never offered any suggestion in either published writings or personal correspondences that one might contradict the other. In fact, although large sections of text were added to later editions of *TMS*, only a relatively small amount of text was ever removed. He also continued to advertise *WN* and his other works at *TMS* VII.vi.37, even when he himself acknowledges that he had "very little expectation" of completing his proposed system (*TMS advertisement*). His announcement seems compelling evidence that Smith saw the works as interrelated.

As is already apparent, while developing my interpretation I rely, whenever it is relevant, on historical fact, context, biographical evidence, and testimony from those who knew Smith. This runs counter to Vivienne Brown's approach in *Adam Smith's Discourse*. Brown uses literary theory as her guide and argues that the authority of the text is best dealt with in isolation. She suggests that each book should "be read in its own terms and not cross-read through the others," explaining that by "reading each text separately" she will be able to treat each one "more discriminately."[5] In doing this, she challenges the editors of the Glasgow Edition who observe that "the same man" wrote both works. It is a mistake, she retorts, to assume that "Smith's personality and his own understanding of his writings are definitive in interpreting the meanings of the texts."[6]

That texts develop a life of their own cannot be denied; such has been a concern since Plato critiqued writing in *Phaedrus*. That Smith's works have multiple voices, as Brown argues, is also certain. His writing, like most great philosophy, is often dialogical. Like Shaftesbury, Smith has to come to terms philosophically with the nature of a divided self. The impartial spectator, like Shaftesbury's soliloquy—an internal dialogue intended to adjudicate thorny moral issues—breaks people into two before it puts them together again. The unity of the person who adopts multiple perspectives is a recurring theme throughout this book.

Thus, Brown's suggestion is helpful. Reading books in different ways assists in exposing their nature. Her project allows Smith scholars to see things we couldn't see before. Nevertheless, as anything more than a temporary inter-pretive framework, Brown's approach is too extreme and becomes untenable. First, why discard evidence regarding the meaning of Smith's text when we have it? Smith is clear that he intended his work to be read as a system. Ought we not take him at his word first and challenge its viability afterward? Second, and perhaps more important conceptually, it seems problematic to impose a lack of unity on texts that we know were continuously revised over Smith's lifetime. It is the fragmentation that seems arbitrary, not the holistic approach; I return to the subject of fragmentation during my discussion of Foucault's critique of philosophy of history in the final chapters of this book. If Brown is right that a single agent who continually attends to a variety of texts is not enough to declare common authorship, what is to stop us from suggesting the fragmentation of each individual book, or each individual chapter, paragraph, or sentence? Either an author retains some identity over time or there can be no coherent assumption of conceptual unity on any level.

I do not suggest that Smith might not have changed his mind over time. But if he did, it was still *his* mind that he changed, and biographical evidence suggests that when this happens he was conscious of it and altered his books accordingly. In essence, Brown forces us to contend with the postmodern critique that now dominates literary theory. As I conclude, this attack does not succeed in challenging Smith's project.[7]

Charles L. Griswold Jr.'s principle of charity seems a better interpretive rule to follow. He suggests that tensions between Smith's works should be seen as intentional on Smith's part first before they are deemed inconsistent or mistaken.[8] This is not to say that one cannot declare Smith contradictory, ambiguous, or incorrect given proper evidence. It is only to recognize that we can learn more assuming deliberation than by supposing coherence by accident.

My comments on methodology can be summarized by observing that any approach that treats Smith's work as fragmented obfuscates the fact that history, ethics, economics, jurisprudence, and aesthetics are necessarily interrelated. This is not simply a claim about Smith's work, but it certainly applies. Nor is it limited to the Scottish Enlightenment oeuvre that informed Smith, although his cohorts appear to have shared the assumption. It is, instead, an assertion regarding the nature of the human experience and the knowledge that people pursue. As we shall repeatedly see, there are no clear lines between aesthetics, education, jurisprudence, history, justice, political economy, rationality, rhetoric, and sympathy. Knowledge is not atomistic in this manner and neither is sociality. Part of the appeal of Smith's theories is that they recognize the depth, richness, and ambiguity in social and political life.

In fact, it is the intimate nature of knowledge, rationality, and perspective that has created many of the interpretive difficulties that Smith scholars address. Smith's name and system are frequently used for partisan purposes. In popular culture, he has become a symbol for a certain kind of conservatism: his face graces neckties, and his moniker has developed into a shorthand for free-market and limited government: the government that governs best governs least. However pervasive, this is an extreme misreading of his work. That Smith relies on government assistance much more often than a libertarian interpretation allows has become a fairly commonplace assertion. However, as we shall see, there are more subtle impositions of libertarian principles than just how much emphasis is placed on Smith's account of the sovereign's duties.

Lauren Brubaker challenges claims that Smith is Burkean in nature and that he relies heavily on the unintended consequences of the market to promote liberty.[9] These are arguments against the conservative interpretation of Smith, and Brubaker is correct to articulate them. Smith sees neither traditions nor continuity as goods in themselves, nor does his anti-mercantilism presume a passive government whose job is only to protect rights and enforce contracts.

In contrast, Doug Den Uyl and Samuel Fleischacker debate the extent to which the left can claim Smith as one of their own (and by this they likely mean the American left). Both reject the notion that Smith is either liberal *or* conservative in any contemporary sense,[10] and Fleischacker adds that "the issues Smith faced and the issues that we face are so different that it is difficult if not impossible to know where he would have stood on the contemporary political spectrum."[11]

While I am sympathetic to these conclusions, contrary to Fleischacker in particular, I would argue that it is precisely because Smith's and our issues are so similar that individuals want to claim him as representative of their political agenda.[12] Certainly, mercantilism has evolved into protectionism, and the division of labor has been forever altered by the industrial revolution. But his fundamental concerns—social and political unity, religious moderation, moral awareness, the need for and nature of education, the regulation of the market, the nature and limits of the sovereign, and so much more—are still very much our concerns as they were his. If Smith's were not ours, then he could not contribute to our contemporary liberal debate, and there could be no discussion between Smith and Rawls, Nozick, Nussbaum, and Sen, let alone Friedman, Hayek, and the other libertarians who often get identified as inheriting his project. Smith's work is a useful font because it allows us to consider common problems from a different point of view, but the problems are still common. They are still ours.

Seeing Smith as an interlocutor in our own controversies understandably nudges readers toward identifying him with current partisan politics. Yet, however appealing it may be to associate Smith with a particular movement, to do so encourages people to read Smith from his conclusions backward, a grave error given the priority of *TMS*. Therefore, while Brubaker's, Den Uyl's, and Fleischacker's cautions against pigeonholing Smith are important, their discussions miss what seems to be the more important element in the debate: what makes the left/right division so problematic for Smith scholarship is not the category he may fit in but the filter through which his readers evaluate the texts. (Here, Brown's reference to "the death of the author" is instructive and helps moderate discussion.) Simply put, making Smith either conservative or liberal to satisfy one's political leanings creates problems where there are none.

In reading this book, therefore, I ask that my readers leave partisanship aside. I have no doubt my interpretation is controversial, but it is not so because of where it may end up politically. I also ask my readers to consider not only Smith's conclusions but also the interpretive framework through which they read him. This requires an examination of many of his sources, an imposition of modern insights regarding the nature of equality and group association, and a reconsideration of the contemporary skepticism regarding progress and the science of human nature. While I do not claim that Smith is either leftist or conservative, I do suggest that he is a link in the liberal chain.[13]

WHY RATIONALITY, EDUCATION, AND PLURALISM?

My argument in this book is for two related conclusions with an eye toward an ulterior motive. First, I argue that Smith offers a theory of pluralism that prefigures twentieth- and twenty-first-century theories of diversity. Second, I show that a particular account of human rationality underpins his moral psychology and political economy. Ultimately, I emphasize that, for Smith, pluralism and rationality are intertwined, and the two are made all the more inseparable by their relationship to the human capacity and need to be educated. My ulterior motive involves an attempt to create a language that allows us to apply Smith's insights and texts to contemporary liberal debate. Despite my comments above that Smith's concerns are ours, Smith scholars do not yet have the *vocabulary* to adequately engage Rawls, for example. My hope is to begin providing one.

Regarding the first claim, Smith's pluralism often seems reduced to a purely economic description. In his theory of natural liberty and the account of limited government that results, it is certainly easy to emphasize the economic. Smith argues, for example, for those conditions under which someone can "change his trade as often as he pleases" (WN I.vii.6) and "where every man was perfectly free both to chuse what occupation he thought proper, and to change it as often as he thought proper" (WN I.x.a.1). Additionally, while he does make the liberal assertion that "articles of faith . . . are not within the proper department of a temporal sovereign" (WN V.i.g.18), Smith's more detailed argument for religious freedom references the role of public competition between sects. It is clear why an economic understanding of liberty may be tempting.[14]

I discuss and reject this economic view and revisit Smith's account of natural liberty and religion later in the book. For now, I remark only that interpreting political freedom simply as the ability to change one's economic circumstances ignores some of Smith's richest and most compelling insights. His system allows for much more than this limited picture of commercial diversity; natural liberty is supplemented by other freedoms as well. Smith's theory can be used to cultivate social and political unity in the face of the cultural, religious, economic, ethnic, gender, and racial differences that have so preoccupied our most recent liberal debates.

Regarding the second aim of the book—to present the account of rationality that underpins Smith's morals psychology and political economy—I show that his picture of decision making is significantly more layered than might be represented by a market-based model of exchange such as rational choice. As I argue, his theory of rational deliberation is complex and context-dependent, allowing for its usefulness not only in economic circumstances but in the full range of human experiences, including but not limited to the moral, political, familial, aesthetic, and personal spheres.

In arguing for Smith's account of rationality, I spend the first part of the book emphasizing those factors that work together to support it, ultimately concluding that decision making for Smith may be helpfully described using the discourse of modern argumentation theory. Rationality presupposes a range of human capacities and desires. It involves human judgment, which is impossible without goals, motivation, moral adjudication, socialization, and education. I therefore rely on Amartya Sen's definition of rationality as "the discipline of subjecting one's choices—of actions as well as of objectives, values and priorities—to reasoned scrutiny."[15] Sen's account allows for, as Alasdair MacIntyre argues, the assertion that the laws of logic are only a "necessary and not a sufficient condition for rationality, whether theoretical or practical."[16] MacIntyre's argument that rationality and the nature of inference are defined within the context of particular traditions plays a foundational role in this book.

This wider conception of rational thought proves essential to my discussion.[17] It does, however, lead to a difficulty. The historical texts that inform Smith do not offer the same analytic precision as do modern discussions of rationality. From a contemporary perspective, these sources do not distinguish between the faculty of reason (the human ability to make inferences), rationality as the ability to improve one's actual inferences, rationality as judgment (the ability to generalize from such inferences and apply those judgments when necessary), and instrumental reason (the ability to determine the best means to achieve an end). Many of the texts, Locke's in particular, use "reason" to mean any and all of these things, often in the same paragraph.

For the most part, I am concerned with the middle two terms, rationality as inference and rationality as judgment, but one cannot fully develop either of them without articulating their relationships to the others. Interpretive jumps must be made, claims that many historians of philosophy will find inauthentic and unsatisfying. But if we are to shift Smith from being simply an exercise in the history of ideas to a modern interlocutor in contemporary liberalism, some anachronisms will have to be tolerated.

These anachronisms are, of course, the very thing that many historians of ideas try to avoid. Quentin Skinner, for example, argues that "the key to excluding unhistorical meaning must lie in limiting our range of descriptions of any given text to those which the author himself might in principle have avowed."[18] Because "classic texts [are] worthy of study in themselves," he argues for "the value of a strictly historical approach.[19]

This is good guidance for a particular kind of project, but mine is a bit different. My hope is to find historically authentic meaning using Skinner's method while *also* reflecting on what Smith might have thought if he had had access to contemporary analytic categories. This is a difficult task and involves immense speculation; I have therefore made every effort to distinguish between the historical and contemporary throughout the book.

Furthermore, while Skinner is concerned with referencing only authentically connected texts, this requirement is particularly well-suited for my current project. Smith explicitly references all of the historical work that I cite as his influences. Locke was Shaftesbury's teacher; Hutcheson was Smith's. Smith was Hume's best friend, and both had a difficult but social relationship with Ferguson. Mandeville references Shaftesbury frequently, and Hutcheson and Hume vociferously rebuke him. Mandeville was also so immersed in Hobbes's philosophies that James Dean Young considers him to be a "popularizer" of the earlier philosopher's work.[20] Smith addresses them both; there are no anachronisms in the lineages I cite.

Similar relationships can be seen in the contemporary authors I reference. John Rawls is most famous for reigniting political philosophy with A *Theory of Justice* in 1971, and MacIntyre did the same for ethics with *After Virtue* ten years later. The two almost never mention each other by name, but both work in full awareness of the other. Both also cite, but badly misrepresent, Smith.[21] Sen and Nussbaum, on the other hand, collaborated, and both see Smith as a central influence. And while there are significant disagreements among contemporary liberal theorists, there is a clearly defined canon and critique; I rarely step outside of this discourse. So, while Skinner and others may find my claim that Smith prefigured or anticipated pluralism as stepping outside the bounds of the history of ideas, there is little but the conservative rules of scholarship to justify their concern.

In the end, I side with Warren J. Samuels over Skinner when he writes, "I . . . believe that it is impossible for a scholar to escape his worldview and to keep it from influencing his work. I also believe in criticism, not necessarily to reach Truth—more likely, to identify the matrix of positions taken by those in the process of working things out."[22] The matrix of positions he refers to has extended over many centuries. I see no reason to exclude our own if we are careful while we do it.

Returning to the question of language, contemporary discussions of rationality often aim for some kind of formalization even if they are not overly symbolic. Gerald Gaus's account of reasoned deliberation in *Justificatory Liberalism*, for example, addresses belief, public reason, inferences, and other tools of practical rationality with virtually no discussion of their content.[23] A similar claim can be made of Roberto Scazzieri's account of Smith's theory of rational choice. He argues that Smith's system

> presupposes binary relations among contingent or 'first-order' states of the universe (states of the universe as immediately experienced by a particular individual at a given instant of time). This means that, given the set Ω of all conceivable first-order states of the universe, individuals are assumed to be skilled social actors in so far as they are assumed to be able to rank all these states (these are also the states in which their own choices are directly involved). Any given individual is supposed to rank first-order states in terms of behavioral beliefs that cover more than a single set of first-order states. In other words, the very possibility of ranking first-order states presuppose the ability to identify a set of 'second-order' beliefs. These are beliefs that individuals may reasonably apply to a multiplicity of circumstances. Second-order beliefs are assumed to be relatively persistent and homogenous across a variety of individuals (and groups).[24]

In contrast, I show that Smith's account of rationality is more complex and more dependent on narrative structures than this passage suggests. However acceptable this outline of rational activity may be, given the predilection of contemporary philosophers, it is not representative of how Smith wrote or taught about rational activity; a different type of language must be developed. Consider the following two passages. First: "Of all the calamities to which the condition of mortality exposes mankind, the loss of reason appears, to those who have the least spark of humanity, by far the most dreadful, and they behold that last stage of human wretchedness with deeper commiseration than any other. But the poor wretch, who is in it, laughs and sings perhaps, and is altogether insensible of his own misery" (*TMS* I.i.1.11).

Second:

> Let it be considered too, that the present inquiry is not concerning a matter of right, if I may say so, but concerning a matter of fact. We are not at present examining upon what principles a perfect being would approve of the punishment of bad actions; but upon what principles so weak and imperfect a creature as man actually and in fact approves of it. The principles which I have just now mentioned, it is evident, have a very great effect upon his sentiments; and it seems wisely ordered that it should be so. . . . Though man, therefore, be naturally endowed with a desire of the welfare and preservation of society, yet the Author of nature has not entrusted it to his reason to find out that a certain application of punishments is the proper

means of attaining this end; but has endowed him with an immediate and instinctive approbation of that very application which is most proper to attain it. . . . Thus self-preservation, and the propagation of the species, are the great ends which Nature seems to have proposed in the formation of all animals. Mankind are endowed with a desire of those ends, and an aversion to the contrary; with a love of life, and a dread of dissolution; with a desire of the continuance and perpetuity of the species, and with an aversion to the thoughts of its intire extinction. But though we are in this manner endowed with a very strong desire of those ends, it has not been intrusted to the slow and uncertain determinations of our reason, to find out the proper means of bringing them about. Nature has directed us to the greater part of these by original and immediate instincts. Hunger, thirst, the passion which unites the two sexes, the love of pleasure, and the dread of pain, prompt us to apply those means for their own sakes, and without any consideration of their tendency to those beneficent ends which the great Director of nature intended to produce by them. (*TMS* II.i.5.10)

These quotes are taken out of their proper contexts, and no extended analysis is possible right now; I return to both of them later. For the time being, I ask only that the reader consider them as exemplars of Smith's overall approach.

In them, Smith's presentation is more like MacIntyre's and Sen's than Gaus's and Scazzieri's; rational deliberation cannot be investigated in isolation. In fact, as I show, Smith's use of the term 'reason' is most frequently paired with other terms, suggesting a multi-ingredient formula for rationality. In just the two passages cited here, reason references the human faculty by high-lighting the tragedy of those who can no longer infer, and judgment, in that the agent in question cannot adequately self-evaluate. In the second passage, the term means judgment but also discovery.

To add complication, over the course of the two excerpts Smith associates reason with humanity, sentiments, imperfections, natural tendencies (this is what Smith means when he uses the term 'principles'), and desires. Reason is a "slow and uncertain" process and not simply the practice of rule following or comparison. It is also a tool of communication. This prefigures MacIntyre, who writes, "It is on what has to be added to observance of the laws of logic to justify ascriptions of rationality—whether to oneself or to others, whether to modes of enquiry or to justifications of belief, or to courses of action and their justifica-tion—that disagreement arises concerning the fundamental nature of ratio-nality."[25] Or, as MacIntyre puts it elsewhere, the problem of competing traditions of rationality—or the greatest difficulty for rationality itself—is "how to describe the relevant examples. . . . There are no preconceptual or even pretheoretical data, and this entails that no set of examples of action, no matter how comprehensive, can provide a neutral court of appeal for decision between rival theories. . . . To put the same point in another way: each theory of practical reasoning is, among other things, a theory as to how examples are to be described, and how we describe any particular example will depend, therefore, upon which theory we have adopted."[26] Rationality here also involves both inference and judgment. Choice, reason, and rationality are so intimately connected that they are easily conflated.[27]

I fully acknowledge that one must connect many dots to get a more modern method of explanation from Smith; purists will object. Nevertheless, I argue that because of Smith's bundling of concepts, we must engage all of these issues while we investigate rationality. Sentiments, nature, imperfection, natural tendencies, and desires are all gateways to and modifications of rationality for Smith, and each of them is altered, cultivated, and identified through education and group identity, or so I argue in this book.

Returning briefly to the partisan nature of what Smith's readers sometimes bring to the text, this shift away from more formal modeling of rational deliberation is itself a shift away from an 'economic' account of Smith. As I shall argue, such an interpretation misrepresents his system. Smith's individuals are not *homo economicus*, and as a result this also means that his mechanism for choosing ends cannot be reduced solely to rational choice. As Sen writes,

> RCT [Rational Choice Theory] has denied room for some important motivations and certain reasons for choice, including some concerns that Adam Smith had seen as parts of standard 'moral sentiments' and Immanuel Kant had included among the demands of rationality in social living (in the form of 'categorical imperatives'). The point of contention is not that these motivations and reasons for choice are not invariably invoked by RCT . . . but rather that RCT does not at all allow these values and motives to be invoked in that form in interpreting either rational or actual choice. Insofar as moral or socially principled behavior is accommodated within RCT, this is done through the device of complex instrumental arguments that are combined with ultimately self-interested behavior. . . . RCT has tended to choose, fairly arbitrarily, one very narrow interpretational story, rejecting other rival understandings of what can lie behind the regularity of choices and the use of goals and values.[28]

The attempt to impose mathematical interpretive models such as rational choice theory on Smith's work is artificial and ultimately represents a non-Smithian commitment to the priority of the market over all other explanatory devices. To suggest that rationality demands that market-based RCT work in tandem with other mechanisms is not to denigrate the market—commercial exchange is still essential. It simply acknowledges the complexity of forces that Smith sees as governing human behavior.

SMITH STUDIES AND THE PLACE OF RECENT LIBERAL THEORY

This book is the first of what I expect to be a multivolume discourse considering proposed "Smithian shifts" for twenty-first-century liberalism. The second book will examine what liberalism might look like if we used Smith instead of Kant to ground political theory; the third will investigate the nature of political participation in a Smithian liberalism. These discussions, however, will be dependent on the interpretation of Smith I present here. Therefore, with only a few significant qualifications, this volume is more a work in the history of philosophy and contains fewer detailed remarks about recent liberal theory than I might otherwise offer. While I am engaged in contemporary interpretation, I am not yet ready to engage recent liberal theory head-on.

This approach, to return to my own terminology, is indicative of what I, as Smith's reader, bring to the texts with me. I am a twenty-first-century philosopher investigating texts written in the eighteenth century. What I find useful about these texts is influenced by my personal, political, and philosophical commitments. I therefore take certain things for granted that Smith might have not. For example, while I emphasize issues related to gender, race, and class, I offer no justification as to why these topics are worth investigating and why we might look at Smith in this light. There may be those who regard these issues as unimportant, but I offer no rejoinder to them. If contemporary political theories and realities haven't persuaded the skeptic that gender, race, and class are important analytical tools for investigating the nature of justice—albeit not the *only* important analytical tools—then there is nothing, in this book at least, that I can do to change their minds.

The organizational model I use for investigating Smith's pluralism also comes from recent debate. I, along with many of my contemporaries, and with Smith himself, presume a vast array of different human experiences, even among those who live in close proximity. Individuals diverge in their needs, thought processes, and actions. Although there are certainly more than I list here, I would suggest that contemporary political philosophy is particularly focused on four such spheres: differences in personal motivations and aims, differences in group identification, differences in experience and education, and differences in rationality and ways of thought. In addition, contemporary political philosophy largely ignores the eighteenth-century commitment to progress, an essential element of social improvement. I use these four modern liberal preoccupations and this one significant absence as a means to organize my approach.

"Pluralism" is a modern term: it did not come into use for more than a century and a half after Smith wrote. In this context, pluralism is to be defined as the political situation in which peoples of different fundamental beliefs and histories share equally in common governance and live within common borders.[29] Under this system, it is the prerogative of the citizen to choose his or her social priorities; in turn, the citizen is thought to be an unfettered agent who can participate in governance. Pluralism may or may not be a kind of liberalism—MacIntyre, for example, is most certainly a pluralist, but he does not consider himself a liberal[30]—but as described here, and as Smith foreshadows, there is continuity between the two. The ability to live among difference depends upon individual rights first and group rights second. If there is such a thing as collective identity, it cannot trump core liberal values. Individuals must preserve their rights as they enter and exit subgroups as well as whole communities. This is often a response to learning and cognitive change, and thus liberalism must have a theory of education.

While most post-Hobbesian political philosophy sees political legitimation as based upon the consent of the governed, contemporary liberalism qualifies it by suggesting that consent is authentic only when it is informed and when it is given through regular participation in fair and open legislative processes. Even if we are to accept, in its most simplistic form, Aristotle's definition of humans as political animals, we cannot expect people to be participatory at birth. Nor can we expect children who reach the age of reason—or some arbitrary or ritualistic age of adulthood—to suddenly be capable of making adequate political decisions. Humans must be taught to be citizens. As John Dewey writes, "Since education is a social process, and there are many kinds of societies, a criterion for educational criticism and construction implies a *particular* social ideal. The two points selected by which to measure the worth of a form of social life are the extent in which the interests of a group are shared by all its members, and the fullness and freedom with which it interacts with other groups. . . . Such a society must have a type of education which gives individuals a personal interest in social relationships and control, and the habits of mind which secure social changes without introducing disorder."[31]

Here Dewey articulates what Smith recognizes throughout his system: we are trained in political deliberation and participation through formal and informal education. Since citizenship requires education, I think it is fair to suggest that some methods of education are to be regarded as being better than others, although a true pluralism must accept the likelihood of coexisting, equally adequate approaches to learning and development. These themes and their foundational concerns drive my discussion, and I devote a significant amount of time to analyzing Smith's educational and curricular prescriptions.

To elaborate, pluralism is committed to the notion that personal motivations and aims differ among peoples and recognizes that there may be multiple reasons for acting: deciding to act depends on multiple tertiary concerns. I emphasize the management of these motivations early on in the book. Pluralism also recognizes that individuals have different associations with different, yet often overlapping, groups. How deeply these associations attach themselves to an individual's identities is a matter of deep disagreement, but few theorists doubt that such experiences go a long way toward shaping a person's attitudes, political views, conceptions of the good, and motivations.

Finally, liberal theory recognizes that individuals have different manners of deliberation. People want things and deliberate as to whether they should want them, what else they might desire, how they can acquire them, how and when to act in order to do so; and they frequently seek objective measures to help evaluate their choices. Liberals and their critics have emphasized these differences in rationalities, especially after MacIntyre challenged liberalism's supposed monolithic notion of rationality and its alleged commitment to a single, overarching "enlightenment project."[32] As should be evident by now, MacIntyre's stamp can be found throughout this book.

But while my book seeks to be a bridge between Smith and contemporary authors, it is also a project within Smith scholarship itself. My account provides the first full-length investigation of Smith's philosophy of education and his theory of rationality. I take explicit stands on how to read his corpus and reject market-dominant interpretations. I examine the nature of motivations in Smith's system and offer an account of sympathy's deliberative aspects. I am explicit about the depth and breadth of Smith's predecessors' influence. I argue that Smith's accounts of motivation and rationality are responses to a debate that prepared the ground for his insights. All of these claims have anticipations in today's vibrant discourse about Smith and the Scottish Enlightenment, but I believe they need further elaboration.

OVERVIEW

This book is divided into two parts: the first focuses on defining rationality, while the second emphasizes the means to improve the judgments that result from rational deliberation. Each part is divided into multiple chapters. The first two chapters present an interpretive methodology for reading Smith, one that takes seriously his Scottish Enlightenment context and understands that both *TMS* and *WN* are responding to existing discussions. In particular, I privilege Mandeville, Shaftesbury, and Hutcheson to highlight a thematic thread emphasizing motivation, self-interest, and morality. I argue that Smith's system rejects some of Mandeville's more extreme claims and accepts but tempers others, a distinction that helps elucidate the relationship between *TMS* and *WN*. I then show that these same thinkers, along with Locke and Hume, represent a progression toward acknowledging the multiple motivations that affect agents, which, in the end, requires a complex notion of rationality. In chapter 2, after establishing the conceptual unity of Smith's corpus, I critique the economic interpretation that Smith sees the market as the unifying framework for his system, arguing in more detail why one should prioritize *TMS*. I then show that, for Smith, pluralism is present at the most basic level of human experience. Human action cannot be reduced to simple self-interest; a diversity of motivations operates in any given situation.

Chapters 3 and 4 are concerned with the nature of sympathy and its connection to education. After acknowledging the moral priority of Smith's system and its complex motivational foundation, I impose the contemporary categories of gender, race, and class on his analysis to show how his theory allows for such group identification and to examine how this fractious heterogeneity can be bridged. I argue that Smith develops a sophisticated account of otherness that is able to cultivate social unity despite the presence of significant differences. This relies upon socialization and education to maximize the ability of a spectator to enter into the perspective of an agent. I also begin to examine the nature of Smith's empiricism and highlight the principles that direct human behavior. These two chapters emphasize that, for Smith, human rationality is the outcome of both experience and natural human tendencies and that the pluralism that results from human difference is a central concern throughout his corpus.

Chapters 5, 6, and 7 investigate Smith's theory of rationality itself. They are the most abstract and also the most foundational discussion of the book since, as I argue, a particular conception of rationality is presupposed by Smith's theories of progress, motivations, sympathy, and education. I show that Smith's rhetoric- and context-based theory of reasoning is an outgrowth of the seventeenth- and eighteenth-century rejection of Aristotelian syllogistic logic, once again emphasizing the lineage of Hobbes, Mandeville, Locke, Shaftesbury, Hutcheson, and Hume. I argue that Smith's account of rationality is narrative in form, not a product of rational choice, and that it can be teased out of his *Lectures on Rhetoric and Belles Lettres*, although its elements are found throughout his writing. I argue that Smith reconsiders the traditional divide between emotion and reason, presenting us with a modern account of argumentation that anticipates recent work in informal logic and critical thinking. I also show that his account of rationality allows for a normative understanding of the role of price, arguing that it presumes analogous deliberative structures in the economic, moral, and political spheres, emphasizing, in the process, that this interpretation is most defensible when read through *TMS*.

Part 2 of the book investigates Smith's method for cultivating rational judgment. Chapters 8 and 9 revisit Smith's account of education, articulating his philosophy of education as it extends beyond his account of sympathy, the fellow feeling that guides moral deliberation and empathetic judgment. This area of Smith's work has received little attention. I offer an account as to why, according to Smith, people learn and why education is so essential to proper market operations. I also describe Smith's ideal curriculum and suggest that, despite its absence at key points in the text, Smith argues for the importance of arts education to cultivate the well-being of individuals. This discussion includes Smith's prescriptions for public subsidies of education and addresses his concerns about religious divisions' adverse effect on social unity. The discussion of pluralism in this chapter once again forces us to consider the nature of Smith's empiricism, and I emphasize the ways in which learning results in specialization, which is both a positive and negative force in Smith's theories. I show that Smith's call for public education is built on his assumption that learning is a precondition for rationality and, ultimately, for virtue and happiness.

In the final two chapters I reconsider the viability of my overall project with an eye toward the postmodern attack on progressivist histories. In doing so, I articulate Smith's philosophy of history, asking to what extent nature informs individuals and communities about normative claims. I argue that Smith's philosophy of history relies on a dialectic between discovery of an ideal history and the recounting of actual historical events, in this case historiography and historicity, respectively. This involves an investigation of the nature of evidence in historical analysis, the viability of particular narratives connecting this evidence, and the role of these narratives in defining and limiting the discovery that comes from historical inquiry. I show that, for Smith, progress is that which reveals the "ought" of nature. In the final chapter I address Michel Foucault's critique that such a project is incoherent, examining his challenge to the unity of discourses and the sciences to show that, in the end, while Foucault and Smith share a range of common methodologies, Smith has the tools to defend his theory against the postmodern challenge.

In summary, I offer the argument that Smith's accounts of pluralism and rationality are intertwined and that they are made all the more inseparable by their relationship to the human capacity to be educated. In making this claim, I suggest that two themes run through Smith's work. First, as already noted in his philosophy of history, Smith's work assumes a constant interaction between an *ideal* that acts as evaluative criteria for human thought, motivation, and moral inquiry and an *actual* but imperfect process of discovery that illustrates well the limitations of the human project. Smith's agents always aim for perfection but never achieve it; progress and comparison must always be the standard of betterment.

A second theme is that that which divides people also unites them. Perhaps one of the most problematic aspects of Smith's work is that the very factors that help unify people in the face of diversity are the same ones that cause them to understand one another as different in the first place. This is an empiricist's dilemma and an accurate account of the human condition; Smith's philosophical problem is everyone's existential one. As we shall see, natural tendencies make individuals want to domineer, but these same tendencies motivate people toward mutual sympathy. Lived experience results in agents' having different perspectives, but this same root empiricism (however limited it may turn out to be) allows people to imagine themselves in another person's circumstance. The division of labor creates political divisions just as it creates universal opulence. How Smith manages these factors and how he overcomes the divisive forces that may also be used to cement society are important questions that guide my investigation.

Part One

WHAT RATIONALITY IS

1

MEDIATING TERMINOLOGY AND TEXTUAL COMPLEXITY

In this chapter I focus on the literary complexity in both my project and Smith's. In the first section I address the difficulties of using the contemporary language of pluralism to analyze an eighteenth-century text. I investigate the manner in which Smith might be said to postulate pluralism and begin to unravel its centuries-old relationship to rationality. In the second I show that such literary tensions were not uncommon in Smith's times. The Scottish Enlightenment thinkers were unified in their opposition to Bernard Mandeville's *Fable of the Bees*, but, as I illustrate, that book is itself a mixture of philosophical argument, maxims, and contradictions. This necessitated a different type of response on Smith's part, one that involved explicit rejection and implicit acceptance, the former finding its voice in *TMS*, the latter being much more subtly placed in *WN*. Ultimately, I show that the debate between Mandeville and Smith is one about the place of rationality in negotiating human motivation.

THE EIGHTEENTH-CENTURY LANGUAGE OF PLURALISM

It would be anachronistic to suggest that Adam Smith offers an explicit theory of pluralism in any contemporary sense. The first published reference to the term as a theory of diversity is found in 1924, one and a half centuries after his death.[1] This seems surprisingly late given the long history of writing on toleration.[2] However, its usage does seem a natural extension of pluralism's first political designation, only seven years earlier, as a theory of politics that prioritizes individuals and organizations over a monolithic state.[3] Tellingly, this earlier definition contains the term "rationality," although its meaning suggests a Weberian account rather than the phronesis that is the focus of this book. From the first, diversity and rationality were intertwined.

Modern theories of diversity concern themselves with ethnic, religious, cultural, sexual, and other group differences. They preserve and celebrate patterns of dissimilarity, recognizing that a truly pluralistic state manages rather than eradicates variation. Thus Kant's categorical imperative is not itself pluralistic because it seeks to find a universal human morality that transcends difference and contingency. It can be used to undergird pluralism, as Rawls and his followers try to do, but the imperative itself is homogeneous and absolute.

Smith explicitly rejects this uniform picture of humanity, acknowledging class, race, sex, religious, and ethnic differences throughout his work. It is, however, in a comment on national identity that Smith comes closest to arguing for some sort of modern pluralism. In *TMS* VI.ii.2, while Smith is elaborating on the nature of loyalties to one's state, he writes, "Every independent state is divided into many different orders and societies, each of which has its own particular powers, privileges, and immunities. Every individual is naturally more attached to his or her own order or society, than to any other" (*TMS* VI.ii.2.7). These subgroups, Smith continues, while sometimes acting "unjust," are not "useless." They tend "to preserve whatever is the established balance among the different orders and societies into which the state is divided." And, while they often seem to disrupt things, any group "contributes in reality to the stability and permanency of the whole system" (*TMS* VI.ii.2.10). Thus subgroups, for Smith, both preserve the status quo and promote national strength.

Shortly thereafter, while exposing the disruptive dangers of fanaticism, a topic Smith revisits numerous times throughout his corpus, he writes,

> The man whose public spirit is prompted altogether by humanity and benevolence, will respect the established powers and privileges even of individuals, and still more those of the great orders and societies, into which the state is divided. Though he should consider some of them as in some measure abusive, he will content himself with moderating, what he often cannot annihilate without great violence. When he cannot conquer the rooted prejudices of the people by reason and persuasion, he will not attempt to subdue them by force; but will religiously observe what, by Cicero, is justly called the divine maxim of Plato, never to use violence to his country no more than to his parents. He will accommodate, as well as he can, his public arrangements to the confirmed habits and prejudices of the people; and will remedy as well as he can, the inconveniencies which may flow from the want of those regulations which the people are averse to submit to. When he cannot establish the right, he will not disdain to ameliorate the wrong; but like Solon, when he cannot establish the best system of laws, he will endeavour to establish the best that the people can bear (*TMS* VI.ii.2.16).

There is a political tension in this paragraph between individuals' and groups' "powers and privileges," a phrase we would colloquially call rights, although they do not meet the philosophical criteria for identifying them as such. This tension requires a negotiation between what individuals are free to do, what groups are free to do, and what limits they all impose on one another. This is more than just liberal individualism. Pluralism gives special acknowledgment to groups and recognizes that while the perspective of one group does not always appear legitimate to others, the association must still be permitted to exist and not simply as a collection of individuals.

These nuances are likely too subtle for Smith's eighteenth-century perspective.[4] The important point is that Smith is not simply acknowledging the existence of diversity but institutionalizing the maintenance and cultivation of group identity and its importance to the state. This is pluralism as a system of governance, not just plurality as a fact.

Smith also references in the passage many of pluralism's great themes while emphasizing his own approach to political stability. Those who seek the public good must respect the different individuals and groups of society. Such people may be understood, from a spectator's perspective, to have different habits and prejudices, but they must still be approached with humanity and benevolence, never violence. Because no system is perfect, the public-spirited person must seek to moderate people's prejudices, but in the end the sovereign should aim to establish the best system of laws compatible with the people and groups already contained within society, remedying the negative consequences of those group behaviors and attitudes that will not change. Replace the phrase "great orders and societies" with "ethnic, religious, and racial groups," and replace the term "moderate" with "teach equality to," and one would be hard-pressed to distinguish Smith's prescription from that of most modern pluralists.

Smith makes a similar point with similar language in WN when he compares the corn laws to laws that effect religion: "The laws concerning corn may every where be compared to the laws concerning religion. The people feel themselves so much interested in what relates either to their subsistence in this life, or to their happiness in a life to come, that government must yield to their prejudices, and, in order to preserve the publick tranquillity, establish that system which they approve of. It is upon this account, perhaps, that we so seldom find a reasonable system established with regard to either of those two capital objects" (WN IV.v.b.40).

This is not democratic theory. Great Britain did not have a true democracy until the reform acts of 1832, and Smith offers no account of democracy in either his published or unpublished writing. Instead, it is a discussion of managing group interests, activities, perspectives, and identities. Obviously, the second passage tempers the first one, in that tolerant laws are seen as more of a compromise, and Smith emphasizes that religions lead to unreasonable attitudes. But my argument is not that Smith offers a full-fledged pluralism, only that he anticipates this type of political system in many ways. Rawls may reject this kind of diversity, a system built upon a modus vivendi, but in a society ripped apart by strife, toleration by compromise is a grand achievement.[5]

Smith's pluralism is too embryonic to be clearly identified as either a "melting pot" or "mosaic" model, where the former emphasizes assimilation and the latter encourages multicultural coexistence.[6] The comments cited so far emphasize mosaic difference, but, as we shall see, the intersubjective elements of Smith's moral theory encourage a kind of melting-pot assimilation. Sympathy, for Smith, involves sharing in the experiences of others. It demands, ultimately, the creation of an imagined impartial spectator who speaks for the community in times of moral myopia, but who can also act as an advocate for individuals determined to challenge a community. An impartial spectator who speaks for a community must be culturally assimilated, but one who is capable of challenging that community must be accepting of difference.

While Smith recognizes that privileges and inequalities are to be preserved in some sense, he also recognizes that these advantages are not absolute. Stable political systems must allow for idiosyncrasies even if, from the perspective of those in charge, these attitudes are illegitimate. Smith makes it clear that these prejudices appear unreasonable, but one of the central questions of this book, and of pluralism in general, is what, in a diverse society, reasonable can actually mean.[7]

In contrast to Kant, Smith's approach presumes human difference; he rejects noncontextual normativity. While he does call into question the breadth of the spectrum of human difference (WN I.ii.5), his analyses and recommendations suggest that variation is both normatively and empirically informative. Continually negotiating the tensions between discordance and commonality, Smith frames his project as a dialogue between otherness and familiarity. To begin with, the full title of TMS as printed in the later editions is *The theory of Moral Sentiments or, an essay towards an analysis of the principles, by which men naturally judge concerning the conduct and character, first of their neighbours, and afterwards of themselves to which is added, a dissertation on the origin of languages,* and each edition begins with the first principle that individuals care for others despite there being no benefit but "the pleasure of seeing it" (TMS I.i.1.1). Smith is arguing that while we care about others and judge ourselves on their account, our doing so creates a philosophical problem that must be addressed. Diversity both interferes with and cultivates moral determinations; that which divides us also unites us.

TMS is intended to describe the moral psychology that allows for communication and judgment amidst differences. In part VII, for example, Smith identifies two questions that "ought to be examined in a Theory of Moral Sentiments," the second of which concerns us: "By what power or faculty in the mind is it, that this character, whatever it be, is recommended to us?" (TMS VII.i.2). In this book I investigate the nature of the human mind from Smith's point of view. In it, I ask how *differently* people think and how they think in the face of these differences. Again, diversity and rationality are intertwined.

Smith is famous for his system of "natural liberty," but liberty is not pluralism. The former is a state of possibilities for individuals; the latter is a description of society. Smith understands this distinction, recognizing that the "liberty of every individual" depends upon the "impartial administration of justice" (WN V.i.b.25). However, the question at hand is to what extent pluralistic principles are implicit in Smith's notion of impartiality. Furthermore, the relationship between pluralism and liberty is dependent on what *kind* of liberty one presumes.

There are times when Smith seems to presume negative liberty, suggesting that what he wants is simply freedom from obstruction. But there are others when he focuses on human development and progress, suggesting that the sovereign has a responsibility to cultivate the moral, social, political, and intellectual capacities of its citizens. To a certain extent, then, Smith's discussion is a preamble to the nineteenth-century German idealist struggle with the state's role in individual actualization. It necessitates reflection on the nature of individuality and its relationship with difference and commonality.

In WN the tension between familiarity and otherness manifests itself as a discussion of cooperation in the face of specialization. It too presumes some sort of natural human differences, some existing from birth and some acquired through experience. In the third paragraph of its introduction, Smith references possible variation in "the skill, dexterity, and judgment" of laborers (WN intro.3) and then refers to these differences again in the first sentence of the first chapter (WN I.1.1). Even the title of WN's first book announces the fact of diversity by describing its subject as "Of the Causes of Improvement in the productive Powers of Labour, and of the Order according to which its Produce is naturally distributed among the different Ranks of the People." Smith's starting point in both published books is that difference in skills, experience, and capacities are matters of fact that must be acknowledged and dealt with.

Smith's comments allude to education as well as diversity. TMS's subtitle summarizes the process by which individuals learn to make moral judgments about themselves and others, and WN's account of skills and dexterity begins a recurring emphasis on specialization and the process of skills development. Rationality, however, is more subtly placed throughout the text, and while it turns out that the rational faculty is tied to education and knowledge of oneself and others, teasing out Smith's theory of it is a lengthy task.

While reconstructing Smith's unfinished corpus is difficult (he ordered most of his unpublished work burned before his death), it is clear that his overall purpose was to provide a systematic account of human activity and its relationship to nature. Philosophy is, for him, the "science of the connecting principles of nature." It seeks to "introduce order into this chaos" and "allay this tumult of the imagination" (*HA* II.12). It is an umbrella discipline that offers both content and method in a vast range of subject areas. Notice how this terminology prepares the ground for rational thought. It presupposes the possibility of imposing order. It allows an individual to moderate and control the imagination, resting on the interpretive and predictive power of 'principles'—a term Smith references in the first sentence of *TMS* and one he uses as a contrast to nonevidentiary supposition (*TMS* I.i.1.1).

Rationality is, for Smith, a response to more than just political pluralism; it challenges philosophical monism as well. Smith presumes not only that there is more than one mind, but that each has more than one motivation. As I emphasize, while some commentators have misinterpreted Smith's text as postulating a monistic egoism or a monistic altruism, the rational capacity, for Smith, is that which allows an individual to act on multiple motivations at once. He inherited this approach to rational deliberation from his predecessors, most specifically Mandeville, Shaftesbury, Hutcheson, and Hume.

These four, like Smith himself, were all empiricists; Daniel Carey usefully employs the word "observational" in describing their approach to evidence.[8] All played with the notion of inborn capacities in different ways, but Hutcheson, at least, explicitly asserts that he is not postulating any innate knowledge (*Inquiry*, xv). Each was bound by the success of Locke's *Enquiry*, assumed the existence of reflection, and struggled with Locke's assertion that humans are born without any knowledge whatsoever. Hutcheson, building on Shaftesbury's terminology, transformed this reflection into a moral sense theory ultimately rejected by Smith and most post–Scottish Enlightenment thinkers.[9]

The moral sense is a response to human diversity; it bespeaks a universal human nature in the face of cultural and personal difference. Whereas Mandeville and Locke embraced this difference as a fundamental human fact, Shaftesbury and Hutcheson worked hard to show that evidence of moral variation was exaggerated. They rejected seventeenth- and eighteenth-century travel literature, the source of much anthropological data, as sensationalistic and sought to show that whatever differences existed had developed only after natural moral unity had been achieved. Although not every modern debate about diversity can be traced to this lineage, "a substantial core of current concerns had its first modern exploration in the work of Locke, Shaftesbury, and Hutcheson."[10]

There is no commonly held understanding of what the moral sense might be.[11] While it may be tempting to read the Scots as collectively moving toward a unified theory rather than posing, revising, and rejecting one, this would be unfortunate. The philosophical discussions that revolve around it are rich and informative. Shaftesbury sets up the moral groundwork, Hutcheson defends it against Mandeville, and Hume integrates it more fully into a coherent and systematic Lockean empiricism, citing sympathy as the epicenter of moral adjudication.

Smith did indeed adopt Hume's project, as Nicholas Phillipson points out,[12] but, as D. D. Raphael argues, Smith saw Hume's notion of sympathy as too narrow and replaced its emphasis on the consequences of judged action with a concern for motive and propriety.[13] Hume "introduced the concept of sympathy, sharing the feelings of those *affected* by an action, to explain approval and disapproval of the action,"[14] but Smith presents a much more complex notion that takes context and the imagination into account. He creates a modern theory of conscience that is the direct outgrowth of previous debates, the lynchpin of which is a response to Mandeville and his superficial Hobbesian account of rationality understood both instrumentally and as judgment.

MANDEVILLE

Smith's philosophical project was consistent with that of the other Scottish philosophers; he used their texts, questions, information, and, in certain cases, rhetoric and vocabulary. More specifically, Smith appeared devoutly committed to rebutting Mandeville's *The Fable of the Bees*, an early eighteenth-century treatise that postulated vice as the driving force in society. A purely virtuous society, Mandeville argued, would be as destitute as an abandoned beehive.

The Fable was a focal point for two generations of Scottish thinkers. It has been called Hutcheson's, Hume's, and Smith's "curious obsession" and can therefore provide a unitary theme through which we can read the Scots.[15] Hutcheson refers to Mandeville's theory throughout all of his philosophical works. He also felt it necessary to respond to him publicly in six letters to the *Dublin Journal* in 1726 and again in *Reflections on Laughter and Remarks on the*

Fable of the Bees in 1750.[16] In the latter he observes sarcastically that Mandeville "must have been scared by a sermon on self-denial in his youth."[17]

Hume attacks Mandeville's doctrines several times as well, in both the *Treatise* and the *Enquiry*, mentioning him alongside Shaftesbury, Hutcheson, and Butler as philosophers who have "begun to put the science of man on a new footing."[18] Smith himself responds to Mandeville in the very first sentence of *TMS*, then offers a full-frontal assault in a chapter titled "Of licentious Systems" (*TMS* VII.ii.4). He also mentions Mandeville in his early "Letter to the Edinburgh Review," in which he associates Mandeville with Rousseau on several points. In particular, he blames Mandeville for providing the foundation for Rousseau's incorrect assertion that the "laws of justice, which maintain the present inequality amongst mankind, were originally the inventions of the cunning and the powerful" (*Edinburgh*, 11).

It was not just the Scots who had an "obsession" with Mandeville. Despite Smith's association of the two, Rousseau criticized Mandeville explicitly (Smith acknowledged some of these criticisms in *Edinburgh*). When *The Fable of the Bees* was translated into French in 1750, it was publicly and ritually burned by the public hangman but then quickly retranslated after Rousseau won the Dijon Academy Prize.[19]

Although not inconsistent with the history of philosophy, this curious hysteria seems misplaced. Sterling Lamprecht writes, "Philosophers seem often unable to appreciate the writings of witty and satirical persons, and miss the point of sallies and clever pens. Mandeville aroused a storm of protest when he should have been met with counter-thrusts of equally shrewd and brilliant repartee."[20] Yet the debates over Mandeville continue today. Among the scholarly literature there is great division, not only regarding what Mandeville meant but whether what he wrote ought to be taken seriously. Writers also attack F. B. Kaye, the editor whose edition of *The Fable of the Bees* of 1925 became both definitive and the standard apology for Mandeville's more "eccentric" conclusions.[21]

At the core of Mandeville's argument is Hobbes's assertion that individuals are solely self-interested, even after the formation of the social contract.[22] In opposition, Smith argues that the social contract is a misleading description of early society (*LJ(A)* v.ii.5).[23] Society, he suggests, is a natural progression that manifests itself in certain stages (*WN* III.i). Accordingly, there has never been a time in which humans found themselves without social structures: people "can subsist only in society" (*TMS* II.ii.3.1) and have "a natural love for society" (*TMS* II.ii.3.6).[24]

The Scots shared Smith's conviction that the progression of human history is relevant to the study of nature and is itself natural. One learns about morality and sociality by learning about natural laws, all of which are manifest in social and political changes over time. Shaftesbury, Hutcheson, and Hume, like Smith, ground many of their claims about "natural philosophy" in the progression of human history. Hutcheson goes so far as to assert that history has its own "beauty" (*Inquiry*, 51),[25] and Carey rightly points out that the celebrated stage theory of history is a means by which the Scots can account for the diversity of beliefs across cultures.[26]

It is not just the social contract in *The Fable of the Bees* that Smith challenges. He argues that Hobbes and Mandeville were also wrong in their egoism. He asserts in the very first sentence of *TMS* that there *are* principles that interest people in the fortune of others (*TMS* 1.i.1.1). Virtue is necessary for social unity, and sympathy is inherently other-oriented. He does accept Mandeville's notion that self-interest plays an important role in both universal opulence and political governance, but he objects to the *extent* of the power of this self-interest, not to its existence or importance. It is therefore useful to understand Smith as making two distinct arguments. The first is a rejection of certain common elements of Hobbes's and Mandeville's theories, and the second is a reluctant but limited acceptance of others.

Mandeville was not a simple writer. He can be seen as a participant in the French intellectual Jansenist tradition as the descendant of La Rochefoucauld, Jacques Esprit, and La Fontaine, but also in the skeptical tradition of Montaigne and Pierre Bayle.[27] At the same time, as Pierre Force puts it, "Mandeville's anthropology is consistent with both the Epicurean and Augustinian accounts of human nature."[28]

Mandeville's mode of presentation is also complex. Some of his earliest work can be found in *The Female Tatler*, a satirical response to Richard Steele's *The Tatler*.[29] In these accounts, Mandeville does not have one clear voice. His dialogues present two sisters, Lucinda and Artesia; it is not always clear which of them is the mouthpiece for his ideas, and in *Fable* Mandeville relies rhetorically on dialogue to present, defend, and criticize philosophical positions. M. M. Goldsmith has shown that *The Fable of the Bees* is actually a conglomeration of three distinct positions presented in his earlier writing.[30]

Mandeville is argued to have an "interest" in "moral satire and that of genetic explanation" of moral norms.[31] He builds on symbolism in Aesop that turns traditional imagery of the beehive and the bee on its edge—beehives had been associated with absolute monarchies, and bees were seen as representative of Dutch frugality, discipline, and commercial success.[32] He is not encouraging vicious actions. He is condemning or speaking out against them while presenting a "genealogy of morals."[33] He is also a satirist and, as the title reminds us, writing a fable, not straightforward philosophy.[34] Mandeville's texts are instead, in Stephen Daniel's terms, "mythic" in form.[35] Or, to put it another way, Norman Wilde tells us, "Mandeville's work is thus a parallel to that of Voltaire. What Voltaire was to the optimism of Leibniz, Mandeville was to that of Shaftesbury — the *Fable of the Bees* is the English equivalent of *Candide*."[36] Given this context, Mandeville's *Fable* seems a more difficult target than often allowed, and Smith's response must also be more complex.

Smith is not always honest about his agreements with his predecessor. Mandeville's name appears seven times in the body of *TMS*, located solely in chapters devoted to Smith's critique (*TMS* VII.ii.4); his name is not found anywhere in the *Wealth of Nations*. In contrast, the Glasgow Edition of Smith's work offers only five footnote references to Mandeville in *TMS* but twenty-five in *WN*.[37] This is understandable. Smith's use of rhetoric, his examples, and what he considered worth commenting on often seem to come straight from his predecessor's pen. Consider Mandeville's comments in *Fable* I, 169: "A Man would be laugh'd at, that should discover Luxury in the plain Dress of a poor Creature that walks along in a thick Parish Gown and a course Shirt underneath it; and yet what a number of People, how many different Trades, and what a variety of Skill and Tools must be employed to have the most ordinary *Yorkshire* Cloth?"

Now compare them to Smith's in *WN* I.i.11: "Observe the accommodation of the most common artificer or day-labourer in a civilized and thriving country, and you will perceive that the number of people of whose industry a part, though but a small part, has been employed in procuring him this accommodation, exceeds all computation. The woollen coat, for example, which covers the day-labourer, as coarse and rough as it may appear, is the produce of the joint labour of a great multitude of workmen."

Both of these examples refer to woolen coats in order to illustrate the vast amount of labor involved in creating the most mundane of everyday objects.[38] Smith's famous passage extends well beyond this selection, since he enumerates many of the possible trades people connected to the manufacture, but his choice of example is curious given Mandeville's earlier use of it.

Consider also the similarities between *WN* I.ii.3 and *Fable* II, 284. Smith writes, "In a tribe of hunters or shepherds a particular person makes bows and arrows, for example, with more readiness and dexterity than any other. . . . Another excels in making the frames and covers of their little huts or moveable houses. He is accustomed to be of use in this way to his neighbours, who reward him in the same manner with cattle and with venison, till at last he finds it his interest to dedicate himself entirely to this employment, and to become a sort of house-carpenter. In the same manner a third becomes a smith or a brazier, a fourth a tanner or dresser of hides or skins, the principal part of the clothing of savages."

In contrast, Mandeville asserts, "Man, as I have hinted before, naturally loves to imitate what he sees others do, which is the reason that savage People all do the same thing: This hinders them from meliorating their Condition, though they are always wishing for it: But if one will wholly apply himself to the making of Bows and Arrows, whilst another provides Food, a third builds Huts, a forth makes Garments, and a fifth Utensils, they not only become useful to one another."

In both quotations the authors emphasize precommercial society, bows and arrows, huts, and clothing in order to argue for the efficacy of the division of labor;[39] a very odd coincidence if accidental.

Other examples abound. In just the first chapter of *WN* Smith uses concepts put forth by Mandeville in the first paragraph of his description of the division of labor (*WN* I.1.1, *Fable* II, 142); they both use fire engines (a coal-fueled furnace) as examples of specialization (*WN* I.i.8, *Fable* II, 167); and they both compare the current standard of living with the poor of precommercial societies (*WN* I.i.11, *Fable* I, 169). Even if these examples were common cultural tropes—an unlikely possibility owing to their specificity—Smith's close reading of *Fable* would have made him aware of Mandeville's use.

Consider also the initial paragraph of *TMS*, in which Smith articulates those principles that even the "ruffian" and "most hardened violator of the laws of society" are "not altogether without" (*TMS* I.i.1.1). It is strikingly similar to Mandeville's description of the horror of watching a mad sow dismember a toddler. Invoking the natural capacity for pity, Mandeville indicates that virtue is not a prerequisite for fellow feeling: "an Highwayman, an House-Breaker, or a Murderer could feel Anxieties on such an Occasion" (*Fable* I, 256). As Force puts it, "To Mandeville's 'house-breaker' or 'murderer' who is taken by pity, corresponds Smith's 'greatest ruffian,' or 'most hardened violator of the laws of society,' who is 'not altogether without [concern for others].'"[40]

Similarities extend to use of language, not just examples. In this first paragraph Smith's rhythm and sentence construction mirror Mandeville's. *The Fable of the Bees* tells us, "How calamitous soever a Man's Circumstances might be, he would forget his Misfortunes for the time, and the most troublesome Passion would give way to Pity" (*Fable* I, 256). Smith writes in response, "How selfish soever man may be supposed, there are evidently some principles in his nature, which interest him in the fortune of others" (*TMS* I.i.1.1). Although the two sentences are not carbon copies of one another, Smith clearly substitutes "selfish soever" for "calamitous soever," "fortune" for "misfortune," and both rely on "pity." Strikingly, commentators regularly point to this first sentence in *TMS* as a direct refutation of Mandeville, not as a signal of their commonality. Even I have done so twice in this chapter already, despite my emphases of their commonality.

Mandeville makes a show of criticizing philosophers for focusing too heavily on ideals. In the very first sentence of *Fable*, he writes, "One of the greatest Reasons why so few People understand themselves, is, that most Writers are always teaching Men what they should be, and hardly ever trouble their Heads with telling them what they really are" (*Fable* I, 39).[41] One might wonder whether it was this particular condemnation that Smith had in mind when he wrote, in an extended footnote, that "the present inquiry is not concerning a matter of right . . . but concerning a matter of fact. We are not at present examining upon what principles a perfect being would approve of the punishment of bad actions; but upon what principles so weak and imperfect a creature as man actually and in fact approves of it" (*TMS* II.i.5.10). This exchange recalls Sen's observation that Smith's theory of justice is comparative, not transcendental, as well as my observation that Smith's work represents a dialectic negotiating between the ideal and the actual.[42]

Smith's criticism of Mandeville in *TMS* mirrors the rhetorical complexity one encounters in the relation between Smith's two books. His condemnation is not as clear-cut as one would expect given that Smith does ultimately reject Mandeville's and Hobbes's egoism in this first sentence and that Smith asserts that Mandeville's "notions" are "in almost every respect erroneous" (*TMS* VII. ii.4.6). His response is further obfuscated by the fact that he comments several times on Mandeville's rhetoric, observing that his text is "lively and humorous" with a "rustic eloquence" that would allow the "unskillful" to be convinced by an "air of truth and probability" in his doctrine (*TMS* VII.ii.4.6). He also refers to Mandeville's argument as "ingenious sophistry" (*TMS* VII.ii.4.11). This rhetorical attack on Mandeville shares similarities with Smith's attack on Shaftesbury's florid text in *LRBL* (i.145) and on Plato's critique of the rhetoricians.

Smith's periodic tempering of his remarks about Mandeville seems to run counter to his more extreme assertions. He writes that Mandeville's system "in some respects bordered upon the truth" (*TMS* VII.ii.4.14), and despite the fact that it "once made so much noise in the world," it "never gave occasion to more vice than what would have been without it" (*TMS* VII.ii.4.13). Smith next asserts that individuals are not easily deceived by a "system" that "pretends to inform us of what passes in our neighbourhood, and of the affairs of the very parish which we live in" (*TMS* VII.ii.4.14) and then reminds us yet again that any system that appears convincing even to the most "injudicious and unexperienced reader" must "bear some resemblance to the truth, and must even have a considerable mixture of truth in [it]" (*TMS* VII.ii.4.14). These comments apply easily to Mandeville.

Finally, in *TMS*, when it is time to condemn Mandeville's assertions about the primacy of self-love, Smith becomes agnostic. He writes, "Whether the most generous and public-spirited actions may not, in some sense, be regarded as proceeding from self-love, I shall not at present examine. The decision of this question is not, I apprehend, of any importance towards establishing the reality of virtue, since *self-love may frequently be a virtuous motive of action*. I shall only endeavour to show that the desire of doing what is honourable and noble, of rendering ourselves the proper objects of esteem and approbation, cannot with any propriety be called vanity" (*TMS* VII.ii.4.8, emphasis added).

Against the traditional formulation of the Adam Smith Problem, this passage seems to be a smoking gun. Even in *TMS* Smith leaves open the possibility that self-interest may motivate public-spirited actions—a theme that dominates *WN*. Thus his rejection of Mandeville becomes framed as a more subtle dispute: Mandeville is wrong that self-love is synonymous with vanity, but not that self-love is an important motivation in human action.

According to Smith, there are three problems with Mandeville's approach. The first is that it "take[s] away altogether the distinction between vice and virtue" (*TMS* VII.ii.4.6), a critique that suggests Smith's objection to anything that subverts the possibility of rational adjudication. The second, or "the great fallacy of Dr. Mandeville's book," is "to represent every passion as wholly vicious, which is so in any degree and in any direction" (*TMS* VII.ii.4.12). This should also be understood as a subversion of a complex rationality because Mandeville presumes a binary rather than a nuanced comparison of sentiments. The third, which does not concern us in this book, is that Mandeville confuses wealth and money. I set this aside because it is primarily an economic argument and because, as Jimena Hurtado-Prieto shows, it is as much a response to mercantilism in general as it is to Mandeville.[43]

According to Smith, Mandeville confuses the desire to do praiseworthy acts with the desire to be praised and, as such, treats any reference "to what are, or to what ought to be the sentiments of others" as vanity, a term Mandeville defines as "a love of praise and commendation" (*TMS* VII.ii.4.12, VII.ii.4.7). The consequence is that "all preference of public to private interest, is, according to him, a mere cheat and imposition upon mankind; and that human virtue which is so much boasted of, and which is the occasion of so much emulation among men, is the mere offspring of flattery begot upon pride" (*TMS*

VII.ii.4.7). Despite the criticism and the foreshadowing of *The Wealth of Nations*, Smith seems to agree that private vices *do* lead to public benefits, thereby adopting Mandeville's observation that luxuries help build a strong commercial society (*TMS* VII.ii.4.12).

In short, Smith's criticism of Mandeville, even in *TMS*, is that humans are not solely self-interested and that an element of self-interest (or even self-love) does not condemn an action to be categorized as vanity. Here my interpretation differs from Force's: community approval is not equivalent to vanity for Smith.[44] Smith wants to preserve the possibility of adjudicating between subtle passions and interests. Additionally, according to Smith, the desire for "luxury, sensuality, and ostentation" does result in public benefits (*TMS* VII.ii.4.13). While he leaves open the question of whether self-love can lead to "public-spirited" or other-oriented actions, Smith condemns the claim that self-love is *all* there is. Had he not done so, he would have an even weaker critique of Mandeville, and his spectator theory would be incoherent.

Smith was a careful writer. He was, in Willie Henderson's words, "extraordinary [sic] cautious and circumspect."[45] It would not have been out of character for him to disguise his agreement with Mandeville even if it was moderate and justified. Smith on occasion misjudged that which would be controversial and that which would not.[46] It is no surprise, then, that Smith's critics find the tension between altruism and egoism an easy target.

The altruism/egoism debate has a long history, as does the related investigation of the balance between public and private goods. As early as Plato's *Republic*, readers are faced with both the puzzles related to the ring of Gyges (*Rep* 359d–360d) and Thrasymachus's claim that Justice is the rule of the stronger (*Rep.* 338c).[47]

The difference between Thrasymachus's claim about power and Hobbes's articulation of a war of all against all is mainly a question of metaphysics. Hobbes offers a mechanistic account of human nature with a positive consequence, thereby justifying his created system of virtue. Since, for Hobbes, the sovereign, granted authority through the social contract, declares good and evil by fiat, it is not so much that vice leads to virtue but that the absence of any ethical system at all allows for the declaration of arbitrary goodness. In *Leviathan* a capricious collective good is an improvement over the lack of any such conception.

Mandeville moves this one step further. He argues not that amorality leads to virtue but that immorality does. Vice, or human beings' natural antisocial dispositions, is the first step toward the discovery and realization of virtuous activity and a strong society. But Mandeville's readers must be careful here. He makes two different points simultaneously that are easily conflated, and "immorality" in this context is not necessarily what it seems to be.

First, building on Hobbes, Mandeville writes, "The first Rudiments of Morality ... were chiefly contrived that the Ambitious might reap the more Benefit from, and govern vast Numbers of them with the greater Ease and Security" (*Fable* I, 47). Here Mandeville agrees with Hobbes that moral virtue began with the desire of some people to govern others.[48] Humans find morality in much the same way that people, for Hobbes, follow the laws of nature. However, and in contrast to Hobbes, for Mandeville, our egoism—our natural hedonism—moves us toward virtue because "the humblest Man alive must confess, that the Reward of a Virtuous Action, which is the Satisfaction that ensues upon it, consists in a certain Pleasure he procures to himself by Contemplating on his own Worth" (*Fable* I, 57).

The difference between Hobbes's and Mandeville's arguments is subtle. Hobbes believes ethics is created, but Mandeville's account suggests more discovery than invention; this is consistent with the Scottish Enlightenment thinkers. Both Griswold and Leonidas Montes suggest that Smith might also be a realist or at least, according to Griswold, for Smith, agents "behave like moral realists."[49] Mandeville might be a realist as well. He was certainly not a relativist. He articulated a very specific and sophisticated account of virtue, defining it as "every Performance, by which Man, contrary to the impulse of Nature, should endeavour the Benefit of others, or the Conquest of his own Passions out of a Rational Ambition of being good" (*Fable* I, 48–49).[50] He adds, anticipating Kant, that "it is impossible to judge of a Man's Performance, unless we are thoroughly acquainted with the Principle and Motive from which he acts" (*Fable* I, 56).

For Mandeville, virtue, by definition, is the act of deliberately acting for the good of others with the intent of achieving that good and is therefore neither purely circumstantial nor relative. Thus Mandeville's readers are led to ask whether the vicious origins of virtue "infect" the morality of an action.[51] Since virtue is discoverable only in a system founded on vice, one might be tempted to suggest that virtue is inherently corrupt. Does virtue have to be genealogically pure? Clearly, Mandeville thinks not, and Smith seems to reject the idea as well. As noted earlier, he tells us that "the great fallacy of Dr. Mandeville's book" is "to represent every passion as wholly vicious, which is so in any degree and in any direction" (*TMS* VII.ii.4.12).

That virtue has vicious elements may seem problematic to the purist, but Mandeville's readers would have expected a certain element of paradox in his work. E. J. Hundert tells us that Mandeville was understood to be a writer of *maxims*, codas or propositions that had, at one time, adorned the houses or tableware of those who sought to emulate Erasmus. Hundert writes, "The maxim writer was expected to draft the 'greatest' or 'universal' truths into a literary code of rules. . . . The best maxims sought to reframe a particular phenomenon in a new dynamic context so as to offer with striking conciseness an unexpected and often disturbing general truth which would intuitively, even if reluctantly, command assent."[52] Mandeville was writing in a rhetorical and literary context that embraced internal tensions rather than in a modern analytic context that eschews them, an interesting anticipation of Foucault and the post-modernists that follow him. In his literary complexity, Hundert writes, "Mandeville had no eighteenth-century peer."[53]

Mandeville offers a second argument in *The Fable of the Bees*. Whereas the first is anthropological, the other is political or economic. The first argues that vice leads to the discovery of virtue, the second contends that the political and economic consequences of egoistic desires result in a strong, affluent, stable society. This is a different point; economics are a matter not of virtue but of success. In the poem that begins the text, Mandeville writes, "Whilst Luxury Employ'd a Million of the Poor / And odious Pride a Million more / Envy it self, and Vanity / Were Ministers of Industry" (*Fable* I, 25). Mandeville defines society as "a Body Politick, in which Man either subdued by Superior Force, or by Persuasion drawn from his Savage State, is become a Disciplin'd Creature, that can find his own Ends in Labouring for others, and where under one Head or other Form of Government each Member is render'd Subservient to the Whole, and all of them by cunning Management are made to Act as one" (*Fable* I, 347).

This account seems entirely drawn from *Leviathan*, but where Hobbes stops, Mandeville continues. Hobbes argues that the formation of the state allows for the beneficial consequences of the moral code: acting under the rule of the sovereign prevents the state of war. Mandeville, on the other hand, claims that peace, concord, family, virtue, and charity do little for the state and that even after the state is formed, vice, not virtue, is the core of social good:

> But let us be Just, what Benefit can [peace, concord, family, virtue, and char-ity] be of, or what earthly Good can they do, to promote the Wealth, the Glory and worldly Greatness of Nations? It is the sensual Courtier that sets no Limits to his Luxury; the Fickle Strumpet that invents new Fashions every Week; the haughty Dutchess that in Equipage, Entertainments, and all her Behaviour would imitate a Princess; the profuse Rake and lavish Heir, that scatter about their Money without Wit or Judgment, buy every thing they see, and either destroy or give it away the next Day. . . . It is these that are the Prey and proper Food of a full grown Leviathan. . . . to procure an honest Livelihood to the vast Multitudes of working poor. (*Fable* I, 355)

According to Goldsmith, even in *The Female Tatler* Mandeville sees vice as contributing to society in two ways: "Vice in the sense of physical deficiency, privation and need makes society necessary for human survival; secondly, vice in the sense of moral defect (greed, vanity, pride, selfishness, lust, luxury, and envy) stimulates production and improvement."[54]

It would be wrong to see Mandeville as a relativist who believes that vice begets virtue in a political context. Morally, instead, vice creates society that then allows for the *discovery* of virtue. Individuals rationally derive virtue "negatively"; they see what it is not. Smith makes a similar point. For Mandeville, vice creates activity that then provides occupation. The subtitle of *The Fable of the Bees* is private vices, public *benefits*, not private vices, public *virtues*. Mandeville is not arguing that vicious acts become virtuous; this would run counter to his definition of virtue. Instead, he argues that vice strengthens society because it offers the occasion for trade, manufacture, and employment.

For Mandeville, vice is not simply an immoral act. It is anything that people think of as an evil: "Not moral defects only, but such things as pestilences, the niggardliness of nature, and all the natural drawbacks that render people discontented with their lot and rouse them to exertion."[55] He defines vice as an action within which it can be observed, "the least prospect, that it might either be injurious to any of the Society, or ever render [the moral actor] less serviceable to others" (*Fable* I, 48). Interestingly, Mandeville knew very well that his title would cause controversy, but he hoped that a select readership would see through the confusion. In *Letter to Dion* he writes, "The true Reason why I made use of the Title, *Private Vices, Publick Benefits*, I sincerely believe, was to raise Attention: As it is generally 'counted to be a Paradox, I pitch'd upon it in Hopes that those who might hear it or see it, would have the Curiosity to know, what could be said to maintain it; and perhaps sooner buy the Book, than they would have done otherwise."[56]

A. K. Rogers has us further temper Mandeville's notion of vice. He tells us that Mandeville did not argue that vices are necessary to society per se. They are instead "only necessary to the sort of society with which his readers are familiar, and which aims at wealth and power and expansion."[57] Thomas Horne adds that Mandeville maintains "a rigorous moral standard, which man is unable to live up to."[58] And Goldsmith notes that *The Fable of the Bees* "does not prescribe what it describes."[59] As F. B. Kaye puts it, a concise summary of Mandeville's position might be the following: "Since you will be wicked in any case . . . whether your country is prosperous or not, you might as well be wicked and prosperous."[60]

In Sterling Lamprecht's interpretation Mandeville categorizes acts into three, not two, groups: vices which are acts resulting from passions, virtues in which reason wholly determines the acts, and a third group of acts which are neither vicious nor virtuous.[61] Reason here is a form of judgment, not a faculty. Acts that are neither vicious nor virtuous do not run contrary to reason, but "reason has not extirpated passion." Lamprecht adds, "To the observer they resemble virtue, but in his inner heart [the actor] knows that he is morally at fault."[62] Notice that all of a sudden this discussion of virtue is also a discussion of rationality. Virtue is directly connected to the rationality of its justification.

Mandeville's account of rationality is Hobbesian. For Hobbes, good reasoning must meet two criteria. First, it must recognize the consistency of a personal language, and, second, it must be the outcome of an ordered thought process. Reasoning is good for Hobbes insofar as there is an identifiable progression of words or beliefs leading to the acquisition of that which is desired. It is the product of the human machine, with the only standard of evaluation being the fulfillment of the desire of the machine.[63]

Mandeville has a similar linear notion of rationality; Force describes it as "a strict determinism of the passions: we can only do what our passions prompt us to do."[64] New circumstances lead to new opportunities, Mandeville tells us; new motivations replace previous motivations. As Rogers describes it, "We are courageous because we get angry and forget our fears, honorable because we do not dare to face public condemnation, industrious from necessity or avarice, public-spirited because it is in this way that our vanity can most easily be fed."[65] For Mandeville, then, there is no sense that motivations may cumulatively affect a conclusion or that information is balanced and harmonized in order to support a moral action. In fact, Mandeville doubts whether rationality can govern a large-scale polity at all.[66] Agents born with the rational capacity develop and use this capacity only after society is formed; it is bound together with the development of language. Mandeville writes, "Man is a rational Creature, but he is not endued with Reason when he comes into the World; nor can he afterwards put it on when he pleases, at once, as he may a Garment. Speech likewise is a Characteristick of our Species, but no Man is born with it" (*Fable* II, 190).

For Mandeville, rationality can govern individual action but not "political administration."[67] Horne explains that "attempts to initiate large-scale reform of society are the result of pride, which causes man to overstate his own knowledge and abilities."[68] There is an obvious place for Smith's invisible hand in this notion of rationality.[69] Smith too is skeptical of social engineering or large-scale governance and uses the positive effect of unintended consequences to help mitigate this skepticism. Nevertheless, even with this addition to Hobbesian rationality, Mandeville does not allow for multiple motivations for human acts—this will be left for Shaftesbury, Hutcheson, and Smith—and because of this Mandeville's account will be inadequate for the political task it aspires to achieve.

Furthermore, with his more complex definition of virtue, Mandeville has laid the foundation for Smith's use of self-interest in WN, including, one can see from *Fable* I, 355, possibly suggesting the title of the book. He also provides a way for helping us conceptualize the relationship between the two books. The first, *TMS*, rejected Mandeville's Hobbesian claim that virtues, in general, are discovered through vice. The second, WN, tempered but did not reject Mandeville's claim that vice leads to public benefits. By dividing the response between the two books Smith is also able to distinguish between moral psychology and political economy.[70] In the end, Lamprecht argues, "it was not until Adam Smith that Mandeville's denial of virtue to most men was effectively answered."[71] It may be the case that of all those who responded to Mandeville, Smith was the only one who actually read both parts of the *Fable*.[72]

I am not making a claim about Smith's personal motivations—I do not purport to know Smith's mind and am therefore reluctant to suggest that Smith explicitly knew he had divided his response to Mandeville in this way. Channeling Brown, in this instance, I would suggest that the author's intention does not take priority. I am arguing instead that the relationship between the books becomes clearer when we understand them in this manner. *The Wealth of Nations* tempered Mandeville's political and economic claims while offering a systematic response to mercantilism and enumerating the limits of the sovereign; there Smith focuses on bettering one's own condition and on choosing the type of society that would take vice into account. *The Theory of Moral Sentiments* complementarily countered Mandeville's moral claims that virtue is the product of political manipulation, but for this, Smith also required Shaftesbury's and Hutcheson's discourses. Both take the political tensions between virtue and vice and convert them into a problem of personal identity and rationality. Whereas for Mandeville the conflict between the two is a public matter, for Shaftesbury and Hutcheson it is a problem of personal deliberation.

2

One System, Many Motivations

I have argued for two claims so far. First, that Smith's books are related in a very specific way: *TMS* rejects Mandeville's argument that virtues are discovered through vice, while *WN* accepts but tempers Mandeville's claim that vice leads to public benefits.[1] Their relationship is one of compatible difference, not contradiction, a conceptualization that flies in the face of the Adam Smith Problem. Second, I have shown that Mandeville, while moving past a binary notion of rational adjudication is, in some sense, struggling to free himself from Hobbesian linear rationality. Smith, learning from Mandeville but needing more than *The Fable* provides, looked toward the dialogical elements found in *The Female Tatler* and in other philosophers. It is my contention in this chapter that a key ingredient for Smith's rationality comes from Shaftesbury's account of the soliloquy. This, combined with Hutcheson's multiple inborn senses, evolves into Smithian sympathy and his conception of the impartial spectator.

SHAFTESBURY AND HUTCHESON

Practically speaking, Shaftesbury's *Characteristicks of Men, Manners, Opinions, Times* was written during the same philosophical period as *The Fable of the Bees*, although their production shared only a relatively short overlap.[2] Mandeville's first mention of Shaftesbury was in 1723, but Shaftesbury could not have mentioned Mandeville in return since the *Fable* had no authorial attribution until after Shaftesbury died in 1713.

Shaftesbury is clearly concerned with denying the power of self-interest and with doing so by attacking Hobbes's doctrines of egoism and the naturally antisocial nature of humans. For our purposes it is useful to think of Shaftesbury as a foundational element in the response to Mandeville, although there is no clear evidence that Shaftesbury ever read his work. Hutcheson certainly thought of the two in opposition. He indicated on the title page of his *Inquiry* that the book was an explicit defense of Shaftesbury's principles against Mandeville's attack.[3]

Mandeville announces his opposition to Shaftesbury in no uncertain terms, stating that "two Systems cannot be more opposite than his Lordship's and mine" (*Fable* I, 324). Although he calls Shaftesbury's comments, "a high Compliment to Human-kind, and capable by the help of a little Enthusiasm of Inspiring us with the most Noble Sentiments concerning the Dignity of our exalted Nature," he adds, "what Pity it is that they are not true" (*Fable* I, 324).

Mandeville is correct in describing them as opposites. In particular, Shaftesbury and Mandeville differ in their optimism regarding the human condition.[4] Whereas Mandeville rooted all actions in self-interest, Shaftesbury had a "large and generous view of human nature."[5]

But, as with Mandeville's *Fable*, responding to Shaftesbury is not simply a task of countering moral assumptions or conclusions. Rhetoric and motivation are intertwined with Shaftesbury's philosophy. First and foremost, where Mandeville wanted to shock, Shaftesbury wanted to be "polite," a central concern in English discourse at the end of the seventeenth century, including Mandeville's writing.[6] Although the term starts off denoting an extension of civility and courtesy, politeness ends up indicating a complex interplay between sociality and philosophy with special attention to a changing idea of virtue.[7] For Shaftesbury, the *Characteristicks* was "to recommend MORALS on the same foot, with what in a lower sense is call'd *Manners*; and to advance PHILOSOPHY . . . on the very Foundation of what is call'd *agreeable* and *polite*" (*Char.* III, 100).

For Shaftesbury, the social nature of philosophy leads to the conclusion that dialogue is the ideal philosophical form. It represents the internal moral debates experienced by the virtuous, but it also brings forth the forms and styles of moral conversation: "Good talk demonstrates good-breeding and ethical character; for Shaftesbury decorum and truth are fundamentally linked."[8] It is here that one begins to see the power of the term 'manners' in Shaftesbury's title. In the eighteenth century it "still carried with it the full force of what we generally call 'morals' . . . they reveal our true character in that which most defines us: our social nature or sociability."[9]

This leads us to the second difficulty in interpreting Shaftesbury's work: the role aesthetics play in moral deliberation. Rationality, for Shaftesbury, includes more than just logical relations, a sharp contrast to our contemporary analytic vision. He sought to unify the good and the beautiful, arguing that they are one and the same.[10] Thus, as in the case of Mandeville, responding to Shaftesbury is a complex project involving attention to multiple aims and to a lack of disciplined systematization; Shaftesbury himself is explicit that his work is not a unified whole (*Char.* III, 176).[11] Also as with Mandeville's work, to attack or develop Shaftesbury's moral system is to walk a fine line between philosophical argument and social and political considerations. Perhaps this can account for the odd fact that both Mandeville and Smith engage in *ad hominem* attacks against Shaftesbury in the midst of their philosophical argumentation.[12]

Shaftesbury is concerned with the relationship between self-interest and the public good but argues that psychological egoism proves to be meaningless. If all actions are self-interested, he explains, then the term 'self-interest' ceases to have meaning.[13] Or, as Force describes, channeling Macaulay's response to James Mill, "If self-interest explains everything, it explains nothing."[14] The solution, according to Shaftesbury, is to return to the Platonic attempt to harmonize the self and public interest. (Plato is also clearly visible in both Shaftesbury's commitment to dialogue and his equating the Good and the Beautiful.) This is done, to a large extent, through personal deliberation, implying again a specific, albeit rudimentary, theory of rationality. Shaftesbury's aesthetic, rhetorical, psychological, and philosophical concerns all meet in his account of personal moral adjudication. They manifest themselves in the locus of the internal dialogue of the soliloquy, the location for the negotiation of virtue and vice.

The soliloquy is the process by which a normal person, aware of his or her own faults, "takes himself to task, without sparing himself in the least." It is a process of self-dissection. "By virtue of this SOLILOQUY [a person] becomes two distinct *Persons*. He is Pupil and Preceptor. He teaches, and he learns" (*Char.* I, 100).

For Shaftesbury, the soliloquy is the means of cultivating moral activity. Virtue requires reflection (*Char.* II, 18). It is the internalization of philosophy and the natural evolution of the Delphic command to know oneself (*Char.* I, 102). Self-understanding leads to virtuous activity. It clarifies a person's intent and character, leading to the will's moral action, the proper resolution of a moral conflict, the clarity of one's own "Meaning and Design," and consistency of character and action: to be "*one and the same* Person to day as yesterday, and to morrow as to day" (*Char.* I, 116). Whereas Locke looked to rewards and punishment to cultivate moral behavior, for Shaftesbury, "virtue was not a matter of prudential calculation . . . but a case of following nature and the disinterested impulses of affection, love, and friendship that animated the soul."[15]

According to Shaftesbury, virtue is a harmony of passions and motives. He argues that there are three types of affections: natural and social, which focus on two or more persons; private or "*Self-affections*," the focus of which is on the person herself or himself; and "*unnatural Affections*," which tend neither to public nor private goods (*Char.* II, 50). Virtue is, then, *"a certain just Disposition, or proportionable Affection of a rational Creature towards the moral Objects of Right and Wrong"* (*Char.* II, 23). Even Shaftesbury's definition of virtue incorporates his notion of rationality.

Shaftesbury writes that a person must bring his or her passions into line with the proper objects of what is appropriately good and harmonize, "Mind and Temper, sutable, and agreeing with the Good of his *Kind*, or of that *System* in which he is included, and of which he constitutes a PART" (*Char.* II, 45). A person must also harmonize his or her own goods with the needs of others: "to stand thus well affected, and to have one's Affections *right* and *intire*, not only in respect of one's self, but of Society and the Publick" (*Char.* II, 45).

Earlier I discussed Mandeville's claim that private vice leads to public benefits and cautioned against the suggestion that vice led to virtue. Shaftesbury complicates this by offering a variation on this suggestion, namely, private goods lead to public goods: "Affection towards private or Self-good, however *selfish* it may be esteem'd, is in reality not only consistent with publick Good, but in some measure contributing to it" (*Char.* II, 13). Selfish passions are, for Shaftesbury, "more than ordinary Self-concernment, or Regard to private Good, which is inconsistent with the Interest of the Species or Publick" (*Char.* II, 13). He argues that there is a normal level of self-interest that is neither morally reprehensible nor a violation of the public interest.[16] Instead, self-interest is "basically [a] narrowness of perspective" and unselfishness is, "by contrast . . . [a] largeness of vision."[17] As Shaftesbury writes, "Thus every Immorality and Enormity of Life can only happen from a partial and narrow View of Happiness and Good" (*Char.* III, 186).

Shaftesbury departs from Mandeville's approach; he refuses to consider self-interest a vice at all. If one's self-interest is against the good of all, then the agent is simply mistaken in thinking the act is in his or her best interest in the first place. It is, instead, "ill and unnatural toward himself" (*Char.* II, 13). Reminiscent of *Republic*, natural tendencies can be harmonized in such a way that all self-interest is made beneficial to the community; only ignorance advises agents to act in ways that are harmful to themselves or society. He also anticipates Smith's impartial spectator, seeing partiality as narrowness of vision and impartiality as the attempt to see circumstances beyond one's own interest.

To put this in terms of pluralism, for Mandeville, self-interest is the means to meeting one's goal in the face of otherness, regardless of the extent of difference one encounters, but for Shaftesbury, difference and otherness are harmonious. Whatever the nature of the diversity of any given society, what is good for one individual is good for all. This supports James Otteson's observation that Shaftesbury anticipated Smith's "invisible-hand explanations of selected social phenomena" and the pursuit of collective good.[18] Shaftesbury uses the phrase "visible band' to point to the coherence of different interests, but he also ends up leading directly into a discussion of sympathy, which leads to the subject of fellowship (*Char. I*, 70–72).

Returning to the question of virtue, for Shaftesbury, something is a vice only when it meets very specific characteristics. An act is vicious, "1. When *either* the publick Affections are weak or deficient, 2. OR the private and Self-affections too strong, 3. OR that such Affections arise as are neither of these, nor in any degree tending to the Support either of the publick or private System" (*Char.* II, 56). With an eye toward Smith's argument, Shaftesbury's comments are advancements on Mandeville's because they challenge the notion that self-interest is inherently vicious. They argue that private good is compatible with public good and that human beings are naturally sociable. In addition, by relying on the soliloquy—an internal dialogue in which a moral actor imagines an interlocutor for the purpose of dialectical reasoning—and by suggesting that the battle between virtue and vice is primarily one of self-identity and personal deliberation, Shaftesbury allows for multiple motivations for any particular act, some of which are themselves virtuous and some of which are not.

Smith's impartial spectator seems directly related to Shaftesbury's soliloquy. For Smith, a moral actor, when faced with a decision, imagines an observer who judges his or her actions from either a community point of view or an even wider humanistic perspective. This "impartial" attitude (exactly how impartial the spectator can be will be addressed later), helps the moral actor overcome immediate self-interest and vanity. The creation of both Smith's impartial spectator and Shaftesbury's soliloquizing is a process of dialogical self-division. Both require using the imagination to enter into another perspective, and both suggest that the passions are a central component of the internal dialogue. Additionally, both presuppose the presence of multiple influential forces that require rational adjudication in some form or another.

Smith's one mention of Shaftesbury in *TMS* is critical. He describes Shaftesbury's system as seeking "a proper balance of the affections, and in allowing no passion to go beyond its proper sphere" (*TMS* VII.ii.1.48). But his criticism is that Shaftesbury's approach does not give "any precise or distinct measure by which this fitness or propriety of affection can be ascertained or judged of" (*TMS* VII.ii.1.49). In other words, he is critical not of Shaftesbury's attempt to harmonize or control the passions but of his negligence in not developing a method by which one is to determine their propriety. Yet this is precisely what Shaftesbury thinks he's doing with the soliloquy,[19] and this is also what Smith seeks to do with the impartial spectator.[20]

Proponents of the traditional formulation of the Adam Smith Problem suggest that *TMS* postulates altruism as the *sole* motivation for moral behavior and self-interest as the *sole* motive for commercial activity. But Smith, inspired by his predecessors, made room for numerous simultaneous motivations: "Thus self-preservation, and the propagation of the species, are the great ends which Nature seems to have proposed in the formation of all animals. Mankind are endowed with a desire of those ends, and an aversion to the contrary" (*TMS* II.i.5.10). As Joseph Cropsey points out, here Smith explicitly lists two simultaneous and opposing motivations; he is also emphasizing the plural in the second sentence. If we are to use the language of egoism and altruism, then we must ascribe both motives to human activity.[21]

The existence of multiple motives is an essential component of Smithian rationality—to be rational is to wade through a plethora of personal and social influences. Building on Shaftesbury, Smith accepts the dialogical model of the divided self. Dialogues can have multiple interlocutors—Rawls and Habermas refer to omnilogues[22]—and while both the soliloquy and the impartial spectator divide the agent into two perspectives, they do so in order to manage these motivations. The rational *debate* may be binary in structure at times, but the content is much more complicated. The required rationality must be as complex as well, a significant departure for the Hobbesian and Mandevillian rationality that simply replaces one desire with another.

A further dialogical illustration of the ways in which multiple motivations work can be found in an allegory in which Shaftesbury describes the romantic longing of a young man who sought to force his love upon a princess. The youth comes to a realization: "O Sir! . . . Well am I now satisfy'd, that I have in reality within me *two distinct separate* Souls. This Lesson of Philosophy I have learnt from that villainous Sophister LOVE. For 'tis impossible to believe, that having one and the same Soul, it shou'd be actually both Good and Bad, passionate for Virtue and Vice, desirous of Contrarys. No. There must of necessity be *Two*: and when *the Good* prevails, 'tis then we act handsomely; when *the Ill*, then basely and villainously" (*Char.* I, 115).

A similar passage is in Hutcheson: "But it must be here observ'd, That as all Men have Self-Love, as well as Benevolence, these two Principles may jointly excite a Man to the same Action; and then they are to be consider'd as two Forces impelling the same Body to Motion; sometimes they conspire, sometimes are indifferent to each other, and sometimes are in some degree opposite . . . that such a Man has also in View private Advantage, along with publick Good, as the Effect of his action, does no way diminish the Benevolence of the Action" (*Inquiry*, 89).

For Shaftesbury and Hutcheson, as for Smith, moral deliberation is the process of rationally adjudicating competing sentiments representing varying degrees of morality.[23] For each, the motivations are coexistent and of varying influence. For both Shaftesbury and Hutcheson, the agent must be aware of the many competing influences that inspire an actor. For Hutcheson in particular, this is most difficult when one turns the moral looking glass upon oneself (*Inquiry*, 75).

Hutcheson does not believe that virtue is derived from vice per se. It is the product of an internal sense (*Inquiry*, 74), a moral reflection in Lockean terms[24] or a moral taste in Shaftesburyan ones.[25] Whatever its form, the moral sense communicates the pleasure of morally good acts and motivates individuals to act to maximize that pleasure.[26] Actors maximize their pleasure simply because it is pleasurable: self-love is a force in our motivation. Hutcheson writes, "Self-Love prompts us to retire from the Object which occasions our Pain, and to endeavour to divert our Thoughts" (*Inquiry*, 153).

Thus, to a great extent Hutcheson represents a synthesis of the philosophies of Locke and Shaftesbury,[27] while also using concepts from Descartes and Malebranche. Hutcheson inherits Shaftesbury's notion of the dignity in human nature and the importance of a social human nature with benevolent impulses, as well as Locke's empiricist framework and the reliance on observation.[28] Yet they both counter Locke's assertion that human experience is irreducibly diverse, returning to the concept of innate ideas to do so. Most relevant to our larger discussion, their solution to moral pluralism is, in some sense, to deny actual difference.

Hutcheson's moral sense was prefigured not just by Shaftesbury's reference to the moral sense—Shaftesbury himself tellingly calls it a reflected sense (*Char.* II, 16)—but also by his use of Stoic prolepsis, that is, the innate predisposition to naturally think in terms of a certain concept.[29] In fact, Shaftesbury seemed bitter that Locke's work demanded such a lengthy response at all, calling the debate about innateness "'one of the childishest disputes that ever was.'[30] The real question was not whether 'propositions' about right and wrong were innate but whether the inclination toward society was natural or the product of art or accident."[31]

Hutcheson also adopts Descartes's and Malebranche's treatment of bodily sensation in which a healthy, functioning body uses pleasure and pain to accurately inform itself of good and bad.[32] The morally healthy individual finds pleasure in morally good acts. Difficulties arise, however, when morally healthy individuals differ on what is morally good or what brings moral pleasure; the seventeenth- and eighteenth-century version of the problem of otherness as it manifests itself in pluralism. Hutcheson was well aware that the cultural diversity of moral opinions suggested a problem for a moral sense theory,[33] but he allows for the influence of custom and education by distinguishing between the moral sense and reason, where reason means inference. This makes room for differing opinions while preserving the universality of the moral sense.

Counter to our contemporary understanding of how education operates, Hutcheson sees custom and habit as divorced from rational justification. For him, education impairs logical inference: "By Education there are some strong Associations of Ideas without any Reason, by mere Accident sometimes, as well as by Design, which it is very hard for us ever after to break asunder."[34] Here Hutcheson follows Locke's discussion of madness and superstition,[35] but a consequence of this claim is that the moral sense operates "prior to calculation of advantage," or before certain aspects of reason.[36] Thus reason is, in some important sense, distinct from, operates separately from, or contains more than just the content of the moral sense. For Shaftesbury, the moral sense, the transformation of pity, is "a direct, immediate reaction to the sufferer's pain," and for Hutcheson, remaining close to Malebranche, sympathy is "a sort of contagion or infection."[37] In preparation for later chapters, the reader should take note of Hutcheson's use of the term 'education' to mean both experience and socialization. This foreshadows Smith's own ambiguous use of the term.

Returning to the topic at hand, the consequence of the distinction between morality and reason is Hutcheson's concern about the balance between benevolent motivations and self-love. Rational justification is, in this regard, the battleground of the passions. Self-love ensures survival while the moral sense governs our social activities—it subordinates self-love to the needs of the community.[38] Judging an act to be morally good is feeling the pleasure of contemplating it.[39] Yet what prevents Hutcheson from degenerating into Mandeville's egoism is that for Hutcheson self-love is not pleasure (*Inquiry*, 70). Pleasure leads to awareness of advantage, he argues, but is not in itself advantageous. This distinction is more complex than Hobbes would allow; Hobbes has singular notions of good and evil derived from singular notions of pleasure and pain.

Hutcheson's view of benevolence is also more complicated, allowing, specifically, for gradations in complexity and intensity: "But we are not to imagine, that all benevolent Affections are of one Kind, or alike strong. There are nearer and stronger Kinds of Benevolence, when the Objects stand in some nearer Relations to ourselves, which have obtain'd distinct Names; such as natural Affection, Gratitude, Esteem" (*Inquiry*, 140).

Thus even with Hutcheson's reliance on a moral sense, the philosophers progress in complexity regarding the types and number of motives affecting an individual. Hutcheson contributes further by adding not simply the complexity of a moral sense to the five familiar senses, but equally complicated senses of beauty, of honor, and of a public sense, all of which are inborn.[40] His account requires this multiplicity because each must offer not only an imperative regarding what to do but also a justification explaining why the act ought to be done.[41] The moral sense provides moral content with a normative conception of the good. It guarantees "distinctions between the natural and unnatural" and provides "a solid criterion for separating good from evil."[42] It "not only reports on moral reactions but judges at the same time."[43]

Here, we return to the problem of moral diversity. Since the moral sense is not simply a means to pleasure but is instead a normative power, it can even inform individuals of what is morally correct for historical figures with whom one has no connection (Smith thinks the same of sympathy). Hutcheson uses the *Aeneid* as an example (*Inquiry*, 76) but then, with an eye on Hobbes and Thrasymachus, asks why people don't simply choose to align themselves with power instead of morality. Why don't people's sympathies always rest with the victorious or "love the successful Tyrant, or Traitor?" (*Inquiry*, 76).

His answer begins with the assertion that people must have a "secret Sense which determines our Approbation without regard to Self-Interest" (*Inquiry*, 76). In other words, although pleasure leads to self-interest, there must be some notions of approbation, informed by a moral sense, that are completely independent of personal interest. Hutcheson's answer continues with a passage that Smith will adopt and modify: "Suppose any great Destruction occasion'd by mere Accident, without any Design, or Negligence of the Person who casually was the Author of it: This Action might have been as disadvantageous to us as design'd Cruelty, or Malice; but who will say he has the same Idea of both Actions, or Sentiments of the Agents? Thus also an easy, indolent Simplicity, which exposes a Man of Wealth as a Prey to others, may be as advantageous a Disposition as the most prudent Generosity, to those he converses with; and yet our Sentiments of this latter Temper are far nobler than of the former. 'Whence then this Difference?'" (*Inquiry*, 76).

It is noteworthy that this passage is immediately followed by a reference to Hobbes. Whereas Hobbes argues that all of our moral actions are derived from self-interest, Hutcheson has finally completely divorced himself from this claim, and in order to do so he relies on literature and accounts of historical persons. As it is for Shaftesbury, for Hutcheson, aesthetics and morality are intertwined. It is this lack of separation that causes so much difficulty for contemporary readers and for the progression to Smith, who will also see literature and historical accounts as central to moral adjudication.

Hutcheson's answer to why people side with morality even in instances that are not related to their self-interest is the moral sense—this "secret sense" that he referred to before introducing his thought experiment—an answer that Smith only partially rejects. Sympathy, for Smith, is also a natural capacity that incorporates moral and aesthetic elements. It is empirical in nature but it assumes a certain a priori capacity that cultivates the social nature of humanity. Like Shaftesbury's Stoic prolepsis, the moral sense "took place prior to any social input, contribution from the will, rational reflection, or intervention of self-interested impulses."[44]

Reminiscent of the moral sense, and in a paragraph immediately preceding a discussion of Hutcheson, Smith refers to sympathy as a "power" (TMS VII.iii.3.3). His use of it is the consequence of an extended discourse, the goal of which is moral adjudication and the management of multiple human motivations. This discourse, as we have seen, is steeped in questions regarding the nature of rationality and the consequences of moral difference. Diversity and pluralism are at the forefront of the philosophers' thinking.

THE ADAM SMITH PROBLEM AND THE PRIORITY OF THE MORAL SENTIMENTS

With Shaftesbury's and Hutcheson's dialogical rationalities in place, I now return to my methodological assertion about the priority of TMS. I do so in order to defend my claim that this dialogical rationality is incompatible with rational choice theory and other economic or mathematical accounts of rationality. I have already argued that TMS and WN play interrelated parts in a response to Mandeville; the early book rejects his most extreme conclusions and the later one accepts but tempers others. I have also argued that Smith builds on his predecessors' understanding of individuals as being moved by multiple motivations at once, and that these predecessors offered different solutions regarding how these motivations were to be reconciled with difference. Both of these claims have interpretive consequences as well as philosophical ones. Let us therefore consider a modern variant of the Adam Smith Problem and examine how my account of Smith's theory of agency further undermines its claims.

The original Adam Smith Problem asserted that Smith offered two radically different schemes of human motivation: TMS's 'sympathy' was said to refer to an altruistic human nature, while WN's 'self-interest' was alleged to be egoistic.[45] The inspiration for this interpretation was as political as it was philosophical. German economists saw Smith's philosophy as a threat in two ways. First, they feared that the "Manchester school," as founded by Smith, sought to monopolize English manufacture. They were threatened by the individualistic emphasis they viewed as "opposition to the older cameralistic tradition that assumed that society and its members needed guidance."[46] Second, they "conflated the ideals of the French Revolution with Smith's legacy" and hoped to "'overcome" Smith's and Rousseau's "rationalistic Enlightenment," assuming that the two thinkers had a common project.[47]

Contemporary scholars have collectively challenged the legitimacy of the Adam Smith Problem, reasserting that sympathy was not meant to be altruistic and that self-interest is neither the single motive for economic activity nor purely egoistic.[48] In the last decades, however, numerous authors, in a wide variety of venues, have replaced the original formulation with a host of other Adam Smith Problems, a diverse list of supposed incompatibilities between *TMS* and *WN* that call the unity of Smith's work into question.

The most intriguing of these can be found in James Otteson's *Adam Smith's Marketplace of Life*.[49] First, Otteson observes that *TMS* rests judgment upon the impartial spectator and its concomitant virtues, but there is no mention of them in *WN*. Second, he claims that *WN* puts forth a singular self-interested motivation that all people share to "better their own condition," while *TMS* offers more complex, more altruistic motivations.[50] An important component of Otteson's solution to the Adam Smith Problem—he does eventually "solve" it—is to argue that Smith presents a single organizational structure throughout all of his work, the market.[51] The dominance of the market model, he argues, is evidence that "central parts of Smith's corpus are, on a deep level, united."[52] Thus, he suggests, Smith's ethical theory as well as his theory of language is best understood if we interpret them as postulating an organizational structure akin to commercial competition.

Vivienne Brown wisely cautions us against an "integrationist approach" that risks moral justification for any market-based action simply because it is an outcome of the market.[53] As we shall see, moral considerations do become lost in the face of this all-powerful metaphor.[54] Were we to accept Otteson's view, not only would we move significantly closer to either the libertarian or economic interpretation of Smith, but we would also assent to the economic models of rationality that inform *homo economicus* and rational choice theory. These would run counter to even the bare bones account of Smith's rationality that we have seen so far, a picture that is far from complete.

As we have seen, Smith inherits from his predecessors a sophisticated notion of multiple motivations for moral acts. This notion strikes a fatal blow to the original Adam Smith Problem and, more specifically, to Otteson's newer version of it. The Adam Smith Problem necessarily presupposes single motivations for human behavior. It describes actors operating out of either some form of altruism or some form of self-love; they do not act out of lesser versions of both. Otteson continues this tradition by claiming that *TMS*'s reliance upon the impartial spectator is in tension with the spectator's absence in *WN*. However, Smith never described the impartial spectator as a tool for *all* deliberation. He introduces it in relation to "indignation" (*TMS* I.i.5.4), calls upon it to control the pitch of a person's emotions (*TMS* I.i.5.4), references its "cool" demeanor (*TMS* I.ii.3.8), uses it to measure proper gratitude and resentment (*TMS* II.i.1.7), rejects fellow feeling with selfishness (*TMS* II.ii.1.3), uses it to help counter the desire to do evil in order to avoid placing one's own happiness above that of others, to help humble the natural tendency toward self-love (*TMS* II.ii.2.1), and in many similar ways.[55] "The real or even the imaginary presence of the impartial spectator" is, for Smith, "the authority of the man within the breast," and it "is always at hand to overawe them into the proper tone and temper of moderation" (*TMS* VII.ii.1.44).

The impartial spectator is, for Smith, a moral voice but not necessarily an economic one. Its role is to define and encourage moderation—the modulation of the sentiments. While this may be useful for judicious economic decisions, it is far from sufficient. August Oncken, in his classic account (1897) of the Adam Smith Problem, writes that "self-love is not the root of *all*, but only of economic actions."[56] Force extends this to assert that "the dividing line" between the two motivations was "between Smith as a moral philosopher and Smith as an economist."[57] These authors are correct if we understand them as making claims about human rationality. The economic and the moral, as themes, are interrelated throughout both of Smith's books and his lectures. But as different styles of rational adjudication, they are distinct but analogous. Thus when Brown argues that *TMS* and *WN* have different models of action—she claims *TMS* allows for free agents, preserving the possibility of moral agency, while *WN* is more determinate[58]—it helps us understand that metaphysical *freedom* as a central concern in *TMS* while *WN* as concerning itself with political *liberty*.[59] *TMS* is a larger discussion, then, since no liberty is possible without free will, but free will is most certainly possible without liberty.

Otteson relies on the original Adam Smith Problem to argue that only singular motivations are present in each book: *TMS* operates on sympathy and *WN* on self-interest. Yet, building on his predecessors and the complex interrelationship between the two books, Smith is explicit not only that there are multiple motivations for any act but also that even benevolence and self-interest are not mutually exclusive. The very first sentence of *TMS* postulates a plurality of motivations, claiming that there are evidently "some principles" (notice the plural) that interest people in the "fortune of others" despite the singular reward of "the pleasure of seeing it" (*TMS* I.i.I.1).[60]

This concurs with Smith's famous comments about the butcher, brewer, and baker. *WN* tells us, "Nobody but a beggar chuses to depend *chiefly* upon the benevolence of his follow-citizens" (*WN* I.ii.2, emphasis added). The key word is "chiefly"; the beggar relies on benevolence sometimes but on barter otherwise. Furthermore, people's motivations change. Sometimes they are altruistic, sometimes they are not. We do "address ourselves, not to [the butcher's, brewer's, and baker's] humanity but to their self-love," but we *could* choose to do otherwise because in each of these agents "their humanity" is present (*WN* I.ii.2). For Smith, "man has almost constant occasion for the help of his brethren, and it is in vain for him to expect it from their benevolence *only*. He will be *more likely* to prevail if he can interest their self-love in his favour" (*WN* I.ii.2, emphasis added).

Again, Smith is reminding us that people cannot expect *only* benevolence from others but *some* benevolence is certainly implied. Additionally, Smith comes to a pragmatic and not a philosophical conclusion. We *can* appeal to benevolence and sometimes it will result in our assistance, but we will be *more likely* to succeed if we appeal to commercial instincts, especially since our needs are constant. This appeal to self-love is a rhetorical choice of the agent and indicative of the role of audience and narrative in argumentation and persuasion.

Otteson challenges this complex schema of motivations, claiming that agents are motivated in *WN* by the desire to better one's own condition, a self-interested motivation, "exclusively so, with no hint of benevolence."[61] As evidence for this exclusivity, he cites Smith's description of "the uniform, constant, and uninterrupted effort of every man to better his condition" (*WN* II.iii.31) and "the principle which prompts [us] to save, is the desire of bettering our condition, a desire which, though generally calm and dispassionate, comes with us from the womb, and never leaves us till we go into the grave" (*WN* II.iii.28).[62]

This fails prima facie. It is certainly possible for someone to want to better his or her own condition to benefit children, a spouse, or other loved ones, suggesting that betterment is compatible with altruism. Smith's contemporary Adam Ferguson makes this very point when he writes that we must "distinguish the selfishness of the parent when he takes care of his child, from his selfishness when he only takes care of himself."[63] More important, Otteson is simply mistaken in regarding "universal, constant, and uninterrupted" as indicating exclusivity. All living people uniformly require a "constant and uninterrupted" heartbeat, for example, yet we also uniformly require constant and uninterrupted breathing, thinking, and other activities. Uniform, constant, and uninterrupted should not imply "sole," but for Otteson they do.

In response, Otteson might suggest that self-interest is different in form from heartbeats or breathing because self-interest is inherently singular, but such is not the case. It is in our self-interest to eat, yet we choose to ingest specific foods based on taste, economic concerns, and what we wish to share with others. It is perfectly possible to be self-interested while having other concerns as well. It may not be possible to be both selfish and altruistic if we define the two terms very strictly, but there is no evidence that *TMS* is even referring to what would eventually be called altruism, let alone defining it narrowly.[64] Instead, Smith is building on Mandeville, who begins adding complexity to self-interest by distinguishing between "self-love" and "self-liking" in *The Fable*.[65] Smith himself relies upon either 'beneficence' or 'benevolence,' which scholars tend to conflate.[66]

The phrase "bettering our condition" is found in both books. In *TMS*, as Otteson himself cites, Smith defines "that great purpose of human life" as "to be observed, to be attended to, to be taken notice of with sympathy, complacency, and approbation, are all the advantages which we can propose to derive from" (*TMS* I.iii.2.1). In fact, I would suggest that *WN* is an attempt to elaborate on the meaning of "bettering our own condition" as first introduced in the earlier book, not an attempt to contradict it.

Otteson offers the narrowest interpretation of the phrase, yet moral betterment was clearly Smith's motive in both treatises. It is present in Shaftesbury and Hutcheson as well. In the end, however, my response to Otteson is likely moot because he himself concludes there is in fact no Adam Smith Problem after all; Otteson's use of it appears to be a rhetorical device.[67] The real difficulty in the book is his advocacy of the market metaphor to describe all of Smith's work—the assertion, as articulated by his title, that Smith postulates a marketplace of *life*.

While Otteson ultimately defends a systematic approach to reading Smith's work, his thesis represents a conflation of the economic and ethical. By subsuming all activity under the market, he gives unjustified priority to *WN* and risks making moral agents *homo economicus*. This implies that Smith held the more recent belief that an economic calculus can explain all human activity, while Smith would never have accepted such a notion.[68]

There are, in essence, two Adam Smiths present in the secondary literature: a caricature that bends A *Theory of Moral Sentiments* into subservience, and an account that regards Smith as a moral philosopher with a theory of political economy fully integrated into his ethics. Jerry Evensky classifies these two Smiths as the "Chicago Smith" and the "Kirkaldy Smith," respectively.[69] The former he

names after the famous Chicago School of economics—theorists such as Frank
Knight, Theodore Schultz, George Stigler, Milton Friedman, and Gary Becker,
who begin "with the assumption that humans can be represented as *homo
economicus*, beings driven by a single motive: personal utility maximization."[70]
They rely on mathematics to describe human activity and dismiss the historical
comments in *The Wealth of Nations* as digressions.[71] Smith, these economists
argue, "made the economic approach to human behavior possible."[72]

The Kirkaldy Smith is named after Smith's place of birth, a town he repeatedly returned to throughout his life, including while he was writing WN. This
Smith, Evensky explains, "does not assume that we are one dimensional in our
motives, does not see history as a 'digression' in his analysis, and does not offer
a deductive analysis that 'cries out for mathematical formulation.'"[73] Instead,

> Kirkaldy Smith sees humankind as a uniquely complex realm of nature that
> does not lend itself to such reductionism . . . this complexity derives from the
> nexus of human reason and human frailty that puts humankind in a peculiar
> and problematic position. Our reason gives us dominion over the earth and
> the ability to transform nature into material wealth far beyond our require-
> ments for survival. But that reason, when wedded to frailty, can lead to
> destructive interpersonal conflict; for, if unbridled, self-interest drives each
> of us to seek a larger share of the human bounty for ourselves, and our society
> degenerates into a 'rent-seeking society.' . . . This dynamic is especially prob-
> lematic in a liberal society where freedom of choice simultaneously
> unleashes both productive capacity and opportunities for rent-seeking.[74]

Ultimately, Evensky argues that the Kirkcaldy Smith offers a compelling
solution to the dilemma of liberal society through his "civic humanist voice
extolling 'active duty'"[75] and is both more accurate and more useful than the
Chicago Smith.

Evensky challenges the economic approach by arguing against a singular
notion of self-interest in Smith's work. He writes that there are "three broad
categories of sentiments in Smith's representation of human nature: self-love,
justice, and beneficence";[76] he later adds a fourth, "resentment," to the list.[77] He
then offers an account of how the progress of society, along with the evolution
of government structures, intertwines these sentiments: "Government authority
emerges to establish order in society, but government is neither the original
source of order nor the locus of control that establishes order in the ideal state.
Order begins and ends with the individual citizen. In the beginning, a rude
order is established by retribution based on a self-defined sense of justice. In the
end, in the limit, a refined order is established by a common acceptance of

social norms, civic ethics, among citizens with the self-command, the self-government, to enforce those norms upon themselves. Between this beginning and this end, in the course of humankind's evolution from the rude state towards the ideal, the internal and external systems of governance—norms and positive laws, respectively—shape one another as systems of justice evolve."[78]

Notice, first, how intertwined Smith's conception of progress is to his theory of normative discovery. This will require elaboration. Notice also that the power of this quote is in the way it summarily incorporates all of the elements of Smith's system. One could not make sense of this integrated approach if one began with the Adam Smith Problem's assumption that *The Theory of Moral Sentiments* and *The Wealth of Nations* are incompatible, at least in part, because both offer complementary accounts of the development of justice. "Positive law serves as an active tool for the inculcation of values," Evensky explains, "so the maturation of the citizenry and the maturation of positive law go hand-in-hand."[79] This leads him to conclude that "indeed, everything in Smith's analysis goes hand-in-hand because in his moral philosophical system, these social, economic, and political dimensions form a simultaneous, evolving system."[80]

There is a notable symmetry in Smith's works. *TMS* asks what virtue is and how it is acquired (*TMS* VII.i.2). *WN* asks what it means for a nation to be wealthy and how this wealth is to be increased. These parallel sets of questions reveal his overall project: the search for principles that govern human social interaction and deliberation. *TMS* starts with an investigation of those forces that motivate individuals, and *WN* ends with a description of the proper method of financing the sovereign. His writing thus conceived describes the continuity of experience within a society of individuals.

With this in mind, I want to return to my suggestion that *TMS* creates an unfinished discussion about bettering one's condition, a conversation that is only concluded in *WN*. I argue that by introducing the concept of bettering one's condition in *TMS*, Smith asks his reader to consider what quality of life might mean and then leaves the question unfinished until he is ready to address it in more detail.

"Bettering our condition" is used once in *TMS*, in a chapter titled "Of the origin of Ambition, and of the distinction of Ranks." In this chapter Smith challenges the notion that riches are attained for necessities, arguing that even the "meanest labourer . . . spends a great part" of his or her money "upon convenien-cies, which may be regarded as superfluities" (*TMS* I.iii.2.1). He then poses the question, in interrogative form, of where our motivation comes from to better our condition. His answer: as quoted above, we better our condition "to be observed, to be attended to, to be taken notice of with sympathy, complacency,

and approbation, are all the advantages which we can propose to derive from it"
(*TMS* I.iii.2.1).

This is the language of morality. Smith mentions sympathy first, then qualifies it with complacency, or self-satisfaction and self-approval, and, finally,
approbation, by which Smith means the approval of others. In other words, he
seems to be suggesting that the primary motivation for bettering our conditions
is to make ourselves better people—to increase our capacity for sympathy and
to eventually approve of our selves.[81] This is not to suggest that the desire for
moral betterment precludes the desire for economic betterment. As Aristotle
writes, external goods and luck are necessary for happiness, and a person may
want conveniences simply because they make life easier, which in turn may
make it easier to be moral. Nevertheless, *TMS* does seem more concerned with
intangibles, while *WN* offers a complementary discussion of tangible assets.[82]

Ultimately, Smith suggests that we wish to be observed and sympathized
with, to be "attended to," which seems to mean acknowledged and interacted
with, and to approve of ourselves. As Smith explains in his discussion of Plato
and the history of justice, "In another sense we are said not to do justice to our
neighbour unless we conceive for him all that love, respect, and esteem, which
his character, his situation, and his connexion with ourselves, render suitable
and proper for us to feel, and unless we act accordingly. It is in this sense that
we are said to do injustice to a man of merit who is connected with us, though
we abstain from hurting him in every respect, if we do not exert ourselves to
serve him and to place him in that situation in which the impartial spectator
would be pleased to see him" (*TMS* VII.ii.1.10).

While Smith does remark that justice "upon most occasions" is a negative
virtue that can be fulfilled by sitting still and doing nothing (*TMS* II.ii.1.9), he
does go on to say that Plato's account "coincides in every respect with what we
have said above concerning the propriety of conduct" (*TMS* VII.ii.1.11). Justice
in the wider meaning suggests positive moral treatment.

As we have already seen, some falsely equate bettering one's condition with
vanity, but Smith's use of the language of morality shows that this desire is
neither vicious nor a superficial attempt at receiving approval. Instead, it is
Smith's attempt to rectify "self-deceit," the "fatal weakness of mankind" that is
"the source of half the disorders of human life" (*TMS* III.4.6).

Compare the moral language of bettering one's condition to Smith's
comments elsewhere in *TMS* that "we suffer more, . . . when we fall from a
better to a worse situation, than we ever enjoy when we rise from a worse to a
better. Security, therefore, is the first and the principal object of prudence" (*TMS*
VI.i.6 and *TMS* I.iii.I.8). Although it might not be evident from the fragment,

this too is the language of morality. The discussion is in a chapter titled "Of the Character of Virtue," and the specific comment revolves around prudence, a particular virtue. For the "economic implications of prudence," the editors of *TMS* direct the reader to *WN* II.iii (*TMS* VI.i.6.fn).

The discussion of bettering one's condition in *WN* is not in the language of morality. In "Of the Wages of Labour," Smith tells us, "A plentiful subsistence increases the bodily strength of the labourer, and the comfortable hope of bettering his condition, and of ending his days perhaps in ease and plenty, animates him to exert that strength to the utmost" (*WN* I.viii.44). Then, in "Of the Accumulation of Capital, or of Productive and Unproductive Labour," Smith writes, "With regard to profusion, the principle, which prompts to expence, is the passion for present enjoyment; which, though sometimes violent and very difficult to be restrained, is in general only momentary and occasional. But the principle which prompts to save, is the desire of bettering our condition, a desire which, though generally calm and dispassionate, comes with us from the womb, and never leaves us till we go into the grave. In the whole interval which separates those two moments, there is scarce perhaps a single instant in which any man is so perfectly and completely satisfied with his situation, as to be without any wish of alteration or improvement, of any kind (*WN* II.iii.28)."

These two comments use the language of economics. If readers were to rely solely on *WN*, then bettering their condition would involve "saving" their money in order to end their "days perhaps in ease and plenty" without focusing on sympathy, complacency, or approbation. There is only the briefest hint of moral discussion here, an allusion to the relative strength of competing desires (notice, once again, Smith's commitment to the rational adjudication of multiple motivations of an act). In *WN* Smith seems insistent that the self-interest of the moment is more powerful than the desire for long-term planning, even though the less-powerful desire remains with us our entire lives. But this difference does not signify inconsistency since Smith discusses the *moral* content of self-interest in *TMS*. He writes, "If we could really believe, however, of any man, that, was it not from a regard to his family and friends, he would not take that proper care of his health, his life, or his fortune, to which self-preservation alone ought to be sufficient to prompt him, it would undoubtedly be a failing, though one of those amiable failings, which render a person rather the object of pity than of contempt or hatred. It would still, however, somewhat diminish the dignity and respectableness of his character. Carelessness and want of oeconomy are universally disapproved of, not, however, as proceeding from a want of benevolence, but from a want of the proper attention to the objects of self-interest" (*TMS* VII.ii.3.16).

In other words, *TMS* tells us that attending to one's economic self-interest is an act of propriety, and *WN* tells us how we are supposed to do it.[83] *TMS* alludes to the economic discussion but never completes it; *WN* assumes moral discussion but doesn't quite acknowledge it. In other words, *TMS* sets up the problem and *WN* continues it as if there were a link that allowed the reader to move directly from the text of *TMS* to the text of *WN*. A hyperlinked edition of the two books would illustrate this relationship perfectly.

A second place in which Smith sets up a question in *TMS* and then resolves it in *WN* involves a moral quandary in *TMS*, one that makes sense only when one understands Smith's commitment to multiple motivations. Here, Smith puts the tension between self-interest and altruism center stage. In the chapter titled "Of the Influence and Authority of Conscience," Smith poses a problem through a thought experiment. He suggests that a person, a European presumably, reading of a terrible earthquake that killed every person in China, would respond with sadness or, perhaps, philosophical speculation, but that he or she would lose much more sleep over a "frivolous disaster" such as the loss of a little finger (*TMS* III.3.4). Nevertheless, Smith asserts, no person, no matter how horrible, would ever sacrifice all the Chinese to save this finger.[84] First, he observes that "human nature startles with horror at the thought, and the world, in its greatest depravity and corruption, never produced such a villain as could be capable of entertaining it" (*TMS* III.3.4). Then he asks, "But what makes this difference? When our passive feelings are almost always so sordid and so selfish, how comes it that our active principles should often be so generous and so noble? When we are always so much more deeply affected by whatever concerns ourselves, than by whatever concerns other men; what is it which prompts the generous, upon all occasions, and the mean upon many, to sacrifice their own interests to the greater interests of others?" (*TMS* III.3.4).

Yet again Smith announces the unfinished discussion with an interrogative. Here he explicitly addresses his reader with questions that will remain only partially answered. This is strikingly similar to Hutcheson's passage identified above, asking why actors reject approbation (*Inquiry*, 76). Like his teacher before him, Smith postulates a great disaster to juxtapose selfish and altruistic actions—not in two separate books, as the proponents of the Adam Smith Problem will have us believe, but in the same book and in the same passage. He does it consciously enough to have adopted the rhetorical form and content of his predecessor. This may be baffling if we read *WN* and the market as the paradigm for interpretation, as Otteson does, but if we understand *TMS* as setting up the rules for how to read the corpus, the reader easily understands Smith as setting up an unfinished problem.

Smith mentions the tension between benevolence and self-interest else-where in *TMS*:

> Regard to our own private happiness and interest, too, appear upon many occasions very laudable principles of action. The habits of oeconomy, indus-try, discretion, attention, and application of thought, are generally supposed to be cultivated from self-interested motives, and at the same time are appre-hended to be very praise-worthy qualities, which deserve the esteem and approbation of every body. The mixture of a selfish motive, it is true, seems often to sully the beauty of those actions which ought to arise from a benevo-lent affection. The cause of this, however, is not that self-love can never be the motive of a virtuous action, but that the benevolent principle appears in this particular case to want its due degree of strength, and to be altogether unsuitable to its object. (*TMS* VII.ii.3.16)

This selection is preoccupied with the purity of virtue and with the multi-plicity of motivations. It also makes it unquestionably clear that Smith was consciously concerned with the relationship between self-interest and altruism in *TMS*, even if he emphasizes one of them in *WN*. The tension between the two motivations returns us to the discussion of the disaster in China and the distinction between active principles and passive feelings.

Smith uses the phrase 'active principles' only one other time in *TMS*, also in the chapter on duty and also in juxtaposition with passive feelings (*TMS* III.3.7). Active principles, for Smith, refer to the self-consciously derived moral rules that are the product of sympathy. He argues that the moral rules are after-the-fact constructs and thus must be *actively* formed over a long period of time using the mechanism described throughout *TMS* (*TMS* III.4.8). Smith's first treatise is a blueprint for people's *actual* moral psychologies. As referenced earlier, *TMS* "is not concerning a matter of right, if I may say so, but concerning a matter of fact" (*TMS* II.i.5.10).

Passive feelings, on the other hand, refer to our passions—those feelings that form the ingredients of our moral deliberation but do not necessarily lead us to moral activity. Only sympathy and the impartial spectator—Smith's version of the soliloquy—can convert competing passions into a harmonious character. Notice the beginning of a formula for rationality here and its connection to the will. Notice also that the question of sympathy for the Chinese is the question of moral responsibility in the face of difference, a global mosaic pluralism. Finally, notice that this approach speaks to the Stoic elements that many ascribe to Smith—moral actors must control their passive feelings in order to make use of their active principles.

In what ways and how much Smith was influenced by the Stoics is a matter of debate. Certainly, he has inherited the prohibition of overly expressive emotions as well as the assertion that the laws of ethics are discoverable through the study of the principles of nature. But whether this comes directly from the Stoics themselves or is filtered through other influences such as Shaftesbury is more difficult to determine.[85] Whatever the case, Stoicism marks a fault line for the debate between Mandeville and Shaftesbury, and it speaks to the complicated forces that influence Smith's approach. Shaftesbury, as we have seen, was heavily influenced by Stoic prolepsis but also by Stoic notions of God and Nature.[86] Mandeville, in contrast, was opposed to Stoic ideas, calling the idea of self-sufficiency, for example, a "pretence to a Chimera, and a Romantick Notion" (*Female* 109). He argued against indifference to the passions as a "ridiculous sort of virtue."[87]

The formation of and adherence to our active principles is the primary concern of *TMS*; it is that which is the goal of any moral psychology. *WN*, however, is much more concerned with our passive feelings. Our self-interest and our preferences guide our economic actions. The impartial spectator is required for moral deliberation and thus the moral actor must divide "as it were, into two persons" (*TMS* III.1.6) as one would in the soliloquy, whereas the economic actor need only concern himself or herself with price and preference (in economic matters). Here we see, once again, that Smith acknowledges both passive feelings and active principles in *TMS* but acknowledges only one in *WN*.[88] And we see that Smith once more sets up a problem in *TMS*, then concludes it in *WN*.

A note of caution: one might be tempted to suggest that this last observation reinforces the Adam Smith Problem since it can be misread to be arguing that the nature of motivations is different in *TMS* and *WN*. I am not suggesting that the two books offer different accounts of motivations; I am instead suggesting that *WN* elaborates on part of *TMS*. The comments in *WN* should be seen as an extension of a particular area of discussion, not a departure from *TMS*.

With this in mind, I now offer several other instances in which Smith begins to discuss problems in *TMS* but concludes them in *WN*. Because my discussions are necessarily truncated, these topics will be dealt with in more detail in later chapters. I have already mentioned that *TMS* concerns itself with freedom while *WN* takes a narrower approach, concerning itself with liberty. Smith's discussion of slavery also bridges the two books. In *TMS* Smith is explicit regarding the immorality of slavery. He writes, "Fortune never exerted more cruelly her empire over mankind, than when she subjected those nations of heroes to the refuse of the jails of Europe, to wretches who possess the virtues neither of the countries which they come from, nor of those which they go to, and whose levity, brutality, and baseness, so justly expose them to the contempt of the vanquished" (*TMS* V.2.9). In contrast, in *WN* he offers an antislavery argument from a different perspective: the perceived economic advantages of slavery are false advantages. Smith opposes the practice on economic grounds in addition to moral ones. The slave owner is motivated to work diligently to increase production. In contrast, the slave, "who can acquire nothing but his maintenance, consults his own ease by making the land produce as little as possible over and above that maintenance" (*WN* III.ii.12). It seems odd that *TMS* and *WN* offer such radically different responses until one sees the two books as complementary instead of contradictory. In *TMS* Smith announces the problem dramatically in moral terms, but in *WN* he finishes the discussion in economic ones. In this example, Smith, like his beggar, appeals to his readers' humanity yet depends chiefly, but not solely, on their self-interest; his rhetorical style mimics his philosophical conclusions. Thus there appear to be multiple motivations for his readers as well as for his agents.

Next, Smith places great importance on the role of education in society. For Smith, education is so fundamental to the development of moral judgment that one can judge the quality of a society's educational system by examining the moral activities of those who have learned from it. Smith highlights this relationship by comparing the ancient Greek and Roman methods of education: two cultures that are used to represent excellence so much that "our prejudice is perhaps rather to over rate them" (*WN* V.i.f.45). Smith uses the term 'education' interchangeably, sometimes referring to socialization or acculturation (*TMS* III.3.7, *WN* V.i.f.47[89]) and sometimes to institutional education (*TMS* IV.ii.1.10, *WN* V.i.f). *TMS* refers explicitly to both, but *WN* focuses almost entirely on institutional education, devoting two important chapters to its role as a social good. Smith presents the problem in the earlier book that he completes in the later one.

In another example, in *TMS* Smith is quick to dispense with the role of the sovereign. He writes, "The civil magistrate is entrusted with the power not only of preserving the public peace by restraining injustice, but of promoting the prosperity of the commonwealth, by establishing good discipline, and by discouraging every sort of vice and impropriety; he may prescribe rules, therefore, which not only prohibit mutual injuries among fellow-citizens, but command mutual good offices to a certain degree" (*TMS* II.ii.1.8).

Yet in *WN* he spends a great deal of time on this topic and on the ways in which the sovereign may discourage vice and impropriety. Smith could not have thought that his brief comments in *TMS* would suffice, especially since the science of the legislator would constitute such a large portion of his corpus.

The passage in *TMS* seems more of a placeholder than an argument; the required argument for the nature and limits of the sovereign is simply too large and cumbersome for a book on moral psychology. Smith locates it in his larger scheme, returns to it later in *WN*, and, in fact, promises a further pass at it in his work on jurisprudence that he would never finish.

Yet another instance of the earlier book leading to the later can be found in *TMS*'s example of a Quaker striking someone who has initiated a fight. He writes, "A very devout Quaker, who upon being struck upon one cheek, instead of turning up the other, should so far forget his literal interpretation of our Saviour's precept, as to bestow some good discipline upon the brute that insulted him, would not be disagreeable to us. We should laugh and be diverted with his spirit, and rather like him the better for it. But we should by no means regard him with that respect and esteem which would seem due to one who, upon a like occasion, had acted properly from a just sense of what was proper to be done. No action can properly be called virtuous, which is not accompanied with the sentiment of self-approbation" (*TMS* III.6.13).

This remark concludes Smith's discussion of religion, in the chapter on duty, in which he calls for toleration (*TMS* III.6.12). This is also the location in which Smith argues that "false notions of religion are almost the only causes which can occasion any very gross perversion of our natural sentiments in this way; and that principle which gives the greatest authority to the rules of duty, is alone capable of distorting our ideas of them in any considerable degree" (*TMS* III.6.12). Yet Smith does not articulate what we are to do to counter the power of religion. He saves this for his discussion of education in the later book.

In the same section of *WN* in which he discusses institutional education Smith describes a process by which the state can discourage fanaticism by encouraging frequent public events (*WN* I V.I.g.15). Public festivals and gatherings offer an opportunity for public scrutiny of the newest religions. The new sects, by virtue of their newness, offer more excitement and appeal than familiar sects do, yet their public scrutiny would make them open to public ridicule, opening them up to perhaps the most effective of all social pressures, a plan, incidentally, that echoes Shaftesbury's suggestion in *Characteristicks* (*Char.* I, 6–14).[90] It is not coincidental that this solution is parallel to the process of sympathy, although, once again, Smith leaves out the moral terminology in *WN*. In *TMS*, then, Smith offers us an example of the public's role in judging and tempering a radical religion,[91] and in *WN* he informs us of the mechanics required for that role to function properly and rationally. I return to this subject later, but I want to note that Smith here is focused on one of the central concerns of modern liberal pluralism: the management of religious difference.

A further example of the connection between the two books involves Smith's most famous turn of phrase. In *TMS* Smith announces how participants in the market "are led by an invisible hand to make nearly the same distribution of the necessaries of life, which would have been made, had the earth been divided into equal portions among all its inhabitants" (*TMS* IV.i.10). He alludes to the benefit of unintended consequences but offers little in the way of elaboration as to how this market works other than a passing comment about "providence" dividing the earth. In fact, his remarks on the invisible hand are sandwiched between a parable about a poor man's son who mistakes riches for happiness (*TMS* IV.i.8) and a wondrous observation describing the human "love of system" that allows people to consider the operations of public policy beautiful.

It is only in *WN* that any of these ideas are discussed in any detail. Books 3 and 4 illustrate the "natural progress of opulence" and systems of economy; book 5 addresses the nature and beauty of public policy. While one could argue that all of *WN* is an elaboration of Smith's passage about equally dividing the necessities of the earth among all people, all such interpretations bolster the fact that *WN* is largely a footnote to this section of *TMS*.

Until now I have focused on the priority of *TMS* in regard to *WN*; its precedence is harder to see with Smith's unpublished work than it is with *WN*. His lectures on rhetoric are presented while he is lecturing at Glasgow College and writing *TMS*. I argue that they are intrinsic to both his theory of rationality and his philosophy of history. His essays on philosophical subjects are attempts at working out ideas, most of which he didn't want published. His lectures on jurisprudence are both attempts to work out ideas that end up in *WN* and that are intended for a separate distinct work. These facts suggest that *TMS* is not the primary text for Smith's corpus per se but just the starting point for *WN*. Thus, if this were all I could demonstrate, then it would be enough, given that the debate about the Adam Smith Problem focuses only on those two books.

However, a closer look does support that *TMS* is intrinsic to *LRBL*. The term 'sympathy' appears ten times in the lecture notes; the term 'sentiments' almost twenty times. Smith's comments are preoccupied with questions of character and the communication of moral values. There is every reason to believe that the unfinished work on his history of the arts would likely continue this pattern. *LRBL*, as much of this book will illustrate, elaborates on many concepts within *TMS*. Analogous observations can be made about *LJ*. The term 'impartial spectator' appears six times, the term 'sympathy' eight times, including the obviously connected statement "The cause of this sympathy or concurrence betwixt the spectator and the possessor" (*LJ*(A) i.37). The term 'sentiments' appears close to a dozen times, including Smith's comment, "This principle is fully explained in the Theory of moral Sentiments, where it is shewn that it arises from our sympathy with our superiours being greater than that with our equals or inferiors: we admire their happy situation, enter into it with pleasure, and endeavour to promote it" (*LJ(B)* 12–13). Here Smith explicitly acknowledges the primacy of *TMS*. Finally, *LJ* is concerned with the working class, slavery, the advance of women, and numerous other subjects that *TMS* introduces and *WN* continues. His concluding remarks and advertisement suggest that the unpublished work on police, revenue, and arms is intended as supplementary to *WN*.

Because Smith did not authorize their publication, it is impossible to be certain about the relationship between the unpublished texts and *TMS*. My suggestion is that we side with the preponderance of evidence and ask what we can learn about these texts from reading them through *TMS*. If we do, as the remainder of this book will show, we learn a great deal about the more subtle aspects of Smith's system.

I have argued in this section that *TMS* ought to be read as the "first chapter" of Smith's corpus and that doing so allows one to see Smith's pluralism better. I have shown that Smith can be said to use the earlier book to set up discussions that connect to elaborations in other works. Therefore, I side with E. C. Mossner: "I would charge Smith with an error of *literary* judgment, the type of error that authors both before and after him have been prone to, that is, the error of assuming that the reader of the second book has also read the first."[92]

My approach to reading Smith's work is not without antecedents. Alec Macfie writes, "It would appear that the *Wealth of Nations* is simply a special case—the economic case—of the philosophy implicit in the *Moral Sentiments*. It works out the economic side of that 'self-love' which is given its appropriate place in the developed ethical system of the earlier book."[93] Donald Winch adds, "The *Theory of Moral Sentiments* contains Smith's general theory of morality or psychology; it consistently operates on a higher level of theoretical generality and with a lower degree of empirical realism than the *Wealth of Nations*. The latter work can, therefore, be regarded as a specialized application to the detailed field of economic action of the general theories of social (including economic) behaviour contained in the earlier work, which means that it can properly be used to supply background assumptions to the *Wealth of Nations*, particularly on questions involving individual motivation and social conduct."[94]

Laurence Dickey refers to *TMS* as "the single 'motivating center' of Smith's thought,"[95] and T. D. Campbell writes, "There is no doubt that the *Theory of Moral Sentiments* is important for the understanding of *The Wealth of Nations* for it presents a broader picture of Smith's social theory, of which the work on economics is only a specialized part."⁹⁶ Both Ian Ross and Nicholas Phillipson recount Smith's biography as if *WN* is the consequence of further thought and not, in any way, a new or distinct project. Glenn Morrow remarks that "it might almost be said that the doctrine of sympathy is a necessary presupposition of the doctrine of the natural order expounded in the *Wealth of Nations*."⁹⁷

I am doing more here than asserting what Dickey calls "the continuity argument."⁹⁸ I am asking us to reconsider Winch's claim that there is no warrant "for regarding the *Theory of Moral Sentiments* as a court of higher appeal on all disputed matters ... [or] as being logically or philosophically prior in all respects" to *WN*.⁹⁹ Certainly, Winch is right that *TMS* does not have priority in *all* matters: if there is conflict, one must look at the dates of Smith's revision and offer an interpretation to defend the emphasizing of one claim over another. *TMS* does not hold an absolute trump card, especially in those matters where added detail changes the nature of the discussion.

However, Winch is wrong in suggesting that *TMS* is not a higher court of appeals in the broader sense: it is precisely because *TMS* is more general that it opens a window onto Smith's overall theory of human nature. More important, because *WN* is a special case, one can and must reject the notion that the economic descriptions of human agents is *the* overarching picture of humanity. Imposing the market descriptor on the rest of Smith's corpus makes *WN* the higher court of appeals, and there is neither textual nor biographical justification for this approach.

With this in mind, what might Smith's system look like if *WN* were to take priority over *TMS*? If we examine those parts of *WN* that I have argued are linked to *TMS* and see them without their moral foundations, we get a bleak picture of humanity.

In this picture, the natural desire to better one's condition would be the simple accumulation of wealth and preparation for retirement.¹⁰⁰ People would help others only if it served their own interests. Education would be structured solely on the basis of institutional needs, often nationalistic and often in service to the needs of the sovereign. The same would be said of religious life, which would become vapid, governed by empty ritual. Doctrinal affiliation would be subject to fad and fashion without appeal to God. The condemnation of slavery would be utilitarian at best, an economic matter unrelated to the injustice implicit in the institution.¹⁰¹ This is unappealing indeed. It certainly takes away those aspects of humanity that most people, Smith included, value the highest.

Consider instead a vision with *TMS* as having priority. In this account, humans strive for moral betterment, a theory of virtue that both encourages and is enabled by economic success. This success would allow moral actors to imaginatively enter into the condition of others and offer their assistance while gaining economic advantage from the process. Society would cultivate an educated people who understood the positive and negative aspects of socialization and who could develop institutions to complement or counter these forces. This would allow for stronger influence on the sovereign and further limit its power over people's moral and spiritual lives. God could be in people's lives and actors could condemn immoral institutions such as slavery because they were wrong, but they would also gain economic advantage from this condemnation as well. This, at least to me, seems a more appealing picture of humanity; one more in tune with Smith's cohort than the previous one. It is also one in which the problem of pluralism, the need to manage individual, religious, political, and economic difference, is of paramount importance to society and the state.

I simply cannot assent to the claim that Smith's overarching method is the market and that every realm, whether economic, moral, or linguistic, ought to be described under the auspices of a market metaphor. Otteson qualifies that "a distinction should be drawn between the concept of a market on the one hand and actual marketplaces on the other. The concept of a market with which I argue Smith works is the theoretical model of a system of free exchange in which the rules of exchange spontaneously develop."[102] This seems to be a distinction without a difference.[103] No one would suggest that Smith thinks his religious system is built on an actual exchange of, for example, silver or groceries. Smith's organizational structure must be theoretical in nature, whether market or not.

Nevertheless, even the market understood as such does not apply because Smith's moral theory does not involve *exchange*. It does not presume that moral activity ought to be described as "give me that which I want, and you shall have this which you want" (WN I.ii.2); this is how Otteson quotes Smith's account of market interaction.[104] Moral agency involves mutual recognition, and the natural desire to cultivate and preserve sociality and relationships that are neither ephemeral nor quid pro quo. As Evensky argues, "socialization" is a more accurate "analytical frame" for understanding Smith's account of moral development than exchange is.[105] Furthermore, the rules of morality are anything but *spontaneous*; they are progressive. Certainly, they are discovered and assented to by different individuals and communities at different times, but this is the product of long-standing inquiry, rational discourse, and the consequences of trial and error. This exploration is dependent on the nature of arts and literature, education and socialization, and a complex account of rationality and historical progress that is far more sophisticated than any economic account of competition of preferences.

Life is *not* a marketplace for Smith. It is often familial, pedagogical, spiritual, and natural; it is only sometimes commercial. Many of these realms are not competitive, and none of them, not even the marketplace, are wholly so. In one of his most famous comments, Smith writes that in a commercial society individuals become "in some measure a merchant," not one in toto (WN I.iv.1). The task before us now is to investigate the nature of social unity in Smith's work to see how Smith balances individual and social needs. This is the purview of sympathy. It necessitates encountering and coping with difference. It also forms the basis for moral adjudication that assumes a sophisticated notion of rationality.

3

EDUCATION AS ACCULTURATION

Independent of the methodological considerations involved in reading Smith's corpus, the previous chapters concerned themselves with the preliminaries of moral behavior. Identifying the plurality of motivations that influences moral agents, they described the relationship between *TMS* and *WN* but also led to unanswered questions: given that there are multiple motivations at play, where do they come from and how are they to be adjudicated? Are our motivations innate or learned, individual or social, or some combination thereof? How much do they differ among actors and cultures, and how strongly can they be influenced? These questions are all the purview of Smithian sympathy.

'Sympathy' is the term Smith uses to denote the means by which moral actors consider normative rules and empirical facts to determine propriety. It is a complicated process, involving both inborn faculties and learned skills. It is fostered and impaired by cultural norms and practices, and Smith himself emphasizes that both sympathy's accuracy and motivational power diminish as cultural and physical distance between individuals increases.

Over the next few chapters I argue that sympathy is a rational process, cultivated by education. This chapter specifically examines the sympathetic process in and of itself, preparing readers for the discussions about social unity and narrative rationality that follow. Here, I examine Smith's claim that increased cultural and physical proximity is a bulwark against mutual sympathizing.

The Theory of Moral Sentiments offers an eighteenth-century moral psychology that mixes rational development with identity construction and self-awareness. It is, among other things, an early understanding of what is now termed a relational self.[1] In contemporary liberal parlance, *TMS* has strong communitarian elements where "communitarian" is understood as acknowledging some priority of the community or society, and "liberal" is understood as commitment to the priority of the individual and his or her identity.[2] While *WN* may emphasize the more individualistic elements, understanding Smith's political economy through his moral psychology emphasizes this relational approach and shows that Smith's account of liberty and individualism is compatible with socially constructed identity.[3] As Robert Urquhart puts it, "It is fair to say that not merely the concept, but the condition of having individuality is inherently problematic: it is indeed a central problem of the modern world. In Smith's account, its problematic character is displayed in a tension between what may be described somewhat loosely as Aristotelian and Stoic elements of his thought. The former pushes toward an idea of individuality as partly constituted by relations, the latter toward an idea of the individual alone."[4]

Briefly, and to foreshadow this discussion, Smith argues that humans are by nature social (*TMS* II.ii.3.1, III.2.6). He asserts that morality is the product of social processes, arguing explicitly that moral adjudication and self-identification are impossible in isolation (*TMS* III.i.3–4). He also insists that general moral rules are after-the-fact constructs developed from social interaction (*TMS* III.4.7–8) and that the most basic of these are enabled by education (*TMS* III.5.1). He argues that the state should foster both secular and religious education (*WN* V.i.5) and that the sympathetic foundation of morality functions best in small communities.[5] He also opposes the social contract (*LJ(A)* v.116, v.128, v.118).[6]

The point, as I see it, is to show that sympathy may be useful in helping resolve perceived tensions between individuality and the collective good, a central problem for any pluralism. For our purposes, this is beneficial because the debate over the nature of group or minority identification in liberal societies often stalls at the point at which one is forced to choose between the priority of the group and that of the individual. Smith's theory does not require this.

According to Smith, there can be no judgment regarding either moral approval or aesthetic beauty without the social structures that evolve around 'sympathy,' the natural capacity that allows for moral judgment and social unity (*TMS* III.1.3–5). He first distinguishes his notion of sympathy from its standard usage—the sharing of "the sorrow of others" (*TMS* I.i.1.5)—by calling it the "fellow-feeling with any passion whatever" aroused in a spectator (*TMS* I.i.1.5). Sympathy allows for the "original passions" that make one person's happiness "necessary" to another and make people "naturally" interested "in the fortunes of others," even though a person "derives nothing from it except the pleasure of seeing it" (*TMS* I.i.1.1). However, Smith is less than precise in his definition of this central concept and spends much of *TMS* investigating and qualifying its limits.

Sympathy is a "cognitive process," inspiring both change of "circumstances" and "personhood" with others.[7] According to Smith, as a result of sympathy "an analogous emotion springs up . . . in the breast of every attentive spectator" (*TMS* I.i.1.4). It is by "changing places in fancy with the sufferer, that we come either to conceive or to be affected by what he feels" (*TMS* I.i.1.3). This adoption of the perspective of another is, according to many commentators, an attempt to "temper the self-centeredness of our perspective"[8] and an effort to "deflect the criticism that sympathy is founded in self-love."[9] D. D. Raphael emphasizes that changing places is "the source of fellow-feeling," a product of the imagination, and is not sympathy itself.[10] This is an important reminder: sympathy is the consequence of the ability to enter into the perspective of others, and in its absence no sympathy is possible.

A person's self-awareness derives from the socially constructed rational self-reflection inspired by the judgments of others (*TMS* III.i.3). It is "the only looking-glass by which we can, in some measure, with the eyes of other people, scrutinize the propriety of our own conduct" (*TMS* III.1.5). "The central point" of this social foundation of sympathy is, according to Knud Haakonssen, "that we only become aware of ourselves—gain self-consciousness—through our relationship to others."[11] Or, as Fleischacker puts it, "The process of moral judgment is the means by which individuals most deeply build the views of their society into themselves."[12] Smith seems concerned with countering the claim that humans are selfish in the vicious sense—that they are egoistic—but also in the sense that they cannot step outside their own perspectives at all. Sympathy allows us to "transcend" ourselves.[13]

While I am unconvinced by Fonna Forman-Barzilai's assertion that sympathy ought to be considered a "social practice" rather than some capacity or power—this would run counter to Locke, Shaftesbury, Hutcheson, and Hume's understanding as outlined in the previous chapter—I find her bifurcation of the process useful.[14] Sympathy, she argues, takes place in two stages: "surveillance," in which the spectator observes the behavior of any moral agent, including himself or herself, and "discipline," which is the influence the spectator has on the agent that "motivate[s] her to modify her conduct, and, ultimately, through repetition, to become a member of a culture."[15] This account serves two purposes. First, it shows the cycle of acculturation and education.[16] The agent acts on the basis of culture, is consciously influenced by a spectator's judgment, and as a result of this education—role modeling is pedagogical by intent—he or she influences the culture that then acculturates others.

Second, Forman-Barzilai's bifurcation shows explicitly how sympathy is connected to our overall discussion of rationality. She writes,

Smith emphasized the "cool" rationality of "proper" behavior. Agents are regularly confronted with a choice—to indulge in present, undisciplined gratification or to calmly pursue a duller but more mature enjoyment of love, approval, and congenial relations with peers. An agent must negotiate these ends, calculating how best to bring her emotions into "harmony and concord with the emotions of those who are about [her]." Experience is surely her best guide. Since she was a small child, startled to discover that her playfellows refused to indulge the selfishness and moodiness once tolerated by her parents, the agent has learned the rules of obtaining love and approval. She has learned through surveillance and discipline to exercise a Stoic-like self-command, to become "master of [her]self" and to adjust her passions (or at least the appearance of them) to a "tone" or "pitch" or "degree" that spectators can "enter into."[17]

As an empiricist, Smith is coping with the fundamentally discrete nature of human beings; the capacity to individualize ourselves is part of our corporeal constitution. Our physical separation then requires a moral theory derived from sensations and events occurring to others.[18] Thus Smith is explicit about the limits of the connections between individuals. It is only the spectator's own imagination that creates the analogous emotion inspired by sympathy, and as a result, Smith argues, such parallel sentiments are always imperfect. Our imaginations "copy" another's sentiments, entering, "as it were," into someone else's body, becoming "some measure the same person" and forming "some idea of his sensations" although these are always "weaker in degree" (*TMS* I.i.1.2).

To sympathize is to experience a sentiment similar to that of an observed actor, but one can also sympathize with oneself, in which case the lens of sympathy "divide[s] . . . , as it were, into two persons" (*TMS* III.1.6) and creates an imagined "impartial spectator" who either does or does not sympathize with the actor who imagines it.[19] As argued, this division echoes Shaftesbury's soliloquy. It is imaginative and dialogical in purpose. Sympathy indicates approval of the sentiment and, by extension, the moral position inherent in the sentiment. When the spectator is unable to adopt the sentiment of the moral actor, this indicates disapproval. The same is true if the imagined impartial spectator disapproves of the actor who created it.

For Smith, the impartial spectator is exact in his or her judgment and is the final arbiter of propriety (*TMS* I.i.5.4). Actors are said to act appropriately "when the heart of every impartial spectator entirely sympathizes with them, when every indifferent by-stander entirely enters into, and goes along with them" (*TMS* II.i.2.2). The impartial spectator also sets limits upon action. He or she "allows no word, no gesture, to escape it beyond what this more equitable sentiment would dictate" (*TMS* I.i.5.4). Thus "the abstract and ideal spectator" (*TMS* III.3.38) is imaginary and exists only insofar as our ideas do. It is an "invo-cation" of an ideal of propriety,[20] an "idealized form" of the "*correspondence* of sentiments that is induced by social interaction."[21] The observer "pretends" to be an impartial spectator, where "pretends" holds to the eighteenth-century meaning 'to claim.'[22]

The impartial spectator acts as an ideal for Smith not in the sense that Smith presents an ideal observer theory.[23] Rather, it provides a tool through which Smith describes the ways agents manage large amounts of information and come to rational decisions regarding the propriety of a particular act. When the actual spectator is in line with the imagined impartial spectator, a person's moral judgment is functioning well. Reminiscent of Shaftesbury, this compar-ison also provides Smith with a useful contrast to distinguish between a person acting with too limited a scope of understanding—when a person does not incorporate all necessary information—and a person acting upon enough infor-mation to form a sound judgment. Thus it is central to our discussion of ratio-nality since, for Smith, rational tools are necessary to help manage the diversity of information required for both moral and economic judgments.

Since the imagined impartial spectator represents an ideal, its creation is in some sense beyond an agent's abilities. The impartial spectator cannot do more than the spectator; the spectator's knowledge limits are also those of his or her creation. Thus we revisit the two tensions I identified as central to Smith's work. The attempt to attain an ideal is limited by the capacities of those who attempt to attain it, and the very acts that divide us unify us and vice versa. The teleolo-gies that we pursue are often those that we cannot, by definition, achieve. Spectators *try* to achieve absolute impartiality but necessarily fall short. They try to completely enter into the perspectives of others, but they can't. By striving for objectivity, they stretch their own capacities past their previous limits but they can never fully succeed because no actor can imagine a truly ideal knower, and no person can become someone else.

Sympathy forms the foundation of moral judgment by devising criteria of acceptable action after repeated similar observations and after determination of community judgment (*TMS* III.4.8). The impartial spectator is the aggregate of a person's experience balanced with what he or she knows of the moderating power of community (*TMS* VI.iii.25); it is an anthropomorphization of the rational process and incorporates the sentimental foundation into the reasoned analysis.

Sympathy is both contextual and perspectival; it involves both reconstruc-tion and interpretation of an actor's experience.[24] The spectators do not look at actors in a "disinterested light."[25] Rather, sympathy respects the differences between people: who one is will greatly influence how one feels about another's actions, decisions, and sentiments. Thus Smith's sympathy is dependent on context, and one must be aware of as many facts as possible. This is true both in order to understand which sentiment originated where and in order to note all relevant facts. Attention to detail in this regard is crucial because, according to Smith, the spectator looks at the cause and the context of the agent's emotions more than at the emotions themselves (*TMS* I.i.1.10).

There is a further tension here. On the one hand, Smith is insistent that the spectator judges from his or her own perspective. He writes, "I judge of your sight by my sight, of your ear by my ear, of your reason by my reason, of your resentment by my resentment, of your love by my love. I neither have, nor can have, any other way of judging about them" (*TMS* I.i.3.10).[26] On the other hand, sympathy does not require that the spectator simply put herself or himself in the situation of another person. It asks more specifically that the spectator determine the appropriate sentiments based on how this *particular* agent should act in this *particular* situation given the facts of the agent's life: "When I condole with you for the loss of your only son, in order to enter into your grief I do not consider what I, a person of such a character and profession, should suffer, if I had a son, and if that son was unfortunately to die: but I consider what I should suffer if I was really you, and I not only change circumstances with you, but I change persons and characters. My grief, therefore, is entirely upon your own account, and not in the least upon my own" (*TMS* VII.iii.1.4).

Thus sympathy is a constant balancing act between self-knowledge and knowledge of others. To determine the cause, context, and possible ends of any situation, the spectator must understand the actor. He or she must investigate the actor's reactions to other similar situations and to the consequence that resulted from them. The farther removed the spectator is from the actor, the more difficult a true understanding of the situation and the agent becomes.

For Smith, the more knowledge any person has about the other, the more capacity he or she has to sympathize. He inherits this localization of sympathy from Hume, who tells us,

> The more we converse with mankind, and the greater social intercourse we maintain, the more shall we be familiarized to these general preferences and distinctions, without which our conversation and discourse could scarcely be rendered intelligible to each other. Every man's interest is peculiar to himself, and the aversions and desires, which result from it, cannot be supposed to affect others in a like degree. . . . Sympathy, we shall allow, is much fainter than our concern for ourselves, and sympathy with persons remote from us,

much fainter than that with persons near and contiguous; but for this very reason, it is necessary for us, in our calm judgments and discourse concerning the characters of men, to neglect all these differences, and render our sentiments more public and social. Besides, that we ourselves often change our situation in this particular, we every day meet with persons, who are in a situation different from us, and who could never converse with us, were we to remain constantly in that position and point of view, which is peculiar to ourselves.[27]

It should be no surprise why commentators have emphasized Hume's account of sympathy when addressing Smith's. Nicholas Phillipson may have put it best when he claims that Hume "provided the philosophical resources Smith needed to develop a theory."[28] This excerpt highlights many of the themes that Smith explores in his book-length investigation: the more interaction individuals have, the more they can sympathize; each person's perspective is unique and must therefore be overcome to enable social intercourse and moral behavior; one's circumstance changes, but this change is necessary to understand the experience of others; the more distanced people are from one another, the harder it is for them to sympathize with one another.[29]

Regarding the last point, for Smith, distance between the spectator and the agent should be understood both literally and metaphorically; both physical and psychological separation affect sympathetic ability.[30] We are most intimately connected with ourselves (*TMS* VI.ii.2.1). Then, we connect, in this order, with our family (*TMS* VI.2.i.2), with those with whom we work (*TMS* VI.ii.1.16), with those in our neighborhood (*TMS* VI.ii.1.16), and finally with those in our "state or sovereignty" (*TMS* VI.ii.2.2). Russell Nieli refers to this progression as "spheres of intimacy," Both Griswold and Forman-Barzilai call it "circles of sympathy," and Otteson describes it as a "familiarity principle."[31] In each case, we sympathize most effectively with those with whom we have common living experiences (*TMS* VI.ii.1.1). For Smith, such proximity emphasizes the tension between self-love and beneficence. To highlight this, recall his assertion that people, reading of a terrible earthquake that killed every person in China, would respond with a wide variety of emotions, but that their feelings would always be of much less intensity than how they might react to a minor personal injury such as the loss of a little finger. Recall also his postulation that despite the natural tendency we each have to focus on our own misfortune, no person would ever sacrifice all the Chinese to remedy the loss of a finger. He asks, "When our passive feelings are almost always so sordid and so selfish, how comes it that our active principles should often be so generous and so noble?" (*TMS* III.3.4).

In response to this puzzle regarding the balance of self-love and benevolence, Smith appeals to conscience. It is, according to him, "the love of what is honourable and noble, of the grandeur, and dignity, and superiority of our own characters" that prevents us from sacrificing millions of people to protect our little finger (*TMS* III.3.4). Furthermore, right before he suggests that conscience prevents us from acting so perversely, Smith writes, "It is not the love of our neighbour, [and] it is not the love of mankind, which upon many occasions prompts us to the practice of those divine virtues" (*TMS* III.3.4). In other words, it is precisely *not* the affection for others that prevents an actor from sacrificing a civilization to save his or her digit.

Although this appears to minimize the importance of proximity, Smith qualifies his comments in the next paragraph (*TMS* III.3.7). There Smith acknowledges that distance, literally as well as figuratively understood, prevents us from tempering our affairs in a manner that challenges our indifference. Smith uses China in the earthquake example because China was so far away and so different culturally from the Scotland that he knew. (Here Smith uses his interest in difference to his rhetorical advantage.) Therefore, he writes as if only the love of what is noble could motivate an actor to give moral consideration to the Chinese; distance suggests that they are not neighbors or of his intimate concern. In this case, something independent of familiarity must be operating, since we cannot use affection or care to motivate morality (*TMS* III.3.4). Again, this is a mosaic rather than a melting-pot pluralism.

These passages are found in the book on duty, in a discussion about conscience. Smith begins with the impartial spectator, remarks about our narrowness of vision, and then demands that before we can see our interests in proper proportion to others', we must overcome "habit and experience." To even see our own actions for what they are involves "some degree of reflection, and even of philosophy" (*TMS* III.3.3), and necessitates that individuals step outside of themselves, act as objectively as they can, and rely on moral rules for guidance. The impartial spectator seems here to be the anthropomorphization of duty.

Smith defines duty as "the regard to those general rules of conduct" and argues that although there may be no passionate sentiment guiding an individual, the person who acts on the basis of a sense of duty does so "without any hypocrisy or blamable dissimulation" (*TMS* III.5.1). To act on duty is to act upon "a serious and earnest desire" to follow the general rules of conduct, and "there is scarce any man, however, who by discipline, education, and example, may not be so impressed with a regard to general rules, as to act upon almost every occasion with tolerable decency, and through the whole of his life to

avoid any considerable degree of blame" (*TMS* III.5.1). In short, the sense of
duty, for Smith, is built upon an actor's "reason, principle, conscience, the
inhabitant of the breast, the man within, the great judge and arbiter of our
conduct" (*TMS* III.3.4). Notice the priority given to reason and principle here
and that the description of the inhabitant of the breast is in terms of arbitration—rational adjudication.

Smith sees reason as linked to arbitration in regard to duty; he also views
education and example—institutional and social learning, respectively—as
inculcating in a person the desire to act on one's duty. Education and socialization can create sentiments—a vital point for Smith—and rational judgment, as
we shall see, builds upon those sentiments in many ways.

One learns the general rules in a variety of circumstances—in family interaction, for example, or via arts and literature, as we shall see—but one also
learns via the market. Recognizing this point is yet another moment when *TMS*
understood as the "first chapter" in Smith's corpus helps us clarify *WN*. The
earlier book tells us that since the spectator in question may have neither affection nor interaction with the victims of the Chinese earthquake, duty demands
that they not be sacrificed for the sake of a little finger. In contrast, on those
countless occasions when a spectator has no affection for others but is forced to
interact with them on a daily basis, the general rules of the marketplace can use
sympathy to create concord without relying upon immediate fellow feeling.
This is the elaboration of *TMS* as put forth in *WN*.

According to *TMS*, an agent's interaction with the butcher, brewer, and
baker is a purely formal one—it operates on the rules of exchange and justice,
and mutual self-interest demands that it be functional enough to achieve the
desired aim. However, these are not unbounded interactions; they are regulated
by a complex system of enforceable norms: "In the race for wealth, and honours,
and preferments, [an economic actor] may run as hard as he can, and strain
every nerve and every muscle, in order to outstrip all his competitors. But if he
should justle, or throw down any of them, the indulgence of the spectators is
entirely at an end. It is a violation of fair play, which they cannot admit of"
(*TMS* II.ii.2.1).

As Otteson points out, like the general rules of conduct, the rules of exchange
are not given a priori for Smith; they are derived from existing practices and
refined over time.[32] However, while the market is the motivating force in
concord, its content and effectiveness are still controlled by sympathy. It is the
spectators who condemn the violation of fair play; censure does not come from
the desire for profit or exchange. Smith is therefore making an entirely different
argument, for example, than Kant's utilitarian example in *Groundwork of the*

Metaphysics of Morals in which the shopkeeper charges everyone a consistent price to maintain his or her reputation and business.[33] For Smith, the rules of fair play are enforced by the sympathy spectators feel with the wronged, not by the negative consequence of bad business practices. Impartial spectators call attention to this psychological and social pressure in order to modify actions in the market; spectators sympathize with the injured party (*TMS* II.ii.2.1).

Were we to see the market as a metaphor for all activities, prioritizing WN in the process, the modification of economic behavior would be just another example of competition; the attempt to assert one's own self-interest over another's. But this doesn't follow from Smith's point. The offender, according to Smith, sees the reaction of others and naturally desires to modify the pitch of his or her sentiments to that of those observing and condemning. This is cooperation, not rivalry. It is certainly not an example of exchange.

Duty and propriety are given support by the laws of justice, "whose violation seems to call loudest for vengeance and punishment" (*TMS* II.ii.2.2), but these too are reinforced via Smith's moral psychology and not simply by economic or jurisprudential means.[34] Violations of justice are inherently antisocial for Smith, not simply because they are violations of the rights of others but because unjust acts and their consequent remorse are experienced by the offender as a removal from society itself: "He dares no longer look society in the face, but imagines himself as it were rejected, and thrown out from the affections of all mankind. . . . The horror of solitude drives him back into society, and he comes again into the presence of mankind" (*TMS* II.ii.2.3).

Even justice is dependent on proximity to a certain extent; its violations bring a person to a psychological position of isolation. It is the horror of feeling alone that causes an agent to experience remorse and reenter society. There is something about an unjust act that moves agents farther away from one another, psychologically if not physically. There is also something about violations of justice that prevent reflection—reasoned self-analysis. We see yet again that sympathy and rationality are connected; the removal of fellow feeling results in the removal of critical capabilities.

Recognizing the importance of proximity in *TMS* first also helps Smith's readers see the most explicit echoes of sympathy in WN. Smith writes,

> A man of rank and fortune is by his station the distinguished member of a great society, who attend to every part of his conduct, and who thereby oblige him to attend to every part of it himself. His authority and consideration depend very much upon the respect which this society bears to him. He dare not do any thing which would disgrace or discredit him in it, and he is obliged to a very strict observation of that species of morals, whether liberal

or austere, which the general consent of this society prescribes to persons of his rank and fortune. A man of low condition, on the contrary, is far from being a distinguished member of any great society. While he remains in a country village his conduct may be attended to, and he may be obliged to attend to it himself. In this situation, and in this situation only, he may have what is called a character to lose. But as soon as he comes into a great city, he is sunk in obscurity and darkness. His conduct is observed and attended to by nobody, and he is therefore very likely to neglect it himself, and to abandon himself to every sort of low profligacy and vice. (WN V.i.g.12)

Recall that WN never uses the term 'sympathy,' one of the reasons some commentators put forth the Adam Smith Problem. In this selection, Smith uses the term 'character' to describe the social modulation of moral activities. If one were to encounter this passage without reading *TMS*, one might interpret this as only an instance of vanity. However, recalling the earlier book, we see that this passage is actually a compact and powerful account of sympathy and how it works. Class and fame, Smith is arguing, help determine the boundaries of the community observing any specific moral agent. For the wealthy, even the largest community can help temper actions because their authority and reputation are well known and easily affected. For the poorer or lesser known, this process of observation works only in the context of a small community, where everyone is known by everyone and authority and reputation must be guarded. In a big city, anonymity prevents significant community influence over the actions of the little known.

Smith makes these comments in his discussion of religious instruction, observing that those small-town people who have moved to the city and who feel alone and anonymous are the most attracted to religious groups (WN V.i.g.12). The desire to be noticed—on the part of both the agent and the religious group—encourages fanaticism; extremism is more noticeable than moderation. We can see why. Religious belief is a ready-made commonality; ascription to a doctrine allows people to find a community of judges who are predisposed to adopt the principles that motivate one's own moral sentiments. It is manufactured proximity for those who feel alone.[35] In this case, the moderating force of sympathy is all the more powerful because denominational allegiance is powerful enough that it often trumps the political expectations of the community that houses it (WN V.i.g.17). Smith seems to be arguing that *all* of these factors—justice, duty, the market, and sympathy—must work together and complement one another to inspire appropriate action.

Returning to the discussion of proximity, when we speak of those who are nearer to us, those with whom we have contact every day, only then does affection for others become an important factor. Otteson's "familiarity principle" articulates Smith's belief that "people's natural benevolence toward others varies directly with their familiarity with them—the more familiar a person is to one, the greater the tendency to feel benevolent toward him; the less familiar, the less benevolent."[36] If this is correct, then Smith must provide examples of alterations in familiarity affecting our apprehensions of another. This will be the case and becomes evident in his discussions of slavery, gender, and class that I emphasize in the next chapter.

Smith's proposal that increased familiarity leads to better sympathy helps resolve the tension between two different natural tendencies. First, Smith writes of the "natural preference which every man has for his own happiness above that of other people," and that each person is "by nature, first and principally recommended to his own care" (*TMS* II.ii.2.1). Humans have a natural tendency both to prioritize their own needs and to be the ones who are most aware of and the most capable of achieving them. Second, and in tension with those principles, Smith writes that "nature, when she formed man for society, endowed him with an original desire to please, and an original aversion to offend his brethren. She taught him to feel pleasure in their favourable, and pain in their unfavourable regard" (*TMS* III.2.6). Smith also argued that people are "naturally endowed with a desire of the welfare and preservation of society" (*TMS* II.i.5.10).[37] People care about others by design and are inclined to cater to their needs.

One cannot frequently prioritize oneself and please others at the same time. Thus, I suggest, Smith reconciles this tension by arguing that the closer people are to one another, the more the natural tendency toward others can be combined with the natural tendency toward oneself. Not surprisingly, then, Smith argues that family life is enhanced by proximity, defining affection as "habitual sympathy" (*TMS* VI.ii.1.5–8). This is true of neighbors as well (*TMS* VI.ii.1.16).

For Smith, it is not the biological commonalities that make families an emotional unit: "The force of blood . . . I am afraid, exists no-where but in tragedies and romances" (*TMS* VI.ii.1.11). Instead, it is the day-to-day living conditions between those who are "naturally bred up in the same house" that inspire affection (*TMS* VI.ii.1.11). Although Smith would certainly have to admit that in the vast majority of cases individuals live together because of the very biological connections he is minimizing, his point is that the source of affection is the living conditions, not the blood connection, a position shared by many who have adopted children not biologically their own. For Smith, it is the shared standards and lives that allow neighbors and family members to care about one another as individuals. Here we see a melting pot pluralism taking shape.

Smith identifies the compromise between an individual's self-regarding tendencies and concern for others as a natural disposition—a tactic he inherits from Locke, Shaftesbury, and Hutcheson. This disposition "accommodate[s] and . . . assimilate[s], as much as we can, our own sentiments, principles, and feelings, to those which we see fixed and rooted in the persons whom we are obliged to live and converse a great deal with" (*TMS* VI.ii.1.17). Thus there is a tension between multiple natural desires that gets mitigated by proximity; the closer we are to people, the more we are able to balance our self- and other-regarding interests. Sympathy is the capacity designed to negotiate these two desires, and, as argued above, how well we reconcile them is based, in part, on our capacity to interpret the relevant information.

This is our most explicit clue so far that sympathy is a component of rationality. Its job here is negotiation and reconciliation of desires—moral adjudication—and it is guided by natural tendencies, dispositions, and principles. The human faculty that we call reason is that which allows us to utilize our tendencies and dispositions in a meaningful and thoughtful way; it allows us to see causation and connection between objects. It is guided, for Smith, by the principles of human nature. Our rationality, as we understand the term today, on the other hand, is that which organizes this information, justifies perceived connections, and generalizes them into rules upon which we can judge. This is more than just instrumental reason since it involves deep values and moral commitments that help frame our character, but it does allow instrumentality when we seek to achieve particular goals. Given that we are building on Sen's wider definition of rationality, it is possible to see these sentimental elements as falling within the purview of reason defined in terms of both faculty and the dictates of logic and inference.

This search for reconciliation between self- and other-regarding interests leads Otteson to refer to Smith's whole theory as a "curious and at times confusing mixture of nature and nurture."[38] I would suggest, however, that this mixture indicates an early struggle with issues of diversity as we tend to understand them in our own contemporary discourse. Smith's comments are not "curious." They are the means by which he addresses social difference and its effects and the relationship between essential and accidental characteristics.

Furthermore, whereas contemporary nomenclature sees a strict divide between 'nature' and 'nurture,' Smith saw no such division. 'Nature' had a wide range of meanings for Smith, included among them the totality of all things, the principles behind all things, and "the result of economic or political conditions."[39] In all of Smith's uses, society and its influences are natural. Since humans are social by nature, since they cannot make moral judgments outside of society, and since Smith himself is reluctant to suggest that there was a time when humans lived outside society, it makes no sense for Smith to compare how people might have been outside of society with what society does to them. Granted, education and socialization have profound effects on individuals, but both are themselves natural. They act on one's natural capacities. To describe Smith in terms of the modern nature and nurture debate is to misrepresent his understanding of their relationship.

There is a further tension between social similarity and difference, but this is epistemological rather than social. First, Smith asserts that humans are in some sense fundamentally similar. He writes, "The difference of natural talents in different men is, in reality, much less than we are aware of. . . . The difference between the most dissimilar characters, between a philosopher and a common street porter, for example, seems to arise not so much from nature, as from habit, custom, and education" (*WN* I.ii.4). Second, and in contrast, Smith suggests that the natural sameness that unifies humanity is mitigated by the fundamental separateness. Humans divide necessarily into spectator and actor. Thus, according to Smith, one may know only one's own sentiments and, consequently, the ability to understand others is, in some important sense, dependent on the ability to deduce or reconstruct the sentiments of others. Sympathy is built on the imagination, which is itself dependent on and cultivated through education. However, for Smith, while socialization and education cultivate difference, they also help to bridge it because they enable spectators to enter into the experiences of others. Imagination is the bridge between people that creates community. Moral judgment is a product of interaction, for Smith, and is enabled by the ability to learn about others. Thinking for oneself, or reasoned critical analysis, he argues, is a group activity. It allows an individual to be constituted at least in part by others, even if persons are, at root, fundamentally separate. It also allows moral agents to use standards of dignity and personhood as criteria for determining how to treat others. Education here is the lifelong process of learning that entails both being taught and figuring things out for oneself.[40] How this relates to dignity and personhood, and how sympathy communicates these ideals over psychological and physical distance, is the topic of the next chapter.

4

EDUCATION AND SOCIAL UNITY

As I argued in the previous chapter, sympathy is built upon the imagination, which, in turn, is cultivated by education. In this chapter I begin to parse what Smith means by education, with special attention to the passive cultural elements that inform self-identity and awareness of others. I begin the process of accounting for the rational process by which a moral spectator enters into the persona of another, particularly those with whom he or she does not share cultural or political commonalities.

The term 'education' is more ambiguous than is often allowed. It encompasses socialization and acculturation as well as schooling in the formal and informal senses. Philosophy of education as it is traditionally understood by Smith's and our contemporaries concerned itself with the latter, schooling. It investigates familial and institutional instruction that presupposes pedagogical intent. This is the type of education that Locke had in mind in *Some Thoughts Concerning Education* and that Rousseau wrote about in *Emile*. Socialization, however, is a different kind of educational concern but also looms large in both eighteenth- and twenty-first-century political discussion. It asks about the role of social, cultural, and political forces in forming one's self-understanding and one's view of the world.

Examinations of socialization in modern liberal debates about social and political diversity emphasize two questions that are often in tension. First, how is one to cultivate group identity? For example, how does one foster authenticity as a Jew, a woman, a Scottish American, or a lesbian (or as a Scottish American Jewish lesbian)? Second, how is a pluralistic society to be organized such that these different associations do not destabilize the state that houses them? Smith focuses on the second question, as do my comments here, although the discourse about authenticity is referenced occasionally and at key moments.

That these two questions are in tension should not suggest that they cannot be reconciled; sympathy offers moral actors the way to do so. Furthermore, anticipating Richard Rorty, Smith understands implicitly that an account of socialization must include a theory of individuation.[1] It is not enough to ask about group membership: we must also ask about the formation of our unique identities.

Our discussion is complicated by the fact that even though Smith's comments on group association and matters of identity are found throughout both his published and unpublished works, there is no central place in which he presents a compact, rigorous argument in support of his position. Although there has been some research on contemporary categories of difference as present in Smith's writing—here I refer specifically to gender, race, and class—little has been done to reconstruct his general theory of managing diversity. Given that rationality, for Smith, is narrative in form, the question of perspective is of utmost importance. Diversity is directly related to rationality for Smith because, as we have seen, who one is and associates with heavily influences the imaginative framework that cultivates sympathy. With limited sympathy comes limited self-criticism and limited self-criticism stunts rational adjudication. I argue here that, for Smith, the wider the pluralism, the more rational an individual can be.

This chapter focuses on social unity, by which I mean the stability of a society that contains within it significant socially recognized difference (a mosaic pluralism), and the possibility of political communication and moral adjudication among members of that society in the face of such difference. Smith most often refers to factionalism when he references a divided public, specifically the effect of political allegiance, economic class, and religion. My discussion in this chapter is an outgrowth of these comments. Although Smith did not share the explicit interest in group identity as liberal theorists now understand it, as I show in this chapter, his theory of sympathy and education both cultivates and arrests forms of social difference that are of contemporary concern. It acts as a bulwark against fractured rational thought.

I conclude that, for Smith, education is the primary means through which perceived otherness is minimized; otherness here is exemplified by focusing on gender, race, and class. In this context, education should be understood in its widest form: as incorporating both institutional and informal means. This broad meaning is due in part to Smith's own treatment. As we have seen Hutcheson do already, Smith uses the term 'education' interchangeably to refer to socialization or acculturation (*TMS* III.3.7, *WN* V.i.f.47) and to formal and informal educative institutions (*TMS* IV.ii.1.10, *WN* V.i.f). *The Wealth of Nations* focuses mostly on institutional education, and there, like Hume, Smith usually refers to "custom" when he means noninstitutional education (*WN* I.2.5).

One might fairly wonder what would not count as education in this definition. This is a difficulty that cannot be avoided. Smith is an empiricist, and it is
unclear how much of a blank slate he would have people start with. Thus it is
unclear how wide education must be (Cf.: *ES* 74, *ES* 52.). My intent is to start
from the broadest possible perspective and move to a more narrow understanding. This helps identify some of the social and political consequences
of human learning. Smith walks a fine line, risking equivocation with his
varied use of the term. In order to avoid my own conflation, however, I offer
the following ad hoc distinction: socialization and acculturation denote social
pressures arising from influences that are largely passive and always collective
in origin. Education, whether institutional or otherwise, denotes the intentional imposition of values, norms, expectations, standards, and lessons on
specific individuals or groups by other specific individuals or groups. For
example, when a seven-year-old girl learns from the culture at large that her
self-esteem ought to be dependent on how skinny she is, this is a form of socialization. However, when this same girl learns from parents, teachers, peers, or
specific media outlets about healthy eating and reasonable body types, this
should be classified as education. This is an imperfect division. Nevertheless, I
suggest that the intentional bridging of divisions caused by the social assumptions about gender, race, and class is to be considered a matter of education in
the latter sense.

Placing a contemporary gloss on Smith's material is difficult because, once
again, Smith's writing cannot always be read as the twenty-first-century reader
might be inclined to. For example, the concept of class did not develop its
contemporary meaning until the early nineteenth century. Smith uses the terms
'rank,' 'social character,' and 'distinction' where modern writers might use
'class.' Rank and its associated terms refer to a "calculus of property, privilege,
dress, education, honor, obligation, residence, occupation, friendship, beauty,
strength and wisdom," while the term 'class,' for Smith, categorizes a thing
"only as a 'species,' 'sort,' or 'type.'"[2] The term 'race' also has multiple meanings.
For example, Smith uses it as a delineation of a category of person, such as a
"race of men commonly called men of letters" (WN I.x.c.37); as a designator for
biological lineage, as in "on account of their descent from a long race of great
and illustrious ancestors" (WN V.1.b.10); as ethnicity or subculture within a
nationality, as in, "The French kings of the Merovingian race had all treasures"
(WN IV.i.30); and as a people, as in, "The Cape of Good Hope was inhabited
by a race of people almost as barbarous and quite as incapable of defending
themselves as the natives of America" (WN IV.vii.c.100). Only the last example
approximates current usage.

Smith refers to Africans (*TMS* V.2.9) and Native Americans (*WN* IV.7.14, *WN* IV.7.16) in ways that leave little doubt that one can tease our current usage out of his discussion, but this approach must also be deliberate and careful.[3] For this reason my comments on race are limited to Smith's discussion of the morality of slavery, a conversation that itself requires reconstruction. I also limit my remarks to the European and American enslavement of Africans, an era of slavery that Smith emphasized.[4] Race, whether an essential characteristic or not, was a major factor in the development of this particular slave trade. My discussion of class is wider, focusing on Smith's comments regarding the laboring classes and perceptions of the rich.

The previous chapter established the initial framework for Smith's account of rationality. Human behavior is guided by dispositions and capacities. By 'disposition,' I refer to natural tendencies, those human actions and desires that Smith references as "principles." Unlike those that govern chemistry or physics, Smith's principles of human action conflict with one another, and the tension necessitates an internal negotiation that determines action and its propriety. The raw material of this negotiation is the sentiments, and the means by which agents learn to adjudicate, revise, and make their sentiments more sophisticated is the natural capacity for sympathy.

Sympathy, the natural fellow feeling that agents have for one another, leads to the discovery and creation of general moral rules that outline community-preferred behavior. How binding these rules are is a matter for another time. For the moment, we are faced with two issues. First, the creation of, evaluation of, and assent to these rules are all rational in nature. Second, how much one can see the other—whom one judges and whom one is judged by—is heavily influenced by the community that houses an individual. As we have seen so far, the nature, size, and intensity of that community will vary the amount of judgment. Now that we turn to more specific divisions, if I am correct that Smith's work prefigures modern theories of diversity, I should be able to show that it can account for these most central modern pluralistic preoccupations.

This chapter should be read as a rejoinder to Michael Frazer, who argues that Johann Gottfried von Herder's "is the first sentimentalist theory to combine a liberal commitment to the importance of each individual with an appreciation of the diversity among both individuals and groups."[5] Frazer argues that both Hume and Smith believed that "the effect of what we now call cultural differences on our ethics is a negative one, serving to block the development of sentiments that would unite all of humanity behind a single set of moral commitments."[6] This is too strong. Diversity is yet another example of Smith's faith that that which divides us also unites us. And, as we shall see, for Smith, individual experience, group experience, cultural background, and moral difference all contribute to the betterment of people's skill, dexterity, and judgment and to the progress of humankind.

As I remarked previously, Smith's discussion of liberty and his struggles with negotiating what would eventually be called negative and positive liberties can be understood as a preamble to the nineteenth-century debate about the idealist actualization of the individual. Because it is just a preamble, Smith will never be as explicit as Herder. Nevertheless, Frazer overstates his claim about Herder, perhaps because he, falsely I believe, argues that "Smith never adequately explains how it is that we can come to share imaginatively in the emotional experiences of even those most unlike ourselves."[7] The previous and current chapters offer just such an explanation.

SLAVERY

Much of Smith's discussion of otherness can be found in his moral condemnation of slavery, a condemnation based on the impossibility of sympathy in a slave-owning society. Many in Smith's "closest circle of friends" were slave owners both abroad and in Scotland, and the first controversies about *TMS* were in response to Smith's critique.[8] We know that Smith was opposed to slavery on moral grounds. At *TMS* V.2.9, he first claims that the slave owner is "sordid" and the Africans who are being enslaved are "heroes." Second, he asserts that the master acts to enslave because he or she is "too often scarce capable of conceiving" the sentiments of the slave, and, in return, the slave owner is faced with the "contempt" of the slave, who is more aware of the injustice.

Slave owners are unable to see the sentiments of the slave because of the owners' personal experiences, events that are largely a product of history. Smith is explicit that those people who live and are raised among impropriety will regard those immoral acts with which they are familiar as simply "the way of the world" and accept them without protest or disapproval (*TMS* V.2.2). Although there is a fundamental similarity between people, Smith explains that historical context and proximity define certain aspects of difference and the capacity of people to overcome that difference. The farther removed someone is from a slave or servant—the less they work together—the less they will understand one another (*LJ*(A) iii.109).

For Smith, slavery exists for a variety of reasons. The first is the perceived economic advantages—but those turn out to be false advantages, and Smith opposes slavery on economic grounds (*WN* III.ii.12). Slavery must, therefore, exist for other reasons. A hint of why is offered in Smith's discussion of authority in *LJ(A)*, an imprecise discussion by his own admission since he writes, "It is very difficult to define what authority is, but every one has an idea of it in his mind" (*LJ(A)* V.129).

Authority, he argues, is caused by a number of factors: "1st, superiority of age and of wisdom which is generally its concomitant. 2dly, superior strength of body; and these two it is which give the old an authority and respect with the young. 3^d, superior fortune also gives a certain authority, caetereis paribus; and 4th^{ly}, the effect is the same of superior antiquity when everything else is alike; an old family excites no such jealousy as an upstart does" (LJ(A) V.129).

As specific as it appears, this list is not particularly helpful. First, Smith's terms are vague. What constitutes superior fortune? Is it only money? Why is it that new money excites jealousy while old money does not? Second, this passage is located in a discussion regarding the legitimacy of the sovereign, and it is not altogether clear that authority here does not mean "legitimate authority," as it does for other political theorists. Third, Smith claims only that these factors "tend" to give authority over others; this is not all-inclusive, and it does not account for those times when these factors do not result in someone asserting authority over others. There must be additional influences.

Recall, first, that despite our natural similarities, people are different because of "habit, custom, and education" (WN I.ii.4). Social norms and customs have influence over social structures. Further, according to Smith, "the pride of man makes him love to domineer, and nothing mortifies him so much as to be obliged to condescend to persuade his inferiors" (WN III.ii.10), and "Slavery . . . has been universall in the beginnings of society, and the love of dominion and authority over others will probably make it perpetuall" (*LJ(A)* iii.117). In other words, there is something natural in human beings that enjoys authority and motivates one person to subordinate another.

What causes slavery then? Economic factors, a love of domination, and incapacity to sympathize. Its moral impropriety is determined through the act of sympathy itself and is further supported by the creation of an imagined impartial spectator who can take the position of the "anyone" and judge the act without bias or conflict of interest. But the judgment of impropriety on the part of the slave owner and society is impeded by the progressive separation of the slave and slave owner cited above. Even when there is proximity, social status and expectations prevent slave owners from seeing slaves as their equals.

Smith offers a brief historical account of slavery to compare the different circumstances in which slaves find themselves and uses it to illustrate how economic conditions help determine the attitude of the master. It also indicates how injustice reverses the historical flow of progress. When the Romans were poor, they treated their slaves "with the greatest humanity." There were not enough slaves for the Romans to be jealous of, so the two groups ate together, and the master "looked on [slaves] as faithfull friends, in whom they would find sincere affection," treating them "the same way as the children of the family." Yet as the society grew more advanced and more prosperous, the Romans inflicted "cruelty" and would even "feed their fish with the bodies of their slaves" (*LJ(A)* iii.109–10).

Continuing this same conversation, Smith adds that the Germans "had very little distinction from their slaves . . . they had the same dress and the same manner of living, and they were accordingly very humane to them." So, too, the "North American planter," who "is often at the same work and engaged in the same labour . . . looks on his slave as his friend and partner, and treats him with the greatest kindness." In contrast, according to Smith, the West Indian, "who is far above the employment of the slave in every point[,] gives him the hardest usage" (*LJ(A)* iii.110).

Smith is quick to point out that the North American's kindness is only owing to "poverty." Smith illustrates the tendencies of individuals to make others' lives worse while they make their own better (*LJ(A)* 109–11); the more successful people are and the freer they become, the more they abuse their slaves. He illustrates that progress has preconditions; society must be a certain way for history to make it better. Perhaps this is because the more secure people are, the more they can afford to engage in the complexities that distance them from others. They lose nothing by treating slaves as chattel (or worse) because they are secure in their power and they have the means by which they can persuade themselves that what they are doing is moral and proper. Again, that which might unify society—in this case, "opulence and freedom, the two greatest blessings men can possess"—divides society even further (*LJ(A)* iii.111).

The imposition of distance by the master from the slave is ultimately a form of self-protection since any attempt to sympathize would only lead toward pain and self-condemnation by the slave owner; where slaves are treated with dignity the slave owners have less to fear. Smith writes, "When we see one man oppressed or injured by another, the sympathy which we feel with the distress of the sufferer seems to serve only to animate our fellow-feelings with his resentment against the offender" (*TMS* II.i.2.5).

Sympathy carries intentionality with it; it is aimed at something. One sympathizes with a particular sentiment. If suffering is unjustly caused, any fellow feeling toward those who are suffering will naturally result in disapproval of the cause of the suffering. The slave owner is the person causing the suffering. By sympathizing with the slave, the slave owner adopts the sentiments of the slave, including the profound animosity the slave feels for her or his oppressor. Sympathizing would then be the process of the slave owner's adopting the attitude of the slave, the necessary consequence of which would be self-hatred.[9]

In the muddiness of the interaction between the universal and the subjective, in the confusion inherent in delineating the universal human experience from that of a particular person, self-hatred is the ultimate form of moral condemnation for Smith because it rests upon the impartial spectator. The capacity of the slave owner to sympathize with the slave is based upon his or her ability to adopt the slave's perspective. As societies develop to separate the two, drama and literature are useful tools to help the slave owner enter into the mind of the slave.

Smith's texts emphasize that the study of literature is necessary for moral education; its pedagogical elements help reveal the normative.[10] Smith's own use of literary references throughout *TMS* highlights its importance as well. His first reference to tragedy and romance is in the fourth paragraph of the book (*TMS* I.i.1.4). As Griswold points out, for Smith, "learning how to judge and how to feel are, though distinguishable, inseparable"; rationality is intimately connected to the passions.[11] Literature lets us enter into the perspective of another, and so Smith praises Voltaire's *Mahamet* as "perhaps the most *instructive* spectacle that was ever introduced upon any theatre" (*TMS* III.6.12, emphasis added).

Smith tells us that even when Greek plays try to communicate physical pain, it is always the character's *circumstances*, such as solitude or mortality, and not their pain that are the focus of the spectators' imaginations (*TMS* I.ii.1.9). This reminds us that the more abstract imaginative sentiments are the more communicative. Given this fact, literature may be the ideal vehicle for character study since it presents all the necessary context, or, as Smith puts it, literature presents us with "the different shades and gradations of circumstance, character, and situation, to differences and distinctions which, though not imperceptible, are, by their nicety and delicacy, often altogether undefinable" (*TMS* VI.ii.1.22).

In the case of slavery, Smith's appeal to literature proved to be prophetic, since history now shows us how influential sentimentalist abolitionist texts like Harriet Beecher Stowe's *Uncle Tom's Cabin* turned out to be.[12] It follows from this argument that since that which might unify society may also divide it, literature supporting slavery, justifying the institution, and arguing for the inhumanity of slaves will only cultivate the practice.[13] As a result, the *content* of the arts is as important as their presence, and if the material is immoral and does not improve sympathetic understanding, it will only lead to factionalism.

Without the assistance of education, literature, and drama, the slave owner may never sympathize with the slave and may never change his or her ways. His or her day-to-day experience reinforces the proximity because it is designed to do so. Moreover, sometimes, even in the face of experience, learning, and literature, attempts to instill morality in others simply fail. Griswold reminds us that there may be a point after which no further discussion can elicit a response from a spectator;[14] this is a major problem for Smith. He never explicitly responds to the case of someone who simply refuses to see the pain of another out of brute stubbornness or incapacity.

The issue is made all the more difficult because Smith argues that spectators are less likely to sympathize with unpleasant emotions than pleasant ones (*TMS* I.iii.2.1). At the same time, as Gilbert Harman writes, sympathy is always "skewed in the direction of the conventional reactions,"[15] a point also made in a letter to Smith by Sir Gilbert Elliot shortly after the first edition of *TMS* was published.[16] Culture preserves itself and works against change because it is dependent on daily habit, ritual, public opinion, and familiarity; it both unites and divides members of a polity. Thus sympathy, all else being equal, runs counter to change, and spectators are even more reluctant to sympathize with those common occurrences that are painful to notice. In short, non-'oppressed' peoples, to use contemporary terminology, find it more difficult by nature to acknowledge and share the pain of those who are experiencing oppression.[17] In the case of slavery, as in the case of women, as we shall see momentarily, this presents an even steeper climb toward social equality than one might otherwise think.

Smith's response to the stubborn unwillingness to sympathize would likely be that the long-term progression of history and the unintended consequences of the market will eventually resolve this issue. He argues, for example, that the market imposed order and quality government on European towns and introduced personal property to feudal subjects (*WN* III.iv.4, III.iv.10, III.iv.17). For Smith, new laws and practices will likely evolve, moving individuals toward greater equality. As John W. Danford writes, "It appears, on Smith's understanding, that historical progress has been a story not only of the spread of general opulence, but also of a gradual transformation in the prevailing moral texture of societies."[18] Smith's comments on the status of women certainly bear out this suggestion, since he is quite explicit that historical change has been beneficial to their treatment by men. In fact, Smith's faith in progress may be the characteristic that is most indicative of his Enlightenment oeuvre, predating Kant's argument for the progression of human morality in "What Is Enlightenment?" and "The Idea of a Universal History from a Cosmopolitan Point of View." My argument here is not that, for Smith, all things progress without loss,[19] at the same rate, or in an uninterrupted fashion.[20] Instead, my point is that, for Smith, human society progresses in general, and when individuals are unable to become morally better, the flow of history may end up being the only possible vehicle for change.

While the enlightenment is alleged to be the age of reason, Smith focused on the moral sentiments as well. It is reputed to be a secular movement, but Smith, as we shall see, saw a very important place for religion. Yet Smith argues that history is itself the unfolding of moral progress, a combination of his stage theory of history and the workings of the invisible hand. I offer a detailed discussion of his philosophy of history in the last two chapters of this book.

GENDER

Race and gender are common areas of focus in the discourse of difference because they investigate ambiguities regarding the distinction between social norms and biological impact, and because they are fault lines on which power has been exerted historically. Debates on gender, in particular, emphasize the distinction between nature and nurture, concepts that have been used both to justify subservience of one sex to another and to argue for social equality. They ask whether or not women are more "naturally" suited to certain tasks than others (again, 'nature' in this usage is not the same as Smith's). In the above discussion of slavery, race is only an accidental feature. All of Smith's comments would apply equally if slaves were Asian or Caucasian; the power is economic or situational and not inherently tied to race. In discussing the role of women in society, however, biology is not accidental, and investigations of physicality are more likely to slip into some form of essentialism. Thus if Smith truly believes that sympathy can overcome group difference, it must do so for women and men as well.

Stuart Justman argues that Smith's theories challenge traditional gender roles by reversing the characteristics that are commonly regarded as belonging to men and women. He claims that Smith makes men more feminine while simultaneously protecting their masculine self-image by using male-coded Stoic philosophy. Capitalism, he asserts, "lives and trades on 'vices' long imputed to women—such as limitless desire and the projection of false but alluring images."[21]

One must be cautious about Justman's assertion. Smith's work predates the gender/sex distinction.[22] Smith does not prescribe vanity for his agents and is highly critical of those who pursue "baubles" and "trinkets" (*TMS* IV.i.6, IV.i.10).[23] Nevertheless, for our purposes it is interesting that Smith might be seen as reversing traditionally gendered behavior because this suggests that the divide between men and women is as artificial as the divide between slave and slave owner.

It should come as no surprise to anyone that Smith's time was bound by such pictures of men and women. However, although Smith's language is a product of his time, his theory is not dependent on it. There seems nothing inherent in Smith's work that either demands a distinction between the genders or must be construed as sexist in our contemporary sense. As we shall see, Smith's analyses foreshadow key assertions made by twentieth- and twenty-first-century feminists, particularly those related to political power and economic circumstance.

This is not anachronistic. As Edith Kuiper illustrates, Smith was in contact with an important emerging feminist discussion, emphasizing "(1) criticism of misogyny and male supremacy; (2) the conviction that the condition of women is not an immutable fact of nature and can be changed for the better, and (3) a sense of group identity, the conscious will to speak 'on behalf of women,' or 'to define the female sex,' usually aiming to enlarge the sphere of action open to women."[24] She also points out that Smith's personal interests would have likely made him aware of differences in education and possibilities for men and women, that his own relationship with his cousin Janet Douglas, who lived with him after the death of her husband, would have made him see the consequences of women's economic dependencies on spouses, and that the Select Club, of which he was a member, discussed the role of women in society.[25]

In contrast, Vivienne Brown argues that Smith has designated all of his readers male.[26] She asserts that his use of the possessive pronoun excludes women, citing *TMS* IV.2.10, where he writes, "The fair-sex, who have commonly much more tenderness than ours, have seldom so much generosity."[27] Kuiper makes a similar point when she references the use of the term "men" in the subtitle of the fourth edition of *TMS*.[28] On the one hand, since Smith's lectures were delivered to an all-male audience and since his books were based on those lectures, these observations are not as significant as it may first seem. On the other, Smith was well aware that many of *TMS*'s readers would be female, and his (probably unconscious) retention of this male-coded "our" or the unquestioned use of "men" as a universal is worthy of note, especially since Smith was, for so long, a professor of rhetoric and because his continual use of "we" throughout *TMS* is designed specifically to pull the reader closer to Smith's own position.[29]

Many women did, in fact, read Smith's work avidly, and he appears sensitive to what some now call women's issues. In 1792 Mary Wollstonecraft cites Smith several times, including using his comments on the rich at *TMS* I.iii.2.1 to make an analogous point about women.[30] In 1798 Sophie de Grouchy, marquise de Condorcet, translated *TMS* into French and attached her own commentary to the publication, adding a feminist voice to the book.[31]

Additionally, as Kathryn Sutherland points out, Smith argues explicitly that women's work, particularly spinning, "never enters the publick registers of manufactures" (WN I.viii.51) and that women laborers are "commonly, scattered about in all different parts of the country, without support or protection" (WN IV.viii.4).[32] Jane Rendall observes that, for Smith, social roles were "the contrivance of man" and not the natural order (in this context, 'man' means humanity and is not gender specific).[33] She also highlights one of Smith's most explicit comments regarding the inequality between the sexes: "The laws of most countries being made by men generally are very severe on the women, who can have no remedy for this oppression" (LJ(A) iii.13). Here, "men" means male.[34]

Observations of this sort are almost indistinguishable from contemporary condemnations of patriarchal society by many feminists, and Smith's moral disapproval is evident in his phrasing.[35] If cross-gender communication were impossible, Smith could not be sympathetic to the historical plights of women, yet he clearly is. His response is to educate, first, his students and then his readers, to the unjust plight of women; as the chair of Logic and of Moral Philosophy in Glasgow, he understood full well that he was educating the next generation of political leaders. Consistent with his theories, Smith always takes a pedagogical approach to social change.

While it is true that Smith is complimentary of Scottish women's education, despite the fact that "there are no publick institutions for the education of women" (WN V.i.f.47), to read his praise as a defense of women's exclusion from advanced schooling would be a mistake. Smith makes this comment in the midst of his critique of purely publicly funded schools and the impractical education that results. Smith argues that in contrast to what is found in such schools, there is "nothing useless, absurd, or fantastical in the common course of [women's] education" because they are taught by their parents or guardians what they need to know. He adds that, unlike men, "in every part of her life a woman feels some conveniency or advantage from every part of her education" (WN V.i.f.47).

This is certainly not the outright condemnation of women's second-class citizenship that many of today's readers might like to see. However, it does serve to show that, for Smith, economic structures can be advantageous to women at least in regard to providing them with the skills they require for life as it actually was most of the time.[36] For Smith, education must be *useful*; it must cultivate skills and judgment. Women need to be educated to do what they are required to do, and anything more would be frivolous, a claim analogous to Mandeville's that since society is wicked, it might as well be wicked and prosperous: since education does not provide women with equality, at least it can be efficient.[37] Furthermore, what these observations emphasize is that Smith's analysis is done under conditions of injustice. He is describing an educational system that does not cultivate natural liberty, and thus the standards must themselves be a compromise from an ideal.

Smith addresses this injustice in *LJ*, where he elaborates on the relationship between women and economics by providing an explicit account of the impact changing societies have on women's status, emphasizing again the progress inherent in the unfolding of history. Chris Nyland presents a clear account of the ways in which women's lives improve according to Smith's stage theory, although his account emphasizes the economic and pays little attention to the role of sympathy in social change. Economic, social, and political progress brings with it improvement in women's lives and rights. Nyland argues that Smith's account "provided a substantive theoretical challenge to the belief that male social domination was natural and that women would always remain the subservient sex."[38] Furthermore, as Nyland shows, as far as Smith was concerned, the only innate differences between men and women are "strength and fecundity."[39]

These theorists have shown that ultimately gender distinctions in Smith's work are superficial at most. This is important since Smith's context was one in which gender contributed significantly to social, political, and educational difference. If his theory—whether intentionally or not—develops so as to minimize the difference between the genders, then it shows significant promise in providing a foundation for social unity and social change, even in the face of sophisticated historical institutions designed explicitly to separate men and women. His theory suggests that there is little that could not be understood between these groups. For example, for Smith, a man can even sympathize with a woman in childbirth, the most exclusive of female experiences (*TMS* VII.iii.I.4).

Those who object to this claim because men cannot themselves experience childbirth—those who assert that such sympathy is only a pretense but not actual commonality—forget that *all* sympathy is imperfect, not just the fellow feeling between men and women.[40] Sympathy results in analogous emotions in the spectator, but that emotion is *always* less in degree no matter what sentiment is being sympathized with (*TMS* I.i.1.2). Smith refers to the original sentiment as the "substance" and to the imagined sentiment as its "shadow" (*TMS* VI.ii.1.1). Therefore, that a man attempts to sympathize with a woman giving birth and fails to do so exactly is typical of every other act of sympathy any spectator engages in.

Women who engage in easier deliveries are also unable to have direct knowledge of difficult childbirth since they did not have the same experience. It should not need to be said that all women are not identical. Their common experience may bring them closer to the pain of labor but it can never be *exact* because sympathy is the product of the imagination and does not provide privileged access. We must, therefore, distinguish between imagining the pain itself and imagining being the person who is in pain, a key element in any diversity theory since it makes a person, not the suffering abstracted from the sufferer, the subject of our concern. Since sympathy is the product of the imagination, the question, ultimately, is not whether a man ever experiences such pain but whether he can ever *imagine* it. It is for this reason that Smith can consistently suggest, as he does, that a spectator can sympathize with the dead (*TMS* I.i.1.13).[41]

For Smith, the fundamental separateness that humans experience is no different between genders than it is within a particular gender. Justman, as critical of Smith as he is, ultimately admits that "the distinction between men and women in the thinking of Adam Smith is wholly specious and artificial, prefiguring 'the artificiality of the binary logic' of Victorian thinking about the sexes."[42] As Rendall argues, Smith's writing "formed an important theoretical stage in that redefinition of public and private spheres which is critical to our understanding of the relationship between the sexes in an industrial world."[43]

EDUCATION AND INTIMATE EXPERIENCE

My argument in this and the previous chapter has emphasized the effects of proximity on persons in society. My purpose is to show that, for Smith, education can overcome social differences, at least in part because these differences are themselves the product of historical developments and of social and political structures. There are rational ways of entering into the experience of another. They are built on learning a person's history and experience and on challenging or becoming more aware of cultural norms. This information is learned through socialization and education, in both passive and active manners, respectively. That these questions are relevant to Smith's pluralism should not require comment. That they are components of his theory of rationality, however, might be harder to see since the project of describing what 'rational' means in this context is so lengthy.

In brief, I argue that rationality is dependent on sympathy, while sympathy is built upon fellow feeling with those whom we are capable of regarding as worthy of observation. As we increase our capacity to observe others, we increase our rational abilities. Historically, two of the most divisive social identifiers have been gender and race, but for Smith there is no reason to think that informed individuals with a cultivated imagination cannot overcome these two barriers. The question before us is how one becomes informed and how one cultivates imagination. This is the purview of education.

As I have emphasized, for Smith, the ability to sympathize rests on either preexisting commonalities or the ability to create commonalities by learning the contexts and perspectives of others. Smith starts with the presumption of natural equality; for him, there is no "originall difference" between individuals (*LJ*(A) vi.47–48). Children in their younger years are "very much alike, and neither their parents nor play-fellows could perceive any remarkable difference" (WN I.ii.4). Significant change comes about when children are employed in different occupations, the effect of the division of labor (WN I.ii.4). Smith rejects the notion that there are different types of people with "fundamentally different 'types' of human psychologies which are not reducible to each other."[44] For Smith, nonphysical, racial, gender, class, and other differences are learned, not biologically determined.[45]

There is a difficulty here. Smith's comment that parents could not note any "remarkable difference" between their children and others can be read as patently false (except perhaps in the first weeks of life). I am certainly aware of the most minute differences between my six-year-old daughter and every other child she interacts with, and I both consciously and unconsciously compare her development with those around her. I have done so since her birth.[46] Smith's statement therefore betrays his lack of familiarity with parenting. However, its veracity depends upon how seriously we take the term "remarkable difference." Although there is no "original difference" between people, he does remark that "the difference of natural talents in different men is, in reality, much less than we are aware of" (WN I.ii.4). The first implies no difference; the second implies only a little but acknowledges *some*. Did Smith change his mind? Or, is what he means by original difference more fundamental than that which he considers natural talents?

The latter is more likely the case. Humans are born fragile; the vast majority will be able to see, run, and speak, for example. Whatever variation exists among individuals, Smith seems to argue, is not so great as to violate their natural claim to equality or to a human nature that requires common endeavor. No individual will be able to see so well or run so quickly that he or she ought to reject the rules of justice, for example, or refuse to participate in some form of economic exchange.

Smith adds that for the first four or five years of childrens' lives, observers "looked upon them as persons of pretty much the same stamp. No wisdom and ingenuity appeared in the one superior to that of the other." Only later does their "manner of life began then to affect them. . . . The difference of employment occasions the difference of genius" (*LJ*(A) vi.46–48). Yes, one child can run faster than another or has more dexterity; this is evident from an earlier age than Smith acknowledges, although, again, this depends on the meaning of 'wisdom' and 'ingenuity.' However, any but the most competitive parent will recognize that most of these differences even out in the end, lending support to Smith's conclusion that "by nature a philosopher is not in genius and disposition half so different from a street porter, as a mastiff is from a greyhound, or a greyhound from a spaniel, or this last from a shepherd's dog" (*WN* I.ii.5).

Smith's point is not that human beings are identical—this is not what original difference means. It is that the natural talents of human beings are similar enough that they all have—and this comment is found in similar discussions in both *LJ* and *WN*—this "disposition to truck, barter, and exchange" (*LJ*(A) vi.48, *WN* I.ii.5). It is one's life, one's experience, one's socialization, and one's education that cultivate the difference to significant degrees.

Returning to the question of noncommunicable difference, modern multiculturalism can be understood to suggest that those members of a group who are bound by similarity—whether it be a culture, a tradition, or a common history—are bound by their own judgments through what I call a lived normativity. In some sense they assent to the standard that binds them; they are subject to their own conclusions. For example, if a Scot morally condemns another Scot, it may hold more weight than if the Scot is condemned by the British colonial power that has imposed itself on Scotland—or so some would argue. While I remain agnostic on whether this multicultural assertion is *true*, we can see anticipations of it in the slave/slave owner example: for Smith, moral condemnation is also more authentic when it comes from within an individual.

In this case it is the slave owner who condemns himself or herself, and it is this particular condemnation that is the most damaging. It is not the external judgment of the community that condemns the slave owner to self-hatred; it is the slave owner's own imagination—the impartial spectator. The slave owner determines that the act is wrong and must then act on it or violate his or her own self-respect. Smith seems to suggest that because condemnation comes from that part of the identity that is most intimate, it has more power than any social judgment the slave owner may be subject to. The impartial spectator is "the man within the breast" and "the great judge and arbiter of our conduct" (*TMS* VI.ii.1.22).

I do not mean to suggest that Smith negates community influence. To do so would run counter to my entire argument so far. Instead, I only mean to propose that community, however influential, is limited in power. At the core of Smith's discussion is an unarticulated claim that central to human understanding is an undeniable experience. The community cannot erase it or prevent it from influencing a person's sentiments or impartial spectator. By "undeniable," I do not mean unfalsifiable. Clearly, in many cases the community can alter an actor's sense, or valuing, of an experience; the community can change the experience's meaning. For example, one friend may show another that what appears to be love is really lust, or a therapist may convince a patient that his or her fear is really paranoia, but no one can challenge the presence of the experience itself. No one can challenge that we feel *something* even if how we articulate what we feel may be culturally defined.[47] In fact, it is precisely because these experiences are emotional—it is precisely because Smith roots his moral psychology in sentiment—that these experiences have power. The reaction to some sentiments simply will not change.

To elaborate: consider my argument that distance adds difficulty to the sympathetic process and that a person sympathizes more easily with those with whom he or she is familiar. The reverse, then, must also be true, that closeness makes sympathy, at least as a general rule, easier, and the actor can most easily sympathize with herself or himself. This is consistent with Smith's claim that each person is "recommended to his own care," is "fitter and abler to take care of himself than of any other person," and that "every man feels his own pleasures and his own pains more sensibly than those of other people" (*TMS* VI.ii.1.1).

Any "unarticulated claim" is, by definition, hard to prove. Yet evidence for this view is available by focusing on Smith's discussion regarding those sentiments that are easily sympathized with and those that are not. Smith argues that spectators tire of hearing lovers discuss each other since they cannot enter into the particulars, even though the spectator understands full well that it is possible for actor *x* to love person *y* and that this situation is an instantiation of such a relationship (*TMS* I.ii.2.1). Smith also claims that physical pains are virtually impossible to communicate, so much so that they are easily forgotten, even by the sufferer soon after the pain has subsided (*TMS* I.ii.I.8). The difficulty in remembering pain shows how important the imagination is; after the pain is finished, a person may have trouble sympathizing with himself or herself. Notice, the more intimate or central an experience, the less communicable it is. For Smith, the ability to communicate is the indication of and the precondition for social interconnectedness.

The consequence of this intimacy of experience is important, although Smith does not explicitly say so. A slave and slave owner may be convinced that slavery is morally correct, that it is just, and that each person deserves his or her place in the social structure, but the slave cannot be convinced that he or she *likes* the experience or that it does not cause pain—again, *Uncle Tom's Cabin* comes to mind.[48] This central conviction is ever present in the slave's life and reaffirmed time and time again; as Smith writes, "It is evident that the state of slavery must be very unhappy to the slave himself. This I need hardly prove" (*LJ*(A) iii.111.

For Smith, this conviction is an outgrowth of the fundamentally discrete nature of the individual. It is this pain that the slave owner must imagine when he or she adopts the perspective of the slave, and to do it properly the slave owner must examine the cause of the pain—the institution of slavery and all its requisite components and consequences, including her or his culpability. It is this recognition that causes self-hatred.

Pain, as has been shown, is the hardest of all sentiments to sympathize with. Yet it is precisely because the slave feels pain that the community cannot make him or her positively value the experience. Again, even if one convinces the slave that he or she deserves what is felt, it is still pain that is deserved, not pleasure and not joy. Pain is not subject to rational persuasion—you cannot *convince* pain to go away.

We have now found the bottom level of Smith's rationality. Pain is an example of what I shall call an emotional *primitive*; it is *simple* in Locke's sense of the term. It can be used as a component of a larger rational argument, it may play a central role in a narrative, or it may play a role in moral adjudication, but it cannot be explained away. It is individualistic and one of the pieces that most separates individuals.

I began this discussion by addressing the connections between rationality— the discipline of subjecting one's choices, actions, objectives, values, and priorities to reasoned scrutiny—and sympathy—the imagination's creation of fellow feeling. There must be explicit connections between sentiments and rationality, and I suggest these primitives are the most basic of them. Recall that Smith inherits his awareness of multiple motivations from the discourse between Hobbes, Mandeville, Shaftesbury, and Hutcheson. In this context, this multiplicity of motivations references primitives as well. Pain may be felt at the same time as desire or curiosity, fear, anger, love, or other such passions.

This need for a new rationality came from the inadequacy of the Hobbesian linear model. Smith did not accept the Hobbesian replacement of less powerful passions by more powerful ones. While these primitive passions exist and while they cannot be denied, they can be utilized, manipulated, referred to, rejected, or embraced by the individual and the community. Their individuality reasserts the discrete nature of human identity; the attention they receive by the community emphasizes the impact of culture. The self-hatred an individual feels after sympathizing with the subject of one's own unjust actions is the moment of active connection as filtered through assent to the general rules of conduct.

Self-hatred is a link between education, socialization, and undeniable experience. It is possible in Smith's system because self-image is quite pliable: the community can influence somebody to dislike herself or himself even when the individual is reluctant to do so. This pliability can both inform and misinform. As noted, self-deceit, for example, the self-persuasion that our acts are appropriate when they are not, is, according to Smith, the "fatal weakness of mankind" and "the source of half the disorders of human life" (*TMS* III.4.6).[49] This is made more complicated by the fact that, according to Smith, self-awareness itself is quite easily deformed. He emphasizes this in an earlier edition of *TMS*: "Unfortunately this moral looking-glass is not always a very good one. Common looking-glasses, it is said, are extremely deceitful, and by the glare which they throw over the face, conceal from the partial eyes of the person many deformities which are obvious to every body besides. But there is not in the world such a smoother of wrinkles as is every man's imagination, with regard to the blemishes of his own character" (*TMS ed.1*, III.i.5).

This passage was removed after the first edition, replaced by material that takes up a great deal of *TMS* III.4.2, "On the Nature of Self-deceit, and of the Origin and Use of general Rules." The new chapter enumerates those times when agents examine their own actions—it uses a paragraph that originally followed the one cited above—and then articulates the difficulties that are involved in accurately describing oneself (*TMS* III.4.4). Smith then provides an account of the general rules of morality and the ways in which they correct the "misrepresentations of self-love" (*TMS* III.4.12).

It is unclear why he made this change, but it is likely that he wanted to theorize the inaccuracy of "moral looking-glass" better. The revisions contain significantly more information but nothing that contradicts the original paragraph. Additionally, the excerpt from the first edition echoes Hutcheson's observation that seeing one's own motivations is more difficult than seeing others'—Smith and his teacher agree that self-knowledge is often more difficult than knowledge of others.

Recall that, for Smith, judgments about beauty, identity, and moral matters are all intertwined. Smith unites them explicitly in his discussion of the social foundation of our capacity for judgment (*TMS* III.I.3–5) but also implicitly throughout *TMS*. As both Shaftesbury and Hutcheson argue, the language of beauty is the language of morality and vice versa. For Smith, fashion and custom "define" beauty and heavily influence the impartial spectator. Regarding beauty, he writes, "Neither is it only over the productions of the arts, that custom and fashion exert their dominion. They influence our judgments, in the same manner, with regard to the beauty of natural objects" (*TMS* V.I.8). Regarding morality, he suggests that custom cannot "entirely pervert" our sense of moral approbation (*TMS* V.2.1)—this is the legacy of Shaftesbury's Stoic prolepsis and Hutcheson's moral sense—but caution is still necessary. For Smith, those who are educated in good company are shocked that agents break moral rules, but those "who have had the misfortune to be brought up amidst violence, licentiousness, falsehood, and injustice; lose, though not all sense of the impropriety of such conduct, yet all sense of its dreadful enormity, or of the vengeance and punishment due to it" (*TMS* V.2.2). For Smith, continuous cultural immersion in impropriety makes a person more likely to misjudge morality. Persistent images of immorality create difficulties for accessing any objective moral judgments. This is the acculturation that education needs to counterbalance.

The same is true of beauty. Smith first postulates the objectivity of beauty at *TMS* V.I.8 and then counters it with an argument regarding its changing standards. Finally, at *TMS* V.I.9, he cautiously concludes that even if there is an objective standard of beauty—perhaps based on utility—there is probably no item that is so objectively beautiful that it can counter a fashion or custom explicitly aimed against it. In other words, the standards of beauty and the forces that influence self-image are as complex and as interwoven as those forces that influence the perceptions of others. Art, literature, and custom—the raw material of a liberal education—can overpower any objective aesthetic.

These realities point to a central difficulty in Smith's system. He implies a universal ethic throughout his work, yet he adopts a context-dependent moral psychology. Smith asserts that acts and institutions like slavery are wrong but relies on culture and context to justify his claims. He does appeal to the impartial spectator upon which he grounds his normative claims, but the spectator is limited by the human imagination and is an imperfect ground. For Smith, moral judgment must somehow be a combination of universal and contextual forces—a grand compromise that he seems to believe is an accurate depiction of the human experience.[50] The product of this compromise illustrates the dual possibilities of education: the potential to unify and the potential to divide. It reminds us of the duality between the ideal and actual that is woven through Smith's corpus. It also forces us to further consider a question I posed in passing: to what extent are the general rules of conduct binding?

Smith argues that education solidifies the moral lessons stemming from sympathetic judgments. Consider yet again the passage regarding the sacrifice of the Chinese for an actor's little finger. In this same section, immediately following his comments about acting toward those with whom we have no connection, Smith writes that the most "vulgar education" encourages impartiality, and the most refined education can "correct the inequalities of our passive feelings" (*TMS* III.3.7). We treat the distant well by following general rules of conduct that are fixed in our minds by "habitual reflection" and that are "of great use in correcting the misrepresentations of self-love." Unless a person has had a "singular" education, he or she will consider such rules "inviolable" (*TMS* III.4.12). In short, all education but the most narrow counters self-love, and there is "scarce any man" who "by discipline, education, and example" cannot be made to obey the general rules of conduct (*TMS* III.5.1).

In each of these citations one can read Smith as referencing either socialization or conscious pedagogical efforts; he believes that there are few who could not be impacted by learning. Notice, then, that Smith first refers to "vulgar" then "singular" education. In each, education is taken at its worst, yet it still holds the power to cultivate morality. For Smith, only minimal education is required to provide a foundation for moral judgment, but in such cases moral judgments will also be basic and spare. The more complex education is, the more complex moral judgments can be.

For Smith, education is so fundamental to the development of moral judgment that one can judge the quality of a society's educational system by examining the moral activities of those who have learned from it. (Here Smith obviously means institutional education.) As I have noted, Smith highlights this relationship by comparing the ancient Greek and Roman methods of education (*WN* V.i.f.45). Smith then presents, as usual, an historical account of changes in education. By doing so, he once again shows how these have resulted in changes of moral standards, an example of the "comparative" approach to justice that Amartya Sen praises Smith for.[51] Without proper education, Smith argues, moral development is severely impeded.

According to Smith, lack of education is as much a barrier to being sympathized with as it is to being able to sympathize. Those without education are both looked upon with contempt and denied happiness (*WN* V.i.f.61); education seems to be a precondition for and therefore necessary to happiness (*WN* V.i.f.60). Comparing two individuals, one who is "mutilated and deformed in his mind" and one who is mutilated of the body, Smith writes that the one who is mutilated of the mind "is evidently the more wretched and miserable of the two" (*WN* V.i.f.60).[52]

The person who is denied education is denied ease of sympathy, and sympathy is essential to social interaction, which is itself a component of happiness, a point we could not have seen if we had read *WN* without *TMS* as its starting point. Since Smith considers happiness to be the "natural and ordinary state of mankind" (*TMS* I.iii.1.7) and since those who are denied education are denied happiness, then those who are denied education are denied the ease of mutual sympathy and the opportunity to live life as a normal person.

What Smith means by happiness is unclear; he does seem to suggest that it is available to all regardless of their educational histories. He speaks highly of the working classes, whom he recognizes as largely uneducated, and at one point references a beggar who lies by the side of the road in perfect tranquility (*TMS* IV.i.10). These observations seem to counter my claim that, for Smith, education is a necessary condition for happiness.

Yet it is precisely Smith's high regard for laborers as people capable of bettering their own lives that likely inspired his concern for their education. His comments about their ignorance are made with a sense of regret. They are not categorical, and they are all responses to the economic conditions implicit in a commercial society. Smith objects vehemently to the circumstances that, in his terms, "benumb the understanding" (*WN* V.i.f.51, V.i.f.61).

What of the beggar on the side of the road? According to Smith, the desire for riches moves commerce forward, and this, in turn, results in large-scale employment. The rich, he argues, select only the finest items from this mass of production, and the rest are divided by the workers (*TMS* IV.i.11). But the poorest of the poor, the beggars, are "in no respect inferior to those who would seem so much above them. In ease of body and peace of mind, all the different ranks of life are nearly upon a level, and the beggar, who suns himself by the side of the highway, possesses that security which kings are fighting for" (*TMS* IV.I.10). Does this counter my assertion that education is a necessary condition for happiness?

Certainly, there is no account of the beggar's previous life, so we do not know whether he or she is uneducated. And one might also argue that Smith refers to happiness only in regard to "ease of body" and "peace of mind," a less holistic definition than the one I am considering now. But these are not persuasive rejoinders. Smith might be arguing that ease of body is exactly what happiness is, or he might be making a smaller point that the beggar is, at the moment, content in a way that others hope to be and is therefore only briefly equal to, if not better off than, the kings who seek that state.

Prima facie evidence suggests the first option; Smith seems to posit that happiness is indeed a form of tranquility. As Griswold shows us, this approach has its roots in Hobbesian felicity and the realization of one's object of desire.[53] When Smith references the happiness of the dead—the restful state at the end of one's life (*TMS* I.i.1.10)—he implies that ease of mind is a form of happiness. This would be consistent with the Stoic influences I discussed earlier. Yet Smith is also clear that the Hobbesian pursuit of desire is a form of deception: the rich are falsely persuaded that material acquisition will make them happy, and this drives the economy. In the end, they discover, as "the poor man's son" who strove for greatness eventually did, that "power and riches appear then to be, what they are, enormous and operose machines contrived to produce a few trifling conveniencies to the body" (*TMS* IV.i.8).

It turns out that each person has the capacity for true happiness—true tranquility—all along, without material good. This is where the beggar comes in. Happiness is a potential that all individuals have, independent of their economic states.[54] This is not a simplistic Hobbesian fulfillment of desire but a mixture of what Griswold calls high and low standards of happiness, the high being the Stoic "greatest possible happiness of all rational and sensible beings" (*TMS* VII.ii.1.21) and the low being the realization of Stoic "proprieties, fitnesses, decent and becoming actions," what Smith calls the Stoic "imperfect, but attainable virtues" (*TMS* VII.ii.1.42). Note the role of rationality in the Stoic conception of happiness. Notice also the ideal aim and the more limited imperfection that might actually be achieved, a continuation of core Smithian themes. Happiness thus ends up being that which would be "approved of enthusiastically by the impartial spectator," the prudent or perfectly just person.[55]

Tranquility in the Hobbesian sense is certainly achievable by the beggar. If one does not want anything, then one need not be unhappy if nothing is gotten. Justice, for Smith, being mostly a negative virtue, can also be realized by the beggar, presuming that he or she is law abiding. But for prudence—a rational capability—and a healthy impartial spectator, education is required. Why? Because, Smith remarks, "Happiness and misery, which reside altogether in the mind, must necessarily depend more upon the healthful or unhealthful, the mutilated or entire state of the mind, than upon that of the body" (*WN* V.i.f.60).[56] The mind must be cultivated in order to engage in virtuous activities.

My argument is further supported by the context of this quote. Smith is discussing the martial virtues in ancient Greece and Rome, referencing cowardice as he does. He writes, "A coward, a man incapable either of defending or of revenging himself, evidently wants one of the most essential parts of the character of a man" (*WN* V.i.f.60). Cowardice was, he asserts, "a leprosy" in this period of time, and Smith offers an analogous leprosy for the commercial age: "the gross ignorance and stupidity which, in a civilized society, seem so frequently to benumb the understandings of all the inferior ranks of people. A man, without the proper use of the intellectual faculties of a man, is, if possible, more contemptible than even a coward" (WN V.i.5.61).

In short, cowardice in martial society and ignorance in civilized ones are both great impediments to "manhood" and represent "mutilations" of the mind that interfere with civic duty, praiseworthiness, and virtue. It is hard to imagine that Smith would describe these people as being happy; education, which, he argues in this same section, was necessary to the Greeks and Romans as well as to the lower classes in his time, is a prerequisite for happiness. How his comments address the gross ignorance and stupidity of a civilized society—and how Smith reconciles this call for education with his high regard for the laboring classes—we shall now see.[57]

CLASS

Some of Smith's most explicit comments on formal education occur in his discussion of the effects of repetitious labor on the working classes. Smith argues that because "the understandings of the greater part of men are necessarily formed by their ordinary employments," industrialization and regular employment result in constant repetition that makes poor workers unnecessarily ignorant (WN V.i.f.50). Emphasizing the impact of historical progression on social structures, Smith argues that in less advanced societies—those that precede "the improvement of manufactures, and the extension of foreign commerce" (WN V.i.f.51)—institutionalized education was not as necessary as in his own time. In earlier societies each person did a wide variety of activities and cultivated numerous skills. Consequently, in those societies "invention is kept alive, and the mind is not suffered to fall into that drowsy stupidity, which, in a civilized society, seems to benumb the understanding of almost all the inferior ranks of people" (WN V.i.f.51).

Each person in these societies is part warrior and part statesman and can "form a tolerable judgment concerning the interest of the society, and the conduct of those who govern it" (WN V.i.f.51). According to Smith, although there is variety in the lives of the individual in this society, there is not much variety in the lives of the various members of society as compared with one another. "Every man does, or is capable of doing, almost every thing which any other man does, or is capable of doing" (WN V.i.f.51). Thus in noncommercial societies it is easy for a spectator to sympathize with any agent since he or she will always be familiar with the situation of those whom he or she encounters. The spectator does not face wide gaps in experience, beliefs, or actions.

In contrast, in a commercial society an individual will have uniform days that will differ radically from the uniformity that others experience (WN V.i.f.51). For example, of two neighbors, one may spend the entire day working in a pin factory while the other may work on a fishing boat. Neither switches her occupation; neither knows what the other encounters. This infinite variety of uniformity makes sympathy much more difficult and makes education that much more necessary, particularly since Smith seems to think that lack of variety in a person's day is an intrinsic part of a commercial society. Again, we see the mosaic reality of diverse society. Thus unless such commercial structures could be radically reconfigured, this diversity of experience has to be pursued via education—it has to be intentionally infused into a person's life by means that do not undermine the necessary hierarchical economic structures. It has to, in a certain sense, be compartmentalized.

Recall that I am using the terms 'socialization' and 'acculturation' to denote social pressures arising from influences that are often passive and always collective in origin, and the term 'education,' whether institutional or otherwise, to denote the intentional imposition of values, norms, expectations, standards, and lessons on specific individuals or groups by other specific individuals or groups. Here is where this difference becomes most significant. Only through education can workers be encouraged to have more diverse experiences. This may involve in-class learning or, conceivably, familial or community-sponsored outings, the express purpose of which is to engage and cultivate the intellectual or creative capacities. I return to Smith's comments on curriculum in chapter 9. However, in either case this would be a kind of education and would help counter the pernicious effects of repetitious work conditions. Furthermore, whatever form this education takes, it must provide not only a different experience for the workers but also a common meeting point for those who have different uniform experiences each workday. Education must be geared toward encouraging a diversity of shared experiences that allow for commonality between those whose own experiences seem farther from those of others. In a mosaic pluralism, Smith asks for people to imagine a melting pot.[58]

'Difference' here refers to class identity as well as to the more mundane activities of work life. Smith is explicit that different groups play different roles in society, identifying, specifically, landlords, laborers, and employers (the merchants and the manufacturers) as "the three great, original and constituent orders of every civilized society" (WN I.xi.p.7). The first "lives by rent," the second "lives by wages," and the third "lives by profit," and while each one has a different relationship with the public interest, the employers, specifically, "have gennerally an interest to deceive and even to oppress the publick" and have done so on many occasions (WN I.xi.p.10).[59]

The key element here is not only the relationship between the classes and the public interest but also the *knowledge* of individual and general interest that varies greatly from group to group. Clearly, the merchants and manufacturers have the greatest knowledge of their own needs and can therefore manipulate policy to benefit their own concerns. Their interest, as a result, often conflicts with that of society. In contrast, the landlords, while "inseparably connected with the general interest of society," are ignorant of both their own interest and others' (WN I.xi.p.8). Their interests do not conflict with society per se but neither do they add wealth to society. Landlords are not productive; they do not work for their income. As Smith writes, "They are the only one of the three orders whose revenue costs them neither labour nor care, but comes to them, as it were, of its own accord, and independent of any plan or project of their own" (WN I.xi.p.8). In comparison, as Dogan Göçmen points out, while only laborers' interests coincide with society in general, their education and social conditions prohibit them from developing judgment.[60] They are not informed enough to promote the social welfare on any conscious level. This, I suggest, is part of what Smith hopes to change.

Smith's analysis of the diversity of group interest illustrates the contextualized way that life experiences and personal concern play havoc with an individual's understanding of "the general interest of society," a phrase that Göçmen rightly associates with impartiality, making explicit, yet again, the connection between WN and TMS's impartial spectator. As I have shown, Smith argues that social unity and impartiality can be cultivated by educating toward a nonpartisan view of society. In short, he develops a philosophy of education that presumes that the more variety a person is exposed to, the more capable he or she is of seeing others.

A wide-ranging education resists ignorance and prejudice; it finds commonality without erasing otherness. Here 'variety' refers to a multiplicity of activities, not the ethnic, racial, or cultural pluralism usually referenced by the term 'diversity.' Yet one can see how Smith's claims might lead to a justification of diversity in the more modern sense, and, as we have seen, he was well aware of the kind of cultural and religious diversity that causes one to doubt universal moral structures.

The division between male and female is a division of task and experience; if the two sexes wish to communicate, they must find commonalities about which to sympathize. The divide between slave owner and slave is also one based on task. The same is true of economic difference. Smith's pluralism based on a diversity of activities is only a small step away from the more modern pluralisms that emphasize gender, race, and class.

Smith's solution to social unity in the face of difference rests on his faith in people's ability to learn about others and their lives, to *imagine* a melting pot morality. Sympathy is the foundation for moral development; it is also the foundation for society. In the absence of sympathy and a proper education a society will be divided into as many factions as there are traits or cultural concerns. Women would be unable to sympathize with men, the rich would be unable to sympathize with the poor, and the English would be unable to sympathize with the Scots. There is no indication that Smith saw such differences as insurmountable, but there is every indication that he was aware of the divisions that traditionally occur near such complicated fault lines. Smith may have been unfamiliar with the cosmopolitan multicultural urban societies that many of us take for granted, but, as Emma Rothschild writes, his disputes are our disputes.[61]

As I have shown, rationality, for Smith, is built on undeniable primitives of varying communicability. The ability to see others, to testify to them or to learn what they are feeling, is dependent on community boundaries and the cultivation of an imagination that can overcome socially cultivated divisions. But these divisions are both politically fractious and socially destructive, and they inhibit the narrative structures that help adjudicate the primitives that then create, support, and interpret the general rules of conduct. How this rationality actually works is the topic of the next two chapters.

5

FINDING RATIONALITY IN REASON

Over the past four chapters I have examined Smith's account of the human experience that creates a framework for rationality. As we have seen, individuals have multiple motivations and must manage any conflicts that result from this plurality. They also have passions that cannot be easily communicated but have a moral agency that necessitates entering into others' perspectives. Finally, individuals are educated to learn about themselves and others as a means of fostering mutual understanding, but the more passive elements of institutional and social education both impair and cultivate this process. In this chapter, I investigate Smith's theory of rationality. In doing so, I pay special attention to the relationship between reason and changing conceptions of logic, emphasizing the rationality implicit in the moral sentiments. This is the first of three chapters specifically on reason and rationality.

As stated in the introduction, I have adopted Amartya Sen's definition of rationality as "the discipline of subjecting one's choices—of actions as well as of objectives, values and priorities—to reasoned scrutiny."[1] This is to be distinguished from reason itself, which is the human faculty for utilizing a range of skills including, but not limited to, inference and judgment. Deliberation, in this context, is the conscious use of rationality to adjudicate between competing positions (regardless of the controversy), and argumentation refers to the dialectical process of rational persuasion. Argumentation differs from rationality in its making reasons, inferences, evidence, and determinations of fact explicit and subject to systematic and critical scrutiny. Thus reason is the psychological capacity that allows for rational deliberation, and one critically and consciously examines these processes using the studies of logic and argumentation.

Logic is traditionally defined as the study of the validity conditions of argument. While readers may begin with this definition, much of the point of the next two chapters is to enlarge the disciplinary conception past the limiting conditions of validity and entailment. I therefore offer a provisional definition of logic as the study of human inference.

In this chapter I argue that Smith's rhetoric plays a central role in his theory of argumentation, thereby allowing him to bring both the role of audience and the psychological elements of persuasion into the foreground. This underscores the rationality of sympathy, emphasizing that despite the passionate nature of the moral sentiments, moral adjudication and interpersonal communication are still rational processes. I also focus on the historical influences that helped lead Smith to his point of view, emphasizing an intellectual lineage that, not surprisingly, is similar to the one described previously: Hobbes, Mandeville, Locke, Shaftesbury, and Hume.

REASON AND THE RETREAT FROM LOGIC

Smith's individuals are decision-making creatures. Humans, he tells us, were "made for action" (*TMS* II.iii.3.3). As such, actors, faced with a significant amount of information, are expected to consider wide-ranging contingencies to make coherent and defensible choices regarding necessities, conveniences, luxuries, virtues, and duties. These choices relate to both immediate needs and long-term planning. They involve both private and collective goods and have personal as well as public consequences. Whether the purpose is the creation of the imagined impartial spectator or determinations about bettering one's condition, Smith's actors are required to create an ordered understanding of how one is to act, judge, and value.

For Smith, agents are neither perfect nor purely objective judges. The impartial spectator is an ideal toward which an agent may strive (*TMS* VI.iii.27), but not one that Smith ever expects him or her to achieve. Smith continually reminds readers of the imperfection in the human condition (*TMS* I.i.5.8, II.i.5.9, II.i.5.10, II.3.iii.3). He resists any direct comparison of persons to perfection (*TMS* I.i.5.9, III.6.12, VI.iii.27) or to "the Deity" (*TMS* VII.ii.3.2, VII. ii.3.18). He insists that sympathy is itself imperfect (*TMS* I.i.1.9, I.iii.2.9) and that moral judgment is fallible (*TMS* III.6.12, VII.4.28). He is also well aware of the impact our emotions have on the process of judgment (*TMS* I.i.5.8, III.4.12). We judge our conduct both before and after we act (*TMS* III.4.2).

A sentiment-based moral system must acknowledge that ephemeral and sometimes unreliable emotions will significantly impact our decision-making process;[2] much of *TMS* is geared toward moderating their effect. It is, for example, the role of the general rules of conduct—the general principles of ethics and duty—to help guide actions when the moral agent is unable to react with propriety. At *TMS* III.4.12, we see Smith's actors struggling to subordinate their desires to their duty, a struggle heightened in times of extreme passion. According to Smith, actions are kept in check by duty, community opinion, and the imagined impartial spectator. Once again, moral approval is not a synonym for vanity in Smith's writing. People act appropriately not only because they want to be thought of in positive terms. Instead, Smith argues, moral people desire to be *worthy* of approbation: "of being what he himself approves of in other men" (*TMS* III.2.7).

For Smith, the desire for approval is both the desire for the pleasure of approval (*TMS* III.2.6) and the desire to do the right thing (*TMS* III.1–4). One must therefore judge not only what one can do in order to be praised, but also what one must do in order to be deserving of praise. As we have seen before, Smith's actors must negotiate competing tensions. In the search for praiseworthiness, the tension is between sentiments and reason.

It is a mistake, however, to think of Smith as seeing emotion and reason as fundamental opposites. The two are, in fact, complementary forces, and they overlap in their contribution to moral judgments. According to Smith, the capacity for reason is an essential component of the human condition. As cited in the introduction,

> Of all the calamities to which the condition of mortality exposes mankind, the loss of reason appears, to those who have the least spark of humanity, by far the most dreadful, and they behold that last stage of human wretchedness with deeper commiseration than any other. But the poor wretch, who is in it, laughs and sings perhaps, and is altogether insensible of his own misery. The anguish which humanity feels, therefore, at the sight of such an object, cannot be the reflection of any sentiment of the sufferer. The compassion of the spectator must arise altogether from the consideration of what he himself would feel if he was reduced to the same unhappy situation, and, what perhaps is impossible, was at the same time able to regard it with his present *reason and judgment*. (*TMS* I.i.1.11, emphasis added)

As we see here, compassion is an act of "reason and judgment." Notice in this passage that the loss of reason diminishes "the spark of humanity" and that reason and judgment are fundamental components of the sympathetic process. Sympathy is a *rational* process; it is not a form of intuition. A person can be persuaded to sympathize or to reject sympathetic inclination. This is done with information, reason, argument, reflection, and normative criteria. If sympathy were not rational, an agent could only be emotionally manipulated. But Smith

clearly thinks sympathy can be rationally altered by spectators and their interlocutors.

Although Smithian sympathy is derived to some degree from Shaftesbury's
and Hutcheson's moral sense, it is inaccurate to think of it simply in terms
of a hunch or instinct. Senses can be refined through practice and learning.
The parts of sympathy that are outgrowths of the moral sense can also be
similarly refined. Recall that sympathy itself is often altered by new information
as well as through the imaginative leap that results from *consciously* trying
to enter into the perspective of the other. That sympathy feels intimate and,
often, instantaneous should not suggest that sympathy lacks either content or
deliberation. Language, for example, is in no way an intuitive process; it only
seems so. It ought not be surprising then that, for Smith, "The rules of
justice may be compared to the rules of grammar" and that other moral rules
ought to be compared "to the rules which critics lay down for the attainment
of what is sublime and elegant in composition" (*TMS* III.6.11). This latter
pairing is why his classroom moral discussions include both rhetoric and belles
lettres.

The assertion that emotions are themselves rational challenges many
assumptions, positions stemming back at least to Plato's chariot analogy in
Phaedrus, in which Socrates describes the intellect and emotions as horses
controlled by a charioteer representing the will.[3] Smith rejects this bifurcation
that underlies many traditional understandings of the "logical." He assumes
that emotions initiate, are the consequence of, and are often indistinguishable
from reason.

Martha Nussbaum explains how emotions may be understood as rational.
She writes, "First of all, [emotions] are *about* something: they have an object. . . .
Second, the object is an *intentional* object: that is, it figures in the emotion as it
is seen or interpreted by the person whose emotion it is. . . . Third, these emotions
embody not simply ways of seeing an object, but beliefs—often very complex—
about the object. . . . Finally, we notice something marked in the intentional
perceptions and the beliefs characteristic of the emotions: they are concerned
with *value*, they see their object as invested with value or importance."[4]

For Nussbaum, as for Smith, emotions are not unintelligent arrows aimed
unthinkingly or spontaneously at some object. They are complex, value-laden
consequences requiring interpretation and reconstruction. They are represen-
tatives of a process of reason and components of larger arguments and deliberations that lie at the core of the human *intellectual* experience. This is a deeper
notion than simply claiming that judgments are cultural; as we shall see, inference itself is fluid for Smith. In this respect, his work anticipates MacIntyre's

accounts of tradition-bound rationality in that a reasoning tradition infuses what individuals understand as reason itself, how rational elements are articulated, and the decisions one makes in order to achieve instrumental goals.[5]

Nussbaum, building on MacIntyre, also provides the opportunity to take Smith's moral sentiments more seriously as "essential elements of human intelligence, rather than just as supports or props for intelligence."[6] If emotions were deemed to be simply reactions rather than judgments, or unfortunate influences that are to be conquered by a pure and unquestionable reason, then Smith's theory could provide neither normative nor rational structures upon which to build a moral or a social and political theory. In such a picture, moral, political, and economic agents would become awash in a sea of uncontrollable forces and would be subject *only* to the invisible hand or social forces that can be neither parsed nor mapped. Under such an interpretation, Smith's theory would also lack any convincing account of human freedom.

However, if we reconsider the traditional Western position that only reason can contribute defensible and normative elements to moral deliberation, and if we regard emotions as legitimate components and consequences of deliberation itself, then Smith's theory becomes that much more powerful—much more *rational*. As Nussbaum writes in her discussion of the work of Richard Lazarus, a cognitive scientist,

> Lazarus notes that goals may be present to an animal in many ways: they may be supplied by biology, by society, or by a process of personal development; they may be objects of conscious reflection, or they may be deeply internalized without being conscious; appraisal may follow set patterns, or it may be done step by step in each case. Emotions need not be 'rational' in the sense of being, in every case, explicit or verbal. But in another, normative sense they are profoundly rational: for they are ways of taking in important news of the world. The suggestion that we might rid ourselves of emotions or cease to be prompted by them is, as Lazarus sees, the suggestion that we should radically reorganize the sense of self that most of us have, and the sort of practical rationality that helps most of us, much as it helps other animals, to carry on our transactions with a world that helps or harms us.[7]

Nussbaum shows that emotions provide ways of "taking in important news of the world." Understanding Smith in this manner helps us see ways in which he may have contributed to Kant's "Copernican Revolution," recognizing that the mind plays an active role in organizing sense data.

Too much should not be made of this. Nussbaum helps to articulate only the small step forward that Smith takes. She continues, for example, that emotions "view the world from the point of view of my own scheme of goals and projects, the things to which I attach value in a conception of what it is for me to live well."[8] She reminds us that "knowing can be violent, given the truths that are there to be known"[9] and that to internalize one's knowledge of these facts one must "accept" and "assent" to the truth of propositions continuously.[10] Like Smith, she argues that emotions can be "true or false" as well, at least in the sense that they are "'appropriate' or 'inappropriate.'"[11] They are "responsive to the way the world already is."[12]

Like Smith, Nussbaum sees the imagination as "a highly discriminating intentional/cognitive faculty."[13] Also like Smith she sees that emotions are "evaluative" and can themselves be "evaluated"; they are necessarily intertwined with socialization. She writes that "a fundamental aspect of treating a person as a person is the recognition that an infant [or any person] has a separate history in a separate body, intertwined with other specific individuals in a history of great depth and intensity. Only from such a history does an infant [or any person] come to be a member of a larger social group."[14] Nussbaum helps us reconceive the traditional divisions of reason and emotions, of judgment and sentiments, and, in her more contemporary voice, offers a defense of Smith's position that reason and judgment are foundational to the sympathetic process.

Returning to the pairing of "reason and judgment," Smith references the two a second time in *TMS*, again tying the phrase to emotion. This time, however, he focuses on happiness: "Since our happiness and misery, therefore, depended chiefly on the mind, if this part of our nature was well disposed, if our thoughts and opinions were as they should be, it was of little importance in what manner our body was affected. Though under great bodily pain, we might still enjoy a considerable share of happiness, if our reason and judgment maintained their superiority. We might entertain ourselves with the remembrance of past, and with the hopes of future pleasure; we might soften the rigour of our pains, by recollecting what it was which, even in this situation, we were under any necessity of suffering" (*TMS* VII.ii.2.5).

Recall my discussion of education as necessary for happiness and that happiness is the "natural and ordinary state of mankind" (*TMS* I.iii.1.7). Since reason and judgment are preconditions of happiness, they must also be natural and ordinary. It follows from this argument that education is natural as well.

Smith uses an almost identical phrase—"reason and sound judgment"—in *LRBL* while discussing the notion of proof in didactic texts. Here, however, he seems to distinguish reason and the passions, explaining that "the Didactic and the oratoricall compositions consist of two parts, the proposition which we lay down and the proof that is brought to confirm this; whether this proof be a strict one applyed to our reason and sound judgment, or one adapted to affect our passions and by that means persuade us at any rate" (*LRBL* II.14).

Despite what it looks like at first glance, Smith is not suggesting that passions and reasons are in opposition. Instead, he emphasizes the aims of different writing styles: his comparison of the rules of morality to the rules of composition again comes to mind. According to Smith, some compositions aim to make arguments while others inspire an instinctive emotional reaction. In fact, as we shall see shortly, the line between logic and rhetoric can be as blurry for Smith as that between emotion and reason.

Smith uses the term 'reason' in several ways. He enumerates particular reasons for arguments and therefore uses it as a synonym for arguments and sometimes for philosophy (cf. *TMS* I.i.4.4, I.iii.2.3, *WN* I.viii.45). He uses it to describe that which is true or to be expected and thus employs it as an indication of that which is correct or reliable (cf. *TMS* V.1.4, *WN* I.iv.4). He uses "reasonings" to describe an individual's deliberative procedure and thus relies upon it as a means by which he can isolate the process of decision making (cf. *TMS* III.3.4, VII.iii.2, *WN* IV.i.34). And, most important for our purposes, he uses the term 'reason' to explain the human faculty itself (cf. *TMS* I.i.1.10, *WN* I.ii.2). With this he focuses on the capacity to reason and not just the process.

Reason in the last case seems to be the capacity that allows for judgment. Smith writes, "The judging faculty, . . . determines not only what are the proper means for attaining any end, but also what ends are fit to be pursued, and what degree of relative value we ought to put upon each. This faculty Plato called, as it is very properly called, reason, and considered it as what had a right to be the governing principle of the whole. Under this appellation, it is evident, he comprehended not only that faculty by which we judge of truth and falsehood, but that by which we judge of the propriety or impropriety of desires and affections" (*TMS* VII.ii.1.3). The phrase "as it is properly called" suggests that he and Plato agree.

Smith repeats a similar assertion later in *TMS*, identifying reason as "the same faculty by which we distinguish between truth and falsehood" (*TMS* VII. iii.intro.2). He also describes reason alongside understanding as the faculty "by which we are capable of discerning the remote consequences of all our actions, and of foreseeing the advantage or detriment which is likely to result from them" (*TMS* IV.2.6).

More often than not Smith pairs reason with other terms. He refers to "the faculties of reason and speech" (*WN* I.ii.2), "dictates of reason and humanity" (*WN* I.viii.44), "the doctrine of reason and philosophy" (*TMS* I.i.1.12,[15] *TMS* I.iii.2.3, *Logics* 6[16]), "reason and experience" in opposition to "the prejudices of the imagination" (*TMS* I.iii.2.2), "superior reason and understanding" (*TMS*

IV.2.6, IV.2.7), "reason and nature" in opposition to "habit or prejudice" (*TMS* V.1.4), "reason and masculine eloquence" in opposition to "frivolous prettiness" (*TMS* V.1.7), "reason and judgment" (*TMS* I.i.1.11, VII.ii.2.5), "reason and propriety" (*TMS* VII.ii.4.10), and he remarks that to treat people as "men" is "to reason and dispute with them upon ordinary occasions" (*TMS* I.iii.2.3). In *LJ(A)* Smith uses the phrase "reason and ingenuity" (*LJ(A)* vi.8),[17] and in *Physics* he uses the phrase "reason and intelligence" in connection to the ether but then revises it in the next clause to read "the very essence of reason and intelligence," suggesting a possible connection between the ether and the deity (*Physics* 11).

We can use these pairings as indications of those faculties and activities that rely on and improve reason. We learn from them that reason is a capacity to be refined, like speech and imagination. It is a tool for scientific investigation, just as experience, philosophy, and understanding are. It helps counter limited perspectives and unjustified presuppositions, such as prejudices, habit, and frivolity. And, importantly, reason is natural. Despite the need for education and practice in the refinement of reason, it is not an artifice. It is akin to the other natural social capacities that make humans what they are.

Smith uses the term 'natural reason' four times in *Lectures on Jurisprudence* in two different ways. The first seems to mean "defensible" or "clear reason" as in, "There is no natural reason why a 1000 acres should not be as easily purchased as a 1000 yards of cloth" (*LJ(B)* 295, also *LJ(B)* 325, 327). This seems to be a literary move and need not concern us. At most, it connects to Smith's use of the term 'reason' as an indication of a correct answer.

Elsewhere, however, and twice in the same paragraph, the term 'natural reason' seems more significant. Regarding "the four real rights" of civil law, namely, property, servitude, pledge, and inheritance, Smith writes, "Some of them are founded on natural reason, and others are intirely the creatures of the civil constitutions of states. [But that] of inheritance is evidently founded on natural reason and equity" (*LJ(A)* ii.27–28).

Here 'natural reason' seems to refer to rational investigations that accurately provide inquirers with a true description of the universe, the product, in part, of progressive inquiry. In this sense, natural reason is distinguished from convention, which, for Smith, is the source of some rights but not of inheritance. This usage coincides with many of the word pairings listed above, including the association of reason with experience, understanding, nature, ingenuity, intelligence, and perhaps philosophy, the "science of the connecting principles of nature" (*HA* II.12).

Smith also associates the term 'reason' with both speech and humanity. This is a pivotal point for Smith since both reason and judgment are inextricably tied to persuasion, and the desire to persuade is itself a central facet of humanity.[18] Smith writes,

> The philosopher and the porter are both of advantage to each other. The porter is of use in carrying burthens for the philosopher, and in his turn he burns his coals cheaper by the philosopher's invention of the fire machine. Thus we have shewn that different genius is not the foundation of this disposition to barter, which is the cause of the division of labour. *The real foundation of it is that principle to perswade which so much prevails in human nature.* When any arguments are offered to perswade, it is always expected that they should have their proper effect. If a person asserts any thing about the moon, tho' it should not be true, he will feel a kind of uneasiness in being contradicted, and would be very glad that the person he is endeavouring to perswade should be of the same way of thinking with himself. We ought then mainly to cultivate the power of perswasion, and indeed we do so without intending it. Since a whole life is spent in the exercise of it, a ready method of bargaining with each other must undoubtedly be attained. (*LJ(B)* 221–22, emphasis added)

He elaborates in *TMS*: "The desire of being believed, the desire of persuading, of leading and directing other people, seems to be one of the strongest of all our natural desires. It is, perhaps, the instinct upon which is founded the faculty of speech, the characteristical faculty of human nature. No other animal possesses this faculty, and we cannot discover in any other animal any desire to lead and direct the judgment and conduct of its fellows. Great ambition, the desire of real superiority, of leading and directing, seems to be altogether peculiar to man, and speech is the great instrument of ambition, of real superiority, of leading and directing the judgments and conduct of other people" (*TMS* VII.iv.25).

These passages underscore Smith's view that there is an intimate relationship between persuasion and speech. He further suggests that there is an intimate connection between these capacities and that other great foundational human capability, "the propensity to truck, barter, and exchange one thing for another" (*WN* I.ii.1). But Smith is reluctant to commit completely to such an assertion, putting the investigation off for another time (*WN* I.ii.2).[19]

For Smith, reason refers to a faculty of decision making, of discerning truth, of making choices, and of persuading others; rationality cannot be reduced to just logic. Inferences have important psychological elements. To see this, we must once again look to Smith's career and philosophical influences. His approach to logic, both in the classroom and in his writing, is inherited from a long-standing discourse about the propriety of the Aristotelian model of reasoning, from which one can also extrapolate a critique of twentieth-century analytic approaches to mathematical logics and formalization.

Persuasion and exchange are central elements in Smith's pluralism; they are the means by which difference can be mitigated or celebrated. Sympathy is, in a certain sense, a mechanism to persuade others about the propriety of one's sentiments, and the propensity to truck, barter, and exchange is itself a means of creating interaction in the face of otherness within a mosaic pluralism.

REJECTING THE SYLLOGISM

Although Smith's first academic appointment was the Chair of Logic at Glasgow University, he taught rhetoric instead of such works as Aristotle's *Analytics*. Aristotle's syllogistic logic was, according to Smith, an "artificial method of reasoning."[20] John Millar, Smith's student, tells us that, according to Smith, "The best method of explaining and illustrating the various powers of the human mind, the most useful part of metaphysics, arises from an examination of the several ways of communicating our thoughts by speech, and from an attention to the principles of those literary compositions which contribute to persuasion or entertainment. By these arts, every thing that we perceive or feel, every operation of our minds, is expressed and delineated in such a manner, that it may be clearly distinguished and remembered."[21]

This comment should not be understood as a complete rejection of Aristotle. Maria Alejandra Carrasco convincingly argues that Smith was rejecting Aristotle's theoretical reason, not his practical reason—his more formal approach to logic. In the section where Smith objects to reason as the foundation of morality (*TMS* VII.iii.2.7), she asserts, "he only considers Cudworth's rationalistic morality," not the larger notion of phronesis.[22]

But we must moderate Carrasco's argument. She explains that "practical reason is nothing but reason that is guiding action."[23] If this is the case, there is no ground to suggest that such a wide definition is necessarily Aristotelian as opposed to simply being compatible with his theories (or others'). If Smith is indeed Aristotelian in his rationality, it is more in his acceptance of the complementary nature of *ethos, logos,* and *pathos* as described in *Rhetoric*. As Stephen McKenna writes, for Smith, rhetoric "takes over some of the heuristic tasks typically assigned to *logos* in classical rhetorical invention."[24] And, as we learn from Edward King, Smith is very attentive to Aristotle's wider account of civic discourse, especially since his "rejection of the parochial concerns of scholasticism was undertaken in favor of a total communications theory that would encompass taste, style, reader and audience reception, the rules governing different media, and the ethics of discourse."[25]

Smith's lack of interest in syllogistic logic is representative of a dominant attitude in early modern philosophy. The fifteenth-century humanists thought scholastic logic was "barbarous in style and unattractive in content by contrast with the rediscovered literature of antiquity."[26] They asked, "Who but a dullard would devote his life to the *proprietates terminorum* when he might read the newly found poem of Lucretius *De Rerum Natura* or learn Greek and study Plato?"[27] The rise of modern physics, including the work of the sixteenth-century natural philosopher Galileo, showed that syllogisms are "useless for discovery, and serve only for verbal fencing."[28] And famously, Locke, in the seventeenth century, wrote of formal logic, "God has not been so sparing to Men to make them barely two-legged Creatures, and left it to *Aristotle* to make them Rational."[29]

Locke's comments on the syllogism are lengthy and dramatic.[30] He is clear that syllogistic logic should be rejected[31] but does not condemn those who find it useful.[32] Instead, he compares formal logic to corrective lenses, asserting that one should not overemphasize the nature of the Aristotelian syllogism and "think that Men have no use, or not so full a use of their reasoning Faculty without them."[33] In short, Locke claims that "as a matter of psychological fact, people do not, in their informal thinking and ruminating, follow syllogistic patterns."[34] Smith, as we shall see, shares this point of view.

There were philosophers who focused on more mathematical logics than Locke and the humanists; Descartes and Leibniz are probably the most recognized and influential. Smith mentions both in his writing, although neither is listed in the holdings of Smith's library.[35] It is not unreasonable to assume, however, that Smith could have chosen to pursue syllogistic logic in his classroom if he saw fit. In this vein, Millar tells us, "In the Professorship of Logic . . . he soon saw the necessity of departing widely from the plan that had been followed by his predecessors, and of directing the attention of his pupils to studies of a more interesting and useful nature than the logic and metaphysics of the schools."[36]

Smith's comments on the nature of logic are limited. We have a very brief fragment of an essay titled "The Principles Which Lead and Direct Philosophical Enquiries Illustrated by the History of the Ancient Logics and Metaphysics" (roughly nine book pages). Its date is uncertain, although it seems likely that it was written while Smith was living in Kirkaldy (1746–48) before he was elected to the chair.[37] The fragment itself contains very little about logic and was dismissed by Smith in 1773 in a letter to David Hume as one of a group of fragments, "none worth the publishing" (*Corr.* 137).

In it Smith defines logic as that which "endeavoured to ascertain the general rules by which we might distribute all particular objects into general classes, and determine to what class each individual object belonged" (*Logic* 1). However, this seems more a definition of Platonic dialectic as exemplified in *Statesman* than syllogistic logic, which he discusses immediately after this comment, and there is no evidence to suggest that Smith saw himself as continuing this "ancient" science in his own lectures. Furthermore, in WN, Smith changes his definition of logic to the "science of the general principles of good and bad reasoning" (*WN* V.i.f.26), a more general and informal definition. It is also noteworthy that the title of Smith's fragment references logics in the plural, not in the singular;[38] Smith seems to recognize what many contemporary logicians take for granted, that there are multiple approaches to logic, and many ways of describing and accounting for inference. This acknowledgment of diverse logics is connected, in the twentieth century at least, to recognition of diverse rationalities, a key element in modern theories of pluralism. Thus Smith's struggle with the nature and limits of logic is itself connected to his attempt to develop what I am calling an early theory of pluralism.

Nevertheless, whatever Smith meant by 'logic,' it wasn't mathematical in the sense that William and Martha Kneale ascribe to Plato and Aristotle[39] or that Frege and the analytics would intend a century and a half after he wrote. Smith was suspicious, both in print and in private, of "political arithmetick" (*WN* IV.v.b.30, *Corr.* 249).[40] In fact, he was suspicious about the use of mathematics in the social sciences in general.[41] He writes only negative things about formalization, condemning the "abstruse syllogisms of a quibbling dialectic" (*TMS* III.3.21). He uses the word "quibble" again, in a slightly different context, elsewhere but with the same critical attitude toward abstruse reasoning (*TMS* VII.ii.1.41).

From the first passage we learn that neither syllogisms nor dialectic are natural. They are instead opposed to "that great discipline which Nature has established for the acquisition of this and of every other virtue" (*TMS* III.3.21). We learn from the second that the attempt to formalize logic is "one of the most effectual expedients, perhaps, for extinguishing whatever degree of good sense there may be in any moral or metaphysical doctrine" (*TMS* VII.ii.1.41). Perhaps rather than Locke's corrective lenses, Smith saw logic as akin to wearing *someone else's* spectacles.

In short, whatever Smith means by logic, it must be more informal in nature (to use more modern terminology) and more closely associated with the natural experience of language and sentiment than the Aristotelian or analytic method of reasoning as expressed in the *Prior* and *Posterior Analytics*. Given this fact, it should not be surprising that Smith's most detailed account of argument occurs in his lectures on rhetoric.

Smith's move to shift reason to a more rhetorical understanding is an outgrowth of the early modern shift away from syllogistic logic to a wider understanding of inference and rational judgment. Locke's pithy remark rejecting Aristotle is itself an outgrowth of Hobbes's shift to a mechanistic deliberation. Hobbes also forces his readers away from a consideration of traditional logic to a more informal understanding of rationality. Smith, reminiscent of his approach to Mandeville's *Fable*, adopts some parts of Hobbes's position and rejects others.

For example, *Leviathan* begins its discussion of reason by espousing a mathematical model reminiscent of Aristotle's syllogistics.[42] According to Hobbes, reasoning, as a faculty, is but *"Reckoning* (that is, Adding and Subtracting)."[43] But Hobbes, while presenting a mathematical analogy, is actually rejecting it. He writes, first, "The Use and End of Reason, is not the finding of the summe, and truth of one, or a few consequences, remote from the first definitions, and settled significations of names; but to begin at these; and proceed from one consequence to another."[44] Here, he emphasizes reasoning as the analysis of understanding inference as opposed to the search for truth. He focuses on the consequence of one particular inference after another, not, as Smith does, on multiple inferences at once. He adds, "Man did excell all other Animals in this faculty, that when he conceived any thing whatsoever, he was apt to enquire the consequences of it, and what effects he could do with it . . . he can by words reduce the consequences he findes to generall Rules, called *Theoremes*, or *Aphorismes*; that is, he can Reason, or reckon, not onely in number; but in all other things, whereof one may be added unto, or subtracted from another."[45]

For Hobbes, like Smith, reasoning involves imagining possible consequences and creating general rules about this process after the fact: "Reason, . . . attempts to resolve effects into conditions (motions) that are necessary and sufficient to generate those effects."[46] Reason seems to involve not the actual act of inference but the rules regarding *how* to infer. Hobbes adds, "By this it appears that Reason is not as Sense, and Memory, borne with us; nor gotten by Experience onely, as Prudence is; but attayned by Industry."[47] As for Smith, reasoning for Hobbes is something that develops over time; it is an acquired skill gained as one acquires information, experience, and effort. Hobbes concludes that individuals are not capable of reason until they acquire speech, and even then reason does not serve them in day-to-day life.[48]

This is where Smith and his predecessor part company. If neither children nor most people have much use of reason, then his notion of an arithmetic reason must be the science of logic and not the faculty of reason at all.[49] (Hobbes uses the term 'science' to describe the outgrowth of reason immediately after this comment.) However, since all humans must be able to make *some* decisions, people must have a different reasoning capacity than he allows for in this selection. This capacity for decision making, Hobbes writes elsewhere, is deliberation: "The whole summe of Desires, Aversions, Hopes and Fears, continued till the thing be either done, or thought impossible."[50]

As discussed, good reasoning, for Hobbes, must meet two criteria. First, it must recognize the consistency of a personal language and, second, it must be the outcome of an *ordered* thought process. Richard Tuck equates Hobbes's notion of ordered thinking to the modern conception of a well-ordered computer program.[51] In addition, A. P. Martinich refers to it as computation: "In pure calculation, 'truth and the interest of men' do not compete with each other. Passions, however, are in perpetual competition."[52] Unlike Smith, rationality, for Hobbes, is a line-by-line process, the act of following one command that succeeds a previous command, and not one of looking ahead at multiple command lines or anticipating what might come later. Deliberation is the sequential conflict between competing desires. Desires are neither chosen nor proposed by reason: "Reason calculates the means to satisfy the ends that passions have."[53] The will is that desire which the person or animal ends with.

Hobbes indicated that deliberation may at times be counter to reason. 'Reason' here must also mean the arithmetic logic referred to above. In making this claim, however, he divorces deliberation from syllogistic logic and from the rules of reasoning understood as he originally presented them: as an analysis of how one adds and subtracts words. For Hobbes, the capacity to rationally deliberate is the capacity of an individual to make decisions for himself or herself on the basis of the desires of the moment. In essence, he is pushing aside syllogistic logic as unnecessary to human reasoning and thereby sets the stage for Locke's conception of reason.

Following Hobbes, Locke acknowledges that the term 'reason' has changed its meaning since the scholastic period, defining it himself as "that Faculty, whereby Man is supposed to be distinguished from Beasts, and wherein it is evident he much surpasses them."[54] Reason, he writes, accounts "both for the enlargement of our Knowledge, and regulating our Assent."[55] It is "necessary, and assisting to all our other intellectual Faculties."[56] It provides the intermediary between our various ideas,[57] and, as it does for Smith, it seeks to "discover what connexion there is in each link of the Chain, whereby the Extremes are held together."[58] He explains that "reason perceives the necessary, and indubitable connexion of all the *Ideas* or Proofs one to another, in each step of any

Demonstration that produces Knowledge; so it likewise perceives the probable connexion of all the Ideas or Proofs one to another, in every step of a Discourse, to which it will think Assent due."[59]

For Locke, reason provides two important services. First, as it does for Smith, it helps connect our discrete ideas into a coherent chain of knowledge.[60] Second, it helps investigate which probability one should assent to. Locke is insistent that "it is unavoidable to the greatest part of Men, if not all, to have several *Opinions*, without certain and indubitable Proofs of their Truths," and, as a result, "however it may often mistake, it can own no other Guide but Reason, nor blindly submit to the Will and Dictates of another." He continues by blending the capacity of reason with the more expansive rational practices of inquirers.[61]

I remarked in the introduction that the term 'reason' is ambiguous in many of the texts I cite. Because early modern philosophers saw themselves as moving away from Aristotle, and because their writings were not always precise in designating the line between reason as a faculty and reasoning as an evidence-based judgment or assent, discussions of this sort risk equivocation. In the passage referenced above, Locke jumps from using reason as the ability to make connections to reason as judgment without any acknowledgment of the shift. Perhaps, for him, there was no difference, but contemporary philosophy recognizes this distinction as important, especially in the context of pluralism.

For Locke, as for Smith, rationality-as-reason is the capacity by which we understand one another's decisions, although for Smith, sympathy is also directly related to the understanding of others. For Locke, we must also use our capacity of reason (now, reason-as-rationality) to reconstruct the argument of another—or have another reconstruct our own argument—and then determine our assent. In this regard, both the faculty of reason and reason-as-rationality are necessary for social life. They are required for us to understand the judgments others make and to assent to or dissent from their beliefs and decisions.

These same roles of reason will be found in Smith—reason as developing a chain of information, as dealing with uncertainty, as the capacity for reconstructing the arguments of others—and Locke's empiricism will, as I have already discussed, make its way into Smith's epistemology. Recalling chapter 2, the basic structure of moral deliberation, for Smith, also finds its source in Shaftesbury's use of the soliloquy.

Shaftesbury responds to Locke's empiricism with a moral realism that, although reminiscent of Plato, is more democratic: more than just the philosophers have access to the truth within nature (*Char.* III, 185). As it is for many, including Plato, Shaftesbury argues that reason distinguishes human from beast: "THOUGHT and REASON [are] *principal* in Man" (*Char.* II, 173).[62] But with this primacy of reason-as-choice comes the Platonic attitude opposing emotion to reason. Shaftesbury tells his audience that "the only *Poison* to Reason, is *Passion*. For false Reasoning is soon redress'd, where Passion is remov'd" (*Char.* I, 58). He then adds "for APPETITE, which is elder Brother to REASON, being the Lad of stronger growth, is sure, on every Contest, to take the advantage of drawing all to his own side. And *Will*, so highly boasted, is, at best, merely a Top or Foot-Ball between these Youngsters, who prove very unfortunately match'd" (*Char.* I, 116). Later, he combines elements of his moral realism more explicitly with the conflict between reason and emotion by indicating how reason (as knowledge) is to access the real moral standards that govern the universe (*Char.* III, 185–86).

While there are many similarities between Plato's and Shaftesbury's approaches, the differences in their metaphors are notable. For Plato, reason is a controlling force that moderates and harmonizes two competing elements of the soul. Each person is to have the right proportion of desire to reason as is necessitated by his or her political role. A just soul, for Plato, is one in which the will is an adequate governing body. While the souls of the philosopher kings, for example, are dominated by their intellect, it is still the will that reinforces the subordinate role of desires. If the will is operating for its own sake, the philosophers would become guardians, and if the will allows sensual desire or greed to take over, they will be relegated to the status of moneymaker.

In contrast, for Shaftesbury, as for Hobbes, the will is more secondary. Shaftesbury's will is a plaything; something that gets bounced back and forth and is always subject to the comparative strength of appetite. Will is not the decision-making element in the above selections. It is something other, something more passive.

Thus, for Plato, there is no problem in understanding the unity of the agent. In *Republic* the individual (and the state) is the ordering of the elements of the soul (and the citizens of the republic). In *Phaedrus* the horses are held together by the charioteer. But for Shaftesbury, since the will is subject to or weaker than the other forces, his readers are justified in wondering what constitutes the binding force that holds character together. We might ask what the dominant identifier that controls the person is. Shaftesbury himself announces this difficulty, asking how a person "shall know where to find himself" and "be warranted *one and the same* Person to day as yesterday, and to morrow as to day" (*Char.* I, 116).

The question of the unity of the person is a relevant concern for Shaftesbury because of the role of the soliloquy. Recall that, for Shaftesbury, "By virtue of this SOLILOQUY [a person] becomes two distinct *Persons*. He is Pupil and

Preceptor. He teaches, and he learns" (*Char.* I, 100). As Ernest Tuveson tells us, "Argument and attack were not Shaftesbury's method; rather, he envisioned something like therapy . . . true soliloquy, self-examination to the very depths of the soul, is what is needed."[63] Since soliloquy is a process of self-dissection, it is necessary to ask how the various parts of the identity are bonded to each other.

It seems that Shaftesbury must revert to his moral realism here and suggest that the moral actor, when acting properly, will allow himself or herself to follow that piece of character that is in line with the true and the right. For Shaftesbury, misalignment is an error caused by the narrowness of vision that does not see the harmony between individual need and collective need; this approach is similar to Plato's. What is essential for our current purposes is to be reminded of the self-division that Shaftesbury sees as a necessary component of reason-as-rationality. The soliloquy, as I have argued, is a progenitor of the impartial spectator.

Shaftesbury's difficulties anticipate some of Smith's. He combines moral investigation with aesthetic inquiry. He sees his philosophical exploration as subordinate to the rules of composition—the third treatise of *Characteristicks* is titled "Soliloquy: or, Advice to an Author"—and he acknowledges that the competing forces of human deliberation are strong enough to be representative of discrete identities.[64] Yet where Shaftesbury has faith in reason's ability to overcome incorrect moral determinations, Smith is not so clear. Smith, after all, has to deal with the ramifications of Hume's famous assertion that "reason is, and ought only to be the slave of the passions" (*Treatise* 2.3.3.4).[65]

Smith never explicitly addresses Hume's famous subordination of reason, but he adopts it implicitly, particularly at *TMS* VII.iii.2.7, where he argues, "Reason may show that this object is the means of obtaining some other which is naturally either pleasing or displeasing, and in this manner may render it either agreeable or disagreeable for the sake of something else. But nothing can be agreeable or disagreeable for its own sake, which is not rendered such by the immediate sense and feeling."[66]

Here, Smith means instrumental reason, but in leading up to this point he mentions reason-as-judgment, reason-as-balance-of-the-soul, reason-as-discovery, and reason-as-determination-of-true-and-false. He begins the passage by partially assenting to the precept that "virtue consists of conformity to reason" (Platonic reason) but then qualifies it by suggesting that reason in and of itself leads only to the (exact) rules of justice. In contrast, it is "experience and induction" that lead to "general maxims of morality," as all general maxims are built on them (*TMS* VII.iii.2.6). He claims that induction is only "one of the operations of reason" and that it is not reason itself that governs behavior but the general rules that are derived from reason. Without such rules, judgments would be "extremely uncertain and precarious if they depended altogether upon what is liable to so many variations as immediate sentiment and feeling" (*TMS* VII.iii.2.5).

While reason-as-rationality is "undoubtedly the source of the general rules of morality, and of all the moral judgments which we form by means of them," it would be "altogether absurd and unintelligible" to suggest that "first perceptions of right and wrong can be derived from reason" (*TMS* VII.iii.2.7). In other words, our first notions of right and wrong come from sentiments and feelings, including pleasure and pain, but reason cannot provide us with what I earlier termed primitives. Reason-as-rationality manages the undeniable experiences that fuel sympathy.

My point is that Smith is Humean in that reason builds on the passions, but, more important, and anticipating Nussbaum, reason-as-rationality is that which makes sense of passions, feelings, sentiments, and other basic ideas. These are the ground for any general rules of propriety supported, interpreted, and motivated by sympathy.

Sympathy references the power of sentiment over actions. As discussed, the principles of nature that operate within human beings, according to Smith, are motivated to a large degree by the pleasure of mutual sympathy and the natural enjoyment individuals derive from being both praised and praiseworthy. While Hume understands sympathy quite differently from Smith, at their core both see sympathy as motivating character and action.

Mutual sympathy is a motivating factor in action; it is also a principle of communication. For Smith, sympathy inspires us to understand others and to project our own situation in ways that spectators can comprehend, hence its role as the groundwork for pluralism. For both Smith and Hume, sympathy is the prerequisite for sociality itself (*Treatise* 2.1.11.2). And, obviously, he and Hume share their empiricism. Although Smith is never explicit in his understanding of the mechanics of the acquisition of sense data, both begin with the fundamentally discrete nature of human beings.[67] As it is for Smith, for Hume, sympathy is a solution to the problem of social unity and understanding in the physical world (*Treatise* 2.1.11.2). He describes the role of external signs and conversation in the sympathetic process; the rules of sympathy are therefore heavily affected by the rules of communication. It is therefore a small leap from Hume's acknowledgment of the importance of conversation to Smith's reliance on rhetoric. As we shall see, rhetoric and logic become intertwined for Smith. Hume makes a pragmatic case for this conflation almost immediately in his *Treatise*. In the second paragraph of the introduction he asserts that in the face of perpetual human disagreement "'tis not reason, which carries the prize, but eloquence; . . . The victory is not gain'd by the men at arms, who manage the pike and the sword; but by the trumpeters, drummers, and musicians of the army" (*Treatise* Intro.2). We might say that, for Hume, reason is (and ought only to be) the slave of rhetoric as well.

One must not put too much philosophical weight on informal musings introducing disciplined treatises, but this glimpse into Hume's heart serves as an acknowledgment of the realpolitik of academic writing. It would be intellectually dishonest to ignore the fact that even in the philosophical treatise the "musicians" lead to victory. Hume is well aware that the nature of persuasion depends not on syllogistic formalizations but on the ability to illustrate with clarity, conviction, and narrative eloquence.

The conviction that rhetoric plays an essential role in the communication of a theory is in no small part the consequence of Hume's converting cause and effect to contiguity (*Treatise* I.1.4; *Enquiry* VII.11). As with Hume's subordination of reason to the passions, Smith is not as explicit about his assent to Hume's contiguity principle as some might like, but he seems to subscribe to it nonetheless, both in *HA*—"When two objects, however unlike, have often been observed to follow each other, and have constantly presented themselves to the senses in that order, they come to be so connected together in the fancy, that the idea of the one seems, of its own accord, to call up and introduce that of the other" (*HA* II.7)—and in *TMS*: "When two objects have frequently been seen together, the imagination acquires a habit of passing easily from the one to the other" (*TMS* V.i.2).

An essential focal point in these discussions is the role of the imagination as well as the role of custom. Habit and familiarity lie at the core of causation for both Smith and Hume—this is why division and unity are cultivated by the same elements of the human condition—and both philosophers spend a great deal of time investigating the nature of the imaginative faculty. As Griswold writes, "Since imagination turns out to be essential to the constitution of morality as well as to that of reason, we are creatures of the imagination no less than of the passions."[68] Imagination and reason are intimately connected, and because the sentiments are themselves influences for and influenced by the imaginative faculty, there is, yet again, a clear connection between rationality and the emotions.

Reason, it is rightly assumed, is built on the role of inference. Again, modern formal logic is frequently defined as the study of or being concerned with the nature of validity. Validity allows for truth preservation among premises in a deductive argument and is based on the notion that there is some necessary connection between the antecedent and the consequent. How useful the formalization of this process is is a matter of debate.

In contrast, the eighteenth-century Scottish thinkers, inheriting a suspicion from their predecessors, rejected syllogistic logic in favor of a more imprecise discussion of the faculty of reason, widely defined. Hume and Smith use this skepticism to challenge the notion of causation itself. In short, if argumentation is based on an understanding of inference, then the nature of the science must change when causation is itself put into question. For Smith, if the imagination is the faculty that brings us closest to truth preservation, and if narrative plays the role of argument, then rhetoric must take logic's place. It is therefore neither an accident nor should it be a surprise that Smith, as the chair of logic at Glasgow University, decided, as his student reports it, to focus on "the several ways of communicating our thoughts by speech, and . . . the principles of those literary compositions which contribute to persuasion or entertainment."[69] There were clearly enough philosophical precedents to justify Smith's decision to teach rhetoric rather, even if the chair was named after logic. The question before us is, What theory of reasoning could result from such a move?

6

REASON AND THE SENTIMENTS

In the last chapter I showed how the eighteenth century withdrew from Aristotelian formal logic and illustrated the difficulties in using rationality-based language for thinkers who did not have as nuanced a vocabulary as our contemporaries. I concluded that Smith required something to replace the Aristotelian model of reasoning, especially since Hobbesian linear rationality was inadequate for his needs. In this chapter I examine his alternative, arguing not simply that rhetoric plays an important role in Smithian deliberation but that rhetoric is in itself a component of reason.

RHETORIC AS REASONING

In his *Lectures on Rhetoric*,[1] Smith identifies four kinds of communication—instruction, entertainment, conviction, and persuasion—and presents four kinds of corresponding discourses—historical, poetic, didactic, and oratorical.[2] That discourse which is most related to syllogistic logic is the didactic, a form whose rules Smith dismisses as "obvious" (*LRBL* ii.97). This "central" mode of discourse, as J. C. Bryce describes it, "emerges as not only a mode of expression but as a procedure of thought."[3] Didactic discourse may be applied either to "our reason and sound judgment" or to "our passions and by that means persuade us at any rate" (*LRBL* ii.14).

Smith defines a didactic discourse as one "in which the design of the writer is to Lay Down a proposition and prove this by the different arguments which lead to that conclusion" (*LRBL* ii.125). Interestingly, despite its importance he limits his comments almost exclusively to lectures 24 and the first few paragraphs of 25.[4] Perhaps this is an outcome of the "obvious" nature of the didactic structure; maybe Smith just didn't want to spend all that much time on material he regarded as self-evident. Maybe, however, Smith limited his comments on the didactic because this type of discourse is itself dependent on and overlapping with all other discourse types and, as such, he is *always* discussing it.

Brown argues that "the distinction between didactic and oratorical/rhetorical discourse is not sustainable in practice in view of the complex interweaving of styles in a particular text."[5] She is probably right about this. However, while she regards this merging of styles as a significant defect, I argue that the didactic model of discourse is strong and fundamental enough that all other forms may possibly be, at their roots, and in certain contexts, didactic as well. Rather than being a weakness in Smith's theory, this flexibility constitutes strength. A rhetoric that is too rigid cannot be of much use given the boundary-breaking nature of literature and composition.

Smith emphasizes simplicity; one ought to present an argument in the form that will "make a greater impression on the mind" (*LRBL* ii.126). As a result Smith argues that in a didactic discourse the author should try never to have more than five propositions. If he or she must, the author should group propositions under no more than five umbrella propositions in support of the primary one. Anticipating the origins of postmodernism, Smith uses architecture as an explanatory analogy (*LRBL* ii.129).

Smith is arguing for a limited, intuitive argument structure because of the nature of the understanding: "When [propositions] exceed this number the mind can not easily comprehend them at one view; and the whole runs into confusion" (*LRBL* 126). As a theory of communication, then, *LRBL* is preoccupied with the success of the audience in understanding the messages both intentionally and unintentionally located in the text. As a theory of pluralism, the goal is to make persuasion as effective as possible by making translation between contexts as easy as possible.

As an example of a treatise whose style makes it too complicated to understand, Smith cites Aristotle's *Ethics* (*LRBL* ii.131), comparing it to Newton's, attacking not only the Greek philosopher's style but also his mode of argumentation. Aristotle branches and organizes knowledge, whereas Newton lays down a chain of reasoning originating from a common principle. This chain gives us a pleasure "far superior to what we feel from the unconnected method where everything is accounted for by itself without any reference to the others" (*LRBL* ii.134).

In short, Smith's logic is inherently audience focused whereas Aristotle's is not. Logic, understood as the science of validity, is independent of the persons doing the work; an argument is valid whether the audience recognizes it or not.[6] Whereas Aristotle felt it necessary to compose separate treatises on logical subjects and rhetoric, including distinguishing between a logical and rhetorical syllogism, calling the latter an *enthymeme*, Smith's argumentation is intentionally rhetorical and necessarily intertwined with the audience.⁷ As Howell writes, "It was Smith who taught rhetoric to . . . assert jurisdiction over what logic no longer wanted to control."⁸

As we have seen, the position of spectator is a normative position, one that influences outcome and participates in the process of discovery. It is for this reason the so-called Newtonian method is so attractive to Smith.⁹ The beauty of the chain-based argument provides the audience with pleasure that motivates them toward the truth. Recall from chapters 1 and 2 that, for Smith, as for many of his influences, natural and moral philosophy incorporate the rules of aesthetics. There are no strict divisions to suggest, for example, that using architecture as a guide to argumentation is not inappropriate.

Smith elaborates on the nature of human understanding in *HA*;¹⁰ the use of the term 'philosophical enquiries' in the title suggests a connection to a wider theoretical purpose than just an account of the history of astronomy.¹¹ The essay's significant overlap with *LRBL* further bolsters my argument that the lectures can be seen as a general theory of argumentation.

In particular, *HA* is concerned with the "subjective side of science."¹² According to Smith, human beings have a natural desire to understand events as a system (cf. *TMS* IV.I.11). Unified chains are pleasurable because the mind seeks discoverable "resemblances"—similarity and organization (*HA* II.1). It naturally sorts events and objects by commonality and uses this scheme as a form of explanation.

Smith's comments naturally relate to his remarks on cause and effect: the habitual identification of events in a chain allows a spectator's mind to move easily from one to another. For Smith, cause and effect motivate individuals to learn more: "There is no connection with which we are so much interested as this of cause and effect; we are not satisfied when we have a fact told us which we are at a loss to conceive what it was that brought it about" (*LRBL* ii.32). Any interruption of this chain of events is unpleasant and necessitates further action to soothe the imagination: "The very notion of a gap makes us uneasy for what should have happened in that time" (*LRBL* ii.37).

He elaborates in *HA*: "But if this customary connection be interrupted, if one or more objects appear in an order quite different from that to which the imagination has been accustomed, and for which it is prepared, . . . we are at first surprised by the unexpectedness of the new appearance, and when that momentary emotion is over, we still wonder how it came to occur in that place. The imagination no longer feels the usual facility of passing from the event which goes before to that which comes after" (*HA* II.8).

In *HA* and *LRBL* Smith develops a narrative theory of the understanding that is directly related to my study of sympathy. By 'narrative,' I mean a linked chain that explains both the cause and the trajectory of an argument. The trajectory can be understood teleologically, as MacIntyre argues. Or it can be understood in terms of more basic storytelling, which is compatible with both MacIntyre's approach and Smith's remarks on how the mind contextualizes sympathy. Newtonian explanations, as Smith describes them, are not teleological because they are derived from principles describing material, efficient, and formal causes but do not necessitate a final cause. Nevertheless, his remarks on system in *HA* suggest a Kuhnian understanding of scientific paradigms: the persuasive power of a scientific theory lies in the cohesive nature of the explanation and how it soothes our narrative imagination (cf. *HA* iv.8, 19).

Yet again we see the importance of prioritizing *TMS*. For Smith, agents' motives and capacity to understand are based on chain-like connections between objects or events; they are built upon a narrative thread. For Hobbes, one desire simply replaces the preceding one. For Smith, however, narrative preserves preexperienced emotions and desires as essential to the teleology or the history so far. Furthermore, as in any good story, a narrative can respect the multiple motivations that inspire a complex character; there need not be only one singular impulse for activity as Hobbes presumes.

However, while narrative allows for all these disparate elements, it also organizes them for deliberation. The mind works best when the spectator can move swiftly from one piece of a theory to the other without getting bogged down in too many simultaneous pieces of information that, as Smith cautions for historical writing, obscures the connection between "the Cause and the event" (*LRBL* ii.36). For Smith, the imagination is powerful enough to fill in basic pieces. In "plain language" discourses, for example, "if we happen to lose a word or two, the rest of the sentence is so naturally connected with it as that it comes into our mind of its own accord" (*LRBL* i.10). Nevertheless, a narrative is best understood when there are no broken links. If there are missing pieces, the moment information is provided to fill these gaps, the unease "vanishes altogether" (*HA* II.9).

Narrative is not the be-all and end-all of thinking. Smith is clear that narration is not enough *in itself* to arouse interest; one must take notice of "the effects it had on those who were either actors or spectators of the whole affair" (*LRBL* ii.5). This echoes Smith's theory of sympathy, reminding his readers that one must work to make a personal history of interest to spectators. However, while narratives aren't sufficient, they are necessary. For Smith, understanding requires a narrative structure, but interest in the subject depends more on commonality or character. *TMS* sets up the problem of overcoming otherness, and *LRBL* explains the mechanics.

We can see how this relates to Smith's theory of pluralism and why he argues that both the community and sovereign have an interest in cultivating attention to difference. In essence, Smith is trying to create a mechanism through which individuals can become interested in others despite their lack of commonality. Narrative becomes more robust as more information is learned and more time passes; as we have seen in previous chapters, the narrative eventually becomes strong enough for judgment. The difficulty with narrative is not that it is, at times, too simple to provide guidance. Rather, it is that as narratives become more complex, the agent finds it hard to distinguish between that which is known and that which is assumed. The cultural components of stories and those influences that would eventually be considered subconscious blind agents to objectivity. Racism, patriarchy, and imperialism are all the result of complex narratives, and it isn't until the second half of the twentieth century that post-modern thinkers like Foucault exposed the dangers that come with narrative complexity.

Yet Smith anticipates this concern. In his account of the history of oration Smith warns his readers: "There can here be no room for a narration, the only design of which is by interweaving those facts for which proof can be brought with others for which no proof can be brought, that these latter may gain credit by their connection with the others. But as nothing is now of any weight for which direct proof is not brought this sort of narration should serve no end. The pleader therefore can do no more than tell over what facts he is to prove, which may often be very unconnected" (*LRBL* ii.246–247).

According to Smith, narratives can be easily corrupted. To mix those pieces of information that can be proven with those that cannot may cast doubt on the entire system, and, given Smith's eighteenth-century worldview, he focuses on the literary form of the confusion. He explains that with too much complexity the narrative thread can too easily be lost by the audience: "Long sentences are generally inconvenient and no one will be apt to use them who has his thoughts in good order" (*LRBL* i.53).

Additionally, during his advice regarding "the proper method of choosing the arguments and the manner of arranging them as well as the Expression," Smith argues there should be little elaboration, "no nicety nor refinement, no metaphysicall arguments" and that "the Expression and Stile is what requires most skill and is alone capable of any particular directions" (*LRBL* ii.138–39). This both introduces the discussion of deliberative eloquence in oratory and concludes his discussion on didactic arguments. It points out the central difficulty in communicating detailed scientific information and the systematic explanations thereof: obfuscation.

Despite all of these qualifications and although narrative is a limited form, it is still the foundation for Smith's use of reason (however we define it). For Smith, the desire to learn is itself a narrative tendency; our natural proclivities move us from wonder to surprise to admiration (*HA* Intro.1–4). Just this progression tells a story—there is a conflict (the anxiety of surprise), action (the inquiry that comes from wonder), and a resolution (the calmness of admiration). Recall that, for Smith, philosophy is the science that organizes and places order upon seemingly disconnected information to ensure coherence. For Smith, the philosopher is more finely tuned to the gaps in the chain of events. He or she sees missing information—"the invisible chains which bind together all these disjointed objects"—and brings with it a "tone of tranquility and composure" (*HA* II.12).

Complexity is problematic in scientific systems as well as in oratory. Smith uses the history of astronomy to show how, viewed over time, the more intricate systems become, the less believable they are. For example, the Ptolemaic system, with its complicated epicycle and its approximate results, was neither pleasing nor satisfying. Its complexity inhibited its greatness, and its unpredictability always elicited surprise (*HA* IV.8).

Smith believes that as systems advance, their complexity decreases. Just as, according to Smith, "the simpler the machine the better" (*LRBL* i.v.34), the less intricate the system, the more believable it is, because a system is simply "an imaginary machine invented to connect together in the fancy those different movements and effects which are already in reality performed" (*HA* IV.19).

Smith gets the term 'system' from Shaftesbury; it serves a variety of purposes.[13] First, it is a way of addressing the connectedness of linked concepts; astronomers put forth systems, as do moral philosophers. Second, a unified system allows for aesthetic evaluation of the linking of said concepts; a person can compare and prefer one system over another on the basis of their beauty, their intricacy, or, presumably, their accuracy and efficiency. Ptolemy's and Copernicus's maps of the heavens come to mind here. Third, the systematic nature of linked concepts emphasizes the role of the imagination and judgment in knowledge; discrete 'facts' are not as useful or as informative as seeing those facts in relation to other facts about the world. Recall that, for Smith, moral and aesthetic judgments are impossible outside of social structures. Comparative knowledge needs a system to offer comparison. Fourth, systems allow for the combining of specialized and general knowledge. As we will see, Smith sees history and the market as contributing to the development of narrow and advanced knowledge and capacities; this is the role of the division of labor. But, as I have argued elsewhere, the division of labor can also be described as the "conjoining of [human] labor."[14] Specialization functions only if it has other specializations to complement. Or, as Cropsey writes, "Marx insists on presenting free commerce as though its essence were conflict; Smith presents it as though its essence is a kind of sociality or collaboration."[15]

Systems allow us to take the bird's-eye view of seeing how these narrow foci interact and enhance one another. Knowledge on the systematic level is therefore the generalization of the more specific tasks. Thus we have Smith's remark that systems resemble machines: a mechanical apparatus presents linked components with a variety of purposes that can be evaluated on the basis of a multiplicity of standards, including aesthetic, efficacy, and efficiency. Its components cannot work or be judged in isolation, and an understanding of the machine in general is different from (although complementary to) an understanding of the specific components and functions of the machine. Finally, Smith's remark that systems are similar to machines echoes Newton's account of the "clockwork" universe.

According to Smith, systems are rejected because they become too complex, and complexity is often the product of too many laws and the lack of one unifying principle. Smith's rejection of Aristotle in *LRBL* is indicative of his rejection in *HA*. In the earlier essay Smith tells us that Aristotle's method of moving from the particular to the general is inferior to Newton's method of theorizing from the general to the particular. By beginning with individual principles, Smith argues, one begins with a multiplicity, but multiplicities inspire surprise and wonder and are therefore both inefficient and lead to anxiety.

At this point we see that the faculty of reason and the understanding are becoming inseparable. While they are distinct concepts analytically, for Smith, individuals must be able to both comprehend and communicate ideas, systems, and sentiments in a manner that is suitable to the structures of the human mind. Reason and rhetoric become one, thereby forming the basis of Smith's rationality.

This is a controversial claim, made more so by an ambiguity in terms. Rhetoric is usually thought of as a science and reason as a faculty. My claim, then, is twofold. First, logic and rhetoric are intertwined; as descriptions of inference and argument analyses and construction, they are necessary elements in mapping human thought. Second, given the centrality of language in Smith's system and given the importance of spectator-based sympathy, an individual's role as audience member and as moral actor is an essential part of what it means to be a human being. Therefore, rhetoric becomes a capacity for Smith in the same way that reason does, or, rather, the faculty of reason is a compound faculty containing both the natural rhetorical perspective and natural reason.

The faculty of reason is the foundation for narrative rationality because the faculty of reason is itself rhetorical.

REASON AND SYMPATHY

Smith never explicitly defines rhetoric. His lectures are a mixture of it and belles lettres. Reminiscent of Shaftesbury's *Characteristicks*, they are as much concerned with aesthetic standards as with persuasion. In fact, not only does Smith not distinguish the two explicitly in his course, there does not seem to be even an analytic distinction within them. He defines his two concerns as "'an examination of the several ways of communicating our thoughts by speech'" and "'an attention to the principles of those literary compositions which contribute to persuasion or entertainment.'"[16]

This division is echoed in lecture II, in which Smith describes the course as first being concerned with "the perfection of stile" and then with that which is "agreable in Stile" (*LRBL* i.133–36). The rules for perfection consist "in Expressing in the most concise, proper and precise manner the thought of the author, and that in the manner which best conveys the sentiment, passion or affection with which it affects or he pretends it does affect him and which he designs to communicate to his reader" (*LRBL* i.133). Agreeability, however, is "when all the thoughts are justly and properly expressed in such a manner as shews the passion they affected the author with, and so that all seems naturall and easy" (*LRBL* i.136). Therefore, for Smith, rhetoric is the science of perfecting agreeable prose, a significantly different definition than Aristotle's "to see the available means of persuasion . . . in each case."[17] It describes the process by which a person *authentically* communicates his or her sentiments.[18] Persuasion is, in some sense, beautiful for Smith.

It is not inappropriate that Smith actually defines the term 'moral sentiments' in *LRBL*. He calls them "morall observations," a definition that incorporates much more than feelings or reactions (*LRBL* i.144).[19] The term is used in reference to Shaftesbury's letters, and thus 'observations' is to be understood not simply as empty viewing without judgment, but as the complete package of observation, reflections, deliberations, and conclusions. We see here similarities with Nussbaum's comments that emotions are complex intentional objects. Moral sentiments are the product of reasoning as well as of reaction. They involve moral judgment and personal commitment.

These definitions point to a further layer of complexity. For Smith, rhetoric is not simply an intended transfer of ideas or beliefs. The audience can also gain information about the author, not just the message; for Smith, the rules regarding how one ought to present one's ideas are partly based on the nature of an individual author's personality. How one speaks and writes is an indication of what kind of person the speaker or author is. Rhetoric is a window into character: "The stile of an author is generally of the same stamp as their character . . . . the flowery modesty of Addison [and] the pert and flippant insolence of Warburton . . . appear evident in their works and point the very character of the man" (*LRBL* i.80).[20]

Smith remarks, for example, that he is judging Lucian based on his works (*LRBL* i.122) and uses the same method to judge the orators Aeschines and Demosthenes much later on in the course (*LRBL* ii.231). He tells us that Addison writes properly for a humble man because "his Sentences are neither long nor short but of a length suited to the character he has of a modest man; who naturally delivers himself in Sentences of a moderate length and with a uniform tone" (*LRBL* i.129).

Smith asserts, "A wise man too in conversation and behaviour will not affect a character that is unnaturall to him; if he is grave he will not affect to be gay, nor if he be gay will he affect to be grave" (*LRBL* i.135). He then condemns Shaftesbury for violating this rule, explaining that he had a "very puny and weakly constitution" and "abstract reasoning and deep searches are too fatiguing for persons of this delicate frame" (*LRBL* i.138–39). He also accuses Shaftesbury of copying Plato's style of writing and condemns him for the false posturing that results (*LRBL* i.146).[21]

According to Smith, Shaftesbury had "no great depth in Reasoning" and would therefore "be glad to set off by the ornament of language what was deficient in matter" (*LRBL* i.144). Although he does compliment Shaftesbury's method of reasoning in his lecture on didactic texts—Smith calls it "perfect" (*LRBL* ii.126)[22]—he summarizes his opinion of both Shaftesbury's rhetoric and character as follows: "Polite dignity is the character he aimed at, and as this seems to be best supported by a grand and pompous diction that was the Stile he made choise of. This he carried so far that when the subject was far from being grand, his stile is as pompous as in the most sublime subjects.—The chief ornament of Language he studied was that of a uniform cadence and this he often does in contradiction to precision and propriety, which are surely of greater consequence. He has this so much in view that he often makes the one member of his sentence an echo to the other and often brings in a whole string of Synonymes to make the members end uniformly" (*LRBL* i.146).

I mentioned in chapter 2 that Smith's ad hominem attack against Shaftesbury may be justified by recalling the classical Greek and Stoic notion that philosophy is as much a way of life as a method of inquiry. Here we see another possible defense for Smith's remark. The suggestion that the attack against the person is a fallacy because it is irrelevant to the argument—that truth is independent of the conveyer of that truth—may be too simplistic. Instead, according to Smith, how one communicates the truth is irrevocably wrapped in the rhetoric one chooses. How one presents oneself is necessarily viewed through the flowers and flourishes of language and behavior. How one sees the world is itself an influence on the argument, and, because of the nature of the impartial spectator, because self-knowledge, for Smith, is an outgrowth of Shaftesbury's soliloquy and the imagination, how one understands oneself is also wrapped in rhetoric.

Smith has this to say about Shaftesbury:

> Shaftesbury himself, by what we can learn from his Letters, seems to have been of a very puny and weakly constitution, always either under some disorder or in dread of falling into one. Such a habit of body is very much connected, nay almost continually attended by, a cast of mind in a good measure similar. Abstract reasoning and deep searches are too fatiguing for persons of this delicate frame. Their feableness of body as well as mind hinders them from engaging in the pursuits which generally engross the common sort of men. Love and Ambition are too violent in their emotions to find ground to work upon in such frames; where the passions are not very strong. The weakness of their appetites and passions hinders them from being carried away in the ordinary manner. (*LRBL* i.138–39)

This is without a doubt an ad hominem. Smith argues here that Shaftesbury was of "too delicate a frame" to reason well, a remark that would most likely be rejected by modern readers. Yet Smith knew what he was doing. Although the history and origin of the ad hominem fallacy is currently in dispute—there is a decadelong disagreement as to whether the fallacy was first introduced by Locke, as is usually argued, or whether its traces can be found in Aristotle even though it is not on his list of fallacies[23]—Smith would have been familiar with all of the relevant texts. He would have known an ad hominem when he saw one.

There are no doubt times when individuals are too sick to concentrate. But Smith's comments are more targeted than that. His remarks concern Shaftesbury's *constitution*, not his circumstance, and are therefore condemning Shaftesbury's intellectual capacities in general. Rather than judging his predecessor on the merits of his philosophy, Smith condemns Shaftesbury's work on the basis of biographical facts. This argument appears as fallacious as they come.

Smith chose Jonathan Swift's writing over Shaftesbury's because the latter was ornate and hard to follow; the argument was buried under superfluities that distracted or misled the reader.[24] For Smith, this style of writing leads to problems because the florid prose inaccurately communicates Shaftesbury's character.[25] When communication is distorted, either intentionally or not—and Smith sees Shaftesbury as doing it intentionally—it interferes with the capacity to sympathize. This impairs the sympathetic process and weakens the capacity to make moral judgments.

Smith believes that Shaftesbury deflects our ability to understand him. He is guilty, to use more modern terminology, of a violation of good faith, a key virtue of most modern pluralisms. According to Smith, Shaftesbury's style interferes with the audience's ability to understand; it impinges upon the lessons Shaftesbury wishes to impart and the sympathy his readers ought to experience toward him. Shaftesbury, intentionally or not, sabotages the community of inquiry.

We can now see why Smith attacks Shaftesbury in the form of an abusive ad hominem. For Smith, attacking character is contiguous with attacking communication, which is contiguous with attacking an argument. Rhetorical style presumes moral assertions, and in Shaftesbury's case—a philosopher who is himself prescribing both moral and aesthetic principles—communication of his character becomes distorted as he obfuscates his writing.

To understand this further, let us consider Douglas Walton's diagram of the ad hominem argument scheme: "The respondent is a person of bad (defective) character. Therefore the respondent's argument should not be accepted."[26] Walton has argued that this logical move may be legitimate because an "attack on a respondent's character, say for honesty, sincerity or trustworthiness, can often undermine the respondent's credibility as a source."[27] As Walton points out, this is relevant in legal argument.

While Walton is probably correct, he is accepting the traditional assumption that the only relevance of the arguer is as the purveyor of testimony. In essence, he argues that because of the questionable character of the source, premises that might otherwise support a conclusion cannot be deemed acceptable on existing (testimonial) evidence.

Smith is doing something else. He is not arguing against the acceptability of the premises. Instead, he suggests that the nature of inference is fluid and that character affects logical consequence. Smith can challenge inferential connections because he is making both a psychological point and an empirical one. The psychological point is that since individuals make inferences justified by their own impartial spectators, the natures of their spectators determine the viability of the inference.[28] D. D. Raphael shows that Smith's psychological grounding helps him derive an 'ought' from an 'is.'[29]

In contrast, Smith's empirical point is that spectators make moral determinations on the basis of observations, and inaccurate or distorted information about an actor or his or her context necessarily leads to inaccurate moral judgments.

Thus, for Smith, Shaftesbury is guilty of two improprieties. First, he intentionally obfuscates his character, thereby preventing individuals from making accurate moral judgments about him—this is a violation of the pluralist ethos. Second, Shaftesbury seems to truly believe that he is right in doing so. In other words, his "puny and sickly" character causes him to violate the rules of transparency and makes him feel good about it.

Given the tone of Smith's critique, it may not be surprising that Smith approves of the use of ridicule in argumentation, a practice "altogether consistent with the character of a Gentleman as it tends to the reformation of manners and the benefit of mankind" (*LRBL* i.v.116). This recalls Shaftesbury's own use of ridicule in truth-seeking and moderating religious practices.[30] It also connects with Mandeville's sardonic method and explains how Smith can praise Swift for his clear, precise writing despite the layered yet never-acknowledged (by Smith) satirical nature of his writings.[31]

Whereas pointed and humorous references to an arguer's shortcomings are deemed irrelevant in a traditional logical argument, for Smith, ridicule is "appropriate when it issues from an appropriate sentiment and communicates clearly the nature of the object that gives rise to that sentiment." For Smith, then, pathos does a good portion of the work that in classical rhetoric is more typically assigned to logos.[32] Thus, we see that, for Smith, his comments on Shaftesbury are not simply an entertaining aside for the benefit of his students but also representative of a particular theory about argument, inference, and character. Given Smith's scheme, his observations about Shaftesbury are relevant and may be necessary.

Given that the rules of logic are, for Smith, really an account of natural reasoning, Smith seems to be calling into question any traditional account of relevance. If I am right that Smith's argumentation theory is a psychological account of inference, then the universe of allowable grounds and consequence becomes much wider. For Smith, reasoning is always a social phenomenon. For example, his famous observation that we get our dinner from appealing not to the butcher's, brewer's, and baker's humanity but to their self-interest is really a comment about persuasion.[33] Commercial activity is itself, for Smith, "the necessary consequence of the faculties of reason and speech" (*WN* I.ii.2) and is built on "the naturall inclination every one has to persuade" (*LJ(A)* vi.56). As a result, according to Smith, "every one is practising oratory on others thro the whole of his life" (*LJ(A)* vi.56).[34]

Again, for Smith, logic and rhetoric, just like reason and rhetoric, are, in some way, one and the same. Given this fact, it makes sense that reasoning necessitates not the abstract identification of noncontextual inference but the intermingling of assertions regarding both the argument and the arguers. If argumentation, oratory, and exchange are themselves interrelated, might it not be possible that argument claims are somehow connected to the character of the arguer? And if this is the case, then might it not be possible that calling an arguer's character into question is a form of calling the claim into question as well?

In Smith's account, Shaftesbury is morally flawed because he can neither see himself accurately nor present himself in a manner that will provide transparency for others to sympathize with him. Agents are self-observers; this is the function of the impartial spectator. Moral rationality is the process of trying to step outside of oneself in order to judge the propriety of one's actions. One must see oneself to do this, and one must allow others to see facts about himself or herself. The core advantage of self-spectatorship comes with wider access to information—one knows more about his or her history and circumstance than anyone else does—but the disadvantage is the feeling of urgency that comes with intimacy; Smith might have felt that this led Shaftesbury astray.

Smith's goal is for the moral agent to become as impartial as possible while still understanding that it is not immoral to prefer oneself to others, but Shaftesbury, Smith seemed to feel, was not as impartial as he should have been. As we have seen, Smith is explicit about the "natural preference which every man has for his own happiness above that of other people" and that each person is by nature "first and principally recommended to his own care" (*TMS* II.ii.2.1, VI.ii.1.1). By hiding his character and capabilities, Shaftesbury puts himself solely in his own care, preventing the community from being a moderating force.

The process of deliberation over the moral propriety of acts and sentiments is the epicenter of Smith's rationality and argumentation theory. The sympathetic process represents a commitment to common sense as a universal starting point for argumentation. The creation of the impartial spectator is evidence that argument analysis is the purview of disciplined, social, and specialized, or context-specific, knowledge. Obviously, communication is of the utmost importance here, and, as Smith argues, moral judgments are impossible outside of society (*TMS* III.1.3). Moral inquiry is predicated on the communal nature of information. McKenna suggests that, for Smith, rhetoric supplants epistemology and that communication is prior to ethics.[35] One might go so far as to say that by inaccurately presenting himself Shaftesbury is trying to step outside of society, an attempt that would arise only from a flawed character. Whereas, as we have seen, the individual who violates the laws of justice experiences this retreat from social life negatively and feels remorse, Smith seems to think that Shaftesbury, in making himself and his argument opaque, revels in the asocial experience and feels no remorse at all.

Leaving Shaftesbury, we are left with the reminder that impartiality is a process of comparing standards—a connection to Smith's theory of pluralism. For Smith, it is impossible to achieve perfection or to be completely outside of one's own experience. The virtue that results from the impartial spectator is itself the result of a continual perspective change: a balance of ideal and pragmatic limitations. For Smith, there are "two different standards of self-judgment that exist: one is comparing our action with the ideal, and the other is comparing it with what is normally achieved in the world."[36] He writes,

> The wise and virtuous man directs his principal attention to the first standard; the idea of exact propriety and perfection. There exists in the mind of every man, an idea of this kind, gradually formed from his observations upon the character and conduct both of himself and of other people. It is the slow, gradual, and progressive work of the great demigod within the breast, the great judge and arbiter of conduct. . . . Every day some feature is improved; every day some blemish is corrected. . . . He endeavours as well as he can, to assimilate his own character to this archetype of perfection. But he imitates the work of a divine artist, which can never be equalled. He feels the imperfect success of all his best endeavours, and sees, with grief and affliction, in how many different features the mortal copy falls short of the immortal original. . . . When he directs his attention towards the second standard, indeed, that degree of excellence which his friends and acquaintances have commonly arrived at, he may be sensible of his own superiority. But, as his principal attention is always directed towards the first standard, he is necessarily much more humbled by the one comparison, than he ever can be elevated by the other. He is never so elated as to look down with insolence even upon those who are really below him. He feels so well his own imperfection, he knows so well the difficulty with which he attained his own distant approximation to rectitude, that he cannot regard with contempt the still greater imperfection of other people. (*TMS* VI.iii.25)

In this excerpt, we see two different and simultaneous processes of self-division. The first is the familiar balance between the ideal and the actual: Smith's virtuous person strives for perfection, uses the ideal as a standard but must be genuinely satisfied with human limitations of virtue. At the same time, the virtuous person judges his or her superiority of character on the basis of the actions of others but refuses to judge others for not attaining the same level. Here we see more of the mechanics of Smith's rationality. The faculty of reason is designed to compare and contextualize, to look for ideals and limits based on an ideal. As the moral judge, the actor must use rationality-as-judgment to determine that which is both within the capacities of human experience and that which the ideal might appear to be.

Smith's rhetoric shows that "the manner in which we organize discourse of various kinds often reflects our own psychology" as well as the psychology of others, reflecting the priority of *TMS* and the role of pluralism in Smith's corpus.[37] As a result, the tension between impartiality and an agent's natural preference for his or her own happiness is as present in rhetoric as it is in moral judgment. Also in both, the closer one is to the incident, the harder it is to be impartial, a point Smith emphasizes by comparing the orator and historian. The orator "treats of subjects he or his friends are nearly concerned in; it is his business therefore to appear, if he is not realy, deeply concerned in the matter, and uses all his art to prove what he is engaged in." The historian, in contrast, "acts as if he were an impartial narrater of the facts; so he uses none of these means to affect his readers" (*LRBL* i.82–83).

The difference in the two cases is based on the different parts of the argument that are being called upon in the construction of the discourse. The orator "or didactick writer has two parts in his work: in the one he lays down his proposition and in the other he brings his proof of that proposition." The historian "has only one part, to wit the proposition" (*LRBL* i.81). This is the legacy of Smith's epistemological framework. In an empiricist worldview, all knowledge is, in part, rhetoric, or all knowledge is filtered through rhetoric: "Men always endeavour to persuade others," and "every one is practising oratory on others thro the whole of his life" (*LJ(A)* vi.56). Smith echoes this sentiment in *TMS* when he writes that since people always desire to persuade others, "speech is the great instrument of ambition, of real superiority, of leading and directing the judgments and conduct of other people" (*TMS* VII.iv.25).[38]

It should be no surprise that rhetoric plays such an important part in Smith's argumentation theory since the necessary preconditions for moral judgment are the ability to know a person's story—to understand their narrative, to read their lives and to present, speak, and write our own. Smith's rhetoric is very much concerned with "what we would now call point of view."[39] Because language and morality are intertwined, Smith's lectures on rhetoric are also lectures on ethics, or at minimum, they are lectures on the *communication* of ethical cases and judgments. Under Smith's system, good writing is both descriptive and prescriptive.

Certain styles of writing and speech are more conducive to imparting information, and Smith is concerned with methods of providing facts as well as ways of describing objects (*LRBL* i.154, and *LRBL* i.172–75). Smith is also clear that some grammatical forms are better at communicating certain sentiments than others: "The Language of Admiration and wonder is that in which we naturally speak of the Respectable virtues. Amplicatives and Superlatives are the terms

we commonly make use of to express our admiration and respect. ...
Diminutives and such-like are the terms in which we speak of objects we love"
(*LRBL* ii.104–5). Smith's lectures on rhetoric assume the problem of sympathy
is a problem of clarity (*LRBL* i.v.57). The mechanics of language are the ground
for sympathy, the result of the discrete physical nature of human beings and the
consequence of empiricism.

Throughout my discussion, I have emphasized the role of narrative and storytelling in the determination of the facts of a moral actor's case. In chapter 3
I showed that, for Smith, the moral determinations about the propriety of an
action are based not on determining how a spectator would act in the actor's
situation but on how that spectator ought to act if he or she were a particular
agent in a particular situation. To determine moral propriety is to know as much
about the person's specific situation as possible. What Smith's rhetoric adds to
this equation is that knowing the context depends on the ability to accurately
communicate the situation *for understanding* as much as it depends on the
ability to receive the information. Smith tells us, "The character of a man is
never very striking nor makes any deep impression: It is a dull and lifeless thing
taken merely by itself. It then only appears in perfection when it is called out
into action" (*LRBL* ii.106–7).

While it is true that, for Smith, the pleasures of mutual sympathy motivate us
to seek the moral approval of others, as a rhetorical problem actors are faced
with the dilemma of making their situations interesting enough for people to
attend to them. This is a central concern of any pluralism; individuals must be
compelling enough to be noticed, particularly in the face of complicated and
confusing differences. In fact, for Smith, even the life of those who receive
acclamation must be described in ways to attract an audience's interest (*LRBL*
ii.107). Description of a person's character, whether one's own or someone
else's, is difficult and important.

Smith is as explicit in *LRBL* as he is anywhere about the impact of knowing
the context and the detail of a moral situation. To describe character "in any
tollerable degree of perfection requires great skill, deep penetration, an accurate observation and almost perfect knowledge of men" (*LRBL* i.189). He also
reminds us of the importance of mutual sympathy (*LRBL* ii.16). Returning to a
previous discussion, when Shaftesbury deflects our ability to understand him, it
impinges on the lessons he wishes to impart and interferes with social unity,
creating, at least potentially, significant fractures in relationships and perhaps in
political society. Smith focuses on the communicative aspect of sympathy
because one of the major unifying themes of *LRBL* is the working of the imagination. I touched on this subject above. Now, we can see more clearly that the

purpose of rhetoric is, in part, the cultivation of sympathy. The proper functioning of the imagination is based in part on how we make information available to ourselves and others.

The very first remark recorded in *LRBL* concerns the imagination's nature
and limits (*LRBL* i.1).[40] For Smith, the root of "perspicuity" is "the quality of
being seen through."[41] In order to be clear and precise, language must not rely
on too many competing, or synonymous, terms, and it must be built on the
familiar; terms must be transparent. Words can be explained both by experience
and by reference to history, background, and culture. According to Smith,
foreign words thus can be admitted into the lexicon over time, but only after a
period during which they become as familiar as their native cousins. Language,
for Smith, is the product of culture, both local and national (*LRBL* i.2–5).

The connection between rhetoric and the imagination is essential because
without the *imagined* impartial spectator, Smith's moral theory has no normative foundation. Smith's theory of conscience acts both as the nexus of deliberation and as the point of intersection between personal and universal perspective.
Rhetoric either cultivates or hinders the imagination and thus allows for the
creation and regulation of the impartial spectator.[42]

Since we are now concerned with rhetoric's role in the creation of the impartial spectator, we can consider analyses that point to the proper imagining and
functioning of this normative device. We have seen how circumstance, particularly economic circumstance, can have both positive and negative impacts on
the sympathetic imagination. Smith's work can be seen as a system, albeit an
incomplete one, and therefore we can take this opportunity to bridge *TMS*,
WN, and *LJ* (as a stand-in for Smith's unfinished work on jurisprudence) with
LRBL, emphasizing, as always, the priority of his first book. In other words,
there are economic concerns in *LRBL* just as there are moral concerns in *WN*.

Smith writes, for example, that use of language is heavily influenced by class
(*LRBL* i.5). He adds that our method of presentation is also adjusted by the
economic class of the audience (*LRBL* i.84). Even artistic endeavors are affected
by economic difference. For example, even the great comedies are rarely, if
ever, focused on the higher classes (*LRBL* ii.91).

To recall my earlier comments, Smith shows how intertwined class is with
the rhetorical and artistic structures of society. Ethics, economics, jurisprudence, and aesthetics are as necessarily interrelated for Smith as they are for
Mandeville and Shaftesbury. Smith's remarks on the economic influence of
language underscore this point since, according to him, the effort to refine
prose is itself the consequence of trade: "Prose is naturally the Language of
Business; as Poetry is of pleasure and amusement" (*LRBL* ii.115). In *LJ*(A),

Smith elaborates how, in the first stages of commerce, trade at great distance was not impossible before contracts replaced oaths and verbal agreements (*LJ(A)* ii.54). These observations are part of a larger anthropology of language. He argues, for example, that commerce brought the transition from cultivating poetry and music to perfecting prose (*LRBL* ii.115–16).

Smith's first point here is that prose and poetry serve radically different purposes. Whereas poetry is created for entertainment, prose is the product of pragmatic commercial endeavors. Smith's comments in *WN* emphasize the relationship between language and "the propensity to truck, barter, and exchange one thing for another" (*WN* I.ii.1). He writes that it was likely that commercial society was "the necessary consequence of the faculties of reason and speech" (*WN* I.ii.2).

But Smith's comments on the role of economics in rhetoric continue to include not only the origin of language but also the influence of class in its refinement because "prose is naturally the Language of Business; as Poetry is of pleasure and amusement" (*LRBL* ii.115). Finally, Smith points to the distinction between necessities and luxuries—one of the defining characteristics of class—to show that as society grows more opulent, commercial and aesthetic considerations merge (*LRBL* ii.115–16).

This anthropology is similar to Smith's other analyses of the development of human capacities and structures. It is historical. It makes no reference to the divine. It assumes that progress follows the law of nature, and it holds an important place for the role of unintended consequences; I go into more depth regarding his philosophy of history in the last two chapters of this book. Smith's remarks on the relationship between language and commerce also parallel his discussions of slavery and the role of women in society.

With an eye toward Smith's anthropological and sociological method, I remind the reader that my discussion of the lectures on rhetoric is intended to emphasize Smith's notion of rationality. While Smith does use rhetoric to displace Aristotelian logic, "he did not openly condemn the syllogistic orientation of ancient rhetorical theory or propose inductive procedures in its place."[43] Smith's lack of comment is often as important as his explicit remarks. As Griswold implies, it is likely that Smith knew the Platonic observation that "the good rhetorician must know when to remain silent."[44] I therefore reiterate that Smith is not completely rejecting Aristotle's logic, only shifting its importance and limiting its role.

7

NORMATIVE ARGUMENTATION

Over the last two chapters I have shown how Smith moves from Aristotelian and analytic models of logic and reasoning to a more rhetorical approach. I have argued that sympathy is itself a rational process by which individuals create a soothing narrative that helps define justified inference. What might this kind of argument look like? In this chapter I offer two examples. The first shows how the impartial spectator and Smith's theory of price encapsulate normative judgment. The second modernizes Smith's language to show that this approach prefigures and fits well into contemporary debates about the nature of argumentation, informal logic, and critical thinking.

THE NORMATIVITY OF PRICE

I have not been arguing that the sole purpose of Smith's lectures on rhetoric is to offer a theory of reasoning. Instead, I argue that if we, as Smith's readers, want to understand his method of argumentation, these lectures offer the best foundation to do so. Smith's theory of argumentation is central to his account of rationality, which, in turn, is the key vehicle for moral and political unity in the face of difference. Human beings pursue language because it is rational to do so; it provides the capacity for exchange and agreement. In the absence of a formal logic, Smith uses rhetoric as a guidepost for reason.

If my argument is defensible, I must show a synchronicity in how the rational method is used within ethics and economics and suggest how this method may be understood as an outgrowth of rationality as derived from the lectures on rhetoric. I do so by defending my assertion that the impartial spectator is the analogue of Smith's notion of price.[1] I remind the reader that this approach further defends my argument regarding the priority of TMS. Here I show that the structures of normativity established in his earlier book prepare Smith's readers for his elaborations on political economy.

Smith's discussion of price is complex. Aware of both the time and detail involved in his discussion, Smith asks readers for "patience," and in the end, he fears, "obscurity may still appear to remain upon a subject in its own nature extremely abstracted" (WN I.iv.18). Part of the complexity results from the variety of similar terms in use. In addition to the single word "price," Smith also uses "first price," which he identifies as labor, or "the original purchase-money that was paid for all things" (WN I.v.2); "real price," meaning "what every thing really costs to the man who wants to acquire it, the toil and trouble of acquiring it" (WN I.v.2); and "nominal price," which Smith defines simply as money. Smith is clear that it is the real price, not the nominal price, that has personal economic consequences (WN I.v.9).

To this list of prices Smith adds "ordinary or average price," which, although he offers no definition, appears to mean the price when supply meets demand (WN I.v.40); "whole price," which, Smith explains, includes the cost of rent, labor, and profit (WN I.vi.16); "natural price," which Smith explains is representative of the situation "when the price of any commodity is neither more nor less than what is sufficient to pay the rent of the land, the wages of the labour, and the profits of the stock employed in raising, preparing, and bringing it to market, according to their natural rates" (WN I.vii.4); and "market price," which is "the actual price at which any commodity is commonly sold. . . . It may either be above, or below, or exactly the same with its natural price" (WN I.vii.7).

The terms can overlap and are sometimes of use to him for only a momentary comment. With this list, however, Smith tries to make sense of both the competing factors that influence price and the deliberations involved in determining the measure. According to Smith, whereas it might be natural to think of nominal price as the true measure of an object's cost, this would be inaccurate. The true cost is the material and services required for manufacture and sale and the profit that motivates the seller. Each of these pieces is mediated by the market. There is, therefore, a thread of relativity that runs through the equation of price. The market price of goods and services varies based on the interaction between supply and demand for any particular good or service. The condition of the seller's life also causes the required profit to vary from person to person.[2] Nevertheless, I argue that, according to Smith, price is not a purely relative phenomenon. It has a normative core.

Jeffrey T. Young's interpretation of Smith supports this conclusion. He argues that Smith inherited many of the themes of medieval just price theory, showing similarities between Smith's approach and both Scholastic and ancient

Greek traditions.[3] Smith refers to a "just proportion" of wages and rent (WN V.ii.i.7) and sees it as "essential to ensure the proper performance of the trades and professions (WN Vi.i.g.42)."[4] Young also shows how, for Smith, in *TMS*, wealth is the "most proper" reward for the virtues of "industry, prudence, and circumspection," acquired through education.[5] In short, "good economics is a necessary, but not a sufficient, input to produce good policy ('good policy' defined as that which promotes the common good). The fact that Adam Smith understood this helps explain why a moral philosopher could become interested in economics without ceasing to be a moral philosopher."[6]

Price can be normative in two respects. The first is the consequence of its connection to labor: "Equal quantities of labour, at all times and places, may be said to be of equal value to the labourer. . . . Labour alone, therefore, never varying in its own value, is alone the ultimate and real standard by which the value of all commodities can at all times and places be estimated and compared. It is their real price; money is their nominal price only" (WN I.v.7). After several pages of discussion, Smith continues: "Labour, therefore, it appears evidently, is the only universal, as well as the only accurate measure of value, or the only standard by which we can compare the values of different commodities at all times and at all places" (WN I.v.17). Smith makes a basic point about the human condition here. As Fleischacker puts it, "An hour's 'toil and trouble' (controlling for the amount and kind of toil and trouble) is an hour's toil and trouble across centuries and vastly different conditions of society, and it can serve as an absolute measure, 'never varying in its own value,' against which all other values can be determined."[7] Labor, for Smith, is a universal and thus a comparative.

Smith's labor theory of value is empiricist. It measures the pain, effort, and energy required of the body rather than, say, the abstract notion of opportunity cost (an inkling of which one can see in his definition of "real price"). A person of a certain body with a certain capacity can only do so much and will only be able to do that much whatever the circumstances. In fact, a human being in general is limited by his or her physicality and thus can only do what nature allows.

Now, one may disagree with Smith, arguing that technological improvements change what a person is capable of doing individually or collectively, but this objection misses the point. The work that the person is doing to operate the machine is still limited by physicality. If the same amount of force is required to pull a lever on a machine as it is to move a massive slab of concrete, a single person will simply not be able to pull the lever. One may then create a machine to pull the lever, but if that machine requires too much force to operate it, then the act fails at this new point in the chain of labor. Labor is therefore an accurate *measure* of value for Smith, although it is not value's cause. By tying price to labor, Smith tries to offer an objective measure that operates independently of the fluctuation of the market. For Smith, effort, necessary consumption, and actual consumption all appear to be constants. Even in his comments about the invisible hand, Smith writes that landlords "consume little more than the poor," even if they choose the best for themselves (*TMS* IV.1.10).

Labor as an objective ground for price is rooted in Smith's belief in the similarity of people (*WN* I.ii.4–5). The most obese of individuals cannot, over a lifetime, consume significantly more food than the most frail, at least not from the perspective of the whole available pool of resources. The strongest person cannot do significantly more work than the weakest, at least in reference to the amount of work that can potentially be done.[8] In essence, Smith makes an Aristotelian claim here. For Aristotle, the relative mean—the virtuous point between excess and deficiency as related to the individual moral actor—is an absolute point. A person of intellectual virtue will determine the proper proportion of extremes in judging the nature of the virtuous action, at least within the limits of precision that ethics allows. An intellectually virtuous person will therefore be *correct*, more often than not, in his or her determination of the relative mean, and an intellectually vicious person will most likely be *incorrect*. For Aristotle, there is an objective standard of virtue even given shifts of context. The same is true for Smith. And, as with Aristotelian virtue, although labor is, in some sense, objective and therefore leads to a normative claim, it is also personal and individualistic. It provides a context-dependent normativity.

There is a second, more powerful way in which price represents a normative outcome. Objectivity in price is the necessary consequence of the complementary relationship between natural and market prices; in a properly functioning market natural prices tend toward market prices (*WN* I.vii.11, *WN* I.vii.15).[9] When the supply and demand for a commodity are in equilibrium, when the supply and demand for the pieces required for manufacture are themselves in equilibrium, when the wages and profits are in order and not perverted by excess greed, then the market price and natural price are the same, and the price is what it *ought* to be. The market is then said to be functioning well and, as Smith puts it, in a state of "perfect liberty" (*WN* I.vii.30). 'Perfect' is, of course, a normative standard by definition,[10] and, as Young points out, Smith tells us that "all policies which raise or lower the market price vis-à-vis the natural price are bad" (*LJ*(A) vi.84).[11]

We are considering a model here, much the same way that sympathy and the impartial spectator are components of a model of moral adjudication. Natural and market prices align only under conditions of transparency, symmetrical knowledge, and zero transaction costs, just as ideal sympathy and impartiality require historical transparency and complete contextual information. It is a "hypothetical, localized, price of a good if there were not all kinds of obstacles preventing the free movement of capital, labor, and goods."[12] As always, Smith is working with an unachievable standard and recognizing the limitations that come with it. Not surprisingly, the forces that direct us to action contain within them the resistance to the action. It is worth emphasizing that the equilibrium of the natural and market price is not always the same. It is a fluid value dependent on conditions at any one time. Smith's just price is a relative mean in an Aristotelian sense; the just price for any given exchange at T1 may not be the same as the just price for the same exchange at T2.

We can presume that the establishment of and deliberation about price will take transaction costs into account, including the very-difficult-to-measure opportunity cost. All else being equal, for example, it would be irrational to spend three hours driving across a major city, missing five hundred dollars' worth of wages in order to save one dollar on a widget. Irrationality is avoided through education, just as irrationally immoral activities are. To put it another way, understanding is implicit in the post-Smith notion of informed consent, since the term 'informed' is an educational term.

At the risk of being redundant, I am not suggesting that sympathy be understood in these economic terms. Instead, I argue that these economic terms are attempts at making sense of the sympathetic process in the economic context—the priority of *TMS*. As Young puts it, "As such, natural price is like a general rule. This consensus is arrived at through the 'higgling and bargaining' which stimulates [*sic*] men's sympathetic faculties . . . the impartial spectator will not go along with ratios which deviate from the natural price. From the standpoint of social efficiency it will be necessary for market price to freely tend toward natural price. . . . Therefore, the promotion of public opulence is the proper basis for policy because it is 'reasonable' when viewed from the standpoint of an impartial spectator, that is, one who is not swayed by the particular interest of the monopolist or the recipient of the privilege."[13]

To use Aristotelian terminology, we can postulate something akin to an "intellectually virtuous consumer" for a Smithian market. Smith does not make this claim, but similar ones can be found in work by William Stanley Jevons and more contemporary commentators.[14] It can also be deduced from the role of the ideal imagined impartial spectator in moral adjudication as well as from the importance of education in understanding context and economics. The intellectually virtuous consumer is the person who knows when the market and natural price are in alignment and who purchases the good or service when it is at or below that price. The complementary "intellectually virtuous merchant" is the one who knows when the good or service is at or above that price. The point of equilibrium is when both intellectually virtuous individuals know the relevant information, and, by definition, ideally the only time when they would both be willing to engage in the commercial transaction would be when the market and natural price are in alignment.[15]

The point of equilibrium is what is best for society as well as what is best for individuals, since both merchant and customer get what they require without undue cost. This contains elements of Shaftesbury's notion that self-interest is aligned with community interest—the invisible hand offers this connection as well—but it also echoes Mandeville's assertion that private aims have public benefits. It recognizes the ideal and unachievable nature of "the economically virtuous" but offers a standard by which one can evaluate the propriety of exchange. Following Young, "Smith's natural price is a just price in that it will fulfil the requirements of commutative justice according to his definition of the term, and that this is so in both the early and rude and the advanced states."[16] Furthermore, "economics sheds light on moral issues. It increases understanding. Smith is not saying that it is meaningless or sterile to ask if market processes are just. He is suggesting that in order for them to be just they must take place within a certain type of social/institutional environment and that individuals must practice the virtue of justice as he understands it."[17]

Price is a means by which large amounts of economic information are encapsulated and is therefore necessary for decision making. It is imaginary in the most literal sense of the word—it is the product of the human imagination—albeit a collectivity of human imaginations in a highly social and complex market system.[18] It is the result of a systematic understanding of diverse human interaction and the propensity to truck, barter, and exchange; it substitutes a general knowledge for a specialized one. It is the outgrowth of language and is a stand-in for value. This is why Smith distinguished between nominal price and real price: a commodity is not worth a particular amount of money, it is worth the value that the money stands for. Price is the signifier for the value and fluctuates given conditions and desires. It is imaginary in much the same way that the impartial spectator is. It also has the same epistemological difficulties. Agents may never actually *know* the natural price, just as spectators can never be ideal observers. Each does the best she or he can with the information and judgment she or he has.

Recall that the impartial spectator is created to balance facts about an individual's life and any other factors relevant to the act being judged. This includes individuals', spectators', and communities' values as well as brute facts about the world. Like Shaftesbury's soliloquy, the imagined spectator is the product of a self-division, the product by which a spectator steps outside of himself or herself to judge the propriety of actions that may be too intimate for immediate judgment (*TMS* III.i.2).

Like price, the creation of the impartial spectator requires the management of vast amounts of information. Like price, the impartial spectator is the outcome of certain rules of human interaction. And like price, individuals make judgments based on the alignment of multiple factors, although with price it is the alignment of natural and market price, which is itself the consequence of the alignment of supply and demand. The spectator sympathizes with the moral actor (or approves of his or her own actions) only if the impartial spectator determines that the spectator's moral sentiments are in alignment with the actor's sentiments (or the community's sentiments). In other words, one may see sympathy, equilibrium of spectator and agent, and the impartial spectator as the final arbiter of this alignment.[19]

We can avoid the economic interpretation, emphasizing the priority of the moral sentiments, if we understand that sympathy is not a moment of equilibrium but that equilibrium is a moment of sympathy. Or, perhaps more guardedly, both sympathy and equilibrium are representative of those moments when rational actors are aware of certain instantiations of the laws of human interaction. This view does not devolve into the argument that moral life is economic in nature because it does not suggest that the moral sentiments are subsumed under the market model; it is intended as a heuristic. Arguments in any given system will always be similar in structure when compared with one another, especially if one presumes, as Smith does, that there are no clear lines delineating the principles that guide the various areas of concern within that system. What makes Smith's theory of rationality powerful is its consistency in multiple arenas. Each of these spheres—the historical, the moral, the aesthetic, the political, and the economic—presumes human agency. The rational structures that govern the decision-making process must therefore work within the human structures of rationality. Otteson and I agree that there is systematic consistency in Smith's work. We simply disagree about the nature of the model Smith describes.

For our purposes, then, I conclude this section by suggesting that price and the impartial spectator can both be understood as encapsulations of or metaphors for arguments. They are the nexus of reason and thus represent the process of balancing information in an ordered fashion. They are created by the individual or society to reference a way that provides justification and explanation for summary judgments. In this context, then, what the invisible hand represents is neither the unfolding of the divine[20] nor the operations of providence but the Scottish Enlightenment faith in the laws that govern human interaction as seen from the perspective of an argument-oriented creature who has limited information. We will see further evidence for this when I examine Smith's philosophy of history.

The invisible hand suggests that from the *perspective* of the moral actor and spectator, moral and economic events unfold as if guided by an unseen force. This force is ordered and regular because it follows natural sociological and economic laws, just as the rotation of the planets around the sun follow the laws of gravity. With the right amount of information and the educated capacity to understand and manipulate such information, moral agents are able to identify basic behavioral patterns, just as economic agents will be able to identify basic market patterns. Certainly, if Smith were not able to assert this much, he would never have engaged in either his moral or economic projects, and he would have had to reject wholesale the Scottish Enlightenment project that Hume referred to as "the science of man." That is, natural laws would not inform Smith or his readers as to what or why humans act. But they do. Smith is committed to a notion of progress that reveals the 'ought' from the 'is.'

In order to understand the impartial spectator and price as *arguments*, we must first expand our understanding of what 'argument' actually means. Following Walton, we can observe that "it is problematic to see how reasoning is related to argument" and then ask, "Are reasoning and argument essentially the same thing? Or is one a proper subpart of the other? Or can you have reasoning that is not in argument? Or could you have argument without reasoning?"[21]

These are important questions. They suggest, as Walton acknowledges, not only an expansion of the term 'argument' but also a widening of the term 'logic.' Therefore, in order to understand what Smith is doing, I suggest that we move away from our natural attraction to the identification of logic as focused on entailment, syllogistic inference, and formalism. I do not propose shifting to phronesis in order to limit the role of mathematical logic in everyday life. Instead, I argue more radically that logic is itself something fundamentally different from what we encountered when we first asked about Smith's relationship to the discipline.

CONTEMPORARY ARGUMENTATION THEORY

In this section I show how Smith's conclusions can be seen as prefiguring, or as complements to, contemporary argumentation theory, the present-day discourse that seeks to define more precisely the nature and limits of informal logic, critical thinking, and argumentation in general. This approach challenges the narrow definition of logic that emphasizes validity conditions. I define 'argumentation' as the dialectical process of rational persuasion that makes reasons, inferences, evidence, and determinations of fact explicit and subject to systematic and critical scrutiny.

We have seen that Smith's account of rationality is too contextual, too interwoven with rhetoric, and too dependent on sentiment to be described by rational choice theory or mathematical logic. I offer argumentation theory as an alternative because, unlike rational choice models, informal accounts of argumentation, persuasion, and critical self-analysis are compatible with the sympathetic narrative approach to rational analysis I have outlined so far.

For Smith, as for our own contemporary world, argumentation acts as a "ground level" tool for interaction in a pluralist society. It is what agents use to persuade one another while maintaining a stable society. The skills of argumentation theory—the nature and methods of critical thinking and informal logic—can be seen as prerequisites for citizenship. Analogs of the impartial spectator and price, the argumentation structures discussed here are the means by which individuals adjudicate personal and community commitments in the light of relevant and often-conflicting information. These wider definitions of argumentation and logic allow for a diversification of standards of inference, criteria that may shift between cultures and subcultures, contexts and circumstances. This is the same flexibility we require to resolve the issues related to Smith's ad hominem attack on Shaftesbury. In general, Smith's system and recent argumentation theory share preoccupations with political participation, education for citizenship, the relationship between logic and rhetoric, and the use of a specific curriculum in the philosophy classroom.

The distinction between argumentation theory, informal logic, and critical thinking is slippery at best. 'Argumentation theory' is meant as an umbrella term referring to the spectrum within the discourse that takes the mechanics of argumentation as its primary focus. This may include rhetoric and nonverbal communication as it relates to argument, accepting, for example, the necessary theoretical link between and complementary nature of rhetoric and dialectic.[22]

Informal logic is narrower.[23] Whereas formal logic focuses on the form or structure of the argument,[24] informal logic argues that the form "is not, by itself, sufficient to enable one to arrive at an evaluation of the argument as weak or strong, reasonable or fallacious. The method of informal logic is to consider the evidence given in the text of discourse in a particular case, and then to evaluate this evidence in light of the context of conversation in which the argument in the given case was used for some purpose."[25]

Critical thinking, on the other hand, denotes a practice rather than a discipline. It is "a skill and attitude of mind whose application has no disciplinary or subject-matter home territory or boundaries."[26] In this sense the Platonic Socrates represents the paradigmatic critical thinker: the person who is open to truth and who does not take any conclusion as given without further examination, even if this includes examining one's own fundamental assumptions.

To be critical is not to be cynical, however. As it was for the Platonic Socrates, and as Smith accuses Shaftesbury of ignoring, critical thinking must always be done in good faith. As Harvey Siegel writes, "The critical spirit . . . involves the *character* of the student. The student who has it not only is *able* to assess reasons well, she is *disposed* to do so, and to be *moved* to conform her beliefs, judgments and actions to the results of such assessments."[27]

Like the early modern thinkers' approach to reason, contemporary argumentation theory represents a retreat from formal logic.[28] However, whereas thinkers in the sixteenth century through the eighteenth moved away from Aristotle, contemporary argumentation theorists see themselves as moving closer to him. They understand the discipline as stepping away from the more mathematical model of logic advanced by Frege and his intellectual descendants. In the current context, Aristotle has come to represent the less formal approach, while for Smith and his contemporaries Aristotle's writing represented a much stricter syllogistic method.

The shift from seeing logic as a narrow discipline to understanding argumentation as a larger amorphous field of inquiry allows for a wider range of considerations when focusing on the reasoning process. Following Stephen Toulmin, Franz van Eemeren and his coauthors distinguish three traditions of argumentation: geometrical, anthropological, and critical:

> The geometrical approach relies heavily on formal logic. Arguments are regarded rationally acceptable only if they start from true or certain premises that necessarily lead to true or certain conclusions. This amounts to saying that the points of departure of valid argumentation must be indisputable and the arguments must be laid out in a formally valid way. The anthropological approach takes the rationality conception of a specific community as its starting point and bases its judgments on empirical evidence. Argumentation will then be regarded as valid if its point of departure and presentational layout agree with the standards of reasoning consented by the community concerned. The critical approach equates rationality with the functionality of the argumentative procedures used for achieving the aim for which they are designed, leaving aside specific logical or empirical assumptions. A rational judge taking this approach will find argumentation acceptable only if its

point of departure and its presentational layout are suitable means for achieving a well-defined aim.[29]

These authors acknowledge that "in practice" different approaches can be combined in a single conception of rationality.[30] They suggest, however, that the largest difference between the various approaches is whether they are to be understood as descriptive or normative in form. They argue that the descriptive appears to have more empirical elements while the normative is more analytic, although they concede that "approaches of the two types are also often combined, or considered as complementary."[31]

Here we see an echo of Smith.[32] Combining both analytic and empirical elements of argumentation, Smith offers an empirically normative theory; we have seen that the impartial spectator, price, and the labor theory of value are all means by which Smith grounded his system in objectivity. Smith is thereby explicitly concerned with some of the basics that these authors take for granted. Consider, for example, their comments on the term 'rational judge,' referred to above: "A rational judge represents an authority to which the evaluation of argumentation is entrusted. It is debatable whether this authority should consist of an existent person or group of people or should remain an abstract ideal. If the first is preferred, it is assumed that the assessors are people capable of setting aside their own prejudices etc. If the second is preferred, it is assumed that a normative construct can be theoretically devised that is fully adapted to the task of making optimum judgments."[33]

First, it might simply be observed that a large portion of Smith's work, certainly a majority of *TMS*, is dedicated to describing the nature of this rational judge. The impartial spectator, the general rules of morality, the rules of beauty and style from the lectures on rhetoric, and price are all manifestations of this concept.

Also, taking the notion of 'judge' that derives from jurisprudence, one might also persuasively argue that the "rational judge" implies the ideal of a legislator. Comparing this ideal with the politician, Smith writes, "A legislator [is someone] whose deliberations ought to be governed by general principles which are always the same, as [compared with] the skill of that insidious and crafty animal, vulgarly called a statesman or politician, whose councils are directed by the momentary fluctuations of affairs" (WN IV.ii.39).[34]

Second, the Smithian might also argue that understanding the rational judge as either pushing aside one's prejudices or developing an analytical construct for optimum decision making is a false dichotomy. The sophistication in Smith's approach is that he utilizes both impartiality and analytical constructs to develop a more holistic notion of argument evaluation as well as a more cohesive pluralism. This form of rational judge is not an ideal observer but a fully capable and fully human agent that balances normative and empirical elements—moral rules, notions of propriety, and the fact of particular circumstance. As Haakonssen puts it, the ideal legislator is "the man of public spirit who will strike the perfect Smithian balance between the enlightenment of 'Some general, and even systematical, idea of the perfection of policy and law,' and the piecemeal action to alleviate concrete evils."[35] This, for example, would counter Todd Weber's argument that "philosophers' conclusions for or against moral dilemmas are driven less by rational argument and more by how the moral world intuitively appears to them."[36]

Weber's comments also represent a false dichotomy. Intuition and reasoning are not either/or situations for Smith. Intuition and argumentation complement each other, at least in part, because the argumentation of the impartial spectator—the rational element of sympathy—is so intimate that it feels like intuition, but, when looked at closely, it is actually a complex bundle of a wide range of balanced influences that require significant time and effort to unpack. Since, as we have seen, sympathy is itself a rational process and the legacy of Shaftesbury's prolepses, what appears as intuition may very well be the product of long-standing deliberation, education, and acculturation. Pluralism demands that individuals reconsider intuitions, but, as we saw in chapters 3 and 4, the more one cultivates understanding the other, the more sympathy across difference feels intuitive.

To return to the informal nature of logic, in *Uses of Argument*, Stephen Toulmin moves away from the mathematical model of argument, suggesting instead that a jurisprudential model is a more appropriate means of analyzing everyday argumentation. Reminiscent of Aristotle, he argues that different areas of interest have different ranges of precision and that context determines the nature of argument. According to Toulmin, although logically normative terms may be "field-invariant," the criteria for actual assessment are "field-variant."[37] In other words, the terms used to designate good or bad arguments remain consistent regardless of context, but the standards that these terms designate are fluid. Just as Locke, Hutcheson, Shaftesbury, and their modern counterparts asked whether moral difference can be regarded as universal once adjusted for cultural difference, Toulmin asks whether the differences between the standards we employed in different fields are irreducible, the argumentative analog to modern pluralism. Toulmin concludes that while "in actual practice, we do not employ any universal battery of criteria" logicians "maintain unabated their ambition to discover and formulate—theoretically, if no more—such a set of universal standards."[38] This is yet another example of the interaction between the ideal and the actual.

In shifting the nature of standards, Toulmin asks his readers to investigate the procedure behind argument rather than the mathematical notion of validity. People then become forced to look at arguments differently, seeing them in numerous forms that incorporate both audience actions and reactions. This point is essential for our purposes, in that Smith's notion of argumentation is based upon behavior rather than argument articulation. His sociological theory assumes a method of reasoning built upon the interaction of social influence and an individual's search for normative standards to which he or she can authentically assent. Smith's notion of reasoning allows for his theory of pluralism. Therefore, in Toulmin's terms, field-variant argumentation, combined with the awareness that action itself is somehow involved in argumentation, makes reasoning much more complicated than mathematical logic suggests. According to Toulmin, the more we understand that argumentation is field-variant, the better we understand that the nature of the field is itself fluid. In Smith's case, the more we understand that rhetorical, behavioral, cultural, and an individual's particulars change the nature of argumentation itself, the more accurate picture we get of the normativity located within the fluid structures of sympathy. Arguments about and inspired by sympathy may share certain conceptions of the good, but the criteria for fulfilling these goods change on fundamental levels because the rational structures necessary to make the relevant inferences also change. Field-variance allows for structural recognition of the tensions between otherness and familiarity.

This shift is not solely about pluralism though. At its root, it recognizes the sentimental elements of Smith's rationality—the primitive experiences that rationality organizes and the sympathy that both forms and is the consequence of rationality, are all built on the moral sentiments or, as he calls them, moral observations. By shifting to a field-variant logic, we also shift the realm of thinking. If argumentation is itself dependent on different contexts for its standards, then the faculty of reason can have within it the capacity to incorporate nonlogical influences on the reasoning process. In the contemporary discourse, this requirement leads to Matthew Lipman's claim that critical thinking is only one component in a threefold categorization of higher-order thinking—critical, creative, and caring—although, as he acknowledges, the boundaries between the three are often unclear and may overlap.[39]

Certainly, the caricatures of the purely rational, autonomous, emotive, or self-oriented person are unwelcome. Smith rejects each throughout his work. For both Smith and today's thinkers, holistic pictures of the thoughtful person take into account an individual's critical framework as well as his or her capacity to create as influenced by social circumstance. Creativity and care are themselves *thoughtful* processes and ones that must be approached critically and rationally. Reciprocally, a critical approach without either creativity or care is the approach of a hard person, one who is inherently closed to anything other than critical procedure. Because, for example, caring is the product of thinking and not solely emotion, Lipman is able to argue, anticipating Nussbaum, that, at their roots, emotions have reasons; to investigate emotions is to examine the reasons behind them and the form of their expression. Sounding a lot like *TMS*, Lipman is able to suggest the possibility of teaching the propriety of emotions: "If we can temper the antisocial emotions, we are likely to be able to temper the antisocial conduct."[40] Relying on the notion of social and emotional propriety while echoing Smith, Lipman writes, "If there can be an education of the emotions in the home, there can be an education of the emotions in the school and, indeed, there already is."[41]

Lipman, along with Smith, suggests that caring is rational, although 'caring' may denote the care one puts into arguments and projects—attentiveness, authenticity, integrity, as Lipman himself intended—or an ethic of care, the active interest one takes in the well-being of ourselves and others, as other critical thinking theorists have expanded it to mean. In either case, the point remains the same: emotionally rooted commitments can themselves be integrated into logic. Reasons are a part of emotions and are, at least to a large degree, critical. Rationality becomes the whole package of deliberative influence—it includes will in addition to motive—and we are then left with the understanding that argumentation, to be authentic, must represent a person's *whole* mode of thinking, at least more so than is traditionally acknowledged. Thus we have a contemporary link to Smith's ad hominem attack on Shaftesbury.

Christopher Tindale's "rhetorical model" of argument adds new dimensions to this holism by providing an account of argumentation that makes explicit the importance of the audience.[42] This is a very important shift for our purposes. It suggests that argumentation is to be understood both as an act and as a relationship. Tindale writes, "This aim of argumentation is not purely intellectual adherence, but includes the inciting of action or creating a disposition to act, which in turn involves attention not to the faculties ... but to the whole person."[43]

Tindale's claim is twofold. First, he asserts that argumentation must be inclusive; it ought not exclude certain reactions simply because they do not fit into traditional modes of reasoning. Second, he suggests that argumentation must inspire action, not just intellectual commitment. This claim echoes the thought of many eighteenth-century philosophers, not least Hume. However, whereas Hume's solution to argumentative motivation is to claim that reason is the slave to the passions, Smith, in a certain sense, equates the two. His emphasis on rhetoric as well as his spectator-based moral theory, when contrasted with Tindale's theory of audience-focused argument, illustrates that the burden of persuasion is bidirectional. The audience must do all in their power to understand the argument and arguer—the critical position is not a skeptical one, for Smith—and the arguer must do everything he or she can to craft the argument for the audience. Failure to do so represents a failure to create the requisite community of inquiry. Shaftesbury, according to Smith, violated this reciprocity.

For Smith, logic is a two-way street. It is not simply the case that an audience analyzes an argument as presented by an arguer, and then the arguer modifies it accordingly. (This description is reminiscent of Ralph Johnson's dialectical tier of argumentation.)[44] Rather, arguing is a sympathetic process, in Smith's sense of the term. It is built on the potential of discrete individuals to come together by modulating their inferences on the basis of the comparison of their own insights with those of the people around them. If an individual's pathos interferes with the accurate communication of his or her ethos, then logos will necessarily be distorted.

Alasdair MacIntyre's work has deeply influenced my comments in this book. His nonliberal (perhaps) account of pluralism assumes that rationalities are diverse and coexistent. More than the other contemporary thinkers noted, he takes an expansive look at argumentation. Rationality, for MacIntyre, is defined by the standards developed by the progression of a tradition. Traditions provide the tools for both internal evaluation of moral adjudication and procedures for analyzing moral conclusions from outside traditions; it is MacIntyre's concern with the external interaction between traditions that makes him a pluralist.

Providing a detailed account of MacIntyre's theory is impossible in the current context; I have done so elsewhere.[45] What concerns us is his assertion that one cannot evaluate from a neutral perspective, that all adjudication and analysis represents the standards of a particular tradition, and that rationality is the product of a lengthy communal history. Traditions, for MacIntyre, are constructed retrospectively, and, to understand and critique standards of rationality, one must reconstruct the progression of argument over time.[46] The tradition forms a narrative, a coherent chronology of events with a goal and understandings of how events contribute to this goal. The telos—MacIntyre's goal is initially Aristotelian—supplies the directionality which then allows for normative standards. This too connects to Smith's approach. For him, histories, personal and collective, are essential for evaluating sentiment propriety, and most argument reconstruction is done after the fact. Actions may be under-taken by looking forward, but they are *explained* and *justified* retrospectively.[47]

It is odd that MacIntyre's work is on the periphery of argumentation theory, since it shares so much with the dominant discourse. What argumentation theorists lack is a large-scale account of human rationality itself; MacIntyre supplies this. What MacIntyre's work lacks is the ground-level discussion of the nature of argument I offer here. I would suggest that Smith's rational moral sentiments are a bridge between these two approaches, providing both an account of human rationality and a picture of argumentation that is flexible enough to bend with context.[48]

When we step back to consider modern argumentation theory as a whole, we see an approach strikingly different from the mathematical model Toulmin rejected in 1958 and Robert Scazzieri's account of rational choice that I refer-ence in the introduction. Contemporary argumentation theory describes a lived argumentation that takes history, perspective, audience, and emotion into account. It regards action as valuable and emphasizes communicative intent. It acknowledges the powerful influence of community and locates reasoning within human relationships.

It is this picture of reasoning that would be most familiar to Smith's readers, although his eighteenth-century contemporaries would not have had the vocab-ulary to describe it in this form. For Smith, argumentation is tied to growth in social awareness. To mature is to absorb and modify socially constructed identity and argument procedures. It is also to gather vast amounts of data and to system-atize them in such a way that one becomes aware of an objective standard of propriety. For example, this may take the form of an account of the standards of beauty, or proper moral action, or of the appropriate cost for a product.

Smith's sociality—the impossibility of making moral or rational judgments outside of society—is not limited to his eighteenth-century commentary. Rather, many theorists argue that critical thinking is best done while a part of a commu-nity of inquiry. Maughn Gregory understands this community as a combination of factors found in Aristotle and C. S. Peirce. He explains that "to formulate procedural (i.e. behavioral) conceptions of ideals such as reasoning well, creativity, emotional maturity, democracy, social criticism, ethical consciousness, etc., is to concretize these notions into matrices of specific behaviors, both individual and collective, that will then serve as normative structures for inquiry."[49]

Gregory identifies two procedural principles that foster good reasoning and democracy in communities of inquiry. Reasoning must allow for universal partic-ipation, and it must be based upon respect and tolerance. David Kennedy offers a more romantic list, suggesting five structural dimensions of the community of inquiry: gesture, language, mind, love, and interest.[50] In either case, the insight is that to divorce human relationships from the process of reasoning is to destroy the potential for reasoning. This again speaks to the Smithian perspective, although it should not suggest that individuals cannot reason alone or that inquiry cannot be engaged in while isolated. It is, however, to remind us that reasoning is first developed socially and is best cultivated with the help of others. The impartial spectator and price are both intersubjective substitutes for the community (or, at minimum, consequences of it); no moral or economic reasoning is possible without social behavior. By imagining the impartial spectator or by understanding price, the actor brings the community with herself or himself at all times.

It is also in the context of the community of inquiry that one might be reminded of Griswold's description of the "protreptic we" in *TMS*. Smith's use of the first-person plural pronoun throughout *TMS* is an intentional rhetorical device designed to pull the reader along with Smith. It makes Smith's audience engage in the sympathetic process he describes. "We" want to feel what Smith is feeling and moderate our reactions to meet his conclusions. As Griswold puts it, "'We' is in part an ideal construction, then—both a mirroring of an ethical community and a vehicle for normative suasion."[51] Argumentation, for Smith, is aimed at discovering both truth and a normative ethics. It is not simply the justification of individual acts of argument or the identification of winning argument strategies. Its goal is intersubjectively and objectively justified cognitive transformation.

My discussion here should not be construed to suggest that the notion of an argument ought to be abandoned. Arguments are a useful way of understanding the chain of reasoning and the boundaries of a particular deliberation. Instead, I want to argue that behavior can itself be perceived or at least explained through the argument structure. Consider how much more compatible Johnson's definition of an argument is with Smith's approach than is a traditional syllogistic understanding: "An argument is a type of discourse or text—the distillate of the practice of argumentation—in which the arguer seeks to persuade the Other(s) of the truth of a thesis by producing the reasons that support it. In addition to this illative core, an argument possesses a dialectical tier in which the arguer discharges his dialectical obligations."[52]

Argument, for Johnson, is a cultural practice, "the main purpose of [which] is rational persuasion of 'the Other' . . . [a process that is] openly and patently rational."[53] This definition widens an understanding of argument to include a broad range of texts or discourses and substitutes persuasion for truth preservation, although a great deal hinges on the meaning of 'rational' in this context.[54]

With an eye toward Smith, let us consider how sympathy as *behavior* can be interpreted as an argument. To do this, I rely upon Mark Weinstein's account of four core problems in informal logic: "premise acceptability; premise relevance; argument reconstruction (the problem of missing premises); and argument cogency (the problem of premise sufficiency)."[55] He (and others) sees informal logic as applied epistemology, a term referencing "constructed and situated knowledge, knowledge as testified to by the practices of successful inquiry, including concern with boundaries and the hither-to [*sic*] unexplored."[56]

Understanding informal logic as applied epistemology is an instructive shift for Smithians since the essential problem for sympathy is the process of spectators' learning all of the information relevant to the context, a problem that, as we have seen, is made more difficult in circumstances of diversity. Ideally, a spectator must determine how an actor thinks, all of the information the actor is taking into account, whether this information is relevant to the moral dilemma at hand, and, ultimately, whether the actor's moral actions are justified—or, in other words, whether the process of moral adjudication warrants the given conclusion.

Using Weinstein's account, we can map out exactly how the sympathetic process translates into the informal logic model: learning the history of the moral agent in order to ask how this particular person should or should not act in this particular situation is a form of identifying missing premises; the spectator's determination of whether he or she knows enough information to judge the agent's act as proper or improper is another form of the problem of argument cogency; the spectator's determination of which information to try to learn about and which to filter out (what background information counts and what does not) is another form of determining premise relevance; and, finally, the impartial spectator's determination of the act's moral propriety is another form of determining premise adequacy—is the act *adequate* given the particular situation? In short, this map is a psychological account of rationality at work.

There are, in Smith's work, five examples of argumentation: historical, moral, economic, scientific, and aesthetic. Each involves the discovery and defense of seemingly objective conclusions derived after an epistemological leap. His theories assert, for example, that a progressive history reveals the 'ought' of nature, that actors construct normative moral rules over time, that participants in the market become aware of a product's natural prices, that theoreticians develop coherent explanatory systems, and that spectators become aware of the rules of beauty and simplicity. The problem for Smith is that all of these objective standards can be derived only from clear analyses of the activities, arguments, and sentiments of the members of a person's community. For

Smith, informal reasoning is, to some extent, applied epistemology, but this epistemology does not imply certitude. In this respect, Smith is Humean; he is not Cartesian. There is an approximation inherent in his system that is unavoidable and is not just the consequence of the tension between the unachievable ideal and the actual. It is also the result of human psychology, idiosyncrasy, luck, and context.

Sympathy is clearly a form of rational deliberation—as I indicated above, it is the result of a reasoned process and can be altered through information, reason, argument, reflection, and normative criteria—but it is constituted by more than just rational deliberation. It is itself a nonrational (but not irrational) process, according to the standard opposition of emotions and reason. But it is deemed rational once rationality is expanded to include the various elements that a wide theory of argumentation can allow for. It therefore requires a wide understanding of reason and the tools required by diagramming deliberation.

Sympathy is a critical, creative, and caring act. According to Smith, the desire for sympathy is a natural part of the human experience: we are born with the capacity and desire to sympathize and with the need for spectator approval. We incorporate into our understanding all elements which may affect our judgment, including the care we feel for other people, things, activities, arguments, and projects; the pleasure and pain of experiences; the subconscious motivations and biases which direct us—this contributes to the difficulty of argument reconstruction—the emotions we feel; the arbitrariness of custom; the randomness of luck; and the lack of control we have over the events we experience. Purely "rational" argumentation cannot account for all of these influences. Human beings are irrational (and illogical) in many ways. The discipline that helps us make sense of the world must have room for all of those influences, not just the idealized ones. Thus we have a further interpretation of Smith's invisible hand: in this context it can denote the combination of the rational decision-making procedure that is overseen by the impartial spectator and the nonrational/emotive procedure that is captured by the natural urge and capacity to sympathize with others.

The invisible hand is a reference to the unfolding of unintended consequences. It suggests that even if history progresses on the basis of specific principles, no person could gather enough information to know exactly what will happen as a result of any specific act or group of actions. Human psychology, human diversity, facticity, and luck are all factors in the unknowable equation that predicts what is coming around the bend. Change, Smith tells us, is so gradual that it is "insensible" (WN II.iii.32), and, as Craig Smith puts it, it "occurs so slowly that we do not notice it until it has happened."[57] The best anyone can expect is to map nature's tendencies and to have a sense of optimism that the invisible hand will move history forward, increase freedom and opulence for all people, and expand human knowledge, or so, it seems, Smith argues.

As previously remarked, here Smith shares his enlightenment optimism with many of his contemporaries. However, even if we had all the necessary information, even if we could forecast what would result from a completely transparent set of conditions, prediction would still be stymied by the vagaries of human psychology. The moral sentiments combined with human desire allow for rational decision making in any individual case, but collectively the rationality of the system gives way to the dominance of general patterns, social tendencies, and large-scale trends that can be described only by reference to an invisible hand that guides us but does not force us.

Human freedom demands the uncertainty of likelihood; the invisible hand preserves its possibility. Propriety demands normativity; the invisible hand preserves that, too. Finally, rationality demands a narrative. The invisible hand preserves that as well—'progress' provides directionality. It supplies the 'plot' to the metanarrative or, in MacIntyre's terms, a *telos*. What Smith offers with this powerful turn of phrase is a way of understanding the connection between individual circumstance and the general state of things, between individuals or groups and the society and histories that contain the pluralist communities within them. His theory of argumentation recognizes that, given these extremes, the most people can do is communicate their situation and endeavor to balance it with the human condition, to hope that others, no matter how different, are motivated to learn about them and to communicate their own needs and their own sentiments. Rhetoric, logic as it is traditionally defined, and sentiment overlap to make this possible. Rationality is therefore a complex phenomenon. Smith, I believe, in conjunction with more recent argumentation theory, offers us a means to think about it in all of its complexity, including, even, its nonlogical elements.

Part Two

Improving Rational Judgment

On the evening of October 12th, 1931, Louis Armstrong opened a three-day run at the Hotel Driscoll in Austin, Texas. Among those who paid 75 cents to get in that night was a freshman at the University of Texas named Charlie Black. He knew nothing of Jazz, had never even heard of Armstrong. He just knew there were likely to be lots of girls to dance with. Then, Armstrong began to play. . . .

"He was the first genius I had ever seen. . . . It is impossible to overstate the significance of a sixteen-year-old Southern boy's seeing genius, for the first time, in a black.

"You literally never saw a black then, in anything but a servant's capacity. Louis opened my eyes wide, and put to me a choice. Blacks, the saying went, were 'all right in their place.' What was the 'place' of such a man, and of the people from which he sprung?"

Charlie Black went on to become Professor Charles L. Black, a distinguished teacher of constitutional law at Yale. He volunteered for the team of lawyers, black and white, who finally persuaded the Supreme Court, in the case of BROWN *vs.* THE BOARD OF EDUCATION, that segregating school children on the basis of race and color was unconstitutional.

—from Ken Burns's Jazz

He was born poor, died rich, and never hurt anyone along the way.
—Duke Ellington on Louis Armstrong

8

EDUCATION FOUNDATIONS

I have been examining the mechanics of rationality. For Smith, individuals have primitive experiences that result in multiple motivations for multiple desires. They form perceptions of the world and cultivate, then modify, sentiments. The ability to judge the propriety of these sentiments is fostered by community standards, practices, and traditions and is both advanced and hindered by differences in experiences, outlooks, and ways of life among individuals and groups. Such judgments are made possible by the inborn faculty of reason. Moral actors use their imaginations to enter into the perspectives of others, reason instrumentally, make moral judgments, and create narratives to negotiate the multiplicity of desires and motivations, often acting on several motivations and desires at once. Thus passions are the building blocks of human rationality, and sentiments are rational in and of themselves.

Reason is inborn, but it, and rationality, develop as people do. How are individuals and communities to cultivate them? My answer to these questions will focus on two specific areas: philosophy of education and philosophy of history. The first focuses on growth of knowledge, judgment, and rational capacities of individuals; the second explores these same questions on the community level, a community that may be homogeneous or pluralistic.

In previous chapters we saw that, for Smith, social and political unity is the outgrowth of a discursive process that enables and cultivates moral judgment. Sympathy, the human capacity to enter into the perspective of another person, works in tandem with the imagined impartial spectator, a theory of conscience that negotiates personal and community judgment. It and the imagination are both nurtured by acculturation and education, education being transmitted through both day-to-day learning and more formal instruction. This, I have argued, forms the foundation of rationality both in its manipulation of the sentiments (even in their most primitive form) and in the interaction between the imagination and the general rules of conduct.

In the next chapter I examine the foundation of Smith's theory of schooling by making his philosophy of education my main focus. The same caveat applies to that chapter as to the earlier ones: education should be understood in its widest sense as the intentional imposition of values, norms, expectations, standards, and lessons on specific individuals or groups by other specific individuals or groups. Nevertheless, it should become even clearer as we delve more deeply into Smith's discussion that the conceptual overlap between pedagogy and acculturation is found in Smith's texts and is a component of his descriptions of how individuals learn in general.

My discussion in this chapter, however, begins with an account of education in Scotland, outlining Smith's historical context and the social and political realities that informed his writing. I then offer his "theory of learning." This examination focuses not on education per se but on the natural desire for creatures to develop intellectually. Here, 'learning' is a more basic concept than education or socialization. I understand it as recalling Aristotle's famous assertion in *Metaphysics* that all people by nature desire to know. My intent is to offer Smith's explanation as to why this is. Chapter 9 discusses education policy.

Despite the renewal of interest in Smith, there has been minimal focus on these aspects of his writing. Smith himself rarely identifies his theoretical comments on education as such, and his remarks on matters of curriculum are dispersed throughout his works. Theoretical concerns specifically identified as philosophy of education are remarkably rare in the secondary literature. Noneconomic comments on Smith's educational theory are usually quite brief and are found in only a handful of disparate sources;[1] a notable exception is a special symposium on Smith and education for the *Adam Smith Review*, which I was fortunate to both edit and contribute to.[2] My position in this chapter is significantly influenced by those of my co-contributors in that volume.

As far as I have been able to identify, the last and possibly the only stand-alone work that focuses on Smith's philosophy of education was published privately in 1945 by Charles Flinn Arrowood, professor of the history and philosophy of education at the University of Texas.[3] The contrast between Arrowood's comments and recent scholarship could not be greater; Arrowood simply does not take Smith seriously as a philosopher. His remarks include such jibes as "Smith's political doctrines reflect a thoroughly naive and inadequate theory of the nature of mind and of knowledge."[4] He repeatedly asserts that Smith saw people as "complete in all their faculties apart from the operation of any social forces."[5] Both of these statements are patently false. As we have seen, Smith saw the development of human knowledge and moral judgment as a social phenomenon, and his philosophy of mind, albeit incomplete, engages some of the most pressing philosophical issues of his day and ours. Both of these issues, and many others with which Smith concerns himself, meet in his philosophy of education.

SMITH'S PREDISPOSITION TOWARD EDUCATION THEORY

Eighteenth-century Scotland offers an interesting context for discussion of both education theory and practice. Some commentators have made great sport of the popular intellectual culture of the time as well as of the fact that the public moral sensibility was centered in the university. MacIntyre, for example, argues that Scotland represented that "rare phenomenon . . . a philosophically educated public."[6] Seeking to describe an ideal education system, he positively juxtaposes his understanding of Scottish education to today's liberal universities—the current education systems do not look very good in comparison. MacIntyre asserts that the Scottish public shared "a deference to a teaching authority, that of the professors of philosophy and especially of moral philosophy. To be called to account for one's beliefs and judgments, in respect either of their justification by deduction from first principles or of the evidentness of those first principles themselves, was a matter from about 1730 onward of being called upon to defend oneself in the forums of philosophically educated opinion rather than in the courts of the church."[7]

Arthur Herman echoes MacIntyre's account, claiming that "only London and Paris could compete with Edinburgh as an intellectual center" and that Scotland's intellectual class was "remarkably democratic. It was a place where all ideas were created equal, where brains rather than social rank took pride of place. . . . Edinburgh was like a giant think tank or artists' colony, except that unlike most modern think tanks, this one was not cut off from everyday life. It was in the thick of it."[8]

However romantic MacIntyre's and Arthur's accounts are, and however nice it would be for the Enlightenment scholar to believe them, they are inaccurate in a great many respects.[9] First, it was certainly not the case in Scotland that secular university values trumped religious moral authority in all matters. Public education was indeed a central political concern for the Scots; the nation developed a school system to educate the poor in 1696. However, whatever attempt there may have been to educate the masses, schooling was never mandated for everyone. Second, although in theory the burgh schools were free from significant religious intrusion because they were under the management of town councils and not the presbyteries, in reality the church did try to influence the curriculum and only sometimes met resistance from individual institutions.[10] Third, Scottish education was an inextricable mixture of theology, philosophy, natural science, and other forms of knowledge: "From the mid-17th century, almost to the end of the 19th century, natural theology not only gave social legitimacy to natural science, but also provided the key ordering principles of natural history."[11]

As David Allan points out, *both* the Kirk and universities were "the principal organs for the dissemination of the enlightened values of tolerance, politeness and learning"; the two institutions worked in tandem.[12] Religious reform led to an opening of the possibilities of discussion, and university reform sought to produce "men imbued with a rigorous training in moral philosophy, rhetoric, science and letters." The scholarship of the time "promised actual moral improvement."[13] As a result, the new roles of the university led to "the emergence of a thriving community of clubs and societies, all of them dedicated to the promotion of polite values, speculative discussion and particular projects."[14] In other words, the Scottish Enlightenment was a convergence of numerous forces, not the simple triumph of a singular academic point of view.

The quality of education that individual students received is hard to gauge. The level varied, often depending on the local teacher. John Rae suggests, for example, that Smith's own school was among the best secondary schools in the country mostly because of the influence of his teacher, David Millar.[15] Thus, although many shared Smith's path through both burgh and grammar schools,[16] and even though "it was usual for the sons of merchants to attend [Glasgow] College for one or two years,"[17] it is impossible to judge how prepared any particular student might have been.

Regarding students collectively, however, more evidence is available, and from this we can determine that the laboring classes simply did not have the same opportunities as those in the middle and upper classes (as MacIntyre acknowledges but Herman does not). They received different educations—a disparity that Smith and many of his contemporaries endorse—and there is disagreement as to how literate the masses actually were. For example, Smith writes in WN that the parish schools taught "almost the whole common people to read, and a very great proportion of them to write and account" (WN V.i.f.55), but Jerry Muller argues that most Scottish adults were "benighted to the point of illiteracy."[18] As noted, Smith points out that women received no institutional education at all (WN V.i.f.4). And while, as also noted, he is complimentary of the practical and efficient nature of the education women did receive, their home-based schooling does not make up for Alexander Carlyle's observation that Glasgow had "neither a teacher of French nor of music in the town . . . the young ladies were entirely without accomplishments, and in general had nothing to recommend them but good looks and fine clothes, for their manners were ungainly."[19]

I do not mean to argue that the "Enlightenment as existed in eighteenth-century Scotland was confined to a tiny minority" but, specifically, that education was neither equal nor universal.[20] While few if any societies can claim an all-inclusive and egalitarian educational system, I emphasize its hierarchical nature both to counter Herman's picture and to elaborate on Smith's own remarks regarding class and education.

Those who did succeed intellectually tended to come from similar economic, social, and religious circumstances. As Bonnie and Vern Bellough show, "An overall profile of the Scottish achiever of the eighteenth century would indicate that he was born in an urban parish. His parents belonged to the Church of Scotland, lived in the midland (the section centered around Glasgow and Edinburgh), and could be classified as upper middle class."[21] Smith himself came from "impressive financial and mental resources," and his mother had the financial security to send him away to school.[22] Not surprisingly, many of his schoolmates and contemporaries grew to hold positions of power and respect, including a member of Parliament, an official in the Church of Scotland, and several prominent architects.[23] Regarding Smith's lectures on jurisprudence, E. G. West writes, "It is clear that Smith had been given the task of providing an education for the sons of aristocrats and for those aspiring towards a life of gentlemanly cultivation and self-improvement."[24] At WN V.i.f.35, Smith himself notes "without any sense of disapproval that most of the young men attending universities were sons of gentlemen and men of fortune."[25]

The class-related issues involved in education can be seen in Smith's British influences as well. In the case of Shaftesbury and Mandeville, education is immersed in the management of moral judgment or economic effect. Shaftesbury wrote, "Perfection of Grace and Comeliness in Action and Behaviour, can be found only among the People of a liberal Education" (*Char.*, I.119), and Mandeville argued that education was harmful to the working classes since, "by bringing them up in Ignorance you may inure them to real Hardships without being ever sensible themselves that they are such" (*Fable* I.317).[26]

Smith discusses many of these same themes, although he disagrees with Mandeville explicitly on the exclusion of the laboring classes from education. He specifically addresses the role of religious institutions in education and casts doubt on the efficacy of universities. As I have shown, Smith's protreptic writing style suggests that he viewed his own lectures and his books as pedagogical projects, and his use of sympathy presupposes the possibility of moral learning as a

mechanism for personal betterment and social unity. Smith's work on education is therefore the convergence of multiple contentious debates regarding
how a society is to educate its members and to what purpose this is done.
As a consequence, his works became a "continuing standard for successive
programmes of educational reform of the revolutionary period, both in
England and in France." They were deeply influential for Condorcet, for
example, and inspired aggressive opposition from his contemporaries Alexander
Carlyle and William Playfair.[27]

Alexandra Hyard shows that Smith's thinking on education "follows a similar
trajectory to that of his French contemporaries."[28] He shared ideas on education
with the French *économistes* and *philosophes* before and after his visit to France.
She observes, "The main dispute at the time was between those who thought
that education ought to be a familial responsibility and those who would
rather see it handled by the state. Between 'domestic education' and 'state
education' — to use the eighteenth century's formulation — the majority of
these French thinkers favoured the latter option." She then adds, however, that,
like Smith, the French thinkers perceived that "the type of education proper for
the superior ranks of society should not be extended to the lower ranks."[29]

Smith most likely read works on philosophy of education. His library
contained Stephanus's edition of Plato, which included *Meno* and *Republic*;
Rousseau's *Emile*; Montaigne's *Essais*, which contains his *Of the Education of
Children*; an anonymously authored book titled *Loose Hints upon Education,
chiefly concerning the Culture of the Heart* that was eventually identified as
Lord Kames's, and *Éducation de la Noblesse Françoise*; as well as other relevant
volumes.[30] He was also a teacher by profession for many years, both at university
and as a private tutor. He refers to the years he spent at Glasgow "as by far the
most useful, and, therefore, as by far the happiest and most honourable period
of my life" (*Corr.* 274). He claims to "have thought a great deal upon this
subject" of how to improve Scottish universities and to "have inquired very
carefully into the constitution and history of several of the principal Universities
of Europe" (*Corr.* 143).

Smith's comments in his books, lectures, and correspondences do indicate a
certain attention to education policy. His focus on rhetoric in his classroom and
his use of particular presentation styles throughout his writing make it evident
that he knew audience awareness was a significant pedagogical factor — that
there are better and worse means of imparting information.[31] Certainly a moral
theory such as Smith's, based on the interaction between spectator and agent,
must also assume this much. Furthermore, Smith was well aware of the role of
audience in his writing and teaching. As Gloria Vivenza shows, Smith adapted

his lectures on rhetoric to account for the better prepared students in the class as compared to those who attended his lectures on jurisprudence; both of these audiences are different from the readership of *The Wealth of Nations*.[32] He clearly understood that teaching required attention to both context and students' capabilities.

There is, however, no reason to think that Smith had any dedicated interest in philosophy of education: he never indicated any plans to write a treatise specifically on the subject. None of the works listed above are cited in his writing; his library contained only the second and third volumes of *Éducation de la Noblesse Françoise*—he may have not owned the first one—and Smith is missing books that would be essential for anyone seriously devoted to the subject. Works by Erasmus, for example, are conspicuously absent; so is Locke's *Some Thoughts Concerning Education*.

Nevertheless, as Vivenza shows, Smith's classical heritage offers numerous discussions of education transmitted through classical sources; he consciously uses them as examples in his lectures. As she writes, "It is worth bearing in mind that in the eighteenth century, the classics were practically inescapable 'authorities' in every discipline" and are now regarded by scholars "as catalysts, so to speak, that are useful in highlighting the fundamental lines of his thought."[33] In short, whereas Smith did not have a specialist's interest in the philosophy of education, the material he drew upon, alongside the influences he encountered in his intellectual growth, make education theory a frequent theme in his writings. This makes it likely that their inclusion was conscious and thoughtful.

A THEORY OF LEARNING

Much of the foundation of Smith's philosophy of education is found in his fragments and early essays. These largely unfinished and unpublished pieces provide insight into the most basic psychological and physiological structures that necessitate education for all people. While their status as drafts requires that they not trump Smith's published writing, they are helpful in offering insights on tangential issues not always raised by Smith's books and lectures. They also consistently support my decision to prioritize *TMS* when reading his corpus.

Not surprisingly, Smith relies on the sentiments at key moments to explain how and why people learn. As we saw in the previous chapter, how much of an empiricist Smith actually was is uncertain. For example, he remarks in the fragment on external senses that "it seems difficult to suppose that man is the only animal of which the young are not endowed with some instinctive perception" that allows them to see immediately upon opening their eyes (*ES* 74). And, although he suggests that human dependency results in people's needing instinct less than animals, Smith entertains the thought that children do in fact have some of these instincts (*ES* 74).

For Smith, the quality of different sense capacities is itself a product of learning. For example, the inequality of visual ability among people is partially dependent upon "some difference in the original configuration of their eyes," but also "frequently" develops because of the "different customs and habits which their respective occupations have led them to contract" (*ES* 52). To illustrate this difference, Smith compares "men of letters" to mariners to show how the "precision" by which a sailor can see objects in the distance "astonishes a land-man" (*ES* 52).

As we have seen, habit makes one's own knowledge seem ordinary, and the commonality between people is often made invisible by differences in experience — Smith will include this theme in his discussion of the imitative arts. For Smith, there is an intimate relationship between the senses and the imagination. He reminds us that the word "feeling," though usually a synonym of "touching, . . . is frequently employed to denote our internal, as well as our external, affections" (*ES* 19). He also reminds us, both in *External Senses* and in *TMS*, that the imagination plays an important part in filling in details when only some are known — a point that foreshadows his narrative rationality.[34] This applies to both visual (*ES* 54) and moral (*TMS* III.3.2) details. Smith assumes this same external/internal division in his discussion of the first formation of languages, arguing that "qualities are almost always the objects of our external senses; relations never are" (*FFL* 12).

Like sensual capacities, the ability to have a language is first dependent on habit. Smith supposes that the first names denoted particular caves or trees, and only later did humans develop the names for species (*FFL* 1). According to Smith, language came about from the necessity of communication; it is an inherently social invention. A good "Rational Grammar" parallels systems of logic and entails, in essence, a "History of the natural progress of the Human mind" since language forms "the most important abstractions upon which all reasoning depends" (*Corr.* 69). This highlights an intimate connection between Smith's comments in *Considerations Concerning the First Formation of Languages (FFL)* and my discussion of the nature of learning. *FFL* is a conjectural history, and Smith "is not concerned with historical fact, which is liable to historical accident, but with the general (or 'natural') features of the human phenomena under consideration."[35] It also connects our discussion of language and rationality, showing how reasoned analysis and language share similar structures. As we have seen, Smith's views on language are essential to his notion of reason because logic and rhetoric are inseparable for argumentation.

Eighteenth-century theorists operated on the assumption that the development of human language was analogous to the development of language in children.[36] Thus Smith would have observed children learning language as a preamble to his discussion. As evidence of his theory, he writes, "A child that is just learning to speak, calls every person who comes to the house its papa or its mama; and thus bestows upon the whole species those names which it had been taught to apply to two individuals" (*FFL* 1). *FFL*, then, is an indication of the process children would have to go through as they learned how to communicate.

For Smith, the fundamental tools humans use to learn and to teach—language, the imagination, and the senses—are themselves subject to some form of learning. As we have seen, they are dependent on proximity, and their cultivation is required to complete tasks. Much of our capacity to know services our capacity to figure out: our knowledge increases itself. As we have seen, epistemology and rationality involve filling in the blanks, so to speak. They also cultivate social behavior and the sentiments.

We can see this explicitly in Smith's earliest account of the nature of human intellectual pursuits. Foreshadowing much of his later work, "The Principles Which Lead and Direct Philosophical Enquiries; Illustrated by the History of Astronomy" is an attempt to explain the human motivation for engaging in natural science and philosophy—two terms that Smith uses synonymously—in terms of the sentiments of the inquirer. It presents a sentimentalist account of the human motivation to acquire knowledge and argues that this desire is caused by those same sentiments that will prove foundational in the rest of moral and political life. The original editors of *HA* write that the essay "must be viewed . . . as an additional illustration of those Principles in the Human Mind which Mr. Smith has pointed out to be the universal Motives of Philosophical Researches."[37]

According to Smith, the motivation to learn is dependent on a series of three sentiments: surprise, wonder, and admiration, a schema reminiscent of Aristotle. Smith equates the sense of surprise elicited by unknown and unfamiliar events to 'panic terrors' (*HA* I.4). It is "the violent and sudden change produced upon the mind, when an emotion of any kind is brought suddenly upon it." It may "confound whole multitudes, benumb their understandings, and agitate their hearts, with all the agony of extravagant fear" (*HA* I.4–5). Upon being faced with the surprise of an unexpected or unfamiliar event, humans search for a way to categorize or organize it. The process of examining the accuracy of our already-accepted categories is called *wonder* and has physical manifestations (*HA* II.3).

Upon successfully ordering events, an agent *wonders* and is then soothed enough to *admire* and appreciate their nature and causes; humans search for inclusive and coherent explanations mostly in the terms of principles or systematic accounts. In his *Lectures on Rhetoric and Belles Lettres* (*LRBL*) Smith suggests that "it gives us a pleasure to see the phaenomena which we reckoned the most unaccountable all deduced from some principle (commonly a wellknown one) and all united in one chain" (*LRBL* ii.133–34). Thus sentiments are soothed when systems and arguments are presented complete, without gaps or contradictions (*LRBL* ii.36).

For Smith, the calming effect of a coherent, inclusive narrative comes from the natural human love of system that inspires thinkers to postulate imaginary "machinery" that itself imposes order and reason on a long series of events; we encountered this in the discussion of narrative in chapter 1. *History of Astronomy* ends with an account of Newton's physics, which Smith, referencing the role of narrative in reasoned discourse, calls a "discovery of *an immense chain* of the most important and sublime truths, all *closely connected together*, by one capital fact, of the reality of which we have daily experience" (*HA* IV.76, emphasis added). This love of system, the human desire to find unifying governing principles of nature, is a direct response to anxiety and is thus the proper object of learning. As we have seen, its power, however, can be seductive and will often corrupt thinkers whose system is inaccurate or too complex. Smith identifies the love of system as one of the major causes of unnecessary social engineering (*TMS* VI.ii.2.17).

Learning is a way to soothe our anxieties and to allay sentiments that are unpleasant to us. It is therefore natural and universal. It is part of the human experience to want to know and to quell feelings of insecurity. In terms of the chronology of his authorship, it is the very first characteristic Smith cites that unifies humanity; it is ever-present in his work. Furthermore, since lack of knowledge necessitates anxiety, the lack of learning prevents human fulfillment. Smith's initial comments in *History of Astronomy* identify the desire to learn as a natural characteristic of human beings. How a society educates its members may be political, as we shall see, but the individual desire for learning itself, according to Smith, is prepolitical.[38]

Similar to Peirce's approach in "The Fixation of Belief,"[39] Smith presents the motivation for scientific knowledge in terms of sentiments and emotion; he subordinates utility to the "intellectual or aesthetic sentiments."[40] This creates a similarity between scientific and moral knowledge, a similarity Smith will extend to artistic knowledge.

To return to the effect familiarity has on knowledge, Smith suggests that those who are already knowledgeable would rather laugh at the uninformed than share the wonder of the ignorant. He proposes that the artisan, for example, does not sympathize with the wonder that those who are not familiar with his or her work feel, even if the artisan fully respects his or her own handiwork: "[The artisan] will be disposed rather to laugh at, than sympathize with our Wonder" (*HA* II.11).

History of Astronomy asserts that an organizing principle for a new science "has generally been selected as an *analogy* from some other art or science;"[41] Smith mentions medicine, ethics, painting, poetry, music, and architecture specifically, supporting my claim that Smith sees unity in the sciences (*HA* II.12).[42] The parallel nature of moral, scientific, and artistic knowledge is underscored in Smith's *Of the Imitative Arts* and is extended to include the appreciation of both craft and beauty. It is, again, sympathetic understanding that allows for pleasure, and in this case Smith is explicit that skill—or education—is required to fully appreciate imitation (*IA* I.16).

Smith argues that people take pleasure in knowing, but learning, which is an effort, is worth it only when the object of knowledge is itself worthy, even if an art is not easily distinguishable as such (*IA* Annexe, 3). This value judgment is paralleled in WN when Smith argues that students will willingly attend lectures worth hearing (WN V.i.f.15).

All these comments suggest that sympathy is that which eases human interaction, yet even more evidence for the priority of *TMS*. Certainly, none of these are economic in nature; none could believably be explained by a market mechanism. They define the ability to sympathize as the product of genius or, in this case, excellence in a particular context—a skill Smith calls specialization in WN. Differences in knowledge and experience contribute to lack of understanding and, by extension, social division—although these divisions are often professional in nature or based on personal interest. Here, Smith's comments again indicate that some of the problems inherent in moral knowledge may very well be the same as in scientific knowledge. That is, the barrier to sympathy in both scientific and moral contexts is the lack of commonality between the individuals who are engaged in the acts of either sympathizing or being sympathized with.

History of Astronomy defines the acquisition of knowledge as a central problem for Smith's theory. Accordingly, scientific knowledge is acquired by creating systems that soothe people's wonder or surprise. Systems organize diverse facts into a general understanding because individuals could not be expected to know and synthesize all information regarding any topic in question; these are the beginnings of what I have referred to as a narrative rationality. Analogously, sympathy organizes the discrete pieces of information regarding moral judgment, and, as I have shown, market price organizes commercially relevant facts. In all three instances—scientific, moral, and economic knowledge—systems are expected to impose order on apparent chaos and to provide information to those individuals who could not possibly acquire and sort through every piece of relevant information in every situation.

This may speak to why some find the market such a compelling metaphor; it does impose order on chaos. However, it is not the only thing that does so; reflection and rationality do as well. So do historiography and storytelling. Narrative is very useful in all of these instances and is more consistent with *HA* than the economic interpretation. The acquisition and ordering of knowledge in numerous contexts are one of Smith's central concerns; the accumulation and transfer of knowledge are the purview of learning and education, not exchange. (Again, education here is widely defined.) Even through the eighteenth century, the meanings of 'oeconomy' tended to refer to organization and management in general, not simply to market concerns. Smith's desire for order is part and parcel of the language he uses.

HA emphasizes the manner in which people are motivated to learn, but it says little about teaching, learning's concomitant activity. As discussed in the previous chapter, there is a back-and-forth relationship between education and human nature. Although "the principles of the imagination" are delicate and "may easily be altered" by education, "the sentiments of moral approbation and disapprobation . . . cannot be entirely perverted" (*TMS* V.2.1), a conviction that bespeaks the connection between Smith and the Hutchesonian moral sense. Additionally, although each person has a "natural preference . . . for his own happiness above that of other people" (*TMS* II.ii.2.1), this is countered by the fact that "the most vulgar education teaches us to act, upon all important occasions, with some sort of impartiality between ourselves and others" (*TMS* III.3.7). Learning is a natural act; it works with the principles that guide us. The mechanism that refines our senses is the same mechanism that refines our sentiments. As our physical capacities develop, so do our moral abilities.

As we have seen, for Smith, "the great secret of education is to direct vanity to proper objects" (*TMS* VI.iii.46). "Self-deceit" is the "fatal weakness of mankind" and "the source of half the disorders of human life" (*TMS* III.4.5–7). "Vanity arises from . . . [a] . . . gross . . . illusion of the imagination" and is "the foundation of the most ridiculous and contemptible vices" (*TMS* III.2.4). Acculturation and education not only help an agent to see others but also cultivate accurate self-image as well. As Griswold argues, for Smith, "education and right ordering of institutions are certainly crucial to checking self-love and containing the disorders it creates."[43]

Education, then, is not designed just to impart information. It provides moral lessons as well as develops critical judgment, reason, and rationality. To focus on the first, however, as Smith shows in his *Lectures on Rhetoric*, discussions of style and communication are intertwined with moral lessons, and often the two roles are inseparable. Certain styles of writing and speech are more conducive to imparting information than others, and Smith offers a full discussion of which methods are best at providing facts and describing objects (*LRBL* i.154, i.172–75).

It is because of the ethical role of writing and speaking that *LRBL* is filled with the language of virtue, including remarks about specific grammar considerations one must take into account during such discussions.[44] Individual words are important for Smith because language is inherently pedagogical. However, it is not simply that virtue makes writing better. For Smith, virtue makes *every-thing* better—the priority of *TMS*. Vice, by contrast, makes all things worse: "Virtue adds to every thing that is of itself commendable whereas Vice distracts from what would otherwise be praise worthy" (*LRBL* ii.101). Here, Smith struggles with the question of whether virtue can be taught. *TMS* suggests it can, but the educational methods for teaching virtue are much more subtle than a simple morality-centered curriculum. Our language choices themselves contribute to the cultivation of virtuous behavior. It is no surprise, then, that Smith's book on moral philosophy is itself a lesson in pedagogical rhetoric.

The Theory of Moral Sentiments was most likely based on lectures Smith presented in his courses on moral philosophy and influenced by his lectures on rhetoric and jurisprudence. It is written in a natural, conversational style and is filled with graphic, yet familiar, examples that may very well have been useful in a classroom context. Smith relies heavily on literature, characters, and verse that would be familiar to his students to communicate moral lessons. As Vivenza writes in her discussion of Smith, the classics, and slavery, this tendency is also found in the lectures on jurisprudence on which *TMS* was likely based.[45]

Vivenza seems to suggest, as has been argued before, that *WN* is simply a specific case of an earlier discussion, in this instance *LJ*. She also shows that Smith's concern is the nature of the audience who would read *WN*; it is a book on political economy, after all. Its readership will be most interested in those types of arguments. While this shouldn't minimize the importance of the economic argument opposing slavery, it should emphasize that presenting only that version of it in *WN* was likely a rhetorical choice for Smith and not a claim that the economic abolitionist argument superseded the moral one.

As Smith modifies *TMS* over the years, the writing style becomes less oratorical and more geared toward print. I would argue that the final edition has more stylistic similarities to WN, suggesting Smith's extended separation from the classroom. It also puts the pedagogical intent of the book in sharp relief. Smith is always conscious of his audience and the medium in which his work is presented. He describes his writing process as deliberate and almost tedious (*Corr.* 276).

Rhetoric and audience are connected to sympathy because the obverse of human equality is physical individuality.[46] Through sympathy individuals can maintain personal and political relationships. Although commentators have suggested that sympathy does not play roles in other works by Smith, as we have seen, it is found throughout his writings. Sympathy is used in those instances in which Smith wants to convey an intellectual or imaginative connectedness. It is also used in those moments when individuals somehow transcend their discrete nature.

First, individuals transcend physical limitations when they feel concern and pleasure regarding the happiness of others (*TMS* I.i.1.1). Acculturation, education, and learning in general allow individuals to have knowledge about the needs of others—those outside of society are incapable of making the necessary judgments because they have no one to learn from or be influenced by (*TMS* III.I.3–5). As Griswold writes, "Moral education" allows "that the impartial spectator's practical reason becomes our own, [it] becomes (as it were) our second nature . . . an acquired form of moral self-awareness."[47] The same imagination that creates systems from discrete scientific facts allows individuals to understand the context and motivation of moral actors, a further example of the connectedness between imagination, sympathy, and rationality. Nevertheless, our understanding of others is bound by our experiences. It is always filtered through our self-understanding (*TMS* I.i.3.10).

The desire to sympathize is natural, as is the desire to learn—both are related to the need to cultivate the imagination and enter into the perspective of others.[48] It is part of the human condition—it is hardwired within us, to use a modern term. Moral judgment and scientific learning are both systematic in nature. They are both based on a foundation of sentiments, yet they require investigation and, ultimately, education, understood as both socialization and institutional learning. It is likely for this reason that Smith uses the metaphor "school" on numerous occasions to point to the "exercise and practice" that is required to develop the "habit" of virtue—this underscores his wide interpretation of the term 'education' as well (*TMS* III.3.36). For example, he refers to "the proper school of heroism" (*TMS* I.iii.2.9, ed. 1); "the great school of self-command" (*TMS* III.3.22); "hardships, dangers, injuries, misfortunes, . . . masters to whom nobody willingly puts himself to school" (*TMS* III.3.36); and "war is the great school both for acquiring and exercising this species of magnanimity" (*TMS* VI.iii.7).

Education serves several purposes in moral growth throughout Smith's corpus. It cultivates our capacity to interpret the sentiments of other; it provides a mechanism by which we cultivate moral judgment; and it offers us standards by which we can temper our own sentiments or suggest to others that they do so. For example, Smith tells us that it is the collective social body that teaches someone not to express joy publicly at the death of his or her enemy (*TMS* III.4.12); Fleischacker points out that this emphasizes the importance of *rules* for the impartial spectator.[49]

What allows the individual to temper his or her anger is an understanding that the moral rule prohibiting public displays of revenge-based pleasure trumps the momentary desire to celebrate. Moral education and its concomitant ubiquitous acculturation therefore allow for a "circular" process that helps us "become ethically sympathetic and sensitive persons who can move back and forth between maxims and context."[50]

Social interaction and community standards play a major role in this process. It is this desire that allows the mechanism of sympathy to be effectual. Learning helps someone create a wider framework from which he or she can create analogous emotions. As we have seen, a wider range of knowledge leads to a wider range of sympathy. This relates to what Haakonssen calls "contextual knowledge," or, "the knowledge we have of human behaviour through the sympathy mechanism . . . concrete knowledge which arises from specific situations and which give rise to common-sense ideas of behaviour wherever people live together."[51] Readers should recall MacIntyre's argument about the need for context in rationality. For him, discrete facts are not helpful for moral judgment unless there is a *telos*, an aim that helps determine appropriate actions.[52] Similarly, for Smith, the contextual reality of knowledge enables individuals to provide sentiments with meaning and value. This is a rational process even though it involves judgments about passions.

Smith's audience is thus forced to ask why any spectator would go through the trouble of sympathizing with others, especially in those instances when it requires so much effort. His answer in *TMS* is the same as his answer explaining the motivation to learn in *HA*. One seeks to sympathize with others because it is enjoyable to do so: "Nothing pleases us more than to observe in other men a fellow-feeling with all the emotions of our own breast" (*TMS* I.i.2.1). Given the role of pain and pleasure as primitives or simple ideas, this suggests that the progression from surprise to wonder to admiration is the foundation of narrative rationality. Agents make sense of their desire through these emotions and direct their inquiries in order to resolve the problem and settle upon a more pleasing passion. This, again, foreshadows Peirce's discussion.

If we define learning as the process of gathering, understanding, and contextualizing information or knowledge, then we can see why education lies at the core of sympathy. Without the ability to learn, no spectator can make moral judgments. Without the potential for education, the capacity for individuals to overcome the fundamental separateness that divides human beings would be nonexistent. Both of these capabilities presume rationality.

What we have seen so far is that, for Smith, all capacities are subject to learning and refinement. This growth allows for differences in familiarity and a separation between those with more refined capacities and those without. This divide is bridged by the imagination and works through sympathy. Thus while sympathy is ubiquitously acknowledged as the foundation for Smith's moral psychology, it is much more. It is the fundamental mechanism for human connectedness. It bridges the discrete individualism that is our physical nature and is modified through learning. Once again, we see that sympathy is the core of Smith's pluralism.

In order for sympathy to function, however, we have seen that the spectator builds on context rather than on perceived sentiment alone. He or she must create a story that allows for understanding as to why the actor responds in a given way, and only then is judgment possible. This is the process of rationality—the means by which individuals create narratives to explain actions, look toward community narratives and balance them with their own, and then judge the propriety of an act based on their intersection. This is also the process of finding social unity in the face of otherness, of creating a stable pluralism. The difficulties lie in relating the stories in such a way that they are understandable to others, and, as we have seen, education is the means by which the community increases individuals' abilities to present or interpret them.

We have seen how community understanding limits or cultivates understanding, regardless of whether we consider a community of abilities or social divisions caused by race, gender, class, community size, or intensity. We have also spent a great deal of time emphasizing the means by which groups socialize one another toward norms. What we have neglected is the means by which the sovereign contributes to this process. If Smith is really presenting a theory of pluralism, then it must be shown that the sovereign, not just the community, has an interest in managing but not eradicating difference. One place this happens is in institutional education.

9

FORMAL EDUCATION

We have seen how sympathy is built on education, how education can overcome group and individual difference, and how learning is connected to the foundation of human experience. It remains to be seen how these concerns are institutionalized in society.

Until now, and following the pattern set forth in chapter 3, my discussion has emphasized education in its widest sense. I have been following Smith's tendency, particularly in *TMS*, to use education as a synonym for the process of lifelong learning, distinguishing whenever useful between socialization and education. In this chapter, I shift the focus to formal education. This involves two related concerns. The first is an examination of what the nature and purpose of schooling might be. The second is the role of schooling in a commercial society, including certain core economic considerations. Both connect pluralism to the duties of the sovereign, the first by suggesting that the basic structure of institutional education is itself a means for managing difference, and the second by prescribing that the responsibilities the government has to fund these institutions is an outgrowth of its effectiveness in cultivating social unity in the face of difference.

INSTITUTIONAL EDUCATION

Smith's economics of education has received the most attention in the literature. This is not surprising, since Smith's discussion of the educational institutions in WN is couched in the language of public finance. As we shall see, the very titles of the related chapters reference the "expense" of education. However, this should not suggest that Smith's justification of education is mainly economic advancement. Quite the contrary—Smith never argues for education to support prosperity. As Emma Rothschild explains, he was "skeptical about the value of occupational training or apprenticeship" and never suggests "that universal education will lead to an increase in national wealth."[1] For Smith, "education is needed as a consequence of economic development, and not as a cause of future development."[2]

Tempering Rothschild's claim, Pedro Teixeira writes that "the influence of the disposition to truck, barter, and exchange, means that the entire community can benefit from the productive outcome" of differences cultivated by education.[3] As a consequence, "most modern economists became convinced that Smith offered the origins of human capital theory," and Smith's writing played an important role in the acceptance of a conception of human capital in its early formulations.[4] In other words, for Smith and his readers, education does have some economic consequences — it is intertwined with need and outcome — but it is not *justified* by them. That economic impact does not change the purpose of education once again emphasizes that there are no clear boundaries between Smith's political economy and his other work.

Interpreting Smith's economic claims is difficult because he proposes policies that may be in tension with one another. Smith calls for commercial competition within the sphere of education as a protection of quality. He was critical of his own education at Oxford and accused the faculty there of being "very indulgent to one another" and to have "given up altogether even the pretence of teaching" (WN V.i.f.8).[5] Market forces, he argues, can help remedy the passivity of those secure in their posts. He also seems opposed to "credentialism," the process by which students attend university to acquire degrees, not to learn.[6]

Despite his call for some competition, Smith also argues that education serves the needs of the wider community, and the public must therefore bear a proportion of the expense; Smith does not say how much. The poor should receive incentives to educate themselves and their children, a prescription that is sure to increase the financial burden on the community. Herein lay the difficulties in Smith's economics of education. His overall theory suggests a wider public responsibility toward educating the working classes, but he is vague as to what those responsibilities might be. Furthermore, his comments on the duties of the sovereign may be read as supporting either more or fewer public subsidies for schooling. Which position one takes depends very much on a wide range of interpretive positions. My aim in this section is to clarify the relationship between Smith's numerous provisions for education and to show how his philosophy of education offers clues as to what position he ultimately held on the public subsidy of education.

These policy tensions are not the only difficulties involved in interpreting Smith's economic claims about education; our project is made even more complicated by conflicting assertions in the text and by what we know about Smith's life. Some of these are made most explicit in a groundbreaking article by Charles G. Leathers and J. Patrick Raines.[7] While some commentators may take it for granted that Smith offers a clear argument for a free-market education policy, Leathers and Raines show that Smith's case is weak at best and that a laissez-faire approach to schooling was likely contrary to his personal beliefs.[8] As they sum up their argument:

> A critical examination of the case that Smith presented in *Wealth of Nations* revealed that it was weakened by contradictions, qualifications and incomplete attention to the institutional functions of universities to the point that it provides no support for making modern universities function more like consumer-friendly firms. In addition, anecdotal evidence from Glasgow University, which Smith implied was operating under the right system, indicated the type of diversity in faculty performances and students' behaviour commonly found in universities in which faculty are paid assured salaries and there is relatively little student-consumer sovereignty. In addition, and perhaps more importantly, anecdotal evidence revealed that Smith himself believed that faculty at Glasgow University should not be guided by their own self-interest but rather by the interest and needs of their students.[9]

Smith's discussion of the institutions of education in WN is divided into two parts, the first of which is a chapter titled "Of the Expence of the Institutions for the Education of Youth" (WN V.i.f.) and the second "Of the Expence of the Institutions for the Instruction of People of all Ages" (WN V.i.g). The main differences between the two are that the latter type of education has a wider range of influence than the former. The latter also focuses on education regarding the afterlife, whereas the former focuses on more secular themes (WN V.i.g), although there is overlap. Both systems maintain that the main responsibility of the cost of education is to be primarily distributed among those who are the most obviously affected, and both regard education as essential to moral development.

Although there is no explicit reference to the term in WN, Smith once again relates the practice of education to the process of sympathy. Smith's argument is that of sympathetic familiarity, a position I have already dealt with in depth. He asserts that the student who travels loses the ability to abide by the standards of the community and gains nothing from it but a poor education in languages (WN V.i.f.36).

Smith's implicit reference becomes evident when compared to similar comments at *TMS* in which he argues that foreign education has "hurt most essentially the domestic morals, and consequently the domestic happiness" (*TMS* VI.ii.1.10). This is yet another instance in which prioritizing the first book adds clarity to an interpretation. Interestingly, *TMS*'s one explicit discussion of the institution of education was added to the sixth edition, *after* the publication and revision of *WN*. This suggests the influence of Smith's further thoughts on political economy and underscores the connection between the two books. Smith, in prioritizing *TMS*, made a conscious attempt to ensure that the two works were coherent, at least regarding the question of education abroad.[10]

In both of these selections, we see Smith observe that education in public schools as well as studying abroad too early makes children lose their sense of family and become conceited, more unprincipled, and incapable of serious application. In essence, children abroad lose their power of self-command, which, according to Smith, is one of the most important virtues and that from which "all the other virtues seem to derive their principal lustre" (*TMS* VI.iii.11). Without self-command a moral actor is unable to adjust his or her actions to the standard set by the sympathy of the impartial spectator. To use Forman-Barzilai's terms, although they may be capable of *surveillance*—and they may not, given their extended separation from cultural norms—they will most certainly be incapable of *discipline*. Students educated abroad will be unable to act on whatever judgments they make. As it was for the Greeks and Romans, one necessary evaluative standard of schooling is the proper cultivation of morals.

Although Smith is critical of foreign education here, he does not suggest the other extreme, what we today would call home schooling: the formal long-term schooling of the child by the parents away from his or her peers. Children need to live at home, he argues, but not necessarily be schooled there (*TMS* VI.ii.1.10). In other words, "domestic education," as the French called it, is an essential part of socialization but need not be the only one.

Smith is moderate in his educational prescriptions and argues that familial and institutional schooling complement each other (*LJ(A)* iii.5). Then, as if to underscore the point, in *LJ(B)* Smith references the long-term dependence human children have on their parents, beginning with their need to nurse. Given this length, he writes, even the worst parents have the opportunity to make their children useful to society (*LJ(B)* 102). While the reference to parental influence in the second set of lectures is built on the utility of the child to society, the first set of lectures relies on sympathetic familiarity. In both, however, his point is the same: education at home is required to temper childish passions.

For Smith, however, this continues only until the child reaches the appropriate age for institutional schooling. Then, being outside the home is necessary for the cultivation of self-command. Ironically, it is life experience itself that he refers to as "the great school of self-command" (*TMS* III.3.22). He then refers to a "weak" person who cannot control his emotion in front of another person as being "like a child that has not yet gone to school" (*TMS* III.3.23).

In other words, institutional education continues practices that domestic education begins; the two are neither competitive nor completely discrete. They build off of one another to solidify each other's lessons. This is further supported by Smith's agnostic posture when pondering which of the two is more important: "Domestic education is the institution of nature; public education, the contrivance of man. It is surely unnecessary to say, which is likely to be the wisest" (*TMS* VI.ii.1.10).

With an eye toward sympathy — prioritizing *TMS* — the problem with foreign education or sending children abroad is that they lose the capacity to judge appropriate behavior using the standards expected in the family and the community; they lose the capacity for even immature rational adjudication or moral judgment. The child, according to *LJ*, ought to be in frequent communication with the parent in order to curb his or her excesses. The parent, in return, must accept the responsibility of observing the child even if it means their "going to ruin before his eyes" (*WN* V.i.f.36).[11]

It is Smith's argument that education — his term despite the familial acculturation that takes place in the home — is the security that ensures that students remain virtuous; an inadequate education results in the deprivation of moral capabilities. Separation from the educational institution, in combination with separation from the familial structure that also enforces virtuous activity, is often too much for young people, and they begin to lose hold of the lessons they have learned regarding moral behavior.

Recall that, for Smith, familial affection is "habitual sympathy" (*TMS* VI.ii.1.5–8). Education solidifies the moral lessons that stem from judgment, which are the result of the capacity to sympathize. It also ensures that children become useful members of society. Here Smith is not arguing that education is good per se for the child, although he does suggest that education is a good in itself. Instead, he is making the point that a child's education benefits everyone — this explains his references to the 'utility' of a child's physical dependency on his or her parents (cf.: *WN* V.i.f.61, *LJ(B)* 330). It also shows the connection between learning and universal opulence — that education is one of the preconditions for the successful functioning of the invisible hand. His purpose, as we shall see, is to further the argument that the sovereign will have a duty to help defray the cost of education for those who need assistance. Social need is a necessary, but not sufficient, condition for demanding the community contribution that is required to educate the lower classes.

In his discussion of the history of education Smith writes that "in every age and country of the world men must have attended to the characters, designs, and actions of one another, and many reputable rules and maxims for the conduct of human life, must have been laid down and approved of by common consent" (WN V.i.f.25). There are two points in this selection which find their origin in *TMS*: first, that morality is based on approval and, second, that moral rules are laid down and assented to with serious attention to other people's actions and characters. Moral rules are context dependent.[12] Without the view from *TMS*, without prioritizing Smith's moral psychology, the phrase "approved of by common consent" would sound much more like the social contract than Smith would likely have supported.

What is relevant here is the intimate connection between society, socialization, and education in maintaining a moral structure. In this section Smith explains that writing, immediately upon its invention, was used as a tool to enumerate and elucidate the rules of morality. In sharp contrast to his comments on the origin of language, Smith does not discuss the evolution of linguistic sophistication in WN; he simply points out that as soon as it was possible, writing was used to codify morality. It was, he argues, the philosophers who attempted to systematize the moral rules (WN V.i.f.25). He then takes the opportunity to offer a history of the structure of the discipline of philosophy.

Smith elaborates on the ancient division of philosophy into three sections (natural philosophy, moral philosophy, and logic), then laments the mistake of the European universities in extending that division to five by adding ontology and metaphysics (WN V.i.f. 25–29). He concludes with a scathing indictment of the European university, then counters with his history of Greek and Roman education (WN V.i.f.28–37). By highlighting historical development Smith shows how changes in education have caused changes in moral standards. Without proper education—understood institutionally here—moral development is severely impeded. As is his wont, Smith uses history to explain and justify change. He assumes that the evolution of educational methods is as natural as the evolution of society. It is related to progress.

Some of Smith's comments on schooling run counter to modern sensibilities. For example, Smith's advice against sending students abroad immediately after university may sound odd to today's parent. In the contemporary world, study abroad is usually encouraged, and it seems clear that, at least in the present day, parents' motivation for doing this would be to expose their children to different perspectives and a wider range of information as well as to prepare them for participation in a global community and marketplace. Travel abroad helps students to learn languages (even if badly, as Smith suggests) and to look at the world with a more critical eye. Many parents also believe that by remaining in one location or one occupation from very early on, children will develop prejudices that they will be unable to see through or be limited in what they believe themselves to be capable of. This attitude takes a more cosmopolitan view of what it means to be a moral and complete person, representative of the global mosaic pluralism that is taken for granted in many parts of today's world. However, a version of this was not foreign to either Smith or his contemporaries.

Smith's texts reveal many of these same concerns: the need for a wide viewpoint, the ability to counter one's prejudices and inaccurate self-image, and the necessity of coming to terms with diversity in the world. There is also no textual evidence to suggest that his prohibition on traveling reflects cultural arrogance, as some might suggest—he did not caution students about going to "inferior" or "backward" countries. Instead, the difference between Smith's approach and the more modern attitude seems rooted in two issues. The first is a matter of class. Boarding schools are and have always been the luxury of the wealthy. Smith himself was sent away to Glasgow College at the age of fourteen and, as an adult, he researched and wrote part of *The Wealth of Nations* while traveling abroad as the private tutor of the Duke of Buccleuch. As discussed above, the most educated people in Scotland came from a wealthy class, and Smith may be responding to student indulgences that come from that type of school as well as to the attention that the duke would have received. Leathers and Raines refer to some of these extravagances in their analysis of Glasgow university life.[13] In modern times, however, when universal schooling is at least the stated goal for most industrial countries, the benefits of traveling abroad are usually thought to apply to everyone, and only a minority of students is treated in the indulgent manner Smith was accustomed to.

A second difference between Smith's comments and contemporary attitudes about foreign travel is the consequence of the modern public's commitment to the contemporary version of diversity and multiculturalism. Education for citizenship in the United States, for example, is very much concerned with overcoming traditional lines of ethnic and cultural difference.[14] As I addressed earlier, Smith simply didn't have this perspective. Although he makes comments that may prefigure modern identity politics, he did not consider multiculturalism as it is now conceived.[15]

Nevertheless, as I alluded to toward the end of the previous chapter, Smith does foreshadow diversity-based education to a certain degree; he seems to agree with the modern belief that motivates today's parents to send their children abroad. Smith argues that most people are surrounded by the same experiences day after day and that such a situation destroys both political unity and individual rationality and judgment. Industrialization and regular employment only complicate matters, as we have seen in chapter 3.[16] Therefore, a closer look at the first few pages of WN is called for. While Rothschild is correct that Smith never makes an economic argument for education to support prosperity, he does look at the effects education has on labor. As I have shown, the beginning of WN is intertwined with a discussion of its importance; both the "Introduction and Plan of This Work" and the first paragraph of the first book are preoccupied with a worker's "skill, dexterity, and judgment" (WN *intro.*3, I.i.1), three capacities that are cultivated through experience and education. The word 'education' itself appears in the third paragraph: for Smith it is education specifically that, supplied by the division of labor, allows a pin factory to increase its production from less than twenty to forty-eight thousand pins per day (WN I.i.3). Thus even the division of labor is enabled by educative elements.

The connection between the division of labor and education lies in the practice of specialization. While the low-production factory employs individuals who make complete pins, the factory that produces forty-eight thousand divides the manufacture into "about eighteen distinct operations." Sometimes each is performed by a different person and sometimes a single worker does "two or three of them" (WN I.i.3). According to Smith, repeated familiarity with a particular process "necessarily increases very much the dexterity of the workman" (WN I.i.6). As a result, "men are much more likely to discover easier and readier methods of attaining any object, when the whole attention of their minds is directed towards that single object, than when it is dissipated among a great variety of things" (WN I.i.8). Increased dexterity and familiarity bring increased innovation, better judgment, and more sophisticated rational capacities.[17]

Despite Christopher Wince's observation that Smith distinguishes between mental and physical forms of labor, Smith's discussion of the division of labor in general glorifies the potential intellect of the common worker.[18] Smith argues that "a great part of the machines made use of in those manufactures in which labour is most subdivided, were originally the inventions of common workmen, who, being each of them employed in some very simple operation, naturally turned their thoughts towards finding out easier and readier methods of performing it" (WN I.i.8). As an illustration he offers a compelling example of a young boy employed to operate a fire engine — again, a coal-fueled furnace — who, out of self-interest, "observed that, by tying a string from the handle of the valve, which opened this communication, to another part of the machine, the valve would open and shut without his assistance, and leave him at liberty to divert himself with his play-fellows" (WN I.i.8). It seems no accident that the combination of specialization and self-interest leads to the boy's liberty, but we should not take this point too far. It is unclear whether the decision to play can be equated with the perfect liberty of changing one's profession, although, in a certain sense, this is exactly what the boy did, temporarily at least.

Those who doubt that Smith sees an intellectual or educative component in specialization need only read the paragraph that follows his example of the fire engine. He compares the mechanical innovation of the common worker with the speculative innovation of the philosopher: "In the progress of society, philosophy or speculation becomes, like every other employment, the principal or sole trade and occupation of a particular class of citizens. Like every other employment too, it is subdivided into a great number of different branches, each of which affords occupation to a peculiar tribe or class of philosophers; and this subdivision of employment in philosophy, as well as in every other business, improves dexterity, and saves time. Each individual becomes more expert in his own peculiar branch, more work is done upon the whole, and the quantity of science is considerably increased by it" (WN I.i.9).

It is, for Smith, this specialization that, "in a well-governed society," results in the "universal opulence which extends itself to the lowest ranks of the people" (WN I.i.10). The increased abilities acquired through practice and education lead to the betterment of all, although, as we saw in the previous chapter and as we will encounter again, excessive specialization on its own will lead to very poor quality of life and low intellect for the worker "unless government takes some pains to prevent it" (WN V.i.f.50).

As further evidence that Smith refuses to see economic life as the sole criterion of quality, he asserts that if the repetition of the division of labor is all that the workers have, then their understanding will diminish. Lack of education, combined with the day-to-day experience of the division of labor, destroys a person's social, political, intellectual, and martial capacities, cultivating only a mental "torpor" (WN V.i.f.50).

Smith's criticism is not that the working classes will be misinformed or lack factual information. It is much larger and touches upon every aspect of humanity that intersects with the rational function. Smith's comments here, even in WN, refer to intellectual capacities, judgments, and moral sentiments. So, additionally, while we are once again focused on rationality, we are also immersed in Smith's response to Mandeville's critique of education for the poor; pluralism with an eye toward economic difference.

Recall that Mandeville wrote that schooling would be harmful to the laboring classes because it would make them see their life for what it really is, a life they could not escape. Smith argues the exact opposite. It is precisely because the poor have no ability to see life differently from what they experience that the state must educate its masses; it seems to be a matter of moral necessity: "But what improves the circumstances of the greater part can never be regarded as an inconveniency to the whole. No society can surely be flourishing and happy, of which the far greater part of the members are poor and miserable. It is but equity, besides, that they who feed, cloath and lodge the whole body of the people, should have such a share of the produce of their own labour as to be themselves tolerably well fed, cloathed and lodged" (WN I.viii.36).

Both expediency and "equity" make society care for the poor. Society must provide basic needs, including, but not limited to, education. Smith's call for equity makes the argument for universal opulence a moral in addition to a political one; his comments incorporate happiness and fairness, or, as Cropsey puts it, "Smith's aim" was "a free, reasonable, comfortable, and tolerant life for the whole species."[19] He makes comparable remarks at WN I.viii.44 and even more graphic ones at *LJ(B)* 330. Those highlight, as bluntly as Smith can, the loss of virtue, intelligence, parental relationships, comfort, and hope that accompanies the lack of education. Smith uses the term 'torpor' to designate a loss of rationality—it references mental stiltedness, not just ignorance, and gives further evidence that education is necessary to cultivate rational thinking.

Smith's comments on education emphasize the holistic nature of the human experience and the effects of unchecked economic influence. Smith's initial remarks regard the economic incentive parents have to sell out their children's education and ends with a polemic decrying that the people who clothe the whole world are in rags. This is the same imagery Smith used in the first citation. In the second, he adds workers' physicality to the mix, arguing that not only their relationships and virtues are at risk but also their physical health. Trapped by their day-to-day lives, they do not have the will or energy to better themselves in a way that will help counter the wide range of negative effects. Moreover, these unhealthy consequences have an impact on workers and their employers alike.

Smith graphically illustrates a central difficulty of commercial society, one that will eventually become Marx's notion of alienation.[20] The laboring classes need an education to better themselves, their intellectual and rational capacities, their conditions, and the circumstances of those around them. They need to perform better for economic advancement, both their own and their employers.' Yet they have not the time, energy, incentive, or financial ability to resolve these issues. Thus, Smith argues, the sovereign must relieve some of these burdens. In book 5, in his discussion of the nature of government, Smith offers a controversial prescription, one I have alluded to already: the sovereign must subsidize public education to help those who, at this point, cannot help themselves, showing Smith's interest in pluralism is about governance of difference, not simply mitigating its brute fact.

EDUCATION AS A PUBLIC WORK

I argue that, for Smith, education improves the mental preconditions for rational thought. Individuals have a multiplicity of motivations derived from passionate primitives that must be negotiated. Analogously, the human senses and capacities for language and thought, while inborn and immature at birth, are bettered through education, widely understood. When agents are skilled enough, they use these capacities and passions to create narratives that contextually communicate and adjudicate actors' and spectators' sentiments. This creates the means to overcome difference-based political disunity. Rationality and pluralism are therefore interdependent in that a person becomes more rational in the face of diverse experiences and diversity becomes more stable as a result of its rational management. However, if I am correct that Smith offers a theory of pluralism that prefigures our own, then I must show that the sovereign is directly involved in the maintenance of diversity. Modern theories of political difference recognize that it is in the best interest of the state to have a pluralistic public, and therefore the sovereign must actively pursue and cultivate such difference. Smith, as I show, argues similarly, as illustrated by his remarks on class.

According to Smith, while the upper classes have time for leisure, learning, and speculation, the lower classes "have little time to spare for education" (WN V.i.f.53). Their lives are a struggle. Lower-class parents barely have enough money for subsistence, let alone education, and their occupation is monotonous and simple and gives "little exercise to the understanding" (WN V.i.f.53).

These circumstances are overwhelming. They interfere with self-betterment, personal relationships, familial life, and an individual's health and well-being. As we have seen, they also destroy the different classes' ability to sympathize with each other, a fact that may lead to factionalism and other forms of social division. Smith, in response, wants to ease the burden of class difference but doesn't want to abandon the class system upon which the market depends, a division he seems to regard as inevitable (WN V.i.b.2–3). There is a tension here between liberal equality and conservative protection of extant social structures. Smith's solution is to promote both physical and economic mobility; at the heart of his embryonic pluralism is also the beginnings of a discussion about equality of opportunity. Smith's pluralistic celebration of difference, as some might call modern diversity theories, rests on the demand that people have access to both necessities and moral acknowledgment, regardless of their economic circumstances. This may not be as much as diversity theorists want today, but compared to, for example, the Dickensian England that would soon follow, it is fairly radical.

Smith, therefore, advises that the sovereign should contribute to the education of the poor: "But though the common people cannot, in any civilized society, be so well instructed as people of some rank and fortune, the most essential parts of education, however, to read, write, and account, can be acquired at so early a period of life, that the greater part even of those who are to be bred to the lowest occupations, have time to acquire them before they can be employed in those occupations. For a very small expence the publick can facilitate, can encourage, and can even impose upon almost the whole body of the people, the necessity of acquiring those most essential parts of education" (WN V.i.f.54).

As referenced in my earlier discussion, here we encounter Smith's call for social responsibility when it comes to education. It is very explicit on Smith's part: the "publick" has a responsibility to both defray educational costs and encourage schooling and can do so for only "a small expense."

WN is, first and foremost, a blueprint for a commercial society—a society that, in Smith's terms, allows perfect liberty for individuals (WN I.vii.6). We have seen how the market creates "concord" among people and how it contributes to "universal opulence," but, famously, it also gives the individual more freedom. Under Smith's ideal, people are free to pursue their own interest in their own ways as long as they do not violate the laws of justice (WN IV.ix.51).[21] Is his call for public support of education therefore a violation of his theory of natural liberty? Or, to ask it another way, are libertarians correct to suggest that the use of taxation and other means of collecting public funds to finance education is a violation of a person's freedom? I argue that, for Smith, they are not. As Jacob Viner put it, in 1927, "Adam Smith was not a doctrinaire advocate of laissez faire. He saw a wide and elastic range of activity for government, and he was prepared to extend it even farther if government, by improving its standards of competence, honesty, and public spirit, showed itself entitled to wider responsibilities."[22] Or, to quote Cropsey, "It goes without saying that Smith did not assume all men to be perfectly wise in their own affairs. The *Wealth of Nations* is replete with instances of individuals misunderstanding their interest . . . the success of the liberal system at large requires some dependence upon the 'wisdom of government' to indicate, and even to make, sane decisions for people."[23] And, as Young points out, Smith does suggest that there are times when the government can demand beneficence from the people, as long as this action is approved by the citizenry (*TMS* II.ii.1.8).[24] He explains, "It is doubly culpable to omit acts of benevolence when the sovereign commands them. . . . Distributive justice . . . is both a private and a public responsibility."[25] Or, as Smith himself writes in *WN*, "Every tax . . . is to the person who pays it a badge, not of slavery, but of liberty. It denotes that he is subject to government, indeed, but that, as he has some property, he cannot himself be the property of a master" (*WN* V.ii.g.11). In short, Smith's use of natural and perfect liberty references an *economic* doctrine, not a theory of negative freedom reminiscent of Hobbes's freedom of restraint.[26] It suggests neither that any form of taxation is a violation of a person's rights nor that governmental manipulations for the general welfare are not *sometimes* warranted.

To elaborate: Smith's definition of natural liberty precedes his account of the duty of the sovereign. It reads as follows: "Every man, as long as he does not violate the laws of justice, is left perfectly free to pursue his own interest his own way, and to bring both his industry and capital into competition with those of any other man, or order of men. The sovereign is completely discharged from a duty, in the attempting to perform which he must always be exposed to innumerable delusions, and for the proper performance of which no human wisdom or knowledge could ever be sufficient; the duty of superintending the industry of private people, and of directing it towards the employments most suitable to the interest of the society" (*WN* IV.ix.51).

These comments are consistent with his remarks about the invisible hand in *WN*, the justification of which is punctuated by his own experience: "I have never known much good done by those who affected to *trade* for the publick good. It is an affectation, indeed, not very common among merchants, and very few words need be employed in dissuading them from it" (*WN* IV.ii.9, emphasis added). The key word here is "trade." Smith's comments focus on merchants. He is not addressing politicians or those engaged in charity works.

Smith's references to 'perfect liberty' are also consistent with the economic limitation of taxation. He defines the term as the condition under which someone can "change his trade as often as he pleases" (*WN* I.vii.6), or, as he writes elsewhere, "where every man was perfectly free both to chuse what occupation he thought proper, and to change it as often as he thought proper" (*WN* I.x.a.1). Later on, he adds that more liberty brings more trade and cheaper goods (*WN* IV.ix.16).

As Viner enumerates, Smith proposes four main economic reforms that require abolishing such practices as apprenticeships, primogeniture, and excessive duties: freedom to choose occupations, to trade land, to trade within a country, and to trade with foreign lands.[27] This does not include a call for laissez-faire approaches to education. He also acknowledges Smith's call for publicly subsidized schooling,[28] but he does argue that subsidy, along with some other prescriptions, is inconsistent with his outline of the sovereign's duties.[29] He asserts that Smith ends up abandoning his own criteria for governmental support.

To rephrase the question of taxation, then, we can ask whether Viner's interpretation is correct. Is Smith inconsistent? To answer this, we must look more deeply into Smith's criteria for public works.

Smith articulates three duties of the sovereign that he regards as "plain and intelligible to common understandings": protect the society from foreign invasion, protect individuals from "injustice or oppression" by other citizens, and create and maintain "certain publick works and certain publick institutions, which it can never be for the interest of any individual, or small number of individuals, to erect and maintain; because the profit could never repay the expence to any individual or small number of individuals, though it may frequently do much more than repay it to a great society" (WN IV.ix.51).

According to Smith, the sovereign must maintain armies, police, public works, public schools, and religious education. In each instance, he adds, these functions ought to be partially financed by the general community but funded to a larger extent by those who use them most.[30] Andrew Skinner tells us that Smith consistently argues that "the state will have to ensure provision where market forces would fail to do so."[31] Furthermore, in each instance Smith tries to balance individual and public responsibility. He takes into account the practicality of maintaining public works with the level of enthusiasm a sovereign must put forth to encourage people's participation in them. As we shall see, he offers practical discussions that are informed by philosophical prescription; they are pragmatic as well as normative.

According to Smith, the defense of society and the chief magistrate should be publicly funded through taxation, since they affect everyone equally (WN V.i.i.1). The main financial burden of the administration of justice should fall upon those who "make it necessary to seek redress or protection from the courts of justice" and "those whom the courts of justice either restore to their rights, or maintain in their rights" (WN V.i.i.2). Society ought to carry the whole financial burden only in those instances when the convicted cannot. Smith continues by asserting that individual municipalities should pay their own costs and that maintenance for roads and communications ought to be paid by those who use them directly and frequently (WN V.i.d).

Interestingly, Smith ties taxation required for roads to the *value* of the goods transported and not to the wear and tear associated with weight. Since, ultimately, it is the consumer who pays the taxes on cargo via price, Smith argues that light but precious goods should be charged more than heavy but inexpensive goods; otherwise more of the burden of repair would be placed on those who are least able to pay for it (WN V.i.d.13). This suggests a priority of equity over use and is consistent with the prescription that convicts who cannot pay court costs should not have to; it is also consistent with prioritizing a moral system over an economic one.

Smith makes a similar prescription in his comments on education finance. It is not the frequency of teaching that raises its cost; it is the quality and outcome of the education. As a result, Smith offers an extended discussion regarding the outlay of education for particular professions as compared to their potential salary (as well as the variety of subjects of study required for several specific occupations). In *LJ(A)* he argues that the expense of much trade education can be covered by the employer with an eye toward the future. Financial investment will, in most cases, be returned to those who are willing to make the expense (*LJ(A)* vi.60–67). He makes the same comments in a more abbreviated form in WN, comparing investment in workers to investment in machines (WN I.x.b.6).

Smith's comment in WN references apprenticeships, a unique case in this discussion since, even though they are a form of education, they are not considered a public work. Apprenticeships are not to be maintained by the sovereign, Smith observes, but are regulated by guilds or businesses. Thus that discussion is found not in the comments about the role of the sovereign (WN V.i) but in the first book of his investigation of labor and its value (WN I.x).

For Smith, apprenticeships are "the epitome of the restrictions of the principles of competition and liberty even though" they had originally "been established with the purpose of ensuring quality";[32] the cost of an apprenticeship is part of the cost of labor and production. He acknowledges that "during the continuance of the apprenticeship, the whole labour of the apprentice belongs to his master" (WN I.x.b.8), an indication of why apprenticeships are not considered a public work. This is not to suggest that apprenticeships do not benefit the general public; it is only a reminder that this form of education is commercial and not the concern of the sovereign. Whatever impact they have is felt through the market.

As Teixeira notes, Smith preferred learning with a strong practical emphasis: "On-the-job training, and learning-by-doing, seemed to be much more important and much more effective in increasing workers' productivity."[33] Nevertheless, here Smith implicitly makes the distinction between what has traditionally been called a liberal education and what would now be considered vocational training. Liberal education is concerned with the human experience—the cultivation of a person as a moral agent and social being—and vocational training is concerned with commercial activity—the cultivation of skills required for workers and merchants. It is for this reason that Smith highlights the role of economic incentives that motivates the apprentice. The apprentice's impetus for pursuing education is different from that of students in general; apprenticeships often promote idle character (WN I.x.c.14).

The two remaining public works under the auspices of the sovereign are institutions for education and institutions for religious study, although they are both considered by Smith to have educational purposes. Once again, ensuring education is not simply ensuring any teaching; Smith wants to cultivate quality instruction, and to do such a thing, he argues that incentives are necessary. Therefore, rather than be salaried or tenured, educators, Smith believes, should be paid per student or per achievement, and each student should have the opportunity to choose the educator with whom she or he wishes to study. Smith believes that opening some areas of the educational sphere to the free market will weed out the less able educators and ensure that each person gets the best education he or she desires. He writes that educators must engage in work of a "known value" in free competition with others vying for the same employment. They will, as a result, be motivated to "work with a certain degree of exactness" (WN V.i.f.4).

Smith is optimistic about student interest. Although he acknowledges that the very young might have to be forced to attend school, students over the age of thirteen can motivate themselves. Smith writes, "Where the masters, however, really perform their duty, there are no examples, I believe, that the greater part of the students ever neglect theirs. No discipline is ever requisite to force attendance upon lectures which are really worth the attending, as is well known wherever any such lectures are given" (WN V.i.f.15). As remarked earlier, this speaks to the natural inclination individuals have to learn that which is worthwhile.

Furthermore, Smith argues, public education is of much lesser quality than private education, probably because it is not subject to the market. In ancient Rome, he argues, unlike in Greece, there were no public law schools, yet the Roman system proved itself much superior (WN V.i.f.44.). Additionally, as mentioned twice before, in Smith's time, since there was no public education for women and since women were educated in the home, there is "nothing useless, absurd, or fantastical in the common course of their education" (WN V.i.f.47).

As a supplement to market-based educational reforms, however, Smith insists that it is the state's obligation to protect the "great body of the people" and to help an individual "exert his understanding, or to exercise his invention" (*WN* V.i.f.782). To fulfill this responsibility, the sovereign, as I have observed, must educate the working classes. Smith believes, therefore, that the state should provide incentives to encourage study. He recounts (without commitment but also without criticism) ancient Rome's state requirement that, independent of the lack of public schools, the "citizen should fit himself for defending [Rome] in war" (*WN* V.i.f.41). He also writes (again, with no explicit commitment yet with a tone of approval) of the "law of Solon" legislating that those children who were not educated were released from the responsibility of caring for their parents during their old age (*WN* V.i.f.42–43). For Smith, education seems to be a sort of continuity between generations; a social contract, if you will, that represents the responsibilities of parent to child and the reciprocal obligations incurred by that child.[34] Thus he writes in *TMS*, "The laws of all civilized nations oblige parents to maintain their children, and children to maintain their parents, and impose upon men many other duties of beneficence" (*TMS* II.ii.1.8).

Solon the Athenian was appointed archon of the city in 594 B.C.E. to help prevent a civil war. He attempted to "balance political power between rich and poor" by allowing for "upward social mobility." Under Solon, the poorest class was excluded from holding public office, but since Solon prohibited "direct taxes on income," the poor had the potential to increase their income and become eligible at some point.[35]

Smith mentions Solon twice in his published works, once in *WN* (at the location above) and once in *TMS*, during a discussion of how the statesman, when unable to provide a perfect system of laws, should still aim to provide the best possible laws he or she can (*TMS* VI.ii.2.16). In both instances the use of Solon highlights an imperfection. It is likely an indication of Smith's belief that, although his system is not perfect, by maintaining some semblance of an education for all, the quality of society will always push toward the better as opposed to the worse. It is also a reference to the role of ideals in rational judgment.

Recall that the impartial spectator is the attempt to reach an ideal objectivity that is limited by human capacities. That which is imagined is limited by the abilities of the imaginer. Analogously, Smith's use of Solon seems to suggest that a utopia is impossible and that the best possible political system is flawed, but only made better by acknowledging the flaw, and by creating institutions that recognize imperfections and act accordingly. Most of the imperfections Smith addresses in *WN* revolve around the differential between differing economic classes.

For Smith, as we have seen, education helps bridge the gap between the classes—yet another reason to invoke Solon in the discussion since Solon was so aware of class conflict. It is, Smith suggests, a necessity to which both the wealthy and the poor should have access. He argues that the wealthy will be compelled to educate themselves and their children both by status and in preparation for their profession, then adds that the leisure of the rich makes room for personal betterment (WN V.i.f.52).

With this background, we can now revisit Viner's observation that Smith's prescriptions for economic support of educational institutions by the sovereign are inconsistent. Again, I suggest that, regarding Smith's overall philosophical perspective, they are not. In all of his economic prescriptions, as we have seen, he prioritizes equity over use when morality or politics requires it. He financially supports those things that promote social unity and mobility, and he recognizes that there are spheres of education—apprenticeships, for example— that are not subject to subsidy. He has therefore subdivided education on the basis of its commercial justification and offered a consistent argument for state support based on moral as well as social and political grounds.

But what of Smith's *economic* prescriptions in WN? Do they also support his call for sovereign support? In this case Smith's text is a bit more ambiguous. In the passage outlining the sovereign's duties, the standard that Smith articulates for governmental economic intervention requires, as we have seen, that the endeavor in question be too large or costly for an individual or small group to recoup their losses and to earn an acceptable profit, "though it may frequently do much more than repay it to a great society" (WN IV.ix.51). In other words, the sovereign is responsible for projects of great public utility whose profit margins are too small to provide incentive for private investors—a market-failure standard that, Viner argues, Smith states then "completely ignores."[36]

Let us suppose for the time being that Viner is correct and that Smith is inconsistent in his prescription regarding government funding of a wide range of institutions. Smith does appear to have two standards, one that he articulates in his discussion of the sovereign—public works must be too costly for individuals or groups—and one which he assumes in his discussion of specific examples— public works must be profitable for the government. If this is the case and if Smith sees the actual criteria of public expense or education as the government being both trustworthy and able to earn a profit, then Smith's readers can take issue with his stated criteria for the sovereign activities, but they still cannot deny that he calls for sovereign-supported education. While his motivations for breaking this standard would, in this case, remain unknown, evidence permits us to speculate that he thought schooling was too important for the poor and for society as a whole to be left *solely* to the market. It repays a great society, as Smith might put it, leading to Viner's related claim that "the modern advocate of laissez faire who objects to government participation in business on the ground that it is an encroachment upon a field reserved by nature for private enterprise cannot find support for this argument in the *Wealth of Nations.*"[37]

On the other hand, one might argue, as I would, that institutions for the education of the laboring classes actually do meet Smith's standard for economic intervention, even if he is not explicit about it. While expensive private schools may be profit-driven enterprises, it is unlikely that a school made up of largely poor and working-class students can be driven by tuition, particularly any school in an underpopulated rural area. The parents of the students would simply not have the money to pay large enough fees for operating costs. Its founders could neither recoup their costs nor earn a significant profit. In this case, Smith would be entirely consistent in calling for public support, and Viner would be wrong in arguing that, at least in the case of education, Smith has ignored his standard.

Regardless of which interpretation one adopts, the end point remains the same: there is no evidence to suggest that Smith asks his readers to disregard his call for sovereign support of education for the masses, just as there is no evidence to suggest his public policy is a violation of his system of natural liberty. While it may be a violation of the articulated purpose of the criteria for sovereign involvement, it does not violate the standards of trade Smith sets forth. As Viner himself summarizes, "The *Wealth of Nations*, though it was from one point of view only a segment of a larger and systematic treatise on social philosophy, was at the same time a tract for the times, a specific attack on certain types of government activity which Smith was convinced, on both a priori and empirical grounds, operated against national prosperity, namely, bounties, duties, and prohibitions in foreign trade; apprenticeship and settlement laws; legal monopolies; laws of succession hindering free trade in land. Smith's primary objective was to secure the termination of *these* activities of government. His wider generalizations were invoked to support the attack on *these* political institutions. Everything else was to a large degree secondary."[38]

Notice Viner's acknowledgment of the priority of *TMS*. WN serves two purposes: it is a tract for its times, but it is also "a segment of a larger and systematic treatise on social philosophy."

Returning to the topic at hand, our examination is not yet complete. Smith's economic prescriptions for education do not end here. While schooling for the laboring classes should be subsidized by the state, this cost will be balanced. The society, as a whole, should contribute money, but, as we have also seen, in order to ensure competition and quality of education, those who attend school should be required to pay a small fee to their teachers (WN V.i.f.55).

Whatever subsidy the sovereign offers to the school, the salary of the master is to be supplemented by contributions from, presumably, the parents whose children attend his or her classes. I use the term 'presumably' because Smith is not as clear as he could be about where the additional funds come from. He is clear that they do not come from the public, but they could be provided by corporate or charitable organizations; Smith simply does not tell us. The upshot, however, is that Smith seems to assert that infrastructure, texts, and general school supplies are to be provided by the sovereign, whereas only the salary of the teacher is to require additional contribution. The justification for the increased income of the school master is one based on quality control, while the justification for governmental financial support is based on the economic and social needs of the poor.

In short, given the question of whether or not Smith sees the state or the market as financing education, the answer is unequivocal: *both*. The state provides its infrastructure, and the market improves its quality. Is this position incoherent or denigrating to the market? No. Smith is setting up what Jerry Evensky calls "a screen on market access," a moderate market-influenced approach that ensures basic quality and adequate funding by marshaling both competition and government financing in order to "secure a public good, an educated citizenry, not a private monopoly."[39] While some may see this as troublesome, it is neither incoherent nor particularly uncommon.

First, it describes Smith's own institutions. As Leathers and Raines explain, this was common practice for Scottish universities of Smith's time.[40] Smith might have been modeling the Scottish education that he was so complimentary of. Second, the twenty-first-century American public education system also operates on a mixture of market and sovereign contributions. Public universities receive funding from their states but pursue grants, tuition dollars, donations, and corporate sponsors to enhance their budgets. Elementary, middle, and high schools regularly join their university counterparts in encouraging private entities such as fast food and soda companies to sell their wares in the hallways and lunchrooms in exchange for a commission. Some schools have accepted corporate-sponsored textbooks, and it is quite common for school sports teams to sell advertising space during their games. While some have taken issue with these methods of fundraising, their propriety does not concern us here. My point is simply that Smith's mixed solution for the funding of education is both plausible and, in his Scotland and in the modern-day United States, commonplace.[41]

Regarding mandatory education for all—also common in the United States and most other industrial countries—Smith seems to be of mixed feeling, however. He speaks of offering the poor "small premiums" and "little badges of distinction" in order to encourage their children's education (WN V.i.f.56). He also suggests instituting an educational requirement and sometimes a probationary period before permitting freedom of corporation, trade, or the holding of certain offices (WN V.i.f.57, WN V.i.g.14). These citations reflect Smith's desire to cultivate universal education. Yet he falls short of making schooling obligatory. Children receive gifts for good schoolwork, and adults have access to trade. But the determined person could abstain from attending school without breaking the law.

Skinner suggests that compulsory education would "indicate a major modification to the claim of individual freedom."[42] Whether he is correct depends on how limiting one sees Smith's comments as being. Again, no adult is *forced* to take the proposed exams. They are obligated to do so only if they wish to establish a corporation or trade in a village or town, or be eligible for office in a range of professions. This might easily be interpreted as establishing a body of minimal business standards akin to those that underlie our contemporary licensing or certification practices.

If natural liberty presumes that all individuals, regardless of qualification, have an inalienable right to trade and choose their professions as they see fit, then Skinner is right that Smith would be inconsistent were he to make education obligatory. The question for interpretation is whether Smith thinks that a system of perfect liberty *presumes* universal education or *leads to it*. If it presumes universal education—that interested individuals ought to be able to pass certification exams after they have been educated—then perfect liberty is compatible with mandatory education because those who want to meet certain requirements can. However, if it presumes that perfect liberty ought to exist prior to universal education—that the freedom to choose one's profession predates a person's ability to pass such tests—then Smith's standards would be violated by mandatory education requirements because they act as barriers to meeting one's desires.

I would argue that Smith presumes the former, that perfect liberty is achieved only when the universal public is educated and when people are rational, competent, at least minimally virtuous, and abiding by the rules of justice. This could be considered a *self-consciously* correcting rather than simply a self-correcting aspect of the market—I follow up on this point in the next chapter—and is the reason I suggest that education is a necessary prerequisite for a properly functioning market. It ties in to morality, pluralism, and rationality.

In both *TMS* and *WN* Smith is trying to develop individuals' capacity to make choices that would allow *for* the capacity to choose one's profession, not just the liberty to do so—a point made clear by not subsuming his moral psychology to the market model.

Smith is clear that rational moral judgment is distinct from the faculty of reason; it is not something someone is born with complete but is made and cultivated over time. Smith is concerned with what it means to be 'informed' in a system built on informed consent. For him, education provides a benefit to the state for little cost and, therefore, funding of public educational institutions for the young is a well-regarded trade-off. The cost of educating the poor is small. The logistics behind "establishing in every parish or district a little school" (V.i.f.55) are simple and easy, and in return the state receives no small benefit, namely, its citizens are less susceptible to "the delusions of enthusiasm and superstition." An educated people is "more decent and orderly than an ignorant and stupid one," and its individuals have a greater sense of personal responsibility and respect. They see through "the interested complaints of faction and sedition" and are "less apt to be misled into any wanton or unnecessary opposition to the measures of government" (WN V.i.f.61).

Smith sees education as a tool for equality, stability, self-respect, and respect for others. He sees factionalism, superstition, and low self-image as burdens on society. Educational institutions can help instill the proper knowledge and self-image of children at a young age, but as children grow they are more susceptible to different and even dangerous forces. Thus I would suggest that Smith sees education as a necessary precondition for perfect liberty and not a consequence of it. And, as he often does, Smith appeals to what is right in addition to what is practical. He remarks that even if it were not helpful to educate "the inferior ranks of people," their education "would still deserve [the sovereign's] attention" (WN V.i.f.61).

Smith addresses another kind of education, one that bridges the passage on mandatory examinations cited above with comments on curriculum. Smith believes that the sovereign has a significant interest in supporting and guiding religious education as basic schooling. These recommendations for the funding of religious education are similar to those regarding secular education. Clergy members are like teachers whose rewards should depend partly on salaries but mostly on fees in order to ensure quality because their jobs depend on "industry and reputation" (WN V.i.g.2).[43]

There are three aspects in which religious education differs from secular education: aim, breadth of influence, and depth of influence. First, the aim of religious instruction is, according to Smith, not to create good citizens in this world but to prepare them for another and a better world in the hereafter (WN V.i.g.1). Second, religious education is for both youth and adults. Third, religious education has a depth which traditional secular education does not have. Smith asserts that many people believe that "the authority of religion is superior to every other authority" (WN V.i.g.17).

By highlighting the supreme authority of religion, Smith cautions the reader in regard to its distinctness from the sovereign. He argues that the goal of religious institutions is to maintain their authority, not to cultivate sympathy, and, as a result, the authority of religion is often falsely deemed to be of more importance than the judgment of the impartial spectator. This is problematic for a variety of reasons, not the least of which is that, for Smith, such authority neither is built on experience and judgments nor relies on the moral rules that stem from them—religious commitment is irrational.[44] It is instead founded on the influence of the institution, its doctrines, and its leaders. Thus its followers are susceptible to fanaticism: the inability to see the impartial spectator correctly. Violence, conflict, factionalism, and fanaticism are the impartial spectator's greatest enemies (TMS III.3.43). And, as Robert Mitchell tells us, political wisdom disappears in "times of public discontent, faction, and disorder" (TMS VI.ii.2.12). He writes, "'Amidst the turbulence and disorder of faction,' the love of beautiful systems—which under normal conditions, further civilized the world—could become separated from both morality and political stability."[45]

To this end, Smith paints a history of competition between the church and educational institutions. In concluding his account of the church from Rome onward, Smith illustrates that when churches are endowed with large benefices (assets or their revenue that provide money for church officials), they drain the universities of their scholars "before they can have acquired experience and knowledge enough to be of much use to it" (WN V.i.g.39). This is in contrast to Greece and Rome, where the vast majority of "men of letters" had been "either publick or private teachers; generally either of philosophy or of rhetorick" (WN V.i.g.40). Smith does acknowledge that the church can attract great names, but only when it can ensure that they are "the most useful to the publick" and not because of the truths that church doctrines espouse (WN V.i.g.40).

For Smith, extreme religious claims corrupt not only education but the political process as a whole. When religious influence is too great, he writes, the sovereign is made to cater to fanatics, even though spiritual matters are rightly outside the influence of the sovereign. This likely pushes the good of the society aside for the alleged good of the sect. In order to remain in power during times of political conflict, the politician must cater to the sect even more so by aligning himself or herself to a particular group and by espousing their specific views.

The sovereign retains authority, and in return the politician grants the sect certain demands, the first of which is generally the destruction of their adversaries (WN V.i.g.7), a violation of the diversity of the state.

As Smith describes it, the sovereign finds it very difficult to compete with religion since theology promises rewards the state cannot offer. Many people give loyalty to their sect before they give it to the society in which they live. This loyalty takes all forms, and, as the members grow more loyal, the mundane aspects of the religion become exponentially more important than even the largest concern of the state (WN V.i.g.7).

According to Smith, clergy members, like educators, should be subject to appointment and reappointment by the people of their sect. In order for clergy to keep their positions, they must show superiority over all other candidates. The people must be convinced that the candidate is the best one for the job and is best representing the religion at hand. But this leads to political difficulties. In campaigning for support, both for themselves and for their religion, the clergy and the religion, Smith believes, necessarily and intentionally breed fanaticism. In order to preserve their influence in popular elections, clergy are pressured to appear extreme and must therefore encourage fanaticism in order to retain loyalty for themselves (WN V.i.g.36).

In this system, Smith argues, the religious sect that backs the winning party has more influence than any other sect. It grows stronger and richer. It may, in turn, force nonbelievers to abide by their religious doctrines and declare the clergy to be exempt from the secular jurisdiction. The more people become exempt from secular jurisdiction, the more insecure a society is and the worse off its citizens are, since liberty, reason, and happiness exist only under the able protection of civil government (WN V.I.g.24).

The system that results is very different from that of the unified society of sympathetic citizens sought by Smith. It may be diverse, but it is nonpluralist. It is a system in which one faction has more power than all others, one group of individuals has advantage politically and economically over others, the perfect liberty inherent in the free-market system is at risk, education is denied or repressed under false doctrines, and the impartial spectator is rejected as a moral authority. In direct contrast, and reminiscent of Locke's *Letter on Toleration,* Smith tells us, "Articles of faith, as well as all other spiritual matters, . . . are not within the proper department of a temporal sovereign" (WN V.i.g.18). Thus, although it is true that religious intervention makes for an unstable society, it is also true, to paraphrase Smith's earlier comment regarding the basic needs of the poor, that it is but equity that the sovereign not intervene in religious matters. Once again, Smith's comments are normative as well as pragmatic.

Smith's solution is yet another example of his pluralism. First, he advocates that politicians avoid allegiance to any religious party. If politicians elude the initial appeal to religion, fanatics will never achieve the foothold that begins the downward spiral to injustice. In addition, political neutrality toward religion will ensure a level playing field and will encourage diversity and competition among religions. As increase in the number of sects reduces each one's size and power, none will be powerful enough to "disturb the publick tranquillity" (*WN* V.i.g.8), a point likely attributable to Voltaire.[46] Smith argues that these sects, being as small, weak, and marginal as they are, would necessarily moderate themselves to protect their own interest and standing in a community. Consequently, the extremists would either be motivated toward more centrist activity or, at worst, be a harmless nuisance that would still be subject to and punishable by civil laws.[47]

An additional method that discourages fanaticism is to encourage frequent public events (*WN* V.I.g.15). Smith believes that the desire for immoderate religion arises in those without recreation or without an outlet for creativity. Religion provides a sense of community for those who feel that the population is too large for them to have a sense of belonging. As we have already seen, Smith observes that large cities often lack the groups that watch and applaud an individual's moral conduct. Public festivals, gatherings, and events would offer such an opportunity as well as allow for public scrutiny of the newest religions. The new sects, he suggests, by virtue of their newness, offer more excitement and appeal. Festivals would make them open to public ridicule, a prescription he shares with Shaftesbury. Like the process of toning down one's sentiments in the search for approval, the religious sect would tone down its claims and activities in order to attract more members.

One might object that my picture of Smith's religious diversity is too contemporary. *WN*, it might be suggested, was concerned with Protestant Christian diversity, not with the encyclopedic religious conflict that today's large-scale societies face. However, there is neither textual nor biographical evidence to support this objection. Smith makes no biblical argument. He never refers to Christ, and while his history of Europe emphasizes the church (comments that seem more Catholic than Protestant), his is a history of institutional abuse, not one of belief or practice. Furthermore, we have no correspondences, comments, or anecdotes suggesting that Smith was addressing a strictly Protestant problem. The one exception is in a letter to his publisher, in which Smith remarks that he reserves the "right of private judgment for the sake of which our forefathers kicked out the Pope and the Pretender" (*Corr.* 50). However, this remark occurs in the midst of a joke and is immediately followed by the comment that he thinks his publisher is "much more infallible than the Pope." Smith, then, uncharacteristically submits to scriptural authority, illustrating that he *could have* used biblical argument had he wanted to, but he didn't.

One could object as well that modern religious diversity is too extreme to be resolved through Smith's religious festivals. This is an empirical question and one that can be answered only in comparison to the Thirty Years' War and the other conflicts of the seventeenth and eighteenth centuries. Toleration and Smith's call for religious diversity are responses to these hostilities, and there is not much compelling evidence to suggest that modern societies are worse off than Europe was before and during Smith's lifetime.

To conclude this section, we have seen how Smith's educational prescriptions connect to pluralism. The sovereign has an interest in moderating fanaticism, which fractures societies, impairs the objectivity of politicians, and interferes with individuals' rational abilities. Those susceptible to the extreme claims of immoderate religions have a much harder job adjudicating social, political, and religious claims and therefore contribute to the downfall of society. Pluralism, education, and rationality are inherently intertwined, and it seems problematic to discuss one's role in Smith's theory without talking about the others. The question now is, what does it actually mean to be educated? what areas of knowledge and skills are best suited for sympathy, religious moderation, and good citizenship in a stable society?

CURRICULUM

Haakonssen argues that "Smith is not concerned with any positive standard of education, but only with preventing men from becoming 'mutilated and deformed' in 'the proper use of the intellectual faculties.'"[48] I disagree. As I have argued earlier, for Smith, instruction is so fundamental to the development of moral judgment that one can judge the quality of the educational system by examining the moral activities of those who participated in it. As we have seen, Smith highlights this relationship by comparing the ancient Greek and Roman methods of education.

According to Smith, every citizen in ancient Greece was educated in the study of gymnastics, music, reading, writing, and "account," by which Smith likely meant basic household record keeping (WN V.i.f.39, 42). Rome educated its youth in reading, writing, account, and gymnastics—leaving out music (WN V.i.f.40, 42).

Here, Smith is explicitly evaluating curriculum for its moral outcome. He does not critique the Romans for excluding the beauty of music from education or chide them for neglecting the skills required to play an instrument. Simply put, it is excusable for the Romans to neglect musical education since, for the Greeks, music "had no great effect in mending their morals" (*WN* V.i.f.40). Smith's belief may, in part, be attributable to his skepticism about the ability of music to transmit certain sentiments. He tells us elsewhere that "when music imitates the modulations of grief and joy it either actually inspires us with those passions, or at least puts us in the mood which disposes us to conceive them." However, other passions, such as anger "and all the passions which are akin to it," are not easily communicable in this medium. On those occasions when music does communicate these "harsh and discordant" passions, it "is not the most agreeable" (*TMS* I.ii.3.6). At Glasgow College, Smith and his classmates were taught to believe that Scottish achievements in "aesthetic and antiquarian matters" made them "the authentic heirs of Roman civilization."[49] It may not be surprising, then, that Smith speaks so positively of their culture and moral system.

Consistent with Haakonssen's approach, these comments are all negative — they tell us what is not required (although, as we shall see shortly, they form the foundation of what Smith will prescribe). In contrast, his positive curricular suggestions appear in his discussion of a third method for the reduction of fanaticism. There he prescribes instruction of the masses in science and philosophy.

According to Smith, "every religion except the true" is "highly pernicious" and will promote superstition and delusion, which scientific education can counter (*WN* V.i.g.6, 14).[50] Smith argues that the more fanatical religions base themselves upon the most absurd claim and that an educated populace would not be as susceptible to inflated boasts. All individuals ought to be instructed in science and philosophy, he argues, because they offer the foundation for intellectual and moral judgment. This is consistent with Smith's comment in *HA* that "philosophy, therefore, may be regarded as one of those arts which address themselves to the imagination" (*HA* II.12).

Whereas Smith offers a clear definition of philosophy in *HA*, what he means by the term in *WN* is unclear. Griswold shows us that it certainly isn't dialogical Socratic philosophy that Smith had in mind: "Philosophy and liberal education generally assist citizens in seeing through fraudulent claims to authority but not, apparently, to evaluate the social or political system as a whole."[51] Rothschild writes, "Philosophical thought . . . for Smith . . . consists in a mild, discursive, and occasionally awe-struck scepticism . . . in which sentiments and reasons jostle together, and which is itself an amusement."[52] And Fleischacker cautions Smith's readers against understanding the notion of philosophical teaching too narrowly. He notes that Smith's colleagues offered lectures on natural science to nonacademics. Thus Smith may be "hoping that the broad vision characteristic of the academy (in his time, at least) can filter throughout society and thereby correct for the limits on people's everyday perspectives."[53] It is likely these acts of public research that MacIntyre had in mind when he portrayed the mass of people in Glasgow as showing deference to the university faculty of moral philosophy.[54]

Smith's commitment to teaching science and philosophy as a bulwark against superstition speaks to his confidence in the cultivation of reason and the ability of all rational people, not just a select few, to make correct decisions. He is expressing his optimism that *knowledge* contributes to more reasonable beliefs, implying along the way that faith can be modified through discovery. He therefore adds his name to a long list of philosophers who saw philosophy as the antidote to ignorance. As we learn from *HA*, philosophy and science do not simply provide alternative answers to life's difficult questions; they model rational thought. They illustrate how systems work and how interconnected facts are to be understood.

We now see that cultivating rationality is a means by which individuals attempt to gauge the truth (or probability) of moral, philosophical, historical, and religious positions and that these requisite skills are developed not just by education generally but by a specific curriculum that prioritizes certain subject areas. A good education makes people more rational, and the sovereign has no small interest in cultivating an educated populace. Education promotes better judgment and social unity. It cultivates a general knowledge and suggests a standard by which to judge the veracity of religious and political beliefs while preserving the individual's capacity to assent. The broader spectrum of knowledge preserves freedom by allowing individuals to not be swept up by religious fanaticism or populist political movements.

Despite their importance, philosophy and science are not the only specific subjects Smith mandates. Learning from both the Romans and the Greeks, Smith argues that the poorer classes should also be educated in reading, writing, and account (WN I.i.f.54). He then qualifies the discussion a bit, adding that a useful curricular move would be to replace the common but cursory smattering of Latin taught in schools with an elementary course of geometry and "mechanicks"—the branch of physics concerned with the behavior of physical bodies. However, these are practical considerations for Smith since he asserts that "there is scarce a common trade which does not afford some opportunities of applying" these studies (WN V.i.f.55)—this may be one of only two points where Smith offers an economic, or at least a utilitarian, justification for education. In the other, he suggests that stubborn feudal land structures can be changed without expropriation by "teach[ing] political economy to the landlords since their interests are, in fact, the same as the public interest" (WN I.xi).[55]

If all these subjects were taught, Smith writes, "the literary education of this rank of people would perhaps be as complete as it can be" (WN V.i.f.55). By literary education, Smith probably meant education from books. As we have seen, in the eighteenth century the term 'literature' represented knowledge acquired from written sources, including drama, verse, history, and a great deal of philosophy, as we understand it.

At this point I wish to insert another subject area in my discussion of curriculum. Although Smith does not list it in WN as a required subject, he makes it clear in practice that the study of arts and literature as we understand them today are necessary for moral education. To recap: Smith's continual uses of literary references throughout TMS highlight their importance; his first reference to tragedy and romance is in the fourth paragraph of the book (TMS I.i.1.4); he praises Voltaire's *Mahamet* as "perhaps the most instructive spectacle that was ever introduced upon any theatre" (TMS III.6.12); when Greek plays try to communicate physical pain, it is always other circumstances such as solitude or mortality that are "agreeable to the imagination" (TMS I.ii.1.11); and literature may be the ideal vehicle for character study since it presents all the necessary context: "The different shades and gradations of circumstance, character, and situation, to differences and distinctions which, though not imperceptible, are, by their nicety and delicacy, often altogether undefinable" (TMS VI.ii.1.22). As he summarizes, "The poets and romance writers, who best paint the refinements and delicacies of love and friendship, and of all other private and domestic affections, Racine and Voltaire; Richardson, Maurivaux, and Riccoboni; are," in cases dealing with propriety, "much better instructors than Zeno, Chrysippus, or Epictetus" (TMS III.3.14).

Smith was hopeful that the general public could be made to appreciate the arts. In discussing the methods for minimizing fanaticism, while espousing the importance of philosophy and science in countering the power of religion, Smith remarks, as I noted above, that what people need quite often is simply something to do. The state should encourage "publick diversion" and give "entire liberty" to those who participate "without scandal or indecency," thereby exposing those who need it to public ridicule (WN V.i.g.15).

His prescriptions—poetry, music, dancing, and dramatic representations— all contain artistic content. They are not simply meaningless diversions but works of art that require a certain attention to their craft to fully appreciate. This recalls his comments in IA that artistic endeavors necessitate cultivation of even the senses if one is to fully appreciate them. It is also the closest Smith comes in WN to prescribing mandatory arts education. Given these comments, it is not far-fetched to suggest that Smith believed in the capacity of the general public to appreciate arts in general and imaginative literature specifically, and, as a result, that presenting a foundation for their appreciation in school would be beneficial morally, politically, and intellectually.

Smith does not include literature or the arts in his discussion of public schooling, and he never claims that the classes ought to have identical education; this last point may be his greatest departure from twenty-first-century liberal democratic principles. I am therefore making an interpretive jump. I am arguing that a case can be made under Smith's system that the study of literature would cultivate moral and political unity and help counter the mind-numbing effects of the division of labor. This would run counter to James E. Alvey's assertion, for example, that, for Smith, "a scientific education, not a liberal education, is needed to make the citizen moderate, orderly and prudent."[56]

Objections to my suggestion are obvious. First, as I have acknowledged, Smith does not include imaginative literature on the list of required subjects; second, Smith writes that his prescriptions might make the literary education of the common people "as complete as it can be"; and third, as we saw in Smith's discussion of Rome and Greece, it is unclear that music, in particular, advances moral behavior. I am suggesting in response, however, that Smith does make an implicit argument for the use of literature and that such an approach is, at minimum, *Smithian*, even if it does not come explicitly from Smith himself.[57]

Finally, education would also include a religious component. Religion is necessary for civil society; it provides a sense of community and meaning for individuals who feel lost or alienated. It also provides a further incentive for people to abide by the moral rules of conduct established through repeated sympathy.

According to Smith, there is an innate sense in all human beings that the rules of conduct are not just the result of personal deliberations but also the laws of the "Deity" (*TMS* III.5.3) — perhaps this is a Shaftesburyian prolepsis. To encourage religion is to give the general rules of conduct the added boost of authenticity that urges fanatics to abide by them even if they are resistant to social pressure and the judgment of the impartial spectator. This innate sense is found even in the rudest form of religion (*TMS* III.5.4), and, for Smith, it is much more important that moral actors consider such rules to originate from God than whether they actually do. The general rules of conduct are social rules; their purpose is to govern people's behavior and to ensure justice.

The nature of the role of the divine in *TMS* is controversial. It is, however, most likely that Smith adopted some form of natural theology as the background to his system. As John Haldane writes, "The philosophers and other intellectuals of the lowland Scottish Enlightenment were religious moderates who inclined toward deism and naturalism. . . . They stood opposed to the fanaticism of the religious parties and associated themselves with the causes of Union and of progressive development. On this account they tended to be secularists both in disfavouring the influence of religious groups on public policy and in seeking natural foundations for ethical and political values."[58]

Certainly, Smith fits this description. It also allows for Smith's notion that moral knowledge is discoverable through sympathy and progress, although he is skeptical of any certitude. As Adrian Pabst writes, "For natural theologians like Smith, such and similar intermediate principles are equally applicable in divine physics, moral philosophy and political economy."[59]

Whatever the metaphysics that underlie Smith's system, it seems that, for him, organized religion is a human construct.[60] Rituals, practices, denominationalism, and the schools of thought behind them are rationalizations of and justifications for the general rules that tie societies together. He therefore argues that each sect ought to be politically equal and that each system of beliefs should be subject to scrutiny because each religion is as valid as the next one— there appears to be no divine revelation for Smith. However, Smith could not permit himself to destroy religions by fiat; this would be a violation of freedom of belief. Therefore, religious sects and their members must be subject to the scrutiny of competition.[61] Religious adherents will decide if the religion is right for them and their community. If they support it, the religion will prosper. If they oppose it, the religion will disband and be replaced by something else. That which guides individuals in choosing a religion is their rationality—their ability to judge what constitutes absurd or unreasonable claims, a product of their education in science and religion.[62] That which provides the motivation to seek out religion is the desire for a sense of community and approval: the natural tendency toward fellow feeling and approval—the mechanism of sympathy, which is itself a rational process. Smith's religious skepticism is merely a practical tempering of religious beliefs. He does not seem to suggest that the majority will discover the true religion by virtue of a theological marketplace. There is nothing akin to Rousseau's General Will in this discussion or to the pragmatists' pursuit of truth in the long run. This supports the claim that Smith, like Hume, is a religious skeptic.[63]

SMITH'S PHILOSOPHY OF EDUCATION SUMMARIZED

Smith never explicitly addresses the philosophy of education by name. All of his comments on schooling, curriculum, and the social and political role of education are subsumed under other discussions. Nevertheless, Smith does offer a coherent philosophy of education that permeates his system. These comments, interspersed through all of his writings, underscore the unity of his project and the importance of learning to every area of human life.

Smith's theory, however empiricist, assumes certain innate tendencies. Two are a desire to please others and the need to see one's own moral codes as stemming from God. In each of these the most intimate qualities are those that relate to a person's moral experience. Yet all behavior, whether learned or otherwise, can be refined, and education, for Smith, is the process of making such abilities more accurate and more precise. Just as artists can be trained to see better, in more detail and with more precision, education offers individuals the ability to make better moral judgments and be happier. It also affords an individual the ability to cultivate his or her rationality, which in turn increases the possibility of interpersonal communication.

Smith believes that education is largely a process of socialization and must therefore remain a predominantly local project. Traveling for one's schooling, while offering some benefits, removes education from its proper context. Education teaches people to understand their most immediate world and the people around them. It helps individuals communicate and interpret the norms and expectations of their communities. Since education allows people to identify the same expectations, it also allows for a more stable political system. According to Smith, the more divisive education is, the more fragile the *polis* becomes.

Smith distinguishes between training and education. Whereas training serves commercial purposes—not an unimportant role in Smith's view—education serves to make people better. 'Better,' for Smith, means an increased ability to sympathize with others, a more diverse sense of one's intellectual abilities, a well-developed sense of self-esteem and self-respect, a strong ability to resist the temptation and easy alliances of superstition, an increased understanding of the moral rules and the potentials of perfect liberty, and a more developed rationality. Thus the sovereign has no small stake in encouraging individuals to be educated. All of society benefits from the education of each of its members, and as a consequence all of society must contribute to its cost.

The quality of any education is to be measured by two distinct markers. The first is the market and the assent of consumers of education. When the market operates properly, teachers do work of "known quality" and in return will be economically stable and well respected. At the same time, education is measured by the ability of individuals within a society to make proper moral judgments. Moral adjudication is an essential part of social and political life, and as a result, when the educational system is inadequate, the moral framework of society would likely fall apart.

Whereas the market plays an important role in enforcing responsible teachers and ensuring quality of education, it is not the sole arbiter. For Smith, certain subjects—philosophy, science, reading, writing, arithmetic, geometry and "mechanicks," and literature and the arts as well, if one accepts my interpretation, ought to be universal for all people, and certain other forms of education must be required before individuals advance in specific economic and technical fields. Education is both a good in itself and a tool that leads to further goods. Quality education, for Smith, is instructive but not wasteful.

The sovereign's job is to ensure that all people have access to at least a minimum schooling. Education is, for Smith, a basic good—a necessity of human life. Without education, humans cannot be happy, and since happiness, according to Smith, is a natural state for people, disallowing education runs against human nature. This responsibility extends also to parents, who, should they neglect their responsibility to educate their children, may lose the claim they have to demand their children reciprocate care when they are older and dependent. At this point, one might wonder if Smith's readers could extend this argument and argue that the sovereign who neglects educating his or her people may no longer demand political allegiance from his or her subjects. However, this argument depends on parallels between the sovereign and a parent, an analogy that Smith would likely be reluctant to endorse. Nevertheless, it is the case that the sovereign who does not use education to insulate his or her citizens against the lure of superstition does, in fact, risk losing their allegiance since fanatical religion lures people away from civic duty.

Socialization and acculturation complement institutional education. For Smith, learning begins at home and at local parish schools and continues through adulthood to expand the understanding of workers, whose repetitious daily life would otherwise make them numb to intellectual activities. It continues further through repeated social interaction and, with long-term religious education, it cultivates proper moral and political behavior. Education is designed to moderate fanatical impulses but also to reinforce the moral codes that are innately tied to the human perception of the creator.

In summary, education for Smith is aimed at cultivating the human experience. It makes people more moral and more social. They become better individuals and better citizens through education. As Griswold writes, for Smith, "sound education is partly a matter of emulating an 'archetype of perfection'"—the ideal versus the actual again.[64] Training in the form of apprenticeships contributes to economic growth: liberal education helps individuals make good decisions, economically and otherwise.

It is unfortunate that Smith is not more explicit about his philosophy of education. As a teacher and as someone with strong pedagogical intent for his writing, Smith had and continues to have a strong influence on what education might look like in a liberal democratic society. If one does not focus specifically on Smith's comments on education, however, this influence continues largely unnoted. This position may be best summed up by quoting Hume rather than Smith. Here I do so via Michael L. Frazer: "The ability to imagine and feel fine distinctions, like the ability to reason about them, is often partly the result of natural gifts, but is always improvable through education and practice. 'A culti-vated taste for the polite arts,' Hume writes, 'improves our sensibility for all the tender and agreeable passions,' and the recipients of a humanistic education 'feel an increase of humanity. . . . Thus *industry, knowledge,* and *humanity* are linked together by an indissoluble chain and are found, from experience as well as reason, to be peculiar to the more polished, and, what are commonly denom-inated, the more luxurious ages.'"[65]

Obviously, Smith's theory of education does not meet all of the modern liberal requirements. He never demands that the lower and upper classes get the same education.[66] As he often is, Smith is concerned with necessities here, not conveniences and luxuries. Differing classes are entitled to equal minimal education but not to identical experiences. In this respect Smith's commitment to universal opulence is like Rawls's *maximin* principle: the goal is to raise the bottom rung, not to create an equality of result.[67] As Young explains, "Smith's ideal vision, then, is of a fluid class structure that may show a high degree of inequality at a point in time, but one that does not condemn any one family to remain on a particular rung generation after generation."[68] Smith's philosophy of education is both a theory of pluralism and a means to cultivate rationality. It argues that the more one develops rational abilities, the more one can create unity in the face of difference.

10

HISTORY AND NORMATIVITY

Previous chapters have focused on education and rationality on the micro level. In contrast, this chapter examines macro processes, investigating the concept of progress through Smith's philosophy of history and explicating the role of historical inquiry in discovering normative claims.[1] I argue that, as in the case of his moral and economic theory, Smith's philosophy of history relies on dialectic interplay between discovery of the ideal and of the actual, in this case historiography and historicity, respectively. My discussion includes an investigation of evidence in historical analysis, the viability of particular narratives connecting this evidence, and the role of these narratives in defining and limiting the discovery that comes from historical inquiry.

The chapter is divided into two sections. The first examines attitudes about Smith's historical writings; I take the editors of the Glasgow Edition of WN and a critique by Michael J. Shapiro as paradigmatic of two competing positions. The second examines Smith's philosophy of history itself, showing how, for Smith, progress is that which reveals the "ought" of nature.

NARRATIVE AND DISCOVERY IN HISTORIOGRAPHY

J. G. A. Pocock argues that Adam Smith was not a historian. Nothing Smith wrote, he claims, "is a history of anyone or anything."[2] To elucidate his point, he compares Smith to Hume, Gibbon, and Ferguson, all of whom regarded history as the main purpose of their major works.[3] Others take a different view. Emma Rothschild and Amartya Sen, for example, emphasize the historical content of *The Wealth of Nations*, suggesting that Smith's economic comments take more of a subordinate role to historical narratives.[4] Both positions are too extreme; Smith's most famous treatise is a work on economics as the discipline understands itself today, but it also has major sections of thoughtful historical exploration. Books 1, 4, and 5, for example, contain impressive, if compact, political, economic, and social histories. The final book of *The Theory of Moral Sentiments* is a critical history of ideas, and the edition published in 1790 almost doubles the historical illustrations.[5] Smith's lectures on jurisprudence rely on pivotal historical elements for their analyses. His fragment on the history of astronomy is, by title, historical writing.[6]

I contend that whether or not Smith was a historian, he is most certainly a *philosopher of history* and ought to be read as such. The invisible hand represents a pivotal moment in his historical theory and is illustrative of the logic that guides collective improvement. All three instances of the phrase reference the intersection between individual acts and the flow of history, and in each case Smith uses the image to help readers understand forces that are beyond prediction or complete understanding. I elaborate on this point in the second section of this chapter.

Eric Schliesser argues that Smith turns to history for four reasons: "the right is articulated by history"; "the historical account provides a normative baseline with which to evaluate moral and social institutions"; "the historical account does justice to the Enlightenment Imperative, one that demands non-miraculous, causal explanations for our practices"; and "the historical account enables a moral theory in which explanation and justification are mutually reinforcing."[7] These emphasize how intrinsic history is to Smith's goals. It is connected to identifying moral content, establishing standards for evaluation, searching for natural explanations, and providing fuel for explanation and persuasion.

Smith was a historical naturalist. He assumed that "science is fundamentally unified" and that history obeys laws.[8] He wrote narrative histories and argued for a conception of progress, most famously categorizing it in terms of historical stages that are irrevocably intertwined with economic conditions and social and political institutions. He also wrote what I refer to as an ideal history, or, in the words of the editors of the Glasgow Edition of *The Wealth of Nations*, "an ideal account of historical evolution, which did not need to conform to any actual historical situation."[9] As we shall see, for Smith, ideal history helps to interpret historical contingencies (historicity), preparing the way for normative discovery.[10] Or, as Schliesser remarks, for Smith, "theories are tools for further research . . . [they make] one ask: how does this theory allow one to find and analyze data that can be turned into evidence? What kind of research can one do to improve the theory?"[11]

Historians from Thucydides onward saw their work as having moral consequences—even Smith's contemporaries Hume, Gibbon, and Ferguson saw history as a moral progression. It has only been in the past century or so that historians have placed an emphasis on neutral reconstruction of events, albeit while simultaneously proclaiming the impossibility of neutral historical reconstruction. The term *historia*, first used by Herodotus, is Greek for "inquiry," but a *histor* in Homer was "someone who passed judgement based on the facts as a result of investigation."[12] Judgment is essential to the origins of the craft.

Twentieth-century historians gave up on this type of history, a rejection resulting from multiple factors: postmodern skepticism about the connected nature of events, analytic philosophy's commitment to logical positivism, and the German "professionalization" of the discipline. But Smith predates these rejections; he is committed to the tradition of grand narrative, a further connection between him and MacIntyre.[13] To ask about the normative qualities of history is to inquire about the unity of the sciences because, for Smith, history and normativity are not fundamentally different from what we now call the hard sciences. The "science of man" and Smith's representation of it presumed a continuity between natural philosophy, moral philosophy, and logic. In the eighteenth century, major disciplinary categories emphasized the difference between philosophy and literature—a concern about research method, not about discrete domains of knowledge. Philosophy, "while employing the written word, . . . emphasized outdoor investigations of nature and the conduct of experiments."[14]

Smith, of course, used literature for much of his research. His historical writing as well as his work in what one would now consider anthropological, sociological, scientific, and economic topics overlap. But he also saw history as a kind of laboratory for human behavior, a millennia-long experiment he could mine for moral conclusions. As we have seen, in WN book 5, he uses Roman and Greek education practices to evaluate Scotland's school systems; he evaluated economic structures partly in terms of the freedom of women; and he used travel literature to provide evidence of worldwide behavior, often referencing these stories instead of classical sources. Smith also claimed to do what social scientists might now call field research: he visited pin factories and immersed himself in patterns of trade as commissioner of customs. Finally, Smith was tremendously attentive to day-to-day life; he wrote of observations made during his daily activities. In fact, the dominant methodology of Ian Ross's biography of Smith is to show, chronologically, how Smith's personal experiences ended up in his writing.

These are all comparative sources, the data Smith used for evaluating the success or failure of economic and social systems. It is "experimental philosophy," even if it is only conceptually so—Rothschild calls it a "virtual conversation"[15]— and while Smith did not have modern experimental mechanisms such as control groups or focused investigations into particular hypotheses, his work is indicative of much modern qualitative research: it brings out patterns and conclusions justified by both collective and individual narratives. For Smith, as we shall see, progress was *apparent*.

Philosophy as a discipline of empirical experimentation runs in sharp contrast to a more modern understanding of the subject, but Smith would have inherited a wider notion of philosophical inquiry from his predecessors: Bacon, Hobbes, and Descartes, the patriarchs of modern philosophy, were all engaged in scientific, mathematical, and philosophical investigations. For each, philosophy emphasized the unity of human knowledge, not its fragmentation. Newton wrote, "If natural Philosophy in all its Parts, by pursuing this Method, shall at length be perfected, the Bounds of Moral Philosophy will be also enlarged."[16] Colin MacLaurin championed experimental philosophy in Scotland in the 1730s and 1740s, founding the Edinburgh Philosophical Society in 1737; he and his students gave public lectures on the subject.[17] It also ought to be remembered that the full title of Hume's first treatise, *A Treatise on Human Nature: Being an Attempt to introduce the experimental Method of Reasoning into Moral Subjects*, prioritized the experimental approach.

As evident by his dabbling in astronomy and physics, Smith would have seen himself as engaged in science in general, with history being simply one piece of it. The endless amount of data in his *Wealth of Nations* is not extraneous. It constitutes evidence for his prescriptions. Smith writes as if his conclusions are, in today's words, reproducible products of his historical experiments. They are used to persuade his readers of the accuracy of his account.

Smith presumes that history reveals facts about nature, truths that become evident in the narratives he constructs. The teleologies he describes are *discoveries*, for Smith, not constructions. Shapiro takes issue with this viewpoint, challenging first and foremost the sufficiency of Smith's evidence. Sources were not simply data, he argues, because Smith's carefully selected evidence obfuscated important factors that challenge the justice of his system. His reliance on narrative, Shapiro claims, "often verged toward the fictive or mythological end of the continuum of historical writing."[18] Furthermore, Shapiro tells us, scholars such as R. H. Campbell and A. S. Skinner, by advocating Smith's histories, actually whitewash details that Smith obscures. Shapiro calls their introductory remarks on history in the definitive Glasgow Edition of the *Wealth of Nations* "naive, celebratory, and lacking in detail."[19]

Shapiro is being unfair: Campbell and Skinner are quite clear about Smith's shortcomings as a historian. They remark that "sometimes Smith's use of a source is less critical than it should be"[20] and that in matters of law, for example, he fails to "distinguish between the intention of [a] statute and the manner and extent of its implementation."[21] They even refer to his comments on contemporary political issues as "excellent political propaganda."[22] True, they dismiss these concerns in part because, they argue, the inadequacies of the history do not taint the majority of Smith's work. But they also point out that Smith himself was critical of many of his sources, acknowledging at times when data were unreliable.[23] Perhaps most important, Campbell's and Skinner's justification for regarding Smith's histories as successful are actually similar to Shapiro's reason for critique. All three are focused on Smith's extensive use of narrative in either revealing or obfuscating patterns that unify historiographies.

For Shapiro, Smith's narratives obfuscate actual facts of the matter. They are, Shapiro argues, "governed by [their] normative properties," and thus the division of labor is regarded as "natural rather than political."[24] Furthermore, by imposing a linear progression on history, Shapiro claims, Smith's writing "constitutes an aggressive denial of his own stories."[25] His history is "aimed at silencing all tendencies subversive to the main, naturalizing, and legitimating story . . . [it] registers no struggles for occupational existence [and] no counternarratives," and "people end up in the occupational positions for which they are destined."[26] If this is true, it would constitute a major threat to pluralism because it silences selected voices.

In contrast, for Campbell and Skinner Smith's narratives shed light and add focus. More so, they emphasize the theoretical underpinnings Smith seeks to elucidate — his progressions are the consequence of his being a philosopher of history and not just an "orthodox historian."[27] Smith's narrative, they assert, is intentionally one of many, a consequence of his theoretical interest and his focus on the logic of progress: "If historical facts indicated a divergence from the ideal explanation, then Smith felt obliged to offer explanations of the divergence. He worked from the system to the facts not from the facts to the system . . . the interesting problem [for Smith] then lay in determining the reasons for the divergence."[28]

Thus the difference between Shapiro's position and that of the editors of the Glasgow Edition is precisely the perceived value of Smith's focusing vision, a question about the internal logic of narrative itself. Isolating particular stories constitutes a violation of accuracy for Shapiro, but for Campbell and Skinner it is a necessary focusing device to highlight accuracies. Furthermore, for Shapiro, the particular narratives Smith chooses misrepresent conditions of the time — there is no discourse of struggle or liberation, for example — but, for Campbell and Skinner, the entire mechanism is itself a story of struggle and liberation — a movement toward bettering collective conditions. In essence, this disagreement asks whether progress is an ad hoc fictive construction utilized to justify arbitrary linkage between events or an empirically verifiable concept that helps expose that which moves discourse. Smith—and apparently Campbell and Skinner—think the latter.

The question at hand is whether Smith's historiography too narrowly limits what counts as evidence. MacIntyre comments that "each theory of practical reasoning is, among other things, a theory as to how examples are to be described, and how we describe any particular example will depend, therefore, upon which theory we have adopted."[29] As in the case of phronesis and its examples, narrative and evidence have a circular relationship. The narrative defines the relevant evidence, and the relevant evidence confirms the narrative. However, when the particular narrative becomes the guide for inquiry, it becomes all too easy to create ad hoc explanations and exclude evidence that would otherwise call the narrative into question. Shapiro charges Smith and his editors with doing just this, creating too limiting an analytic frame for analysis, whereas Smith, Campbell, and Skinner each regard the master narrative as all-encompassing. Over time, they assert, progress will reveal the relevant evidence and engage the proper counterexamples.

Smith is aware of this problem, rebuking any so-called man of system who prioritized the beauty of the theory over the truth behind it.[30] According to Smith, the human desire for theoretical explanation is powerful enough that advocates sometimes bend evidence to fit their hypotheses rather than use data to accurately critique their veracity.[31] This manipulation may be governmental—a penchant for social engineering—or it may manifest itself philosophically, as an aesthetic desire for order.[32] Smith writes that "the man of system . . . is apt to be very wise in his own conceit; and is often so enamoured with the supposed beauty of his own ideal plan of government, that he cannot suffer the smallest deviation from any part of it" (*TMS* VI.ii.2.17). A prime example of such steadfast behavior, for Smith, is the "artificial system" of Ptolemy, each revision of which "rendered it still more embarrassing" (*HA* IV.8, 25).

Inspired by Shapiro, one might then ask whether Smith is guilty of ignoring his own advice. Is he himself putting aesthetics or politics ahead of the facts? I suggest not. First of all, despite Shapiro's charges, Smith is quite clear that counternarratives do exist; he just doesn't present them in any detail. He acknowledges, for example, that different cultures can coexist while experiencing different economic periods—his comparison of the Americas and England comes to mind (*WN* iv.vii.c.23). He argues against empire (*WN* IV.vii.c) and recognizes the oppression of Africans by Europeans (*TMS* V.2.9, *WN* III.ii.12). He advocates for colonial independence (*WN* V.iii.90–92). As we have seen in great detail, he warns against the invisibility of and frequent injustice toward women (WN I.viii.51) and presents class-based critiques (WN V.i.f.50, *LJ*(B) 330, *LRBL* i.5). He takes an interest in those who have no necessities (WN I.viii.36), concerning himself with finding a remedy for famine (WN IV.v.b.5–30). And, while it is true that some of these are references in works other than WN, this book was never intended to stand apart from the rest of his system.

To be fair, there is a danger that Shapiro's critique hints at, and it is a hazard of the integrationist thesis that argues for, as I have, the connectedness of Smith's corpus. As Brown argues, if one views Smith as holding a single continuous philosophical position in both *TMS* and WN, if one suggests that there is seamless moral support for his political economy, then one risks creating apologetics for the shortcomings of the market without seeking any solutions.[33] In other words, if we accept that the market is not by nature a mechanism of perfect justice,[34] the integrationist position risks obfuscating injustice by suggesting that anything that derives from legal exchange is inherently moral. This moral presumption is the core of many radical libertarian and neoconservative views on capitalism and is perhaps most famously found in Robert Nozick's *Anarchy, State, Utopia*.[35] While I have shown that this is not Smith's position, Brown's point is still important. If one's goal is to put forth *TMS* as a moral argument for commercial society and then move uncritically from this foundation, then the integrationist approach undermines Smith's moral authority because it fails to distinguish between economics and ethics in any meaningful way.

In contrast to the integrationist stance, Brown argues for a different position, what she calls the "problematicity thesis,"[36] holding that the relationship between Smith's moral and economic work is "complex, problematic, and unresolved."[37] The two works have much in common, she explains, but they are not part of a unified philosophical vision, and they have, at their core, very different conceptions of moral agency.[38]

Brown is no doubt correct that the relationship between morals and the market is tremendously complex. It does, in fact, inspire both ambivalence and trepidation in many actors. But this is not just a textual problem for Smith. It is an accurate depiction of people's real experiences, an illustration of the book's relationships to nature and the human condition. Whatever tensions exist between *TMS* and WN mirrors the world Smith is trying to describe. Smith's commitment to presenting a corpus is related to his commitment to the unity of the sciences. Morality and political economy are part and parcel of the same inquiry, and Smith could no more see morality and political economy as discrete than he could see astronomy and history as unrelated.[39]

While Brown's concern calls attention to the relationship between history and nature, her textual approach to reading Smith (as described in the introduction) severs the possibility of natural discovery. Text-only readings do not ask about truth, only coherence. Even more so, Brown's criticisms ignore the internal logic that drives Smith's progressive narrative. The "self-correcting" aspects of the market, to quote a contemporary concept, function only if actors are *self-consciously* correcting; I referenced this phrase earlier. My point is that since the market is made up of agents, it will be attentive to injustice, poverty, and alienation only if participants are full moral agents, as *TMS* sees them.

Shapiro's concerns also neglect the internal logic of Smith's narrative; his critique is based on his perception that Smith's history is too narrow to allow for the attention to injustice, poverty, and alienation. As a question of *narrative*, his attack represents a lack of attention to the invisible hand.

The invisible hand should not be seen as an excuse to be passive economic actors. It describes only that system with active, informed, and self-consciously just and sympathetic moral agents. These agents do not seek social engineering or market manipulation (c.f. *TMS* VI.ii.2.18); they need only to strive to be good, moral people who fulfill their duties toward themselves and others. In other words, sympathy promotes what contemporary feminists might call *care*,[40] while economic and political structures help promote moral action among those who are too distant from one another to benefit from emotional connections.

As quoted above, Shapiro claims that Smith sees people as inevitably ending up in their economic positions and that in Smith's system individuals hold the "occupational positions for which they are destined."[41] This is a brazen misinterpretation of Smith and representative of exactly what Shapiro misses about Smith's narrative — its holistic quality. One of Smith's core justifications for the free-market system is that *as a whole* it provides the best possible chance for upward mobility; he holds neither Plato's static position in *Republic* nor Aristotle's commitment to natural-born slaves. I have articulated Smith's set of preconditions for moral and just marketplaces already. I have also examined his account of self-criticism. Together, these go a long way to answer Shapiro's criticisms. However, I do concede to both Brown and Shapiro that *WN*'s history appears significantly less self-critical than *TMS*. Part of this is Smith's attention to micro-sympathetic processes in *TMS* as opposed to his macro-progressive approach in *WN*, but it is also the result of the dialogical element of Smith's moral writing that Brown brings out so well in *Adam Smith's Discourse*. If Brown is correct that *WN* is uniquely monological, any self-critical aspect must exist in a different form than it does in *TMS*. It must be a product of the grand narrative and not a consequence of the text.

My argument here is that self-criticism in *WN* is a combination of market forces and the logic of history; it exists within the narrative itself. However, if it turns out to be true that *TMS* is more inherently self-critical than *WN*, then Smith's choice of titles is ironic. It is, after all, with a definite article that Smith begins *The Theory of Moral Sentiments* but only an indefinite article that announces *An Inquiry into the Nature and Causes of the Wealth of Nations*. For Smith, political economic criticism is larger than the one book. He is well aware that there are counternarratives; his title announces it.

In the end, Shapiro's argument begs the question. His attack on Smith is based on his assertion that the division of labor cannot be natural and that there cannot be a singular universal narrative—an unproven assumption of Shapiro's and many other self-identified postmodernists. This position represents a grand narrative in itself—the primacy of the political over the natural. For Shapiro, all social arrangements are purely political, and Smith's grand narrative is suspect because we all inherit different stories, an outgrowth of Foucault's position that I address in the next chapter.[42] Yet, for Smith, sympathy and the impartial spectator, price, and the invisible hand are indeed all tools for aggregating multiple histories.

Smith is well aware that every single person has his or her own story and that every particular community has its own history; insofar as each life is a piece of historical evidence, Smith considers them unique and contextual. The free market is a system designed to manage this seemingly chaotic reality. Smith is attempting to create a system in which all of these disparate elements can find a single meeting point—to make a single narrative out of the smaller ones. Shapiro's a priori rejection of grand narrative makes Smith's evidence invisible before it can be considered. It is he who has too limiting an analytic frame.

I find it odd that in our time, when environmentalists caution that all people live in the same world and when those who seek peace and universal justice want everyone to consider strangers to be neighbors, that so many can advocate these positions while simultaneously arguing against a grand-narrative history. One of the core values of cosmopolitan arguments for justice is that grand narratives help people see the impact they have on others. Smith is clear how interrelated we all are, a useful reminder for those who seek global justice. While it is certainly true that the nature of narrative truth is a core issue in the philosophy of history, its limited nature is not a necessary shortcoming. To paraphrase Mark Day, we need not be reminded that the historian is not omniscient. Even though liars select details for their stories, selecting details does not make one a liar.[43]

HISTORICAL PRINCIPLES,
NORMATIVITY, AND THE INVISIBLE HAND

Smith does not believe that his narrative is either arbitrary or constructed. For him, as for Kant, a universal history is in some sense natural. But Smith's use of the term 'nature' is itself ambiguous and illustrates that historical laws are fuzzier than the laws of physics. Sometimes, for Smith, 'natural' is a normative term, as when he references natural liberty, but it can also be empirical, describing normal tendencies found in individuals and groups, as when Smith writes that humans are endowed with a natural desire for the preservation of society.

Griswold identifies seven uses of the term 'nature' in Smith's work: it can (1) indicate essence and form; (2) denote imperfection, as when Smith distinguishes natural justice from positive law; (3) distinguish the natural from the artifact; (4) indicate that which is given to us, imposed upon us, or is seen by us—the empirical, as Smith understands it; (5) distinguish the natural from the supernatural; (6) indicate teleological elements of creation or the purpose an object is to serve; (7) denote 'the whole,' 'the world,' or 'the universe.'[44] Several of these are of particular interest to my discussion of history, including Smith's focus on imperfection; his distinction between the natural and the artifactual—historical narrative is an artifact we now call historiography, while history itself is the natural progression of events; his acknowledgment of the teleological—progress and narrative presume some sort of end; and his recognition of the whole, meaning both nature as what is currently understood by the term but also Smith's tendency to think in terms of systems.

Similarly complicated, while Smith's references to the 'principles' of human and political behavior are ubiquitous, one so-called principle may be in tension with another because human tendencies are not inviolable in the same way that the laws of physics are. Thus, for Smith, natural historical laws are of a different form than the laws of natural science.

This is not idiosyncratic in the way that Smith's slippery use of the term 'nature' might be. For example, Isaiah Berlin, in the inaugural issue of *History and Theory*, points out that historical laws require "judgment," which scientific laws do not, and thus cannot be applied to an "electronic brain" in the way that deductive scientific conclusions can.[45] Yet, for Berlin, historical laws are still appropriate to the context: "The explanations that they provide are usually quite satisfactory."[46] History is a science, he asserts. It is, however, a science of a different type than physics or chemistry, and its principles are also of a different measure. Berlin's point here is similar to Aristotle's famous comment that different domains of knowledge are judged by different standards of precision.[47] That historical laws are more flexible than scientific ones does not make them fictitious.

Despite having a lower standard of precision, for Smith, these ambiguous laws may be constant. Human proclivities do not alter, he assumes, most explicitly referring to "the uniform, constant, and uninterrupted effort of every man to better his condition" (WN II.iii.31). This continuity of principle helps clarify Smith's philosophy of history—it is indicative of the forces that move humanity forward. Skinner argues that three principles drive Smith's history: "social change depends on economic development," "man is self-regarding in all spheres of activity," and "the normal process of development will generate four distinct economic stages, each with a particular socio-political structure reflecting the mode of subsistence prevailing. . . . hunting, pasturage, farming and commerce."[48]

I would argue with the details of Skinner's interpretation, especially his account of the role of self-interest, but his point is still clear: Smith believes that *principle* drives history forward. These laws are universal and perpetual, and they *explain* human behavior. For Smith, they would be as true now as they were in the eighteenth century, and one might equally apply them to current historical analyses as Smith does to eighteenth-century circumstances. His discovery therefore contributes to our knowledge.

My argument here should not suggest either fate or determinism. As I have shown, human agency plays a large part in the accidents of history, contingencies that are themselves a consequence of the conflict of the natural principles that guide human endeavors. Bad government can lead to an "unnatural and retro-grade" political system (WN III.i.9). However, even though, for Smith, agents appear to have free will, they still follow basic desires and still act on specific needs, and the science that will eventually be called sociology will still be able to (imperfectly) predict group behavior. This is the logic of history in action.

In other words, Smith's approach to the discipline of history was, ironically, nonhistorical. As David Wootton explains, like Thucydides, Smith thought the best historians were those who experienced events: "It never occurred to Smith that it was the peculiar characteristic of history that it dealt with the past, or that historians faced a particular methodological difficulty because they were depen-dent on the testimony of others."[49]

Wootton's claim lends credence to Pocock's assertion that Smith was not a historian per se. His political economy and moral theory are particular mixtures of anthropology, economics, philosophy, political science, psychology, and sociology, all of which permeated both Smith's and his contemporaries' writ-ings. Therefore, if Pocock is right and Smith is not a historian, then one would have to exclude all pre-Gibbon philosophers from the pantheon of historians as well. As Wootton argues, early historians never hoped to "supplant their predecessors. . . . the notion that history had to be continuously rewritten was an invention of the eighteenth century."[50] Smith, like those before him, saw history as an attempt to complete a picture, not to negotiate differing interpretations.

In this sense alone, Shapiro's depiction of Smith as selective is correct: competing narratives do not concern him on the historical level. Yet, for Smith, as we have seen, these same narratives are necessary because of human nature and the structures of rationality; it is through them that people learn and communicate stories. Sympathy is narrative in structure. So is historical writing (*LRBL* ii.36). Sympathy is pedagogical and ought to be built upon impartiality. Historical writing is also (*LRBL* ii.17). As we have already seen, *LRBL* is as much about ethics as it is beauty.

Narrative is intertwined with evaluation in both sympathy and history. Certainly, there may be debate about whether particular historical consequences are themselves good or bad, but if one accepts Smith's belief that human nature is both discoverable and largely constant, then there ought not be too much debate about whether one should do particular things to achieve specific goals (such as bettering one's condition). There are religious traditions and cultures that reject the acquisition of material goods, but, as we have seen, bettering one's condition is not solely material, and those who do reject worldly goods often do so for otherworldly reasons. They are bettering their *eternal* condition, which is why in book 5 of *WN* Smith recognizes the civic purpose and dangers of religion. That he does so further counters Shapiro's claim that Smith has no eye toward counternarrative.

Historical writing for Smith is instructive in exactly the same way that the moral sentiments are: an impartial observer can construct and utilize criteria or propriety to help determine future action just as a historian builds a historiography to guide judgment. Since the general rules of conduct are after-the-fact constructs, they are the product of personal and collective experience, just as historical writing is (*TMS* III.5). Thus my discussion of Smith's philosophy of history as I described it—naturalistic, built on laws, derived from narrative, built on a stage theory, and ideal in structure—is largely complete. It requires only an account of one final characteristic, the relevance of stage theory, which in turn involves the invisible hand.

Regarding stage theory, my concern is not the nature of the individual stages. Instead, I seek to analyze the natural principles manifest in history that help direct societies' commercial and political progress. In other words, while Smith offers us descriptions of nations of hunters, of shepherds, of agriculture, and of commercial interaction (WN V.i.a, see, also, LJ(A) i.27; see also I 25, 27, 149, 233), my focus is on what brings people out of one stage and into another.

Specialization and technological advancement are, of course, key factors in human progress. Yet Smith is also famously insistent that individuals cannot themselves force the progress of history. Principles other than innovation drive it forward, and he illustrates this conglomeration of factors by means of the invisible hand.

The invisible hand references two themes: the inadequacy of human knowledge—people can neither predict consequences nor know all relevant information—and the forward momentum of progress. Both uses of the phrase published in Smith's lifetime rely upon the language of morality. (The third, published posthumously, does so only if one ascribes moral consequence to divine favor.) In WN Smith is explicit that the interest of society is advanced when actors, pursuing their own self-interest, keep capital within national borders. He observes that trying to consciously advance the public good through manipulation of investment is mostly ineffectual. This is a moral claim because Smith is referring to the best way to pursue public good, not individual interest. However, his reference in TMS is even more explicitly moral: he states that the rich act on "selfishness" and "rapacity." They seek only their own "conveniency" and the "gratification of their own vain and insatiable desires" (TMS IV.1.10). Yet, because of the invisible hand, the goods of the earth are equally divided so that all individuals have almost the same access to necessities they would have had if they were distributed by providence. Smith's claim is one of natural law, then, the constancy of history. This providential division is predictable, reliable, natural, and normative. It also indicates that the invisible hand is somehow more than the sum of its parts. The aggregative tool becomes qualitatively more than the aggregate.

Smith argues that one ought to cultivate the invisible hand because it is in everyone's best and long-term interest to do so; no one loses more than they gain by cultivating universal opulence. To borrow from MacIntyre's account of Hume, this assertion derives an 'ought' from an 'is.'[51] While such a move is never morally justified, it does represent a sociological and psychological reality. Just because individuals naturally want to act in their own best interest, it does not follow that they should. To assume the rightness of their tendencies is to place moral value on fact.

Smith has two kinds of histories in *The Wealth of Nations*; their relationship is that which allows for this derivation of the normative from the factual. The first, the empirical history, is an account of data regarding price, behavior, and political structures among the ages. Here he compares time periods to find identifiable patterns and develops prescriptions as to the economic conditions that lead to efficient markets. He also offers, as Hume and Gibbon do, a philosophical history, or a progression of normative claims about equality, liberty, and political structures. This would be, in his terms, a "natural history," just as his account of freedom is, when normative, a theory of "natural liberty"; his account of price is, when normative, an account of "natural price,"[52] and possibly, following Hanley, his account of religion is an account of natural religion and natural belief.[53] Thus when he points to "unnatural and retrograde" moments, as I highlighted above, he is doing so to investigate what went *wrong* and how it is to be fixed. The invisible hand is the moment of intersection between these two types of history—the ideal and the actual. It represents the instance when human activity no longer inhibits the natural progression of freedom and opulence and when the data articulating price, behavior, and political structures align to create a system of "perfect liberty." History leads to normative claims.

The invisible hand is an instance of Smith as rhetor elegantly moving from the descriptive to the prescriptive, from the 'is' to the 'ought.' From Smith's perspective, he has *discovered* the normative power of history from his analysis—history here being the 'instructive' narrative he himself defends as true. That it takes a very long time to do so is no objection. Histories are the tools that allow for comparing facts over vast lengths of time.

Notice that while I describe the invisible hand as a 'moment' or 'instance' when two aspects of Smith's theories intersect, I am not claiming that Smith wrote with such an intention; I have no biographical evidence to suggest Smith's consciousness of the multiple uses of the phrase. In fact, when it comes to the invisible hand, scholars are wildly divided as to its very meaning. William D. Grampp counts nine different interpretations of the term in the literature: "(1) the force that makes the interest of one the interest of others, (2) the price mechanism, (3) a figure for the idea of unintended consequences, (4) competition, (5) the mutual advantage in exchange, (6) a joke, (7) an evolutionary process, (8) providence, and (9) the force that restrains the export of capital."[54] Grampp then adds a tenth, his own interpretation that the invisible hand represents the self-interest of those who profit from keeping capital in national boundaries when doing so also benefits the public.[55] Warren J. Samuels supersedes this discussion with an exhaustive twenty-two-page list of identities and functions of the phrase, most of which cannot be dealt with here.[56]

The differences between these interpretations are frequently, but not always, subtle. They stem from a variety of factors, not the least of which is that each of Smith's references is different. There is very little suggestion that the three uses of the phrase represent the same claim.[57] His comment in *HA* references primitive minds and their false interpretation that divine intervention is the cause of irregular natural events (*HA* III.2). In *TMS* he points to a just division of necessities among all people in the entire world, and in *WN* he illustrates the public benefit of self-interested restriction of capital to national markets. The only thing the three uses have in common, despite the actual words, is that each points to an instance of a limited point of view. The primitive, the rapacious eater with too small a stomach, and the capitalist are all unaware of what is actually happening; they believe only what they themselves assume to be the case. The invisible hand is epistemological in nature.[58]

Nevertheless, the invisible hand is not in itself an argument. It does no philosophical "work."[59] It is instead a rhetorical device Smith uses to emphasize claims of varying importance. In this respect, Grampp's insistence that the phrase is a simile and not simply a metaphor is relevant to my discussion.

A metaphor, in the widest sense, takes a term and converts it into something that it is not. A simile, on the other hand, is a specific type of metaphor that invites comparison while maintaining the distinct identity of the objects in question. If Smith's use of the invisible hand is meant to suggest only that the forces of nature work *as if* they are an invisible hand, then his meaning might be significantly different than if he means that the forces *are indeed* invisible hands. If one assumes the latter, then the invisible hand becomes closer to a hand of God or providence, as some commentators argue. Assuming the former—that natural forces are only *like* invisible hands—makes Smith's remarks more akin to a particular way of perceiving the world. It becomes a pedagogical phrase rather than a metaphysical claim.

In Smith's remarks in *HA* he clearly ascribes literal identification to the primitive mind—the people he describes actually believe in a real hand of Jupiter (*HA* III.2). Here, then, Rothschild is correct that Smith's remarks are "sardonic."[60] He assumes that his readers understand such superstition to be false. In *TMS*, however, the use is likely not mocking, as Rothschild would have us believe. Smith seems altogether genuine in his description of the "trickle down" effect of wealth.[61] He is also most certainly condemning of the landowners who care little for their workers or for the impact of their greed; "providence" steps in and remedies the situation.

Smith frames his discussion of the invisible hand in *TMS* by extolling the imagination and the false beauty individuals place on wealth—again, here is the epistemic element. But then Smith argues that it is "well that nature imposes upon us in this manner" since the desire for wealth motivates people to cultivate land (*TMS* IV.1.10). This foreshadows Smith's use of Mandeville's argument about the economic power of vices. According to Smith, the rich continue to cultivate land "to no purpose" because their eyes are bigger than their stomachs, but by doing so landowners distribute produce and work among those in their employ (*TMS* IV.i.11). Smith then closes his discussion in *TMS* with an assertion that the poor are happy when it comes to the real valuables in life and continues his epistemological point by condemning the person of system who sees the aesthetics of machinery as superior to actual positive effect.

This passage does not explicitly suggest simile. Smith does not write that rapacity is guided *as if* there is an invisible hand, although one can insert the phrase without changing the meaning. In fact, the clause following the invisible hand remark is itself a conditional—the world gets divided in the same way that it *would have been if* providence had divided it explicitly. This also adds credence to Grampp's point, but it is certainly not definitive. Smith claims not that the divisions of goods and work are *exactly* what providence would have chosen, but rather that the invisible hand leads the wealthy to make "nearly" the same distribution. This suggests a move away from divine providence—God is likely capable of being exact—while further emphasizing the point that historical laws are approximate and not identical to scientific principles. We see here the tension between the ideal and the actual that is found throughout Smith's system.

These same approximations appear in Smith's use of the invisible hand in *WN*. While the annual revenue of society is "always precisely equal" to the exchangeable produce of industry, individuals only "generally" disregard the public interest. This only "frequently" promotes the good of society and only does so "more effectually," not perfectly. And while Smith has never known "much good done" by those who invest capital to benefit the nation, this doesn't mean no good is done at all. These are the same kind of qualifiers Smith uses in his comments about the butcher, brewer, and baker (*WN* I.ii.2).

Smith's reference in *WN* does not explicitly suggest simile either, but one could insert the required grammatical structures there as well, without changing the meaning. Does the hand of the capitalist become the invisible hand? No, it doesn't. Does the hand of the rapacious landowner become the hand of providence? No. Are they both directed by principles of nature to act *as if* they were being guided by an invisible hand? It certainly appears this way, however approximate the results may be. In the case of *WN*, Grampp appears to be correct: the invisible hand is a simile. In the case of *HA* and *TMS*, he seems to be mistaken.

This debate helps Smith's readers understand how he addresses his audience and reinforces the point that the invisible hand is not part of Smith's philosophical argument but part of the pedagogical structures of his text. Consider Rothschild's literary history of the term: she points to its use in Shakespeare's *Macbeth*, Voltaire's *Oedipe*, and Ovid's *Metamorphoses* to begin with.[62] She then enumerates its religious uses, emphasizing Smith's familiarity with the relevant texts in every case.[63] In each of these instances the phrase is used for emotional appeal, to drive an image forward, and to connect with a reader; it does not have a history of being used in either deductions or inductive arguments. I therefore suggest that Rothschild and others are likely correct that the term was probably not all that important to Smith himself but was simply a good turn of phrase. It has minimal scientific or philosophical value—again, it does not do "work." However, it does have tremendous rhetorical value and has become immensely important to us over time. Thus those who try to minimize its influence by arguing that Smith did not intend much by its use miss the point.

The power of metaphors are that they tell a story, especially metonyms, which the *TMS* reference to the invisible hand probably is because the hand *replaces* the notion of providence. In *WN* the phrase is likely a root metaphor because it gives life to a whole new lexicon of related terms and meanings; but there too it tells a story. Thus we once again consider the nature of narrative. If the invisible hand were *only* a simile, the phrase would not seem to the reader as if it were an actual argument; in this sense Grampp misses the mark as much as anyone. The power of the phrase lies not in what it meant for Smith but in what it has meant for generations of readers.

In contrast, Samuels objects to calling the phrase a metaphor because, he argues, it is a metaphor for nothing. His critique has two parts; the first is historical. He claims that most commentators do not indicate what the invisible hand is supposed to represent.[64] My response, as I indicated above, is that the invisible hand denotes those moments, in argument, when the ideal construction intersects with the actual rational deliberation. It is a way of bringing an audience to an awareness of that intersection. It indicates, if I may, an instance of *aletheia* (ἀλήθεια).

His second point is conceptual. The invisible hand, he argues, "corresponds to nothing in reality," and calling it a metaphor or figure of speech "adds nothing to knowledge. Doing so is a distraction and a diversion."[65] Furthermore, the invisible hand "is not amenable to proof."[66] It is "mythopoeic."[67] And, finally, "There is nothing substantive about the invisible hand. The term adds nothing to economic theory . . . only an ideological patina to the account in terms of competition."[68]

Insofar as Samuels's point is that the invisible hand is not an argument in and of itself, I agree. And, since I, along with Grampp, argue that the phrase was intended by Smith to be a metaphor, all three of us also agree that Smith did not think there was an *actual* invisible hand as either a deity or a natural principle, in and of itself (although the question of Smith's notion of progress is dealt with in the next chapter). The invisible hand is indeed mythopoeic, insofar as any imagined ideal is, and history has shown us that Samuels is quite right that it tends toward ideology. However, his claim that because it is a metaphor it cannot contribute anything to economics is nonsense and the legacy of the obsolete positivism that leads to both rational choice theory and exaggerated claims of economics being a hard rather than a social science.

Metaphors contribute greatly to human understanding. From the notion of "seeing" knowledge that Richard Rorty famously emphasizes to the Cartesian notion of the human body as a container, metaphors are essential components of how human beings interact with reality.[69] For example, as George Lakoff and Mark Johnson write at the beginning of their foundational work *Metaphors We Live By*, philosophers are immersed in the notion that argument is war.[70] They explain: "Metaphor is for most people a device of the poetic imagination and the rhetorical flourish—a matter of extraordinary rather than ordinary language. Moreover, metaphor is typically viewed as characteristic of language alone, a matter of words rather than thought or action. For this reason, most people think they can get along perfectly well without metaphor. We have found, on the contrary, that metaphor is pervasive in everyday life, not just in language but in thought and action. Our ordinary conceptual system, in terms of which we both think and act, is fundamentally metaphorical in nature."[71]

I cannot do justice here to such a lengthy, complex discussion. I hope it will be enough to argue that if Samuels is correct that such turns of phrase cannot contribute anything to economics, then the discipline itself is committed to an untenable notion of human knowledge.

In the end, the invisible hand is a rhetorical device; it is a metaphor that tells a narrative story. It has a main character, the owner of the hand, whoever or whatever that is. It has a plot; it promises betterment or progress. There is an antagonist, the person who seeks only self-interest or rapaciousness, and a protagonist, Smith himself, who seeks the universal opulence of the moral society (or perhaps the moral nature of human beings; this is ambiguous). The story has a setting—chaos and disorder—and a resolution—order, meaning, and justice. In each of Smith's three uses, the invisible hand brings with it similar elements, and in each instance it has powerfully captured the reader's imagination. As we have seen, Smith saw storytelling as part of the human condition, and the need to resolve these stories is also part of human nature.[72] The invisible hand tells a short one, no doubt, written with efficiency and aplomb, but it is a narrative story nonetheless. Given its power over the past century or so, it is a quite successful one at that.

The narrative structure of the invisible hand helps bridge ideal history with actual history. It is, as Samuels points out, mythopoeic. As Plato shows repeatedly in *Republic, Symposium, Timaeus,* and elsewhere, myth is oftentimes the best means to get people to grasp an enlightened vision of the whole. Yet, as Plato himself struggles with, for Smith, the existence of facts necessitates a moral reality and accessing the normative reality is a challenge for philosophy: "The natural sentiments of man . . . are in rebellion against the natural course of things."[73] For Smith, nature tells us the right thing to do via history; empirical investigation of progress is the means of discovery. The 'is' of history, for Smith, reveals the 'ought' of nature, and humanity is to help nature along as much as it can (while recognizing that people and their actions are natural as well). We are to create the structures of society that most allow for the advancement of interests that in turn allow the freedom that nature can provide. This freedom allows us not only to better our conditions but also to be critical in the process because this criticism helps create the framework for a well-functioning market. And although historical laws and the rules of nature are not as precise as what we would now call scientific principles, they still accurately describe the human condition and each of our normal tendencies.

Thus actual and ideal histories are related in the same way that the impartial spectator and morality are related. Actual history provides information for the *histor* to judge, but because human beings are fallible and because we have imperfect knowledge, we can neither accurately socially engineer nor come to correct normative conclusions. Smith's ideal history provides an imagined perfect standard by which individuals seek to guide their activities, but, as in the case of the imagined impartial spectator, this is no ideal observer theory. The imperfection is bound by the epistemological limitations of the inquirer. Smith retains his commitment to fallibilism.[74]

Smith is quite aware that the imperfections of the human condition are perpetual and that even as we strive to get better, humanity will likely never have perfect justice, absolute truth, or crystal clear and achievable normative prescriptions. The desire to better one's condition is constant because the need to do so is also constant. In this, Smith anticipates the ever-shifting "long run" of the philosophical pragmatist, who believes that the community of inquiry will converge on the truth in the long run. In opposition to Dogan Göçmen's claim, Smith is not utopian in any meaningful sense of the term because he never presumes the realization of his ideal.[75] Thus we see Smith's use of imagined ideals to guide imperfect human knowledge and desires.

Smith thinks humanity progresses. While there are many who use repeated instances of genocide, war, poverty, and other forms of injustice as evidence that humanity does not, these objections can be countered with all of the predictable appeals to the advancement of women and minorities in many countries, the almost universal lip service paid to democratic structures, and the ubiquitous personal desire for peace and justice regardless of the differing meanings thereof. There is no way I can resolve the empirical debate about progress here, just as it would be impossible to prove that core elements of Smith's analyses are true in themselves.[76] What I can do is engage the critique that challenges even the *possibility* of progress and in doing so ask whether that argument successfully counters Smith's belief that progress and history are both natural. It is therefore to the postmodern attack on progressivist history that I turn my attention in the next chapter.

11

PROGRESS OR POSTMODERNISM?

Adam Smith was a man of his time, an Enlightenment scholar with the optimism that came from a scientific belief in progress and moral betterment. He lived among literati committed to a philosophical ideal of cosmopolitanism and role-model cultures. To him and those around him, Europe and the British Empire spoke of success, inevitability, and the refined manners of the sophisticated, although he was critical of empire on commercial grounds. This is a worldview now discredited by many, frequently described as a culture of bigotry that made voices of dissent invisible, as a time of aristocratic white men who told themselves self-serving mythologies in order to justify their places in the world. In this critique, the "modern" gets pushed aside, rejected by those who seek psychoanalytic rather than natural explanations. Untethered from the natural, the notion of progress becomes problematized. Grand narrative, the orphan child of a long-dead absolutist history, is now historiography, the subjective story that connects interpretation rather than fact. Discovery is no longer an acceptable component of the philosophy of history.

While contemporary liberals rarely acknowledge the impact of postmodern attacks, the continual theorization of moral chaos from continental philosophers provides a reason to abandon progressive views in the face of twentieth-century horrors. Individuals may advance morally, they seem to say, but societies never do. A commitment to utopian theories of justice has replaced the slow and (perhaps) steady approach favored by Smith and his contemporaries.[1] Martin Luther King's famous claim that the "moral arc of the universe is long, but it bends towards justice" is regarded as rhetorically powerful but philosophically specious.[2]

The last two chapters of this book constitute an attempt to bring the question of progress back to the foreground. No society or theory is perfect from the start, and in the absence of a coherent progressive conception of history, the role of learning disappears from long-term political deliberation. Rawls's *A Theory of Justice* did not consider progress at all.[3] *Political Liberalism* suggested evolution of the overlapping consensus but not collective human betterment over time (comprehensive moral doctrines tend toward agreement but not toward truth). It was only with *The Laws of Peoples* that Rawls inserted a neocosmopolitanism into his theory.

It is amidst this cultural rejection of the eighteenth-century worldview that I examine Smith's theories, arguing, as I have already shown, that much of his work anticipates contemporary debate about difference in liberal pluralistic societies. Smith's philosophy is not a romantic conservatism or a laissez-faire moralism but a forward-looking corpus with a commitment to justice and diversity. Yet his approach does rely on a defense of commercial markets and on beliefs in historical law, human nature, and the cosmopolitan perspective that leads to Truth—commitments sometimes dismissed as hackneyed naïveties or, worse, tools of imperialist propaganda. I am therefore forced to ask whether my project is even plausible and whether we, as twenty-first-century theorists, can learn from someone who published two and a half centuries ago.

To do this, I address Foucault's critique that such a project is incoherent.[4] I examine his challenge to the unity of discourses and the sciences to show that, in the end, while Foucault and Smith share a range of common methodologies— more, in fact, than is usually acknowledged—Smith has the tools to defend his theory against this postmodern challenge. In the absence of a coherent philosophy of history, the potential for normative discovery in history is virtually nonexistent;[5] normativity must have theoretical underpinnings.[6]

I do not pretend to offer a complete summary of Foucault's work here, nor do I claim to examine or advance the interpretive literature extending his project. Instead, my hope is to address a narrow area of discussion that calls Smith's historical project into question,[7] with special attention to the philosophy of history articulated in *The Archaeology of Knowledge*.[8]

The possibility of a conversation between our time and Smith's requires either the presumption of discourse simultaneity, as Foucault describes it, or Smith's commitment to the unified development of concepts and knowledge over time. The former suggests that we learn nothing from the past because history is simply a politicized justification of the present, while the latter holds that the present is the consequence of slow, deliberate, and progressive knowledge building. As I conclude, deciding between these options involves not only an investigation of the arguments behind truth claims but also a commitment to the particular worldviews they continue to create. This discussion puts us face to face with core questions in the philosophy of history, including dilemmas involving the role of truth in historiography, the nature of evidence, the place of narrative, and the relationship between history and natural law.

FOUCAULT AND THE DISCONTINUITY OF HISTORICAL NARRATIVE

Foucault was familiar with Smith and remarked extensively on *The Wealth of Nations in* both his published writings and his *Lectures at the Collège de France*.[9] Iara Vigo de Lima argues that Smith's work played a "central role" in the development of both archaeology and genealogy.[10] Foucault cites *FFL* several times in *The Order of Things*, and there are significant similarities between Foucault's concept of genesis ("the process by which imagination connects and orders impressions") and Smith's *HA*.[11] Foucault is backhandedly complimentary of *WN*, arguing that book 1 is the only place any of the classical economists ever analyzed labor.[12] He is also attentive enough to Smith's context to observe that he and his cohorts offer "a naturalism much more than a liberalism"[13] and to claim that the central principle of political economy is that "a government is never sufficiently aware that it always risks governing too much."[14]

Nevertheless, Foucault is also critical of Smith, both in his ancestry to liberalism—at one point Foucault claims that liberal economic policies necessitate a "super-state" that leads directly to Nazism—and by asserting that political economy is not to be understood as one of the human sciences.[15] He sees eighteenth-century liberalism (including Smith's) as beginning the project of defining freedom in the context of a police state that could not be questioned[16] and accuses political economy of focusing on government practices and consequences, not on whether they are "legitimate in terms of right."[17]

Foucault's most detailed comments concern Smith's economics. He saw *WN* as transitioning between the classical and modern ages.[18] Smith's work marks a step away from the discussion of wealth per se and toward the nature of production and capital. For Foucault, this is as much anthropology (as he defines it) as political economy, since *WN* tries to describe the natural relationship between human beings and the acquisition of their needs.[19]

This is plausible. As mentioned, Smith critiques the mercantilist notion that money is wealth (*WN* II.ii.14),[20] and his stage theory is the description of a natural process. He is very much focused on the world from the human perspective, and, as we have seen, Smith tries to define what it is to be a human being, tying the definition to exchange. Nevertheless, it is not Foucault's comments on economics that concern us. Arguments for or against commercial society or the reconsideration of economics since Smith are large-scale projects in and of themselves. Instead, my interest is in Foucault's bird's-eye critique of Smith: that which takes aim at his historical writing.

As is true of Smith, some people challenge the claim that Foucault is a historian. Others go further, suggesting that he seeks to "undermine the legitimacy of history, and of all disciplines, as exclusionary and limiting of knowledge."[21] Neither of these descriptions rings true. Foucault declares his work to be "autochthonous," born of discussions in the discipline of history itself.[22] As he observes, the studies of history—history of ideas, science, philosophy, and thought, in particular—have moved away from concerning themselves with historical periods and instead focus on "rupture" and "discontinuity" of given chronologies.[23] He sees himself as bringing out the central debate in contemporary historiography: "By what criteria is one to isolate the unities with which one is dealing; what is *a* science? What is an *oeuvre?* What is *a* theory? What is *a* concept? What is *a* text?"[24]

Foucault neither questions whether history *per se* is legitimate nor seeks to challenge the integrity of the disciplines themselves.[25] Instead, he asks about conceptual unity, arguing the now-familiar points that the rules that govern the logic of the disciplines come from within them rather than from without[26] and that practitioners are not conscious of the rules that govern their discourses, inquiries, or culture.[27] He "objects to historicism and Western humanism to the extent that they assume a continuous development, progress, and global totalization."[28] In other words, Foucault takes issue with grand narratives that presume human progress, particularly when it comes to political economy. To this day, economics sees itself as "continuous and progressive."[29]

For Foucault, there are no a priori theories or organizational structures through which one can understand any discipline, history included.[30] All interpretive filters are imposed retrospectively on a study, including those, in the case of historiography, that define the meaning and nature of history itself.[31] "If there really is a unity," he writes, "it does not lie in the visible, horizontal coherence of the elements formed; it resides well anterior to their formation, in the system that makes possible and governs that formation."[32]

Foucault argues that these internal disciplinary logics are the product of institutional relations and interactions of power and that they are discoverable only through analysis, not just of a particular discourse "[but] on its frontier, at that limit at which the specific rules that enable it to exist as such are defined."[33] Together, human thought constructs historical knowledge not by conscious choice but by the collective understandings that develop from everyday contact, interactions, relationships, negotiations of power, and the influence that social and political institutions have on the community. Discourses are the conversations, inquiries, practices, and investigations that grow out of these interactions. Culture, as Foucault calls this collectivity, is therefore "studied through technologies of power—not class, not progress, not the indomitability of the human spirit. . . . [Instead,] power exists as 'an infinitely complex network of "micropowers," of power relations that permeate every aspect of social life.[34]

Foucault shares a certain perspective with Smith, echoing, in some sense, the commitment that life feels guided by an invisible hand. The complex relationship between individuals and institutions lead to unconscious, unpredictable, and unintended unfolding of attitudes, events, and understandings, including perpetually changing debates and practices that evolve unintentionally from the culture.[35] This collective 'knowledge,' as Foucault sometimes calls it, becomes a part of the culture, limiting the worldview and possibilities that direct the culture as it moves forward in time.

Discourse rules are thus created by culture, but culture, in turn, is modified by these same discourse rules. Recovering the patterns, identifying the logic of a discourse and its history, is first identified by Foucault as an "archaeology" rather than a history because it seeks to uncover the silent "monuments" of the past and convert them to "documents" that can be "read" and analyzed. This is the reverse, he argues, of traditional history, which takes documents and makes them into silent monuments.[36]

Foucault's archaeology seeks to understand why a discourse becomes a science. It asks "what it is for that science to be a science" in the first place,[37] focusing on "the very different domain of knowledge," where knowledge is a holistic mixture of practices, culture, assumptions, and *episteme*.[38] Foucault explains that "archaeology does not try to restore what has been thought, wished, aimed at, experienced, desired by men in the very moment at which they expressed it in discourse. . . . It is nothing more than a rewriting: that is, in the preserved form of exteriority, a regulated transformation of what already been written."[39]

In other words, and in essence, Foucault is trying to retrace and map the large, unpredictable sweep of the invisible hand that he and Smith both use to describe the changes in culture and experience, a fact that becomes explicit late in the book:

> The analysis of discourse formations, of positivities, and knowledge in their relations with epistemological figures and with the sciences is what has been called, to distinguish it from other possible forms of the history of the sciences, the analysis of the *episteme*. This episteme may be suspected of being something like a world-view, a slice of history common to all branches of knowledge, which imposes on each one the same norms and postulates, a

general stage of reason, a certain structure of thought that the men of a particular period cannot escape — *a great body of legislation written once and for all by some anonymous hand*. By *episteme*, we mean, in fact, the total set of relations that unite, at a given period, the discursive practices that give rise to epistemological figures, sciences, and possibly formalized systems.[40]

Foucault's "anonymous" and Smith's "invisible" hands differ in their capacities to be mapped. For Smith, histories can be reconstructed. Foucault, however, is much more skeptical regarding the possibility of uncovering the story that leads to "the great body of legislation" that feels to agents as if it were "written once and for all." Furthermore, while an invisible hand implies agency (an invisible agent is still an agent), an anonymous one suggests intentional obfuscation. Foucault's legislator has taken great pains to hide authorship. Smith's term evokes a deity, while Foucault's is more Kafkaesque.

Nevertheless, Foucault tries, perhaps harder than Smith, to recount the historical pathways that lead from one "slice of history" to another, spending his lifetime seeking those anonymous discontinuities that represent the true workings of the technologies of power. Since we have seen that Smith has no more commitment to an *actual* invisible hand than Foucault does, the disagreement between the two appears to be an epistemological matter rather than a metaphysical one. They disagree about how much anyone can know.

Smith is obviously committed to a more robust epistemology than Foucault. He believes in the possibility of knowledge while Foucault is less clear on the matter, emphasizing the impact of psychoanalysis and the power of the subconscious or unconscious on the human understanding. How much of Foucault's skepticism is the consequence of the "linguistic turn" — the antirealist notion that language constitutes reality — is unclear, but since language is not transparent for Foucault, the archaeologist must renegotiate the nature and limits of knowledge.

It would be false to suggest that Foucault subscribes to Smith's social theory any more than he adopts Smith's economics. Nevertheless, it is clear that they are both committed to the sociological claim that culture formation is the unintended consequence of interactions among individuals and that these same interactions are heavily influenced by the governing social and political institutions, including, presumably, the modes of production. It feels to both Smith and Foucault as if human experience is, in some way, directed by an unseen hand, even if this hand turns out to be only a metaphorical or heuristic description of an experience.

For Foucault, the examinations of these technologies of power — the institutions and relations that develop from social, political, and economic structures — provide the most fruitful clues to the theoretical underpinnings of culture and change. This is also the governing principle in Smith's stage theory: only by examining the economy can one fully identify the appropriate political and social structures. Furthermore, for Smith, and similar to Foucault, these technologies of power (referencing, again, Foucault's term, not Smith's) are so essential to self and collective understanding that their forms either cultivate or inhibit mutual sympathy.

Like Smith, Foucault is as much a critic of culture as he is of history, and for both philosophers the two analyses often meld into one. Separating the prescriptive and descriptive elements in their treatises is a complex interpretive problem for their readers. Despite their common approaches and difficulties, the two disagree about a great deal, and certain of Foucault's criticisms are tremendously problematic for Smith—his assertion that history is concerned with validating the present, in particular. As H. D. Harootunian explains, for Foucault, "history itself is a Western myth that needs to be laid to rest."[41] It is both "a form of knowledge and power at the same time," and the product of "the urge to domesticate and control it in order to validate the present."[42] Foucault rejects "progressive history, which [for example] tells the story of the rise and spread of rational knowledge and the final extinction of 'unreason' everywhere."[43] While Foucault's account references Hegelian consciousness, given Smith's faith in progress and his commitment to the natural spread of universal opulence, and given Foucault's attack on political economy in his classroom lectures, it would be hard to suggest that he is not also a target of this critique.

Foucault grounds his attack on progressive history on a more foundational criticism of the possibility of an a priori approach to the connection between statements. There are, he states, four possible ways in which statements could follow from one another: they refer to the same object, they define a group of relations, they reference a group of permanent and coherent concepts, and they rely upon unitary forms of identity and persistent themes. All four possibilities must be rejected, he argues, claiming that each has too many variables to describe any definitive unity.[44] This leads him to conclude that "instead of reconstituting *chains of inference* (as one often does in the history of the sciences or of philosophy)," or "instead of drawing up *tables of differences* (as the linguists do)," proper analyses should "describe *systems of dispersion*."[45]

Foucault seeks those moments of discourse that don't logically follow from one another—instances of contiguity that suggest a hidden discourse or, rather, a hidden chaos.[46] Foucault therefore shares with Smith a faith in the duality of historical analysis—for Smith the ideal history reveals the anomalies of actual history, whereas, for Foucault, the lack of natural connection between statements exposes the disorder of culture, the chaos that lies beneath it.[47] Smith's and

Foucault's fundamental disagreement revolves around the natural connectivity of events and statements rather than around the content of their historical narratives.

On a certain level Foucault's conclusion about the discontinuity of statements is about the formation of analytic structures. Foucault argues that rather than look for similarities between statements, the archeologist should look for discontinuities. However, this is a methodological claim, not a metaphysical one. It is nothing more than an articulation of a "possible line of attack," in his words,[48] and says nothing about the viability of history.[49] In this regard, while his prescriptions may offer the historian a better way to learn about culture, they do not indicate anything about the nature of cultural or historical change qua change.

On a different level, however, his conclusion is about rationality. Foucault believes that human reason is malleable enough that inferences become cultural products; they are no longer representative of self-evident logical connections or entailments. Rationality, then, becomes a much larger category, the intermingling of life experience, habit, culture, and power relations.[50] This turn is more than just an extension of phronesis. It is instead a challenge to logical structures themselves. Foucault takes a more daring approach to enlarging reason than, for example, MacIntyre, who suggests that "logic is only a necessary and not a sufficient condition for rationality."[51] Like Smith, Foucault calls certain inferential structures into question.

I do not wish to "confuse rupture and irrationality," as Foucault cautions.[52] My point is not that his discontinuities are irrational. My claim is larger, namely, that he is preserving the "rational" nature of discourse by redefining rationality itself. This struggle to liberate discourses from being analyzed by logic alone is never more prominent than in his lengthy and often ambiguous attempts to define what he means by "a statement."

Recall that the lack of logical connection between statements is that which permits Foucault to question the unity of disciplines. Yet a statement is neither a proposition nor a sentence or speech act.[53] Its individuation is not the product of grammar, logic, or "analysis," where the latter refers to the psychological study of behavior.[54] It is, instead, a "function of existence that properly belongs to signs and on the basis of which one may then decide, through analysis or intuition, whether or not they 'make sense,' according to what rule they follow one another or are juxtaposed, of what they are the sign, and what sort of act is carried out by their formulation (oral or written)."[55]

A statement is a function because it plays a certain role in a culture but is also created by and defined by that same culture: "There is no statement in general, no free, neutral, independent statement . . . no statement that does not presuppose others."[56]

The intricate relationship between statements, and between statements and their cultures, causes their meaning to be contextual—their meanings are in flux because of "differences of material, substance, time, and place."[57] As a result—and in the clearest articulation of what it might mean to be a statement—Foucault argues that "the affirmation that the earth is round or that species evolve does not constitute the same statement before and after Copernicus, before and after Darwin."[58]

This example is the core of Foucault's insight in *The Archaeology of Knowledge*. Because statements about the nature of the Earth as a planet and its position in the universe have such tremendous cultural power, because this information could be revolutionary only before Copernicus and never would be again, and because the meaning of both the terminology in the statement and the consequences of its utterance was so unclear before *De revolutionibus orbium coelestium*, Foucault is likely correct that astronomical statements change meaning before and after the Copernican revolution. To explain why this is so would require no small discourse: histories of ideas, psychology, anthropology, religion, power, cultural life, and many aspects of the human experience would all inform the difference. Given the change in the nature of inference and the fluidity of meaning in statements, one must now question what counts as historical evidence. For Smith, an account of an event or the juxtaposition of political structures can reveal progressive patterns in history, but, for Foucault, neither events nor comparisons have any clear or over-arching meaning. Archaeology can uncover the discontinuities and the technologies of power at work, but since there are no meaningful or implicit connections between two historical items, narratives have to be imposed rather than discovered.

The fluidity of statements does not limit their structure. For Foucault, they are not just single propositional utterances with varied cultural power. Language itself is also a statement,[59] suggesting that what Foucault must mean by the term is not simply the source of meaning in discourses but also an assertion of individual human existence as it is intertwined with meaning and enacted within the boundaries of culture.[60] A statement is the interaction of consciousness and the world. It is an activity, not just an utterance, and it relies on the subjectivity of culture for meaning and definition.[61] Statements constitute a limited assertion (or *enunciation*, to reference the French cognate)[62]—they are of a particular time and place. But statements are also unique. They are contextual and dependent on all the other assertions of individual existence, yet they help to formulate those others. All agents can assert themselves only insofar as others assert themselves; statements are dependent on one another.

If Foucault is right, then moral sentiments and commercial exchanges are also statements, since both are contextual while being intimate and meaningful assertions of individual human existence. Smith sees commercial exchange as a fundamental human activity (*WN* I.ii.1–2), and, as I have shown, the moral sentiments are inherently related to the announcement of identity. As statements, these activities share similar difficulties. Just as language cannot fully communicate the content of statements for Foucault, for Smith it cannot accurately parse sentiments: "It is impossible, indeed, to express all the variations which each sentiment either does or ought to undergo, according to every possible variation of circumstances. They are endless, and language wants names to mark them by" (*TMS* VII.iv.4). And, "It is impossible by language to express, if I may say so, the invisible features of all the different modifications of passion as they show themselves within" (*TMS* VII.iv.5). Regarding exchange, as we have seen, the rise of prose is the result of the growth in commerce (*LRBL* ii.115). Both exchange and sentiments are communitarian constructs that are dependent on culture in its largest sense.

For Foucault, the amorphous nature of the statement is a melding of the logical, linguistic, psychological, and contingent. Yet his assertion that one does not follow from the other is still a radical conception of human rationality because it still presumes that the agents who "state" something are ultimately arbitrary in their moving from one statement to another. For Foucault, the power of culture is so strong that human actions are themselves subordinated to the masterful, albeit nonconscious, manipulations of the technologies of power.

A central component of the drive to state is habit and familiarity; the rules of discourse and culture must have a certain "regularity";[63] otherwise individuals could not act accordingly. Therefore, I would suggest that Foucault extends Hume's famous argument against cause and effect, asserting that inference is the product of *perceived* contiguity. Foucault's contribution to Hume's theory is the recognition of the immense cultural complexities involved in perception. He also substitutes 'culture' for 'custom,' the eighteenth-century equivalent term. Since Foucault's notion of culture is more complex than Hume's custom — Freud's psychoanalytic approach permeates Foucault's writing, and Hume did not anticipate the modern notion of the subconscious[64] — the heaviest analytic work must focus on the nature of perceiving in the phrase 'perceived contiguity.' Full-scale analyses must be developed to investigate which technologies of power influence which inference, why, and in what way they make discontinuities seem inferential. Foucault tried to do this in his book-length histories.

Yet while Foucault's argument is conceptually deeper than Hume's, Hume's is ultimately stronger because it is built on a fully articulated epistemology. For Hume, the limits of cause and effect are the result of empiricist limitations. For

Hume, causation cannot be perceived, only recognized through habitual observation (*Treatise* I.1.4; *Enquiry* VII.11). In contrast, Foucault's argument is conceptual; he offers very little epistemological theorizing. As described above, he justifies his conclusion by systematically eradicating the possibility of four disjuncts in a list of possible connections between statements that he portrays as inclusive of all options. He uses logic to discredit logic. He also presents the interference of culture as a historical given, as if it were true of every time and place. As a result, his own argument is itself either an a priori critique or one simply bounded by his culture at his time. If it is the former, it is self-contradictory. If it is the latter, the discussion can only regress into familiar battles over relativism.

Foucault would no doubt recognize this criticism.[65] Self-referential difficulties have plagued the history of philosophy since its inception. From Eubulides to Nietzsche to MacIntyre to contemporary multiculturalists, philosophers and theories have fallen prey to the identification of internal contradictions. Yet this charge often fails to persuade because the argument does not speak to the experience that the contradictory theory tries to articulate. Sometimes (although not always), attacking a statement as internally inconsistent feels more like smoke and mirrors than cogent argumentation, since by attacking with a logical technicality (no matter how correct it may be to do so) the critic appears to be suggesting that the content of a given issue is not worth addressing. When Zarathustra states that truth is a lie, for example, the reader knows what he is getting at, at least to a certain degree. Zarathustra's proclamation has guided many to action. Similarly, when Foucault implies that inferences are formulated by culture—not that culture interferes with proper functioning logic but that one infers correctly within a specific culture only[66]—there is also something intuitively truthful about the claim regardless of the fact that it is an absolutist statement asserting the universally relative.

Cultures *do* create inferences where there may not otherwise have been any. At WN V.ii.k.3, for example, Smith tells us that custom creates absolute necessities, a paradox of self-reference of the same type. A European worker would be ashamed, Smith writes, to appear in public without a linen shirt, and leather shoes have become necessities in England. While Smith recognizes that he is changing the definition of necessity from its usual meaning signifying those things that human beings need to subsist qua human being,[67] he is still accurate when he describes owning such clothing as necessities per se.

Is Smith's claim nothing more than another example of phronesis? Is he simply equivocating, changing the meaning of 'necessary' to "socially necessary"? Maybe, but disregarding his claim as such misses the point. Doing so ignores the power of and the intimate relationship between culture, identity, and logic, the very connections Foucault is trying to articulate. It ignores the fact that clothing is itself a statement, in Foucault's sense of the term. Rationality must include phenomenological elements, at least insofar as Foucault and Smith both understand it.

If logic alone does not justify Foucault's descriptions of culture, what does? As I suggested above, his histories of madness, sexuality, and punishment are evidence for his larger theoretical claim, however ambiguous the nature of historical evidence might be. Not surprisingly, *The Archaeology of Knowledge* was written after several of his full-length histories, including *Madness and Civilization*, *The Birth of the Clinic*, and *The Order of Things*. Foucault himself claims that the later book is intended to give the others "greater coherence."[68] And while he struggles with his understanding of history throughout his career, changing his dominant methodological metaphor from archaeology to gene-alogy,[69] it remains the case that *The Archaeology of Knowledge* is still the most compact theoretical account of his philosophy of history. Even more so, it is not as radical a departure from the history of thought as some assert. As Hayden White illustrates, Foucault's conclusions are themselves part of a long-standing tradition of rhetorical analysis, and all he appears to do is "rediscover the importance of the projective or generational aspect of language" and call attention to the poetic in science.[70]

While Foucault is challenging the teleology of progressive disciplines, he is immersed in its logic, forcing us to ask, as Smith wants us to, whether progress is unavoidable because it is the natural state of human affairs. Furthermore, while Foucault questions the unity of narrative, he still relies upon its existence. Narrative, too, seems natural. Thus, if the ultimate justification for Foucault's theory is that the evidence supports it,[71] and if he is simply continuing a philosophical lineage of his own, then he is in the exact same predicament as Smith, in that the evidence for Smith's philosophy of history is the information provided by WN.

That over his lifetime Foucault's data set outnumbered Smith's in terms of page number, diversity, and subject area is irrelevant to the larger question, since the manner of justification is the same for both. The main justificatory difference between Smith's work and Foucault's lies only in the type of ideals they juxtapose with their historiographies. As we have seen, Smith compares actual history to an ideal one, but Foucault ironically builds his theory on a neutralist ideal that seeks to eradicate the influence of culture. Foucault shares the penchant for neutrality with the liberals that postmodernists so often seek to delegitimize.

To elaborate: in the absence of an ideal philosophy of history, Foucault writes, "one is led therefore to the project of a *pure description of discursive events* as the horizon for the search for the unities that form within it."[72] White explains that, for Foucault, texts (or instances of historical activity by individual persons) "are not *analyzed*; they are simply 'transcribed.' And transcribed for a specific purpose; they are to be 'diagnosed' to determine the nature of the disease of which they are *symptomatic*. . . . Foucault proceeds in the manner of the pathologist. He 'reads' a text in the way that a specialist in carcinoma 'reads' an X-ray."[73]

Such description, Foucault argues, frees the archeologist from the traditional unities of history and disciplinary work and allows the archeologist to uncover new connections.[74] Yet Foucault would have to argue that no *pure description* independent of culture is possible; this claim is ever present in his work. The archeologist is always bound by the present, by his or her situation, and by the technologies of power. Thus Foucault aims at neutrality while recognizing its impossibility, a dualist approach to understanding that we have already seen in Smith and that continues to frame my discussion.

For Foucault, neutrality is pursued (but not achieved) by turning the fact of discontinuity against itself.[75] He starts with particularity and seeks contradictory information to develop a theoretical picture that is in some sense unified and is in some sense a more accurate account of cultural reality because it is constructed by the technologies of power and the interactions of individuals who are governed by the technologies of power the people create. One can see common methods with Smith's impartial spectator. For Smith, a moral actor examines a circumstance by entering into the perspective of another—this is the particularity. He or she looks at the context and considers social opinion in order to find contradictions or similarities, thereby imagining a new perspective that is more authentically representative of what has actually happened. This balances individuals' experience with that of the other, their own, and the community's. Smith's impartial spectator never achieves impartiality, just as Foucault can never offer a pure description of discursive events. It is not a perfect analogy. But it shows a common problem for both philosophers.

DEFENDING THE PHILOSOPHY OF HISTORY

I have identified Foucault's and Smith's methodological similarities in order to show that their two projects are not as disparate as some might believe.[76] I have argued that the evidence for their theories is of the same type—large-scale empirical studies such as those in WN and *The History of Madness* that claim to report unseen facts about the world. (Foucault does not challenge historicity.) I have shown that their ideal analysts have common investigative techniques;

both the historian and the impartial spectator move imaginatively from perspective to impartiality while recognizing the impossibility of their goals. I have also illustrated that both are committed to sociologies that presume individual lives are framed, to a large degree, by the powers, customs, and relationships that govern societies, while noting that Foucault's technologies of power are not identical to Smith's economic structures. I have not yet fully addressed their locus of difference, the role of progress, and the presumption on Smith's part that progress is natural.

Foucault argues against the possibility of an ideal history of philosophy[77] by presenting a method of analysis that challenges the necessary connection between statements. Thus, he suggests, one should not be concerned with cause and effect in the most literal sense. For Foucault, this involves giving up a search for "origins" and looking instead for "beginnings."[78] In *The Archaeology of Knowledge*, Foucault brackets truth for the sake of a new methodology, the tension between the undeniable chronology of events and the archaeologist's attempt to investigate them as if they were simultaneous: examining the past as defined by the present means acting as if all discourse events happened at the same time.[79] This is another example of the duality of actual and ideal.

The upshot of this critique is that, for Foucault, there is no way to identify what causes history to move, not only from one event to another but also from one stage to the next. The closest one can come is to uncover contradictions in discourse—the drive to identify, resolve, and "escape" from the irresolvable contradictions of disciplines is what moves discourse.[80] This, obviously, is a direct challenge to Smith's stage theory, especially since, as we have seen, Foucault sees historians as giving up the search for periods in favor of identifying discontinuity. When all is said and done, Foucault's *critique* of Smith's philosophy of history can be reduced to three propositions: (1) the assertion that history is natural must be false, (2) the division of history into four stages is arbitrary, and (3) the commitment to historical progress is a fiction (or a mythology). All of these are related to the ways in which Smith relies on a dominant narrative, one he treats as a discovery rather than a construction.

Regarding criticism (1), that history cannot be natural, as we have seen, the terms 'natural' and 'nature' are ambiguous for Smith. They relate to the fuzzy nature of historical laws and may have as many as seven diverse meanings. Only one of these runs afoul of Foucault's approach, the claim that history is teleological, and it does so only if history is *essentially* so, since an ad hoc teleology is not a violation of the arbitrary nature of statement-relations. (If any connection is arbitrary, then a progressivist connection can be no better or worse than any other.) No essentialist teleology has been established, but if there is a *telos* to history, its existence would make a case for a theory of progress against Foucault's third objection, which I address shortly.

Regarding Foucault's objection (2), that Smith's division of history into four stages is a fiction: in *The Order of Things* Foucault himself divides periods of thought into four great epochs, although *The Archaeology of Knowledge* does not continue this practice. Foucault seems to be opposed not to periodization per se but to what he refers to as "totalitarian periodization," the claim that all individuals think identically in the same period.[81] Smith does not argue this, and, frankly, I don't know anyone who does. But even so, Smith's four stages represent shifts in the modes of production and the social and political relations that result. They do not identify specific dates or events that mark the transition. Instead, they represent, again in Foucault's terms, shifts in the technologies of power that influence the nature of interaction. Smith's insight is that as these technologies of power shift, the nature of society shifts. This does not happen universally, nor does it happen simultaneously. Each society follows its own economic progress. Described as such, at least given the theory he outlines in *The Archaeology of Knowledge*, Foucault could not disagree.

In response, one might argue that Smith claims more than that as technology changes, culture changes; he claims that all societies *necessarily* proceed through these four stages. He may therefore be accused of relying upon an a priori theory of progress—or at least making the claim that nature *requires* this progression, an approach that paves the way for the idealist histories of Hegel and Marx (German Idealism being the true object of Foucault's scorn). If so, this again represents Smith's commitment to an ideal history, and we have shifted to criticism (3), since (2), in and of itself, does not address the reason for the stages, only their existence in the organized historiography of human events. Furthermore, the identification of these stages is the result of a narrative, one emphasizing the roles of the modes of production, but one that may remain invisible when looking at a different narrative theme.

Focusing on criticism (3)—a progressive history is perfectionist in the sense that progress implies betterment—the standard Smith relies on in WN integrates natural liberty, universal opulence, and the natural drive of individuals to better their conditions. Each of these has been discussed throughout this book, but each represents the content of the progression, not the fact of progress itself, which is what Foucault seems to object to.

Despite Smith's claim that progress is in some sense natural, the term itself is a cultural one. The meaning of progress has changed throughout history (as has the meaning of nature).[82] Progress as it is currently understood is primarily an Enlightenment concept. Throughout most of the human experience, people regarded history as either static or cyclical. Parents expected their children's lives to be very much like their own, and basic knowledge remained the same over many generations. The archetypical modern experience of children rejecting their parents' attitudes as naïve, inadequate, or corrupt is the product of a rapidly changing world; it is not human nature manifested through inevitable adolescent rebellion.

There is nothing in the human experience that demands progressive commitment. For most of history, when radical change did take place it was usually viewed as the result of accident, the consequence of a particular political will, or intervention by a divine figure. Such change was more likely to be viewed as regressive than progressive; things got worse, not better. The expulsion from Eden is a primary example of a story glorifying an unsullied past. Furthermore, Burke's eighteenth-century conservatism provides the obvious counterexample to Smith's approach.[83] The Enlightenment discourse, with its political transitions, provided a variety of ways to consider the future.

The English word 'progress' is etymologically Latin, a combination of *pro* and *gradi*; literally, it means to 'walk forward.' The first use of the term is likely that by Lucretius in *De Rerum Natura*. In his description of humans distinguishing themselves over time from the beasts of nature, he writes, "These things practice and the experience of the unresting mind have taught men gradually, as they progressed step by step."[84]

For the Roman poet, however, there is no growth past his epoch; humanity may have progressed, but it does so no longer. As far as Lucretius was concerned, whatever advancement humanity had managed was already complete; only the possibility of destruction was ever present.[85] Progress, which contemporary minds understand as a continuous movement forward that provides society and inquiry with direction, was absent from his picture of the future.

But 'continuous' here is a misleading term. As mentioned before, that history moves ever forward does not suggest that history always moves forward. I do not mean to argue that contemporary visions of progress must offer an uninterrupted narrative absent of temporary setbacks, or one whose progress is absolutely secure without any hint of regression. Smith doesn't suggest this either. Progress can be complicated and is often fragile. The twentieth century is a prime example of a time fraught with unlearned lessons and rife with degeneration, but one could certainly make the case that significant progress was made in the midst of the century's horrors.[86]

During times of significant growth and complexity, progress can be particularly hard to spot. As Willson H. Coates writes, "Since there has always been in periods of rapid social change a dual process of breaking down and building up, it is possible to regard the disintegration of moral and social traditions as a necessary part of the moral and social reconstruction which the twentieth century demands."[87] In other words, despite the destruction of institutions and the chaos and barbarism of the twentieth century, a bird's-eye view—perhaps the only view that permits any unfettered glimpse of progress—allows one to see advancement: "Progress may be no less progress for its being precarious, for it has never been, and by definition can never be, identified with stasis."[88] Part of what Foucault would object to in WN is the bird's-eye view that it presupposes with its large-scale narrative focus. The impartial spectator is indeed such a perspective, as are the narratives that Smith described in HA. To attack the possibility of such a view is most certainly to attack Smith's whole project.

As the existence of HA suggests, the intellectual shift leading to the contemporary concept of progress began during the sixteenth and seventeenth centuries with the introduction of the modern scientific method and attitude. Science assumed predictability and coherent explanation. To describe nature was to describe *logos*: "Man had to see that it was not fortune but general causes that govern the world."[89] In 1566, for example, Jean Bodin argued against the classical image of a golden age. Summing up Bodin's argument, Sidney B. Fay writes, "The powers of nature have always remained the same; and . . . it would be illogical to suppose that nature could at one time produce the men and conditions postulated by the Golden Age theory, and not produce them at a later time."[90] Bodin argued that while there are periods of progress and regress, since history "depends largely on the will of men, which is always changing . . . there has been a gradual ascent from the time when men lived like wild beasts to the social order of sixteenth century Europe."[91]

This approach to progress is quintessentially modern: the laws of nature are timeless, and different outcomes are therefore the result of human intervention, not of a fluctuating physics. If there is a connection between the physical reality of the universe and human experience (which there no doubt is), then Foucault's challenge to progress must also challenge the consistency of the laws of nature, something he does not do in *The Archaeology of Knowledge*. This would move him even further away from the linguistic turn. As we have seen, Smith argues for the consistency of principles that guide nature, and this continuity is essential to progress. We are once again immersed in the question of historical discovery: can we learn facts of nature from the unfolding of human events?

I do not mean to beg the question by suggesting that since the laws of nature presume progress, Foucault is right only if there are no laws of nature. Instead, my argument is that *if* there is something progressive in the human experience currently, then there must have been this potential throughout history. *Whether* that progressive potential exists is still on the table.[92]

As Foucault would no doubt agree, progress is not a simple idea. It requires a background culture and a network of social, epistemological, and metaphysical assumptions that provide explanations of the human place in the world, the nature and limits of inquiry, the role (or lack thereof) of the divine, and a complex, sophisticated account of the nature of history itself.[93] It also requires background conceptions of justice and the good life in that a history that progresses must progress toward something. It was not until the Enlightenment that these were identified.

For eighteenth-century thinkers, beginning with Turgot and including, especially, Condorcet, progress includes social, political, and moral components. It was not just scientific knowledge that advanced as history unfolded; the human character and circumstance bettered themselves as well. In *A Philosophical Review of the Successive Advances of the Human Mind*, Turgot postulated that human society moved back and forth from barbarism, closely identified with thought governed by superstition, to civilization, characterized by the centrality of reason.[94] While still cyclical, in a certain sense Turgot contributes a stage theory that will be of immense importance to Smith and his commentators, and it supplies the essential notion that one stage can be identified as *morally better* than another. Without such gradations, progress becomes indistinguishable from chronology. The teleology inherent in the advancement of history assumes that the closer one gets to the goal of history, the higher the moral value of the current moment is.

Ultimately, though, it is the Marquis de Condorcet who offers us the most dramatic account of moral progress, placing its identification at the center of his treatise *The Progress of the Human Mind*. The "aim" of this work, he writes, is to show that "nature has set no term to the perfection of the human faculties. . . . This progress will no doubt vary in speed, but it will never be reversed."[95] Smith's progressive theory is immersed in all of these notions and likely influenced Condorcet.[96] His cultural conditions were such that he put forth a particular idea of progress, one that recognized both the successes and the failures of the world he lived in.

There should be no doubt that this brief, selective sketch of the history of progress is indicative of an agenda, and it certainly makes invisible most of the experience of those who oppose the notion of progress or those who are its victims; bird's-eye views neglect detail by definition.[97] It ignores questions of empire and the tensions between those who have battled for supremacy. It excludes voices; it is a political document disguised as a neutralist academic narrative. Shapiro would have a field day with it. Furthermore, it is understandable that Foucault or any mid- to late twentieth-century French philosopher would oppose a natural conception of progress. Nineteenth-century Prussia, the end of progress for Hegel (again, the actual target of Foucault's critique), met all of the historical criteria of a nation that actualized its progressive teleology, yet it still gave birth to a movement that proved to be one of the most evil (or regressive) in human history—progress under the National Socialists became ideological rather than a fact of nature. The French saw two world wars on their soil, and there can be little doubt that the existentialist call for authenticity is in part a therapeutic response to the *collaberateurs* who assisted the Vichy government. These are the colleagues, institutions, and technologies of power that frame Foucault's philosophical discourse. Reminiscent of his claim about the change in astronomical statements before and after Copernicus, it is certainly worth inquiring whether the phrase "human beings progress" can possibly mean the same thing before and after the Third Reich.

Nevertheless, while Foucault may have had every motivation in the world to reject progress, and while the discourse itself may have changed irrevocably in his lifetime, none of this should indicate that his moment in time is enough to justify the rejection of the notion of human progress in and of itself. The question at hand is not what challenged him to reject the narrative of progress but whether the narrative account of progress as I have described it is *untrue*. If Foucault can show that those who postulate the progressive narrative are excluding relevant counterexamples, and if, as I discussed earlier, a proposed analytic frame turns out to be too narrow to allow inquirers to see evidence against their own theory, then he can cogently argue that their methodology is flawed and that the inquirers have failed at their task. But if this is the case, then the inquirers have, once again, failed at seeing that their narrative is *untrue*. It is still the veracity of the narrative that is at stake.

A critique of narrowness is a powerful challenge to any narrative, but that all narratives are more limited than reality is a claim not that they are false, only that history is not encyclopedic. Historiography does not contain *all* information and *all* perspectives; if such an endeavor were even possible, how large would it have to be and how would anyone read it? As I described above, histories are selective by necessity, and which elements to leave out and to put in are matters for debate. The political discourses of the twentieth century in particular were about finding a model for inclusive histories and political structures; a central motivation in writing this book is my belief that Smith prefigured and can still contribute to these conversations.

There are also a variety of fluid concepts in this history. Progress, obviously, is one of them; freedom, individuality, and humanity are others. It is certainly unclear as to whether the term 'progress' in Smith means anything close to what it did for Lucretius, just as its meaning may have changed before and after the National Socialist regime. However, Foucault would have us believe that there is no *implicit* connection between the concepts of progress in any given time periods, even those contiguous with one another, and that there is nothing inherent in progress that lets human minds naturally comprehend that Lucretius, Smith, and the Nazis are talking about something related. This is a hard sell.

As indicated above, if Foucault is right, his discovery calls into question not just historical methodology but human rationality itself, because the narrative structure described above is both rational and understandable. It *makes sense*, and whether it makes sense to the modern mind alone (which I doubt) doesn't change the fact that it makes sense to someone. The human experience of chronology—of before and after—appears to be universal even if metaphysical and religious systems sometimes play fast and loose with them. Time provides the understanding with an organizational structure. Kant taught us this, and, as de Lima notes, Foucault has explicitly commented that he is in agreement with Habermas that we should not abandon Kant or we would give up rationality itself.[98]

Foucault's discontinuities are designed to provide cognitive dissonance, to make the invisible visible—they are pedagogical and epistemological, not just linguistic—they must still presume a coherent and rationally understandable world, otherwise the term 'discontinuity' would itself be meaningless. The power of the challenge from discontinuity comes from the ever-present nature of continuity. Without the presumption of the possibility of continuity, epistemological chaos would reign and the human psyche would flounder. For Smith, this coherence is narrative in structure; Foucault clearly presumes the same. His agents are not individuals arbitrarily making their way in the world without any meaningful grasp of what is happening to them. They are narrative creatures who look to a world they can grasp, while archeologists study the fact that their understanding is built on connections and foundations invisible to them, or ones that are taken as given when they shouldn't be. Excluding his pre-Freudian perspective, there is nothing here that Smith would disagree with. Foucault is most certainly correct that there is no *definitive* narrative—one that is *inherently* superior to others. This is what Shapiro is getting at in his critique of Smith, and, in this sense, I concede that Smith's emphases on liberty and universal opulence are to a certain extent idiosyncratic. It is Smith's *intellectual interest* in these topics that constructs the narrative, but whether the narrative is correct, whether it is *true*, whether there has or has not been progress in

opulence is not arbitrary. This is an empirical matter depending on the definitions of progress and opulence, accepting the fact that no single meaning may
be definitive. Certainly, there might have been progress for *some* people and
regress or stasis for others, and Smith's narrative may not illustrate these
instances well enough, but, again, this particular criticism moves from being
about truth to being about the encyclopedic nature of a text. As Maureen
Harkin suggests, in addition to Smith's recognizing that progress does come
with some loss, he seems to suggest that his own narratives are "local to a time
and place, neither unconditionally true nor unqualifiedly certain."[99] For Smith,
this is yet again the tension between the actual epistemological limitations of
inquirers who create the narratives and the ideal theoretical constructs they use
to investigate nature.

Furthermore, Smith never claims that suffering is required for progress.
While he does think that lessons come from tragedy and suffering—the experiments of history yield results—he never makes an argument for the necessity of
oppression. As a result, his philosophy of history is not susceptible to the postcolonial critique that any notion of progress *justifies* historical injustice. To use
Kipling's phrase, there is no "White Man's Burden" in any of Smith's work.[100]

From the twenty-first-century perspective (or twentieth, in Foucault's case),
eighteenth-century notions of progress are guilty of the most egregious sins. They
presume European societies are the measure of enlightenment; they claim that
some societies are civilized while others are not; they tend to disregard the possibility of *individual* progress, subsuming personal advancement under the collective (although Smith himself does not do this). In short, they are "triumphant."[101]
They are also inarguably the outcome of technologies of power and of an impe-
rial worldview. But if this is the case, a twenty-first-century "archaeologist" still
faces a familiar dilemma. The assertion that narratives of progress are *wrong*
because of their exclusionary nature is itself either an absolutist theoretical
construction or a moral belief bound only by the culture.[102] If one narrative is
better only because of contingencies such as personal interest, then attacks
against the exclusionary nature of eighteenth-century progress cease to have any
weight. If connections between statements are arbitrary, then there is no reason
to prefer a nonprogressivist to a progressivist link. Foucault's reader is faced with
either the self-referential paradox or the regress into relativism.

To illustrate my point, consider an abridged version of Gary Gutting's
biographical account of Foucault in his *Foucault: A Very Short Introduction*. He
presents three competing accounts of Foucault's life without prioritizing one
over the other: one emphasizing Foucault as a politically connected academic
star, one as a tormented homosexual, and one as an activist. "None of these

stories are false," Gutting writes, "but their mutual truth keeps us from forming any definitive picture of Foucault's life, which is just what he wanted."[103]

On first glance, Gutting's claim that none of these accounts is complete is just silly. There is nothing preventing him from creating a more inclusive picture of Foucault's biography, intertwining the three stories. What makes the point important, though—I have no intention of casting aspersions on Gutting's work—is his admission that their selection is *intentional*. The biographies are designed specifically to selectively impart information as Foucault would have "wanted." They intentionally hide some aspects and emphasize others. Either Gutting is intentionally obfuscating truth or each paragraph is trying to teach readers something. I claim it is the latter.[104]

We are yet again engaged in a methodological discussion, one in which the rhetoric is framed by pedagogical considerations. But by what standards do writers or archeologists choose their pedagogies? *The Archaeology of Knowledge* offers no answer. The most likely criterion, one confirmed by Foucault's later career, is the value of the oppositional. Focusing on the marginalized and the invisible makes history more inclusive and thus more just. This is the position held by queer and feminist standpoint theorists; it is suggested by Shapiro's critique as well. I have no quarrel with this view.

The technologies of power—contemporary culture—do have a logic to them, and, given the current injustice in the world, the three outlines Gutting provides can be organized in a moral hierarchy in terms of the importance of telling a particular story at a particular time. For example, the plight of those who are marginalized because of their homosexuality is a story that very much needs to be told, given current political battles about gay marriage and adoption. It is therefore likely first on the list of political importance. However, the hierarchy I describe is particular to current circumstances in specific societies. It has no cross-cultural weight unless oppositional archaeologies are absolute goods in themselves, unless diversity and inclusion are moral imperatives regardless of culture or time period. If this is so, then queer or feminist standpoint theory is still built on an absolutist framework: inclusivity is to be desired for a variety of reasons, and only by following the archaeological method can one maximize inclusion.

If one responds that inclusivity is to be desired simply because the technologies of power are such that archaeologists working under their auspices prefer inclusion, then one is faced with the same relativistic problems. If culture is a good-in-itself and particular archaeologies are justified by their adherence to either accepting or undermining the cultures in which they are found (recognizing that the desire to undermine is itself a consequence of the technologies of power), then the Foucauldian project ends up being strikingly similar to MacIntyre's. Archeological choices are rational, but the rationality is tradition bound and only internally justified. MacIntyre himself does not consider this relativism, although many others do.[105]

But if inclusion is a good in itself, then the ultimate rejoinder is not the self-referential attack but the observation that the Foucauldian project is, at some level, indistinguishable from the liberalisms and neoliberalisms it attacks. If this is the case, then Foucault is eminently compatible with Smith, although Smith may require the input of John Stuart Mill and Karl Popper to connect the demand for liberty with the demand for truth. Foucault's archaeology would be yet another liberal methodology, useful but not particularly radical.

However, neither of these possibilities seems justified by *The Archaeology of Knowledge*. According to the method it outlines, there are no criteria for choice other than personal interest. If not, then deciding between Smith's perspective defending natural progress and Foucault's notion that progress is mythological is simply a matter of preference, unconscious choice, or cultural manipulation, depending on how deterministic one sees Foucault as being. If so, then the Foucauldian has no warrant to critique the Smithian in any binding manner. The Smithian, however, has every advantage because he or she has an empirically justified system upon which to fall back: a theoretical structure upon which to justify belief, one that claims that progressivist narratives are not on equal footing with their nonprogressivist counterparts because progressivist narratives are *true*. In short, there is no reason for the Smithian to listen to the Foucauldian because the Foucauldian has nothing but instrumental reasons for what he or she claims.

I would suggest, then, that the Foucauldian is left with a powerful choice reminiscent of the one described in *After Virtue*. MacIntyre argues that in the face of the contemporary dominance of emotivism one must choose between Nietzsche and Aristotle: radical individualism and its lack of rational foundation or the Classical Greek teleological virtue ethic with its rational core.[106] Analogously, Foucault's readers must choose between the optimism of progress and the order that it provides human history or the pessimism of chaos with its existentialist radical freedoms in which no narratives are ever justified for any morally binding reasons. Is knowledge unified or arbitrary? If it is arbitrary, there can be no absolute argument for justice because there can be no claim to universal integrity. There is only a personal allegiance to a *discourse of integrity*.

Smith would argue that human connections are natural and that history unfolds as these relationships are explored, tested, reevaluated, affirmed, and denied. It may be easy to break up a discourse into its component parts and see the statements as randomly following one another for reasons of power, but it is infinitely more difficult to *live* with this breakup because nothing follows from it. Nothing, that is, but the individual displeasure one feels from being treated badly. If all that exists is resentment, then we are left with Hayek's claim that justice is simply the demands of envy,[107] the modern version of Thrasymachus's long-refuted position in *Republic* II that justice is the will of the stronger.

There is a direct line connecting this position to Nietzsche's, and Nietzsche's to Foucault's, but Smith would have no part of it because he thinks of the science of man as a science—an account of the natural. His theory of history bears this out, as do his empirical studies that outline human progress. Ideal history presents the logic of historiography, but historicity documents the evidence. For those who reject this on principle, Smith may have nothing to say, but they, in turn, have no means of refutation. All that is left is a battle of the wills, and, as the Platonic Socrates insists in *Apology*, this may be a powerful force, but it is not philosophy.

One final note in Foucault's defense. Part of the point of the archaeologies is to illustrate that particular constructions make facts, people, and assumptions invisible. Madness was seen as such—homosexuality and other traits considered deviances were *genuinely* understood as illness. Getting society to shift this understanding meant changing the culture in such profound ways that the very meaning of truth might feel like it changes. To tell someone that the mad are not mad may feel equivalent to the incredulity Wittgenstein felt at Moore's suggestion that one take seriously the notion that his hand was not his hand.

I think Foucault is right about this, and insofar as Smith is working within disciplines, there are going to be elements of unquestionable, indisputable, and foundational ideology that inform the rest of the discourse. Economists, for example, may not be able to see that 'exchange' is a constructed concept. Smith himself sees it as part of being a human being, remarking that no one ever saw dogs exchange bones (WN I.2.21). He was most certainly unable to see the levels of interpretation involved in such an observation. What Foucault points out, perhaps better than anyone else, is that the construction of meaning goes to the very ground level of our language and experience. Smith did not have phenomenology to inform his thought.

It is the power and intimacy of these imposed meanings that make exchange seem such a self-evident notion. If exchange were not so essential to our worldview, an economic interpretation of Smith would not be as compelling as it is. After all, a marketplace of life is a comfortable notion to people who think of marriage as a *contract*, love as an *agreement*, parenting as a *partnership*. The language of liberal modernity is built on the language of political economy, and a rejection of this foundation would most certainly, as Foucault had hoped, bring the edifice down. Smith did not and perhaps could not see this, and, as a result, we learn a great deal about him and about us from Foucault's critique. But this doesn't change the empirical nature of the question. In the end, once you grant the existence of something like liberty or of a notion such as history, there will or will not be progress. It flows *naturally* out of these concepts.

CONCLUSION
A SMITHIAN LIBERALISM

I have been defining 'pluralism' as the political situation in which peoples of different fundamental beliefs and histories share equally in common governance, and live within common borders. Under this system, it is to be the prerogative of the citizen to choose his or her social priorities, and, in turn, the citizen is thought to be an unfettered agent who can participate in governance. In return, the sovereign accepts responsibility for maintaining pluralism, for respecting and cultivating difference, and for making space for citizen participation.

Following Sen, I have been defining 'rationality' as "the discipline of subjecting one's choices—of actions as well as of objectives, values and priorities—to reasoned scrutiny." I hope it is self-evident how these two concepts relate. Individuals in a pluralist society must be rational, they must be critical of themselves, of others, and of the government, and they must exist in a society that cultivates these abilities. Rationality, a critical standpoint and imaginative capacity, is itself the product of a diversity of experiences, of lengthy and attentive observation, and of narratives that provide the preconditions for communication between discrete individuals whose differences only compound over time. Pluralism is impossible without rationality, and rationality is severely impeded without pluralism.

Keeping this relationship in mind, I have argued for two separate but related conclusions: first, that Smith offers a theory of pluralism that prefigures modern systems of diversity and, second, that he presents an account of human rationality that is representative of a holistic picture of human agency. In the process, I have shown that, for Smith, pluralism and rationality are intertwined and that the two are made all the more inseparable by their relationship to the human capacity and need to be educated. Attention to these conclusions helps clarify the way in which, for Smith, social structures balance individual and communal practices and needs.

However unintentional it may be, Smith offers us an eighteenth-century version of our contemporary theories of pluralism. He shows us that social and political unity in the face of difference is the result of a complex interplay between progressive history, individual freedom, commercial activity, and universal education. We cultivate society by nurturing both our individuality and our humanity; neither has absolute priority, and neither is completely divorced from the other. Economic life is just one of many spheres in the modern state.

I offer very little *defense* of Smith; my comments are largely interpretive and explanatory. In the end, his conclusions, like those of many other philosophers, may turn out to be indefensible or incomplete. I would never argue that Smith offers all the answers to our contemporary political woes, nor would I assert that his theories could not have benefited from modern insights unavailable to him. Smith did not anticipate the industrial revolution, for example, nor did he have any conception of the subconscious.

Nevertheless, I would not be truthful if I did not acknowledge my underlying assumption that Smith got a lot of it right, that he was on a productive track, and that philosophy has been worse off because it has neglected his voice. The industrial revolution makes Smith's comments on the dangers of the division of labor all the more relevant; his concern for the worker is as necessary today as in his time. Modern psychologies are not inconsistent with Smith's account of sympathy; cognitive science and sociology only make it harder to articulate all the information necessary for entering into the perspective of the other. Finally, if it is true that those very forces that divide us may also unify us, then the question of substantive content in education, economic arrangement, and political deliberation becomes all the more pressing. Leni Riefenstahl may drive the democratic citizen to embrace fascism with her compelling film *The Triumph of the Will*, but Frank Capra may equally inspire the disenchanted with *Mr. Smith Goes to Washington*. The reality of the human condition is that what we teach is as important as whom we teach. Smith's comments on curriculum bear this out.

I ask that contemporary liberals revisit their foundational commitments. There is an ever-growing body of sophisticated and impressive interpretive work developed by a diverse group of Smith scholars—I have had the good fortune to learn from much of it. With the right attention, Smith can once again become a central voice in the discourse about the nature of society. This would not be the caricaturish libertarian Smith that leads theorists nowhere, but the holistic, systematic Smith who eloquently articulated the nuances of the complex community that houses a commercial society.

Contemporary liberalism faces challenges from its adherents as well as from its critics. Rawls's later writing is significantly different from his earlier work (or so I would argue), and William Galston's account of a liberal society differs notably from Brian Barry's. There is no clear vision as to the nature and limits of entitlement or justice, and liberals use this ambiguity to challenge the legitimacy of each other's theories. Some feminists have argued that liberalism has neglected to acknowledge the family, the dependent, and the role that caring plays in any society. Others suggest that any political theory that does not regard human emotion as a serious and important component in political debate misrepresents the human experience. And theorists of many stripes suggest that the account of the self implicit in most liberal theories is inadequate: individuals do not reason without society, they argue, and moral principles divorced from context cease to be persuasive. Bridging all of these criticisms is the concern that liberalism is generally too skeptical about religious claims and that fundamental beliefs are both marginalized and disregarded in large-scale secular civic discourse.

Although I do not argue for the position here, I contend that many of liberalism's shortcomings are the product of its Kantian foundation. The conceptions of autonomy and universal reason that Rawls and others build on do not allow for complex notions of identity, political consideration of affection for individual persons, the importance of subjectivity, the emotions in moral and political commitments, and variations in human reason. I suggest that a Smithian foundation has the potential to resolve many of these issues.

Smith's theory contains positions that, in the latter years of the twentieth century, would have been called communitarian. In *TMS* he argues that humans are by nature social, morality is the product of social processes, moral reasoning and self-identification are impossible in isolation, general moral rules are after-the-fact constructs developed from social interaction enabled by education, the state should foster both secular and religious education, the sympathetic foundation of morality functions best in small communities, and political society is not derived from a social contract. I contend that liberalism has never adequately answered these challenges.

Smith offers a wide variety of liberal arguments as well: he calls for a significant range of both political and economic freedoms, regards individuals as ultimately responsible for their choices, sees justice as largely a matter of refraining from harm, claims the government is responsible for protecting individuals' private pursuits, and hints at a proceduralist conception of justice distinguishing the rules regarding moral and religious interaction from the content of specific belief systems. It is not inconsequential that Smith is generally regarded as an important early contributor to the liberal canon.

Smith also foreshadowed the feminist concern for an ethics of care—sympathy is most certainly an early formulation of this approach—and he is able to postulate a theory that cultivates civil discourse in the face of different conceptions of rationality. These two critiques, that liberalism has not accounted for an individual's care for others and that it has not taken seriously how bound to tradition moral and political adjudication is, constitute two of its most significant weaknesses. On the basis of my arguments in this book, I suggest that a Smithian liberalism would be able to meet these challenges, accepting their initial premises while staying true to the liberal vision. In short, Smith resolves these concerns by postulating a relational self that can be adequately and authentically governed by an individualist state. He shows how socially constructed identity is compatible with individual choice and how substantial social unity is a complement of, not a barrier to, personal liberty. He also offers an economics that can anchor contemporary "capability" approaches to liberalism. Welfare economics is, in some sense, a return to the priority of labor that dominated economics before the Marginal Revolution. Smith shows that there must be some balance between welfare and predictive economics; his liberalism can provide this.

Smith also offers contemporary liberals a mechanism that adequately represents the interdependent nature of reason and emotion. Emotions are themselves rational for Smith; reason is derived from and cultivated by our sentiments. Emotions motivate us to pursue our own ends, but they also encourage personal relationships. In combination with the sympathetic imagination, emotions and rationality create the possibility of entering into the perspective of others and balancing moral judgments on the basis of our commitments, the convictions of others, and a normative ideal that, although unreachable in practice, allows for negotiation between a multiplicity of views. The educated and practiced imagination holds firm to a conception of conscience that is motivational but never regarded as infallible.

Human rationality is wider in scope and nature than many of our modern pluralisms suggest. I contend that no theory of difference will ever allow for true communication if it does not recognize the central importance of the moral sentiments. Actions, commitments, and emotions are themselves rational while also being passionate.

Perhaps most useful for contemporary liberal theory, moral beliefs, for Smith, are never final. They are always checked against the community and continually revisited in the light of new information. Anticipating John Stuart Mill and the pragmatists, Smith sees progress as driving inquiry, but whatever perfectionist teleology is implicit in the system is never to be realized. A Smithian liberalism recognizes and accounts for this fact. Progress informs because human behavior is the consequence of natural laws. Moral rules, discovered and verified via a community of inquiry, are intersubjective values, a collective discovery that allows for perspectival vision of proper moral and political action. The most we may be able to hope for is to think of ethics as driven by best practices rather than by transcendental principles.

Perspectivism is not relativism, especially if it is committed to an objective reality discoverable through collective knowledge and experimentation. The Scottish Enlightenment's lack of separation between the natural and the social—the exclusion of the nature/nurture dichotomy—offers a political community the opportunity to commit to these moral rules while still recognizing the social forces that blind us to injustice and vice that would never be permitted to flourish in a purely moral world. This blindness, to both our own needs and those of others, has always been the most dangerous element of freedom, directing liberty to a narrow few rather than to entire populations. Rectifying injustice requires truly seeing and learning from one another. We must, in Smith's words, be attended to and attend to others.

For me, the most instructive element in Smith's theory has always been his notion that all individuals are both spectator and agent, that individuals are continually role models, and that each one of our acts puts forth moral standards for others to consider, while also providing the opportunity for personal rational reflection. Smith's agents and spectators are continually learning; they are being educated, and they are educating others. This is a liberalism, whether Smith called it that or not, in which citizens are mentors to one another and difference provides evidence for or against theories of justice. It is also a democracy, regardless of Smith's personal political convictions. It recognizes that participation is not just electoral in nature but a product of day-to-day activity, the outgrowth of the shared project of human personal and political actualization.

Smith famously tells us that in the fourth stage of history "every man thus lives by exchanging, or becomes in some measure a merchant, and the society itself grows to be what is properly a commercial society" (WN I.iv.1). However true this may be, the economic revelation tells only a small part of the story. Intrinsic to Smith's theory is the assertion that sympathy leads to the moral and political acknowledgment of others. Our natural predilection for concordance of sentiments inspires each of us to learn more about others and, in the process, learn more about ourselves. This creates a stable community that is more than just a collection of individuals governed by a common set of laws. It recognizes that every individual offers a unique reflection of the society in which he or she lives and that these understandings, given a strong enough narrative and a well-cultivated rational imagination, can be communicated and entered into rationally,

When we look at society to investigate its failures and successes, Smith reminds us, we must look not just at sociological patterns but at individual lives as well. We must take seriously the experiences of others and use their self-understanding to moderate our individual and political passions in an effort to make society better, government more responsive, and individuals more attentive to the needs of others. Only interconnectedness gives us liberty. This is not a paradox. It is an empirically verified truth confirmed by history as it has progressed over time.

With the natural desire for interpersonal connection and approval that Smith calls sympathy, we can focus on ourselves and others while balancing our needs and theirs. We are continually being observed, and we are vigilantly observing. To paraphrase Smith, every person thus lives by example, or becomes in some measure teacher and student, and the society itself grows to be what is properly called just.

NOTES

INTRODUCTION

1. Ross, *The Life of Adam Smith*, 18.
2. Brearley, "The Persecution of Gypsies in Europe," 589.
3. Bill Bryson reports a case shortly after Smith's death in which a kidnapper "was charged with stealing the child's cap and gown because that was the only part of the offense that was illegal." He also documents an incident in England from 1812, in which a mother found her missing son sweeping a chimney at the inn where she happened to be staying (Bryson, *At Home: A Short History of Private Life*).
4. Unless otherwise noted, I cite the final editions of Smith's life, those now considered definitive by the scholarly community. For *TMS*, this refers to the sixth edition, and for *WN*, the fourth.
5. Brown, *Adam Smith's Discourse*, 21.
6. Ibid., 20.
7. In personal conversation Brown has assured me that her work was not motivated by postmodern skepticism; I take her at her word. But, as she acknowledges in her introduction, the theoretical nature of her literary theory and the challenges to the unity of the self are both derived from a body of postmodern theorists, most notably Bakhtin, but also Barthes, Derrida, Foucault, and Rorty (ibid., 3n, 13n, 21–22). It is this theoretical structure that I question here.
8. Griswold, *Adam Smith and the Virtues of Enlightenment*, 27. Griswold also argues against Brown's approach by focusing on her use of Bakhtin (27–28).
9. Brubaker, "Why Adam Smith Is Neither a Conservative nor a Libertarian," 197–202.
10. Den Uyl, "Critical Notice: Samuel Fleischacker, *On Adam Smith's Wealth of Nations*," 180.
11. Fleischacker, "Response to Den Uyl," 176.
12. Urquhart, "Adam Smith's Problems: Individuality and the Paradox of Sympathy," 182.
13. The question of whether he is a link in the liberal chain is different from whether he is himself a full-fledged liberal. The latter would be a more controversial assessment.

For a debate on this topic, see Harpham, "Liberalism, Civic Humanism, and the Case of Adam Smith"; Khalil, "Is Adam Smith Liberal?"; Letwin, "Was Adam Smith a Liberal?"; and Winch, "Adam Smith and the Liberal Tradition."

14. Consider also (WN IV.ix.51, emphasis added). Justice itself Smith describes as a negative virtue (TMS II.ii.1.9).

15. Sen, *Rationality and Freedom*, 4.

16. MacIntyre, *Whose Justice? Which Rationality?*, 4.

17. The literature on rationality is vast, and I avoid engaging Sen's or MacIntyre's justifications here. Instead, my argument is that Smith too subscribes to this particular and wide account of rationality. If it turns out that such a position is untenable, Smith's approach would be just as susceptible to critique as Sen's or MacIntyre's. I present a more detailed account of MacIntyre's approach in Weinstein, *On MacIntyre*.

18. Skinner "Some Problems in the Analysis of Political Thought and Action," 283.

19. Ibid., 279, 281.

20. Young, "Mandeville: A Popularizer of Hobbes."

21. See Weinstein, *Adam Smith and the Problem of Neutrality in Contemporary Liberal Theory*, 4.1.2–4.1.3, especially nn181, 189.

22. Samuels, *Erasing the Invisible Hand*, xix

23. Gaus, *Justificatory Liberalism*.

24. Scazzieri, "A Smithian Theory of Choice," 25–26.

25. MacIntyre, *Whose Justice? Which Rationality?*, 4.

26. Ibid., 332–33.

27. Sen, *Rationality and Freedom*, 26–30.

28. Ibid., 28.

29. Walter Feinberg, in *Common Schools/Uncommon Identities: National Unity and Cultural Difference*, makes a distinction between pluralism and multiculturalism. Pluralism, he argues, is based on the notion of a multiplicity of different private spheres that revolve around a central but neutral public sphere. He suggests that pluralism regards with suspicion and regret any overlap in the public and private spheres. In contrast, Feinberg defines multiculturalism as being committed to the notion that there is no neutrality in the public sphere. He argues that multiculturalists "suspect that this idealized common identity is just a disguise for the dominance of one cultural group over others, and they believe that such dominance is inherently wrong" (22). Although his discussion is helpful, Feinberg's description of the two theories is mistaken. There is nothing in pluralism that demands neutrality. The common political culture may be a modus vivendi, it may be an overlapping consensus, or it may be numerous other forms of organization. Multiculturalism is a *form* of pluralism, one that emphasizes community-defined identities and histories. Pluralism, if one wants to force a distinction, can allow for individual differences as well as group differences and is, therefore, wider in scope.

30. For my response to this self-identification, see Weinstein, *On MacIntyre*, 76–77.

31. Dewey, *Democracy and Education*, 99.

32. For a challenge to MacIntyre's view that the Enlightenment was homogeneous in its aims and assumptions, see Schmidt, "What Enlightenment Project?"

1. MEDIATING TERMINOLOGY AND TEXTUAL COMPLEXITY

1. This discussion references the terminological history outlined in the *Oxford English Dictionary*. 'Pluralism' in the first sense appears in Kallen and Whitfield, *Culture and Democracy in the United States*, 43.

2. Toleration as a political solution to diverse religion first appears in English in 1609, in Henry Jacob's "To the High and mightie Prince, Iames by the grace of God, King of great Britannie, France, and Irelande: An Humble Supplication for Toleration and Libertie to Enjoy and Observe the Ordinances of Christ Jesus in th' administration of His Churches in Lieu of Human Constitutions." The concept itself, however, has a much older history, appearing at least as early as Tertullian's second-century *Apology*.

3. This reference actually casts doubt on individualism's viability. The author argues that "pluralism, in an ultimate sense, is therefore impossible; for it would make unintelligible any rational interpretation of society" (Laski, *Studies in Problems of Sovereignty*, i.6).

4. Glenn Morrow describes the liberalism of Smith's time as follows: "It was an age of criticism, consciously and ruthlessly directed against the lingering structures of the medieval system. The political liberalism, the religious liberalism, and the economic liberalism of the eighteenth century were merely separate manifestations of one and the same attempt to break down the older institutional forms and set free human energies and allow satisfaction to human aspirations that could no longer find expression in those forms. Liberalism in all its manifestations was essentially a doctrine of the rights of the individual, and a criticism of the claims of existing institutions to regulate his activity. Individual liberty, in politics, in religion, in industry, was felt to be the first and sometimes the only thing necessary for the introduction of a better social and political order" (Morrow, "Adam Smith: Moralist and Philosopher," 325–26). It is against this strict individualism that I postulate a pluralism inherent in Smith's system.

5. Cf. John Rawls, *Political Liberalism*, 149.

6. Cf. Peach, "The Mosaic Versus the Melting Pot: Canada and the USA."

7. Again, see Rawls, where he distinguishes between the reasonable and the rational (Rawls, *Political Liberalism*, 48–54).

8. Carey, *Locke, Shaftesbury, and Hutcheson*, 10, 159.

9. For a counterexample, see Wilson, *The Moral Sense*. Although he argues that his work "is not a book of philosophy," Wilson does identify his project as "a continuation of work begun by certain eighteenth-century English and Scottish thinkers, notably Joseph Butler, Francis Hutcheson, David Hume, and Adam Smith" (xiii).

10. Carey, *Locke, Shaftesbury, and Hutcheson*, 201. This paragraph largely follows his book-length discussion.

11. Raphael, *The Moral Sense*, and Turco, "Moral Sense and the Foundation of Morals."

12. Phillipson, *Adam Smith: An Enlightened Life*, 71, 141, and cf. 89, 206. See also Weinstein, "Review of Nicholas Phillipson, *Adam Smith: An Enlightened Life*."

13. Raphael, *The Impartial Spectator*, 25.

14. Ibid.

15. Goldsmith, "Regarding Anew the Moral and Political Sentiments of Mankind," 596.
16. Ibid.
17. Horne, "Envy and Commercial Society: Mandeville and Smith on 'Private Vices, Public Benefits,'" 558.
18. As quoted in Goldsmith, "Regarding Anew the Moral and Political Sentiments of Mankind," 601.
19. Hundert, "Bernard Mandeville and the Enlightenment's Maxims of Modernity," 577.
20. Lamprecht, "The Fable of the Bees," 561.
21. The term 'eccentric' is Lamprecht's. See ibid., 562.
22. It is unclear how much of a social contract theorist Mandeville was. M. M. Goldsmith argues that Mandeville rejects the social contract, arguing instead that the cynical but "skillfull Politician" is a substitute for the collective consent required of individuals in the state of nature (Goldsmith, *Private Vices, Public Benefits*, 55). In contrast, F. B. Kaye argues that "in his account of the origin of society in Part II Mandeville is closer to Hobbes's discussion of this matter in his *Philosophical Reduments concerning Government and Society* and his *Leviathan* than to any other predecessor ("The Background," *The Fable of the Bees* [Indianapolis: Liberty Classics, 1988], cx). A discussion of which argument is more persuasive is beyond the scope of this chapter.
23. Khalil, "Is Justice the Primary Feature of the State? Adam Smith's Critique of Social Contract Theory," and Berry, *Social Theory of the Scottish Enlightenment*, 30–33.
24. For a discussion of the role of the "communitarian" interpretation of Smith, see Weinstein, "Author's Response."
25. He also argues that theorems are beautiful (*Inquiry*, 20–25).
26. Carey, *Locke, Shaftesbury, and Hutcheson*, 5.
27. Horne, *The Social Thought of Bernard Mandeville*, 19.
28. Force, *Self-Interest before Adam Smith*, 63.
29. Mandeville wrote thirty-two issues of *The Female Tatler* beginning with number fifty-two, originally released on November 4, 1709. These are collected in M. M. Goldsmith, *By a Society of Ladies: Essays in the Female Tatler*.
30. Goldsmith, *Private Vices, Public Virtues*, 51–53.
31. Rogers, "The Ethics of Mandeville," 16.
32. Hundert, "Bernard Mandeville and the Enlightenment's Maxims of Modernity," 586.
33. Scott-Taggart, "Mandeville: Cynic or Fool?," 230.
34. Harth, "The Satiric Purpose of the Fable of the Bees."
35. Daniel, "Myth and Rationality in Mandeville."
36. Wilde, "Mandeville's Place in English Thought," 231.
37. Haakonssen, *Index to the Works of Adam Smith*, 67, 170.
38. *An Act for the Better Regulating of the Manufacture of Broad Woolen Cloth*, passed by the House of Commons on February 6, 1662, suggests that Mandeville's use of the term 'Yorkshire Cloth' refers to wool of a specific quality from a specific location.
39. These excerpts represent a fundamental disagreement. Smith argues that hunters and shepherds practice the division of labor, while Mandeville suggests "savages" do otherwise. My point is not that they agree with one another completely, but that Smith was influenced enough by Mandeville that he adopts his language and his problematic.

Given Smith's attention to language, it seems unlikely that these similarities are coincidental.

40. Force, *Self-Interest before Adam Smith*, 15.

41. Horne reads this correctly, I think, as a direct repudiation of Richard Steele's "spokesman" Bickerstaff in *The Tatler* (see Horne, *The Social Thought of Bernard Mandeville*, 10–11).

42. Sen, *The Idea of Justice*, 15–18.

43. Hurtado-Prieto, "The Mercantilist Foundation of "Dr. Mandeville's 'Licentious System.'"

44. Smith explicitly rejects the notion that seeking the approval of others is either vain or vicious, suggesting an objection to Force's claim equating community approval and vanity. See Force, *Self-Interest before Adam Smith*, 44–47, 86, although this depends on an ambiguous use of 'self-love,' 124–25, 132, 161–62. Here Force seems to continue the argument substituting "bettering our own condition" for vanity, a technique he continues at 179–80.

45. Henderson, "A Very Cautious, or a Very Polite Dr. Smith?," 61.

46. Famously, Smith received great criticism for his effusive obituary of Hume, much more so, he thought, than for WN (*Corr.* 208).

47. One might be tempted to locate the discussion even earlier depending on how one might interpret Protagoras's remark that man is the measure of all things.

48. For Mandeville, the desire to dominate is natural. He writes that it is this natural desire that motivates children to like animals, because with dogs and cats, "they can do with them what they please, and put them into what posture and shape they list" (*Fable* I, 281). Smith also thinks the desire to dominate is natural. He writes, "The pride of man makes him love to domineer, and nothing mortifies him so much as to be obliged to condescend to persuade his inferiors" (WN III.ii.10).

49. Griswold, *Adam Smith and the Virtues of Enlightenment*, 54; Montes, *Adam Smith in Context: A Critical Reassessment of Some Central Components of His Thought*, 52.

50. Kaye, *The Fable of the Bees*, xlvii–xlix.

51. 'Infect' is my term.

52. Hundert, "Bernard Mandeville and the Enlightenment's Maxims of Modernity," 578.

53. Ibid.

54. Goldsmith, *Private Vices, Public Benefits*, 44.

55. Rogers, "The Ethics of Mandeville," 8.

56. Mandeville, *A Letter to Dion*, 38.

57. Rogers, "The Ethics of Mandeville," 10.

58. Horne, *The Social Thought of Bernard Mandeville*, 22.

59. Goldsmith, *Private Vices, Public Benefits*, 59.

60. Kaye, *The Fable of the Bees*, l

61. Thomas Horne disagrees, arguing that Mandeville is unique among Shaftesbury, Hutcheson, and Hume in having only a twofold classification. See Horne, "Envy and Commercial Society: Mandeville and Smith on 'Private Vices, Public Benefits.'"

62. Lamprecht, "The Fable of the Bees," 573.

63. Tuck, *Hobbes*, 46–47.

64. Force, *Self-Interest before Adam Smith*, 96.

65. Rogers, "The Ethics of Mandeville," 3. In this section Rogers is critical of this interpretation but only insofar as it relates to a conception of virtue "usually credited, or discredited," to Mandeville. As discussed above, Mandeville has a specific and nonrelative definition. Nevertheless, Rogers is not critical of this as a method of rational deliberation, and he should not have been. This is a notion, as I state above, that Mandeville inherits from Hobbes.

66. Daniel, "Myth and Rationality in Mandeville," 602.

67. Ibid., 603.

68. Horne, *The Social Thought of Bernard Mandeville*, 28.

69. Smith makes a similar comment about individuals overestimating their pride. The inability to see ourselves accurately, "this self-deceit, this fatal weakness of mankind, is the source of half the disorders of human life" (*TMS* III.4.6).

70. The original meaning of the phrase "economy of something" refers to the relationship of the whole thing to its parts. As Force argues, this is particularly powerful when seen in the context of Smith's invisible hand. See Force, *Self-Interest before Adam Smith*, 68–69.

71. Lamprecht, "The Fable of the Bees," 576.

72. Rashid, "Mandeville's Fable: Laissez-faire or Libertinism?," 317.

2. ONE SYSTEM, MANY MOTIVATIONS

1. Obviously, I do not claim that these are the only ways in which they are related.

2. The first edition was published in 1711, although it did contain elements that appeared as early as 1699. A second, expanded edition was released in 1714, shortly after the author's death. In comparison, the poem that began Mandeville's *Fable* was first published anonymously in 1705 and then expanded with commentary in 1714. An expanded edition appeared in 1723, then in 1724, 1725, 1728, 1729, and finally 1732. The second part of the *Fable* was published in 1728, then in 1730 and 1733. The two parts were eventually combined and published together in 1733, the year of Mandeville's death.

3. Goldsmith, *Private Vices, Public Benefits*, 596.

4. Bernstein, "Shaftesbury's Identification of the Good with the Beautiful," 309.

5. Wilde, "Mandeville's Place in English Thought," 224.

6. For example, *Fable* II, 17, and II, 128.

7. Here I follow Klein, "The Third Earl of Shaftesbury and the Progress of Politeness," 186–214.

8. Prostko, "'Natural Conversation Set in View,'" 49.

9. Ibid., 50.

10. Bernstein, "Shaftesbury's Identification of the Good with the Beautiful," 305ff.

11. Also cited in Otteson, "Shaftesbury's Evolutionary Morality and Its Influence on Adam Smith," 107.

12. Mandeville: *Fable* I, 331–32. Smith: *LRBL* 1.137–53. I examine the legitimacy of such attacks in the next chapter.

13. Grean, "Self-Interest and Public Interest in Shaftesbury's Philosophy," 38.

14. Force, *Self-Interest before Adam Smith*, 10.

15. Carey, *Locke, Shaftesbury, and Hutcheson*, 99–100.

16. Otteson argues a variation of this point, suggesting that, for Shaftesbury, "the crucial mistake Hobbes made was not in thinking that human beings were self-interested, but rather that they were only self-interested." (Otteson, "Shaftesbury's Evolutionary Morality and Its Influence on Adam Smith," 121.) This coincides nicely with my discussion of the development of the idea of multiple motivations.

17. Grean, "Self-Interest and Public Interest in Shaftesbury's Philosophy," 42.

18. Otteson, "Shaftesbury's Evolutionary Morality and Its Influence on Adam Smith," 114.

19. Interestingly, Smith's criticism of Shaftesbury parallels Adam Ferguson's attack on Smith in his late dialogue "Of the Principle of Moral Estimation: A Discourse between David Hume, Robert Clerk, and Adam Smith." See Merolle, *The Manuscripts of Adam Ferguson*. See also Weinstein, "The Two Adams: Ferguson and Smith on Sympathy and Sentiment."

20. The editors of the Glasgow Edition suggest that Smith misunderstands Shaftesbury's theory: "Here 'proportionable affection' means an affection proportionable or suitable to the moral objects, but Smith may have taken it to refer to a balance of one affection to others" (*TMS*, p. 293n50). If this is what Shaftesbury meant then there is even more similarity between the soliloquy and the impartial spectator since the latter also seeks to determine appropriate sentiments.

21. Cropsey, *Polity and Economy*, 128.

22. Rawls, "Reply to Habermas," 140.

23. It is imperative to distinguish between moral deliberation here and the motivations to be moral. I am not engaged with the discussion as to whether Shaftesbury and Hutcheson are themselves moral realists or to what extent morality is dependent on God. For further discussion on this topic, see Trianosky, "On the Obligation to Be Virtuous: Shaftesbury and the Question, Why Be Moral?," and Rauscher, "Moral Realism and the Divine Essence in Hutcheson."

24. Sprague, "Francis Hutcheson and the Moral Sense," 796.

25. Hirst, "Moral Sense, Moral Reason, and Moral Sentiment," 147.

26. Hutcheson is a utilitarian and asserts his own version of the greatest happiness principle (*Inquiry*, 117).

27. Carey, "Hutcheson's Moral Sense and the Problem of Innateness."

28. Carey, "Method, Moral Sense, and the Problem of Diversity," 103.

29. Carey, *Locke, Shaftesbury, and Hutcheson*, 110–16.

30. Ibid., 117.

31. Ibid. Carey illustrates well the debate as to whether Hutcheson had postulated innate ideas at all, or whether he was successful in his project and developed a set of reflections that could not be associated with Lockean *ideas*. See ibid., 162–63.

32. Kail, "Hutcheson's Moral Sense: Skepticism, Realism, and Secondary Qualities," 60.

33. Carey, "Method, Moral Sense, and the Problem of Diversity," 285.

34. As quoted in ibid., 287.

35. *Essay* II.xxxiii.

36. Carey, "Hutcheson's Moral Sense and the Problem of Innateness," 106.

37. As quoted in Force, *Self-Interest before Adam Smith*, 30–31.

38. Turco, "Sympathy and the Moral Sense: 1725–1740," 81.
39. Frankenna, "Hutcheson's Moral Sense Theory," 369.
40. Ibid., 365.
41. Hirst, "Moral Sense, Moral Reason, and Moral Sentiment," 147.
42. Carey, "Hutcheson's Moral Sense and the Problem of Innateness," 107.
43. Carey, *Locke, Shaftesbury, and Hutcheson*, 166.
44. Ibid., 151.
45. See Hildebrand, *Die Nationalökommie der Gegenwart und Zukunft*; Knies, *Die Politische Oekonomie vom Standpunkte der Geschichtlichen Methode*; and von Skarzynski, *Moralphilosoph und Schoepfer der Nationaloekonomie*.
46. Montes, *Adam Smith in Context*, 20–24.
47. Ibid., 22–28.
48. Ironically, it is WN that Jeremy Bentham refers to as "a treatise upon universal benevolence." As quoted in Mossner, *Adam Smith: The Biographical Approach*, 18.
49. Otteson himself refers to his articulation as "the real Adam Smith Problem" (Otteson, *Adam Smith's Marketplace of Life*, 168).
50. Ibid., 169.
51. The second element in his argument involves what he calls "the familiarity principle." While I am critical of Otteson's use of the market metaphor, I am in agreement with him regarding the role of familiarity.
52. Ibid., 289.
53. Brown, "Adam Smith: Between Morals and Markets."
54. Samuels helpfully insists that the claim that the term 'the market' is a metaphor ought to be followed with an indication of what it is a metaphor for. I address this more specifically in chapter 10, but, for Otteson, "the market" appears to be a metaphor for aggregated exchanges — or, rather, actual markets collectively understood (Samuels, *Erasing the Invisible Hand*, 146–51).
55. I do not offer a complete list here. He uses the phrase sixty-seven times in the sixth edition of *TMS*.
56. Oncken, "The Consistency of Adam Smith," 447.
57. Force, *Self-Interest before Adam Smith*, 259. The reader has to be cautious here. Force takes Oncken's point too far. Multiple motivations in Smith, of which Force is well aware, are found throughout both *TMS* and *WN* and, as we shall see, self-interest and the appeal to sympathy are also found in both books.
58. Brown, "Agency and Discourse: Revisiting the Adam Smith Problem," 69.
59. Brown's analysis goes too far if she portrays Smith's economics as fully determinate.
60. Here, 'singular' refers to reward, not motivation.
61. Otteson, *Adam Smith's Marketplace of Life*, 193.
62. Ibid., 94–95, 193–94.
63. Ferguson, *An Essay on the History of Civil Society*, 14.
64. Smith could not have used the word 'altruism' or its derivatives since it was coined by Auguste Comte in the nineteenth century. According to the OED, the word first appeared in French as *altruisme* in his *Système de politique positive*. The translators suggested the English variation.

65. For Mandeville, self-love refers to self-preservation, and self-liking denotes an instinct "by which every individual values itself above its real worth" (as quoted in Force, *Self-Interest before Adam Smith*, 65.) As we will see in the next chapter, Smith's call for impartial self-observation is more of a discussion of self-liking than a tempering of self-preservation.

66. See Montes, *Adam Smith in Context*, 106n.

67. Ibid., 198. Because Otteson sets up a false Adam Smith Problem only to show that it cannot be defended, Chris Berry, accurately, I think, calls Otteson's argument "a straw man" (Berry, "Review of James R. Otteson, *Adam Smith's Marketplace of Life*," 185).

68. Smith is not doing economics. He is instead doing political economy, a much less specific discipline incorporating political, sociological, historical, and anthropological questions alongside those that are now termed economic (WN IV.i.intro).

69. Evensky, *Adam Smith's Moral Philosophy*. See also Weinstein, "*The Wealth of Nations* and the Morality of Opulence."

70. Evensky, *Adam Smith's Moral Philosophy*, 245.

71. Ibid., 246–47. Otteson has more respect for Smith's corpus as a whole and should not be regarded as identical to the economists Evensky mentions. I relate him to this list only insofar as his conclusions prioritize the economic and minimize the moral.

72. Ibid., 245.

73. Ibid., 247.

74. Ibid.

75. Ibid., 212.

76. Ibid., 35.

77. Ibid., 60.

78. Ibid., 60–61.

79. Ibid., 62–63.

80. Ibid., 63.

81. I do not mean to suggest that "sympathy, complacency, and approbation" are alternatives. They are all related, and each is present for those agents whose conditions are good.

82. Aristotle NE 1153b17–19.

83. Maria Pia Paganelli suggests that *TMS* has a more positive view of self-interest than WN. She argues that the abuses of self-interest are tempered in the earlier book but have more deleterious consequences in WN. If this is true, then it supports my claims that WN continues the conversation about self-interest started in the earlier book. She does also seem to make room for multiple motivations, using qualifying phrases such as "'some' self-interest" and "the virtue of prudence is based at least in part on self-interested considerations." See Paganelli, "The Adam Smith Problem in Reverse: Self-Interest in *The Wealth of Nations* and *The Theory of Moral Sentiments*."

84. Hume also uses the example of a finger when he writes, "'Tis not contrary to reason to prefer the destruction of the whole world to the scratching of my finger" (*Treatise* 2.3.3.6).

85. For a view espousing a heavily Stoic influence, see Vivenza, *Adam Smith and the Classics*. In contrast, Leonidas Montes argues that the Stoic interpretation is incorrect, that for Smith "the virtue of self-command is also pervasively linked to the *vir virtutis* tradition" (Montes, *Adam Smith in Context*, 11). And, as discussed above, Force sees Mandeville as

representative of the Epicurean/Augustinian tradition. If he is correct, then by his and my argument Smith would be as well (Force, *Self-Interest before Adam Smith*, chapter 4).

86. Grean, *Shaftesbury's Philosophy of Religion and Ethics*, 65.
87. Goldsmith, *Private Vices, Public Benefits*, 131
88. Smith does not use either term in *WN*. The word 'passive' never appears, and the word 'active' refers to conscious and deliberate effort but is not paired with principles.
89. The latter passage is interesting in this context because Smith uses both meanings in discussing women's education.
90. Otteson has a useful discussion of Shaftesbury's account of wit and his call for free speech (Otteson, "Shaftesbury's Evolutionary Morality and Its Influence on Adam Smith," esp. 107–12.)
91. Given the contemporary concern about religious violence, it may seem odd to portray Quakerism as being radical. Nevertheless, as a sect committed to complete pacifism, it certainly qualifies. Given Smith's insistence that "the first duty of the sovereign, that of protecting the society from the violence and invasion of other independent societies, can be performed only by means of a military force" (*WN* V.i.a.1), it is not unreasonable to consider a denomination that would refuse to participate in the armed services as a more radical wing of society. I do not, however, intend to suggest a value judgment on Smith's part. The term 'radical' is, for my purposes, only a matter of comparison.
92. Mossner, *Adam Smith: The Biographical Approach*, 17.
93. Macfie, *The Individual in Society*, 75–76. In this section I follow Dickey, "Historicizing the 'Adam Smith Problem.'"
94. Winch. *Adam Smith's Politics*, 10.
95. Dickey, "Historicizing the 'Adam Smith Problem,'" 585.
96. Campbell, *Adam Smith's Science of Morals*, 16.
97. Morrow, "Adam Smith: Moralist and Philosopher," 341.
98. Dickey, "Historicizing the 'Adam Smith Problem,'" 584.
99. Winch, *Adam Smith's Politics*, 10.
100. I refer to the passage about saving as a form of betterment here, although this may well apply to Evensky's list of economists. I do not think it applies to Otteson's view of Smith.
101. A case can certainly be made that *WN* allows for a condemnation based upon considerations of freedom. My point is that *WN* does not offer a complete enough account. For a discussion of the role of economics in the abolition of slavery, see Levy, *How the Dismal Science Got Its Name*.
102. Otteson, *Adam Smith's Marketplace of Life*, 284.
103. Otteson himself models this point. In a later essay he describes his position as follows: "I have argued elsewhere that the rules of moral propriety and merit arise, according to Smith in *TMS*, as the result of a marketlike process involving negotiation, sensitivity to local detail and micro-motives leading unintentionally to macro order. Here I shall suggest that the set of standards that arise with respect to property, the rule-of-thumb instructions for judges that constitute Smith's aversion to the Impartial Spectator and the pragmatic reliance on 'reasonableness' are all consistent with a

'market model' laid out in *TMS*." In the first half of the paragraph he claims *TMS* is "marketlike," in the second he argues more strongly that it actually is a "market model." In the end, there is no meaningful difference between the two positions (Otteson, "How High Does the Impartial Spectator Go?," 95.

104. Otteson, *Adam Smith's Marketplace of Life*,176.

105. Evensky, *Adam Smith's Moral Philosophy*, 38n9.

3. EDUCATION AS ACCULTURATION

1. Glenn Morrow put it this way in 1923: "The individual moral consciousness is the result of social intercourse, the individual moral judgments are the expression of the general sentiments of the society to which the individual belongs. Smith's theory thus goes beyond the analytic assumptions of the century." In Morrow, "The Significance of the Doctrine of Sympathy in Hume and Adam Smith," 70.

2. The phrase "some priority of the community or society" is intentionally ambiguous. My argument is not that Smith is communitarian, but that some elements of his theory can be seen as such. My intent here is not to offer a strict definition of either liberal or communitarian, but to suggest briefly that Smith's approach may cause one to recast many of the currently accepted definitions. See my "Author's Response," 194–96. I revisit this discussion in this book's conclusion.

3. On this point, see also Urquhart, "Individuality and the Paradox of Sympathy," 190.

4. Ibid., 188.

5. Nieli, "Spheres of Intimacy and the Adam Smith Problem."

6. See also Khalil, "Is Justice the Primary Feature of the State?"

7. Fontaine, "Identification and Economic Behavior: Sympathy and Empathy in Historic Perspective," 264.

8. Nieli, "Spheres of Intimacy and the Adam Smith Problem," 617.

9. Sugden, "Beyond Sympathy and Empathy: Adam Smith's Concept of Fellow-Feeling," 75.

10. Raphael, *The Impartial Spectator*, 14n1.

11. Haakonssen, "Introduction," xiv.

12. Fleischacker, *A Third Concept of Liberty*, 49.

13. Griswold, "Imagination," 32–33.

14. Forman-Barzilai. "Sympathy in Space(s)," 190.

15. Ibid., 192.

16. Craig Smith refers to education as acculturation as a form of "social control" that prevents "disputes that may arise from the susceptibility of a deadened workforce to the forces of religious 'enthusiasm.'" See Smith, "Adam Smith on Progress and Knowledge," 308.

17. Forman-Barzilai. "Sympathy in Space(s)," 195.

18. Bitterman, "Adam Smith's Empiricism and the Law of Nature I," 510.

19. The nature of the impartial spectator is quite controversial, and some scholars have argued that Smith's account is inconsistent. They have proposed a 'genetic' view, suggesting that *TMS*'s impartial spectator ought to be regarded differently depending on the citation. There is something to be said for this view, but I do not think various

descriptions imply inconsistency. I have already referenced Raphael's "The Impartial Spectator." For a second and more radical account, see Harpham, "Enlightenment, Impartial Spectators, and Griswold's Smith." Also relevant is Griswold's reply to Harpham: Griswold, "Reply to My Critics."

20. Haakonssen, "Introduction," xvii.

21. Sugden, "Beyond Sympathy and Empathy," 78.

22. Harman, *Moral Agent and Impartial Spectator*, 12.

23. See Campbell, *Adam Smith's Science of Morals*, 128–38. The term 'ideal observer' references Firth, "Ethical Absolutism and the Ideal Observer," 317–45.

24. 'Reconstruction' and 'Interpretation' are Griswold's terms. They build from Smith's theatrical metaphors. See Griswold, *Adam Smith and the Virtues of Enlightenment*, 101, and Marshall, *The Figure of Theater*.

25. Marshall, *The Figure of Theater*, 189.

26. Raphael calls this assertion a "ridiculous generalization of the concordance view." See my response in Weinstein, "Review of D. D. Raphael's *Impartial Spectator*."

27. Hume, *An Enquiry Concerning the Principles of Morals*, 5.2.42.

28. Phillipson, *Adam Smith: An Enlightened Life*, 237. Phillipson describes Smith as a "perfect Humean" to whom the elder philosopher was "ready to hand over the problem" of the science of man because it was "now as complete as it would ever be" (71, 141; see also 89, 206).

29. I do not mean to suggest that Smith is unquestionably Humean. *TMS* is critical of many of Hume's conclusions, "especially his theory of justice and its grounding in sympathy with the public interest" (Frazer, *The Enlightenment of Sympathy*, 89).

30. Ryan Patrick Hanley suggests that physical proximity is not as important as what he terms "moral connections" (Hanley, *Adam Smith and the Character of Virtue*, 156). While I would suggest caution in reading this kind of egoism into Smith, the point underscores the role of imagination in overcoming difference.

31. Nieli, "Spheres of Intimacy and the Adam Smith Problem," 620–23; Griswold, *Adam Smith and the Virtues of Enlightenment*, 94; Forman-Barzilai, *Adam Smith and the Circles of Sympathy*; and Otteson, *Adam Smith's Marketplace of Life*, chapter 5.

32. Otteson, *Adam Smith's Marketplace of Life*, 277.

33. Kant, *Grounding of the Metaphysics of Morals*, 10.

34. I am obviously not purporting to offer anything close to a complete account of Smith's notion of justice. I am only singling out one aspect — its antisocial element.

35. The term 'manufactured' should not imply any theological positions on my part.

36. Otteson, *Adam Smith's Marketplace of Life*, 171. As discussed in the previous chapter, it is this component of Otteson's book that I find most persuasive.

37. Otteson pairs these quotes, and I am grateful for his discussion. However, his purpose for citing them is different from mine. His citations are found in a discussion of the normativity of Smith's standards, not in his remarks on the familiarity principle (Otteson, *Adam Smith's Marketplace of Life*, 204–5).

38. Ibid., 203.

39. Here I follow Bitterman, "Adam Smith's Empiricism and the Law of Nature," esp. 705.

40. I hold to the notion that autodidacticism constitutes education.

4. EDUCATION AND SOCIAL UNITY

1. Rorty, *Philosophy and Social Hope*, 116.
2. Here, my conversation follows Wallech, "'Class versus Rank': The Transformation of Eighteenth-Century English Social Terms and Theories of Production," 409–10.
3. I am not suggesting that 'Native American' constitutes a distinct race. I point to this example only as a signal that Smith does, at times, approximate modern usage of racial concepts.
4. Harkin writes that "the primitive, of course, figures less as a stage in a European Enlightenment narrative of the European march towards an age of capitalist freedom and prosperity, than as a category of spatial, and racial, otherness begging comparison between the progress of Europe and the other societies it was trading with and coloniz-ing" (Harkin, "Natives and Nostalgia: The Problem of the 'North American Savage' in Adam Smith's Historiography," 23.)
5. Frazer, *The Enlightenment of Sympathy*, 139.
6. Ibid., 144.
7. Ibid., 147.
8. Rothschild, "The *Theory of Moral Sentiments* and the Inner Life," 31.
9. There is a potential difficulty given this view. Since analogous emotions are always imperfect, the slave owners' self-hatred would necessarily be of a lesser degree than the original hatred felt by the slave. It is therefore necessary for those who wish to convince the slave owners to change their practices to ensure that the information which the slave owners learn is powerful enough for them to feel enough self-hatred to change their ways. This should be taken as a general observation regarding all oppressive rela-tionships. The greatest difficulty is rarely liberation. Escape and violence are often mechanisms with which to achieve freedom, although they do not guarantee perma-nence. It is much more difficult to convince the oppressors to understand the oppres-sion and to change their ways. With this shift in attitude come both liberation and prevention of further oppression.
10. Griswold, *Adam Smith and the Virtues of Enlightenment*, 215–217.
11. Ibid., 215.
12. On Smith and abolitionist literature, see Howard, *Publishing the Family*, 227, and Robison, "An 'Imperceptible Infusion' of Blood," 450.
13. The American institution of slavery was endorsed and propagated by a wide range of literary mechanisms. These include biblical argument, scientific "evidence," media support, and more amorphous cultural influences. My argument here is that each of these contributed to the inability of the slave owner to sympathize with the slave because they thickened the wall of separation that was constructed when the slave and master ceased to work side by side. While Smith himself would not have been immersed in the American argument, it still represents an appropriate venue in which to examine the means by which culture enforces the institution of slavery. For biblical arguments on slavery, see Shanks, "The Biblical Anti-Slavery Argument of the Decade 1830–1840," and Epps, "The Christian Doctrine of Slavery: A Theological Analysis," 243–49. For arguments from nonfiction material (pamphlets, tracts, speeches, sermons,

addresses, and books), see Wesley, "The Concept of Negro Inferiority in American Thought"; among the intellectual class: Faust, "A Southern Stewardship: The Intellectual and the Proslavery Argument"; among the new media: Perkins, "The Defense of Slavery in the Northern Press on the Eve of the Civil War," 501–31; and racism and bias in science in general: Gould, *The Mismeasure of Man.*

14. Griswold, *Adam Smith and the Virtues of Enlightenment,* 201.

15. Harman, *Moral Agent and Impartial Spectator,* 10.

16. The letter has not survived, but, as the editors of *TMS* show, Elliot asked, "If conscience is a reflection of social attitudes, how can it ever differ from, or be thought superior to, popular opinion?" Smith responded to this criticism in the second edition (*TMS* editor's introduction, 16).

17. Emma Rothschild associates Smith's use of the term 'vexation' with the modern term 'oppression' and articulates a long list of relationships that oppress moral and commercial actors. She writes, "Vexation is indeed a particular, personal form of the abuse of power, characteristic of the enforcement of commercial and fiscal rules" (Rothschild, *Economic Sentiments: Adam Smith, Condorcet, and the Enlightenment,* 27, 33).

18. Danford, "Adam Smith, Equality, and the Wealth of Sympathy," 686.

19. For a useful discussion of loss as history moves forward, see Harkin, "Natives and Nostalgia," 21–31.

20. Samuel Fleischacker offers a useful summary of the stops and starts of Smithian progress, emphasizing *TMS* V.2.9, *WN* V.i.f.58–60, *WN* II.iii.42, *LJA* iii.111, *WN* V.i.f.50–51, 61. See Fleischacker, "Review of Jerry Evensky's *Adam Smith's Moral Philosophy,*" 194–98. For a different account of Evensky's book, see Weinstein, "*The Wealth of Nations* and the Morality of Opulence."

21. Justman, *The Autonomous Male of Adam Smith,* 4.

22. According to the *OED,* the first use of 'gender,' in 1380, is grammatical, referencing sex in objects. It did imply reference to human sex shortly after, but an early and explicit association of the feminine gender with the term 'woman' isn't found until 1642. It wasn't until the middle twentieth century that it came to have its current meaning (by A. Comfort in 1963): "a euphemism for the sex of a human being, often intended to emphasize the social and cultural, as opposed to the biological, distinctions between the sexes."

23. James E. Alvey is highly critical of Justman's book, arguing that he "did not take sufficient care with his topic." He rightly points out the numerous places where Justman neglects Smith's more progressive comments on women—some of the same points I make in this chapter as well (Alvey, "Adam Smith on Gender"). Griswold, however, is more sympathetic to the project, calling it "worthwhile" and "provocative" (Griswold, "Review of S. Justman, *The Autonomous Male of Adam Smith*").

24. Kuiper, "Adam Smith and His Feminist Contemporaries," 51. Also, as quoted in Kuiper: Akkerman and Stuurman, *Perspectives on Feminist Political Thought in European History: From the Middle Ages to the Present,* 3–4.

25. Kuiper, "Adam Smith and His Feminist Contemporaries," 49.

26. Kathryn Sutherland extends this argument to suggest that capitalism as a whole is gendered male (Sutherland, "Adam Smith's Master Narrative: Women and *The Wealth of Nations*").

27. Brown, *Adam Smith's Discourse*, 32n17.
28. Kuiper, "Adam Smith and His Feminist Contemporaries," 51.
29. Griswold, *Adam Smith and the Virtues of Enlightenment*, 49.
30. Wollstonecraft, *Vindication of the Rights of Women*, chap. 14, par. 20.
31. De Grouchy's commentary is in the form of letters, probably initially written to her brother-in-law but then appended to the translation. The commentary is both complimentary to and critical of *TMS* and offers useful insight to the debate at the time. Unfortunately, the introduction to the critical edition of the letters (2008) is not adequately representative of Smith's own philosophy. Karin Brown falsely claims that Smith "makes no use of the concept of pain" (10); oversimplifies by asserting that "Smith is uncomfortable with a strong expression of emotions" (16); incorrectly suggests that only instrumental reason plays any role in Smith's theory because he explains "the entire scope of morality through sentiments" (22, 28, 29); and even asserts that Smith "claims that we do not help others because we love them. We help them because we love the general, objective point of view of the impartial spectator" (25). See Karin Brown and James E. McClellan III, *Sophie de Grouchy: Letters on Sympathy*.
32. As quoted in Sutherland, "Adam Smith's Master Narrative," 99–100.
33. Rendall, "Virtue and Commerce: Women in the Making of Adam Smith's Political Economy," 61.
34. As quoted in ibid., 64.
35. As Goldsmith points out, Mandeville shares some of these key thoughts. He argued that "women are capable of as great virtue as men" and "identifies women's [social] position as unjustifiable slavery, and their capacities as equal to men's." The fact that he used women in *The Female Tatler* is itself "subversive" (Goldsmith, *Private Vices, Public Benefits*, 146–48.
36. Ronald C. Bodkin cites this passage as evidence of Smith's patriarchy. Bodkin both misses the point of the passage and offers polemic instead of argument. It is precisely the fact that women's education is useful that suggests Smith's sympathy toward women and their rationality. The education supplied in the home respects the reality of their lives. Smith is not proscribing a plan for women's education in this paragraph; he is describing the effectiveness of their lessons with regard to the actual lives they will lead and the actual skills they will be required to have (Bodkin, "Women's Agency in Classical Economic Thought: Adam Smith, Harriet Taylor Mill and J. S. Mill," 46–47).
37. Another parallel can be found in Paganelli's observation that "what Smith describes in *The Theory of Moral Sentiments* may very well be 'a nation of shopkeepers,' but what he describes in *The Wealth of Nations* is not 'a nation of shopkeepers; but . . . a nation whose government is influenced by shopkeepers" (Paganelli, "The Adam Smith Problem in Reverse: Self-Interest in *The Wealth of Nations* and *The Theory of Moral Sentiments*," 381).
38. Nyland, "Adam Smith, Stage Theory, and the Status of Women," 618.
39. Ibid., 637.
40. Smith was probably unaware of the phenomenon known as *couvades*, men having sympathy pain in response to childbirth. But anthropologists have observed extensive

systems of *couvades* in many tribal situations, and their conclusions are certainly compatible with Smith's. There is little suggestion that it is artificial or a disrespectful "put on." See Hall and Dawson, *Broodmales: A Psychological Essay on Men in Childbirth*.

41. This is, Smith suggests, an "illusion of the imagination."

42. Justman, *The Autonomous Male of Adam Smith*, 19.

43. Rendall, "Virtue and Commerce," 44.

44. Danford, "Adam Smith, Equality, and the Wealth of Sympathy," 682.

45. Racial and biological differences are learned insofar as their meanings are imparted by society. So, while skin color is largely the product of biological factors, ascribing people a certain color—and identifying variations on color as the same color (i.e., light-skinned and dark-skinned as both black)—is the product of socialization. In fact, there is likely nothing inherent in one's skin color or other biological features that necessitates associating them with another person's characteristics. The desire for social grouping is probably learned as well; Smith's account seems to support these observations.

46. By 'compare' I do not mean to imply a form of competition.

47. Forman-Barzilai illustrates well the complex, culturally laden beliefs that sympathy has to overcome as well as the fact that when difference is encountered it may cause spectators to bristle (Forman-Barzilai, "Sympathy in Space(s)," 209).

48. Harriet Beecher Stowe's contemporaries were known to argue that slaves were, in fact, happy, sometimes citing the slaves' dancing and singing as proof. Even at the time, the response to this was vehement. Frederick Douglass argues that the songs can be understood as expressions of happiness only when one does not understand the lyrics. Douglass, for whom the songs are not "unmaning jargon" (jargon that takes one's personhood away), writes, "I have sometimes thought that the mere hearing of those songs would do more to impress some minds with the horrible character of slavery, than the reading of whole volumes of philosophy on the subject could do" (Douglass, *Narrative of the Life of Frederick Douglass, an American Slave, Written by Himself*, chapter 2). Additionally, Richard Whately showed that what was often called dancing was misinterpreted. He asks, "What is the meaning of the countless advertisements, offering rewards for the apprehension of runaway slaves, to be recognised by marks sufficient to prove the 'happy' state they left, and which they were too dull or too ungrateful to appreciate?" He also compares calling slaves being happy with the assertion that a woman who was abducted "wished in her heart to be carried off," and the Romans, when invaded by the French, "in their hearts wished for the overthrow of the Republic . . . and were glad of the coercion" (Whatley, "Review of *Uncle Tom's Cabin*," esp. 248–50).

49. For a more detailed account of self-deception, see Mitchell, "'The Mysterious Veil of Self-Delusion' in Adam Smith's *Theory of Moral Sentiments*."

50. Recall that contra Mandeville, Smith writes that TMS is "not concerning a matter of right . . . but concerning a matter of fact" (*TMS* II.i.5.10). In other words, here Smith is being descriptive rather than prescriptive and thus the main question is whether TMS is an accurate depiction of how humans actually are. Certainly, much of WN meets these criteria as well.

51. Sen, *The Idea of Justice*, 15–18, 96–105.

52. This passage is a confusing one. Ostensibly, Smith is discussing the "martial spirit" and order in Greece and Rome. The sentence preceding the comments regarding mutilation of mind and body refers to the capacity of a person to defend himself or herself and to avoid cowardice. Nothing in this passage suggests liberal education. However, Smith's readers ought to notice, first, how intertwined moral and educational claims are in his writing. Bravery is a virtue in this context, and it is not unfounded to see these comments in terms of the unity of the virtues. The sentence that follows refers to happiness and misery, healthfulness, and asks readers to consider the mind as a whole. Second, Smith implies that mental health is a precondition of physical health.

53. Griswold, *Adam Smith and the Virtues of the Enlightenment*, 220.

54. Cropsey makes a similar point, emphasizing, more than I do, the role of the moral law in happiness (Cropsey, *Polity and Economy* 63).

55. In this paragraph I follow Griswold's discussion, *Adam Smith and the Virtues of the Enlightenment*, 225–26.

56. Smith is reluctant to ignore the body completely. In strikingly similar phrasing, he condemns Epicurus for focusing only on the mind. Epicurus, he reports, sees "happiness and misery [as] depended chiefly on the mind, [and] if this part of our nature was well disposed, if our thoughts and opinions were as they should be, it was of little importance in what manner our body was affected." But this radical interpretation, Smith writes, is "altogether inconsistent with that which I have been endeavouring to establish" (*TMS* VII.ii.2.13).

57. In other words, it is out of respect and honor for the laboring classes that Smith calls for their education. Unlike Mandeville, as we shall see in the next chapter, Smith felt that workers' minds and aspirations should be cultivated.

58. Rawls's overlapping consensus also asks for a limited melting pot, although for Rawls the imagination is unnecessary because of the political conception of justice that allows for cross-group debate. For a comparison of this aspect of Rawls and Smith, see Weinstein, "Overlapping Consensus or Marketplace of Religions?"

59. My discussion of class interest and knowledge follows Göçmen, *The Adam Smith Problem*, 131–33. See my review of his book: Weinstein, "Review Essay: Adam Smith: *The Rhetoric of Propriety* by Stephen J. McKenna; *Adam Smith's Moral Philosophy*: A *Historical and Contemporary Perspective on Markets, Law, Ethics, and Culture* by Jerry Evensky; and *The Adam Smith Problem: Reconciling Human Nature and Society in the* Theory of Moral Sentiments *and* Wealth of Nations by Dogan Göçmen."

60. Göçmen, *The Adam Smith Problem*, 133.

61. Rothschild, *Economic Sentiments*, 47–48.

5. FINDING RATIONALITY IN REASON

1. Sen, *Rationality and Freedom*, 4.

2. As Smith would likely argue, a decision-making process that relied on reason alone would be as significantly distorted as one based entirely on immediate emotional reactions.

3. A similar division of the soul is found in *Republic*.

4. Nussbaum, *Upheavals of Thought*, 27–30.

5. A kernel of this idea can be found in Eric Schliesser's comment that "Smith has a decisively social epistemology. . . . Smith realizes that natural philosophy is more than just measurement and inference; there is a whole process of setting standards, deciding on criteria, and offering reasons to other inquirers that can involve sympathetic judgments" (Schliesser, "Review of *The Cambridge Companion to Adam Smith*").

6. Martha Nussbaum, *Upheavals of Thought*, 3.

7. Ibid., 109.

8. Ibid., 49.

9. Ibid., 45.

10. Ibid., 46.

11. Ibid., 47.

12. Ibid., 49.

13. Ibid., 84.

14. Ibid., 173.

15. This reference does not contain the phrase "the doctrine" but is used so as to imply it.

16. Again, Smith uses Plato to make his point.

17. I have not included those instances where the terms are separated by a comma, since those do not suggest synonymy, or those instances where Smith uses the term to cover multiple situations, as he does at *HA* IV.44.

18. Force, *Self-Interest before Adam Smith*, 133.

19. For a helpful discussion that emphasizes the role of persuasion rather than the role of reason in many of these same citations, see ibid., 126–30, 232–35.

20. Stewart, "Account of the Life and Writings of Adam Smith, LL.D," I.10.

21. Ibid., 1.16.

22. Carrasco, "Adam Smith's Reconstruction of Practical Reason," 84.

23. Ibid., 89.

24. McKenna, *Adam Smith: The Rhetoric of Propriety*, 143.

25. King, "From Logic to Rhetoric: Adam Smith's Dismissal of the Logic(s) of the Schools," 48.

26. Kneale and Kneale, *The Development of Logic*, 300.

27. Ibid.

28. Ibid., 313.

29. Locke, *Essay*, IV.xvii.4, 671.

30. Ibid., 676–77.

31. Locke may appear to be inconsistent. At *Essay* IV.xviii.2 he writes, "*Reason* therefore here, as contradistinguished to *Faith*, I take to be the discovery of the Certainty or Probability of such Propositions or Truths, which the Mind arrives at by Deductions made from such *Ideas*, which it has got by the use of its natural Faculties, *viz.* by Sensation or Reflection." However, as David C. Snyder points out, 'deduction' in this context refers not to "logical entailment but to the process of finding connections between ideas." (See Snyder, "Faith and Reason in Locke's *Essay*," 201.) Additionally, although the word 'proposition' appears to be a logical term to the modern eye, for Locke it means "objects of the understanding when a man thinks." (See Cohen, "Reason and Experience in Locke's Epistemology," 72.)

32. Locke, *Essay*, IV.xvii.4, 678

33. Ibid.

34. Woolhouse, *Locke*, 75.

35. Bonar, *A Catalogue of the Library of Adam Smith*.

36. Stewart, "Account of the Life and Writings of Adam Smith, LL.D," I.16.

37. Wightman and Bryce, "Introduction to *Essays on Philosophical Subjects*," 8.

38. King, "From Logic to Rhetoric: Adam Smith's Dismissal of the Logic(s) of the Schools," 60.

39. Kneale and Kneale, *The Development of Logic*, esp. chapters 1 and 2.

40. The phrase 'political arithmetick' likely references William Petty's book by the same name. He writes, "The Method I take to do this, is not yet very usual; for instead of using only comparative and superlative Words, and intellectual Arguments, I have taken the course (as a Specimen of the Political Arithmetick I have long aimed at) to express my self in Terms of Number, Weight, or Measure; to use only Arguments of Sense, and to consider only such Causes, as have visible Foundations in Nature; leaving those that depend upon the mutable Minds, Opinions, Appetites, and Passions of particular Men, to the Consideration of others." Smith's objection to the approach should be obvious (Petty, *Political Arithmetick*, preface).

41. Montes, *Adam Smith in Context*, 150.

42. Hobbes, *Leviathan* 18.

43. Ibid.

44. Ibid., 19.

45. Ibid., 20.

46. Leshen, "Reason and Perception in Hobbes: An Inconsistency," 431.

47. Hobbes, *Leviathan*, 21.

48. Ibid.

49. A. P. Martinich suggests that Hobbes saw reason as the exercise of syllogisms in *The Elements* but grew to change this view. See Martinich, *Hobbes: A Biography*, 125.

50. Hobbes, *Leviathan*, 28.

51. Tuck, *Hobbes*, 46–47.

52. Martinich, *Hobbes*, 125.

53. Ibid., 124.

54. Locke, *Essay* IV.xvii.1, 668.

55. Locke, *Essay* IV.xvii.2, 668.

56. Locke, *Essay* IV.xvii.1. 668.

57. Here I refer to Locke's definition of an Idea: "It being that Term, which, I think, serves best to stand for whatsoever is the Object of the Understanding when a Man thinks, I have used it to express whatever is meant by *Phantasm, Notion, Species*, or whatever it is, which the Mind can be employ'd about in thinking; and I could not avoid frequently using it" (Locke, *Essay* I.i.intro.8, 47).

58. Locke, *Essay* IV.xvii.2, 668.

59. Ibid., 669.

60. Snyder writes, "Reason is Locke's general term for our capability to reason about ideas arrived at by using our natural faculties, i.e., sensation and reflection. Knowledge

consists in 'the perception of the connexion and agreement, or disagreement and repugnancy of any of our Ideas' and reason is our capability to recombine these ideas in order to give us knowledge" (Snyder, "Faith and Reason in Locke's *Essay*," 203).

61. Locke, *Essay* IV.xvi.4, 659–60.

62. Shaftesbury also rejects the importance of formal logic. See Grean, *Shaftesbury's Philosophy of Religion and Ethics*, 39–40.

63. Tuveson, "The Importance of Shaftesbury," 276, 290.

64. Recall the graphic self-division of the young man who considers forcing himself upon the princess whom he desires (*Char.* I, 115).

65. Ben Mijuskovic presents a compelling argument suggesting that Hume's notion of a reflective self is an outgrowth of Shaftesbury's *Characteristicks*, particularly in his development of the notions that "a man may alter his entire character and yet continue to be the same man" and "it is memory, *qua* reflection, that is the psychological mechanism which effects our ideas of personal identity." See Mijuskovic, "Hume and Shaftesbury on the Self," 333.

66. The editors of the Glasgow Edition of *TMS* suggest that Smith's comments here are derived from Hume's *Treatise* III.i.1–2.

67. As we have seen, Smith presents the fragments of a physical account of empiricism in *ES*.

68. Griswold, *Adam Smith and the Virtues of the Enlightenment*, 15–16.

69. Stewart, "Account of the Life and Writings of Adam Smith," 1.16.

6. REASON AND THE SENTIMENTS

1. *LRBL* are records of lectures given at Glasgow during the years 1762–63, after the first publication of *TMS* but before *WN*. In many regards, these lectures represent the best possible scenario for found notes. For a sensitive account of the lectures, with special attention to some possible mistakes, see Howell, "Adam Smith's Lectures on Rhetoric: An Historical Assessment," 11–43.

2. Skinner, *A System of Social Science*, 8.

3. Bryce, "Lectures on Rhetoric and Belles Lettres," 14.

4. Howell suggests that Smith seems to change his mind about the importance of didactic texts since his comment about the obviousness of didactic texts in lecture 22 is made in the context of explaining why he chooses *not* to discuss the topic at all. See Howell, "Adam Smith's Lectures on Rhetoric: An Historical Assessment," 30.

5. Brown, *Adam Smith's Discourse*, 17.

6. I ask that the reader not take this point too far. I am not suggesting that mathematics is necessarily Platonic, nor do I wish to suggest any conviction regarding, for example, Frege's definition of number. My point is simply that mathematical and syllogistic logic are independent of the audience to such an extent that neither hypocrisy nor an argument ad hominem is said to affect the truth of an argument. As we shall see, Smith can be understood as calling this fallacy into question.

7. See *Rhetoric* 1355a, for example.

8. Howell, "Adam Smith's Lectures on Rhetoric," 33.

9. Leonidas Montes argues for a reconsideration of the common assertion that Smith is Newtonian in his methodology. In doing so, he does not so much disassociate Smith from Newton as he disassociates Newton from Newtonianism. See Montes, *Adam Smith in Context: A Critical Reassessment of Some Central Components of His Thought*. See also Weinstein, "Review: Leonidas Montes: *Adam Smith in Context: A Critical Reassessment of Some Central Components of His Thought.*"

10. Scholars are unsure as to when *HA* was written. The best guess is some time before 1758, when Smith was in Edinburgh lecturing on rhetoric, but in fact there is enough information to suggest that he began writing it while still at Oxford as a student (*EPS* 7). If this is true, he would have written *Astronomy* while he was still in his early twenties. In either case, *Astronomy* predates *TMS*, *WN*, and the lecture notes in *LRBL*. Nevertheless, we can be more secure about citing *HA* than *LRBL* since Smith himself suggests the value of the essay. In a letter to Hume, Smith writes, "As I have left the care of all my literary papers to you, I must tell you that except those which I carry along with me there are none worth the publishing, but a fragment of a great work which contains a history of the Astronomical Systems that were successively in fashion down to the time of Des Cartes. Whether that might not be published as a fragment of an intended juvenile work, I leave entirely to your judgement; tho I begin to suspect myself that there is more refinement than solidity in some parts of it" (*Corr.* 137).

11. I am concerned with the people Smith describes, not his method of developing that description: for the latter, see Lindgren, "Adam Smith's Theory of Inquiry."

12. Skinner, *A System of Social Science*, 37.

13. Mitchell, "Beautiful and Orderly Systems," 82n4.

14. Weinstein, *On Adam Smith*, 60–61.

15. Cropsey, *Polity and Economy*, 152.

16. Bryce, "Introduction," 12.

17. *Rhetoric* 1355b. From Kennedy, *On Rhetoric*.

18. Vivienne Brown points to an ambiguity in Smith's definition of rhetoric. In addition to the broad interpretation cited here, she argues that Smith asserts the more traditional Aristotelian definition, which requires, in her words, persuasion "at all costs" (Brown, *Adam Smith's Discourse*, 16).

19. This is wider than the generally acknowledged definition of sentiments. It is interesting that commentators tend to take the term for granted and as given. Raphael and Macfie do not define it in their introduction to the Glasgow Edition of *TMS*. Neither does Haakonssen in the introduction to his recent Cambridge edition. Griswold sees the term as synonymous with "passions" and "emotions" (Griswold, *Adam Smith and the Virtues of Enlightenment*, 76), and both Otteson's and Vivenza's indices direct readers to their entries on "passions" rather than address the issue exactly. This may, in the end, not be problematic, but given the fact that Western philosophy has historically viewed emotions and passions in opposition to reason, this simplified approach tends to distort what Smith had in mind. (This is not to suggest that Griswold, Otteson, and Vivenza do not address the role of reason in the sentiments within their individual works.)

20. I edit this quote more than usual because the student taking notes appears to have missed several key words and an additional example. These omissions do not affect the meaning of the sentence.

21. For an alternate discussion of Smith's criticism of Shaftesbury, see Otteson's "Shaftesbury's Evolutionary Morality and Its Influence on Adam Smith."

22. I see this as further evidence that Smith does not regard didactic method as incompatible with the poetic, historical, or oratorical discourses.

23. Walton, "Searching for the Roots of the Circumstantial Ad Hominem"; Chichi, "The Greek Roots of the Ad Hominem Argument"; Walton, "Argumentation Schemes and Historical Origins of the Circumstantial Ad Hominem Argument."

24. Commentators seem evenly divided as to whether Shaftesbury was a good writer, stylistically. Smith's student Hugh Blair, whose own lectures on rhetoric are so important to the discipline of English, continues many of Smith's objections, but Swift himself claims that Shaftesbury's *Letter Concerning Enthusiasm* is "very well writ" (Alderman, "The Style of Shaftesbury," 214).

25. This approach is consistent with Griswold's claim that Smith was influenced by Theophrastus's *The Characters*, in which the classical Greek writer offered character studies as moral types. (Griswold, Jr., *Adam Smith and the Virtues of Enlightenment*, 59–60.) See also Locke, "Adam Smith and 'The Man of System,'" 42.

26. Walton, "Argumentation Schemes and Historical Origins of the Circumstantial Ad Hominem Argument," 361.

27. Ibid.

28. I argue that this foreshadows MacIntyre's plurality of rationalities: context affects the very nature of reason. See my "The Invisible Hand of Rationality: On the Intersection of Adam Smith and Alasdair MacIntyre."

29. Raphael, *The Impartial Spectator*, 134–35.

30. Aldridge, "Shaftesbury and the Test of Truth," 129–56.

31. See Brown, *Adam Smith's Discourse*, 15.

32. McKenna, *Adam Smith: The Rhetoric of Propriety*, 92.

33. Ibid., 134.

34. Ibid.

35. Ibid., 78, 138.

36. Carrasco, "Adam Smith's Reconstruction of Practical Reason," 108.

37. Skinner, *A System of Social Science*, 16.

38. Griswold finds a similar comment at WN I.ii.3. Although Smith is discussing trade "by treaty, by barter, and by purchase," which, he states elsewhere, is the result of the capacity of speech, it seems a stretch to me to understand I.ii.3 as a comment on oratory. See Griswold, *Adam Smith and the Virtues of Enlightenment*, 43.

39. Phillips, "Adam Smith, Belletrist," 67.

40. The first lecture in the records is actually the second of the course. We do not know the content of Smith's introductory class.

41. Bryce, "Introduction," 15.

42. Ibid., 18–19.

43. Howell, "Adam Smith's Lectures on Rhetoric," 42.

44. *Phaedrus* 272a, as paraphrased in Griswold, *Adam Smith and the Virtues of the Enlightenment*, 41.

7. NORMATIVE ARGUMENTATION

1. In *On Adam Smith*, I write the following: "We can see that education allows the consumer to have a better understanding of the market price and whether it is in alignment with the normative standard. Natural price, then, is the economic analogue of the impartial spectator. It encapsulates all related knowledge. As always, there is a danger in this comparison that the reader may revert to a conception of the impartial spectator as an ideal observer theory, especially since natural price seems to be implicitly Archimedean. It must be emphasized that this is not the case. The consumer is limited in his or her *awareness* of the natural price in the same way that the impartial spectator is limited in its ability to make moral judgments. All judgments are the product of human reason, and human reason is limited" (75). Although emphasizing many of the themes dominating this chapter, the presentation in this earlier book was flawed, at least in part, because of a mistake I made regarding the relationship between price and profit. Both Lauren Brubaker ("Adam Smith's Enduring Relevance: Review of Jack Russell Weinstein's *On Adam Smith*") and Samuel Fleischacker (*On Adam Smith's* Wealth of Nations, 296nn2, 3) address this error, and they were right to do so, but only Fleischacker addresses the normative aspect of the claim. My acknowledgment of the mistake and a response to Brubaker's overall reading of my book can be found in Weinstein, "Author's Response." This section should be read, in part, as a response to Fleischacker.
2. Smith is explicit that "the occasional and temporary fluctuations in the market price of any commodity fall chiefly upon those parts of its price which resolve themselves into wages and profit" (WN I.vii.18).
3. Young, *Economics as Moral Science*, 7, 27, 68, 144.
4. Ibid., 144.
5. Ibid., 75.
6. Ibid., 7.
7. Fleischacker, *On Adam Smith's* Wealth of Nations, 127. His entire discussion spans pages 124–31.
8. These points echo my earlier comments that the differences between individuals do not vary so greatly as to affect their equal entitlement to justice and rights.
9. I am not concerned with the mechanics of *how* prices align. For a helpful discussion, see Schliesser, "Some Principles of Adam Smith's Newtonian Methods in the *Wealth of Nations*."
10. 'Natural liberty' and 'perfect liberty' are different terms. Natural liberty denotes the conditions under which economic liberty is to be achieved—it is met when the sovereign limits governing activity to the three duties as articulated in WN. 'Perfect liberty' seems instead to be a description of the realization of the proper functioning of the market—when the market and natural price are in accordance with one another.
11. Young, *Economics as Moral Science*, 69.

12. Schliesser, "Some Principles of Adam Smith's Newtonian Methods in the *Wealth of Nations*," 37.

13. Young, *Economics as Moral Science*, 68–69.

14. William Stanley Jevons postulates a "perfectly wise" consumer to establish a standard for measuring maximum utility (Jevons, *The Theory of Political Economy*, 65). More recently, Chiara Baroni and Maria Pia Paganelli both refer to a virtuous "man of credit," or "a virtuous man to whom it is worth lending" (Paganelli, "Vanity and the Daedalian Wings of Paper Money in Adam Smith," 285, and, as quoted in Paganelli, Baroni's "The Man of Credit: An Aristocratic Ethics of the Middle Class").

15. I reference an ideal; normal reactions to price are approximate at best, and most people (if not all people) do not know the exact moment of equilibrium.

16. Young, *Economics as Moral Science*, 118. Schliesser suggests that Smith jettisons the term 'just price' so he "can ignore the intellectual baggage associated with it" (Schliesser, "Some Principles of Adam Smith's Newtonian Methods in the *Wealth of Nations*," 41).

17. Young, *Economics as Moral Science*, 123.

18. Schliesser refers to natural price as a "theoretical fiction" (Schliesser, "Some Principles of Adam Smith's Newtonian Methods in the *Wealth of Nations*," 45).

19. Montes argues against the perception that Smith's work is a precursor to general equilibrium theory (Montes, *Adam Smith in Context*, chapter 5).

20. As Cropsey puts it, understanding the invisible hand as the manifestation of the divine "is intelligible only in so far as the behest of God is conceived as identical with the behest of passion" (Cropsey, *Polity and Economy*, 31).

21. Walton, "What Is Reasoning? What Is an Argument?," 400. Walton cites and follows Trudy Govier, who writes, "An argument is a publicly expressed tool of persuasion. Typically it takes thinking to construct an argument. Reasoning is distinguished from arguing along these lines: reasoning is what you may do before you argue, and your argument expresses some of your (best) reasoning. . . . But much reasoning is done before and outside the context of argument" (Govier, "Critical Thinking as Argument Analysis," 117). For a related discussion from the perspective of formal logic, see Parsons, "What Is an Argument?"

22. Hohmann, "Rhetoric and Dialectic: Some Historical and Legal Perspectives."

23. To elaborate: Ralph Johnson outlines five different and often incompatible conceptions of informal logic, including but not limited to those presented by John McPeck, Gilbert Ryle, Harvey Siegel, Mark Weinstein, and John Woods (Johnson, "The Relation between Formal and Informal Logic." See also Govier, *Problems in Argument Analysis and Evaluation*; Hintikka, "The Role of Logic in Argumentation"; McPeck, *Critical Thinking and Education*; Ryle, *Dilemmas*; Siegel, *Educating Reason*; Weinstein, "Informal Logic and Applied Epistemology"; Woods, "Fearful Symmetry."

24. Tim Hysee writes, "Formal logic will not provide us with an interpretation of rationality adequate for describing what happens when a hearer is convinced by the arguments of the speaker" (Hysee, "Why Logic Doesn't Matter in the (Philosophical) Study of Argumentation," 211, 224).

25. Walton, "New Methods for Evaluating Arguments," 45.

26. Blair, "Argument Management, Informal Logic, and Critical Thinking," 89.
27. Siegel, "On Some Recent Challenges to the Ideal of Reason," 3.
28. Johnson argues that it is best to understand formal and informal logic as engaging in "complementary tasks" (Johnson, "The Relation between Formal and Informal Logic," 265–66).
29. Van Eemeren, Grootendorst, and Henkemans, *Fundamentals of Argumentation Theory*, 23.
30. Ibid., 24.
31. Ibid.
32. I do not suggest these thinkers see themselves as inheriting Smith's theory of argumentation, only that they are engaged in a similar project.
33. Ibid., 23.
34. Haakonssen, *The Science of the Legislator*, 97.
35. Ibid.
36. Weber, "The Moral Dilemmas Debate, Deontic Logic, and the Importance of Argument," 459.
37. Toulmin, *The Uses of Argument*, 38.
38. Ibid., 39.
39. Lipman, "Caring as Thinking," 6–7.
40. Ibid., 10.
41. Ibid.
42. A different approach with similar consequences is taken by Nicholas Rescher, who argues that even if one is to define rhetoric specifically in opposition to argument (the latter referring to persuasion by "substantiating reasons" and the former is "inducing agreement by representing certain contentions in a favourable light"), it will still be the case that "reasoned argumentation is ultimately dependent on rhetoric." In other words, Rescher argues, "it is not the *presence* but the *extent* of a recourse to rhetoric that is at issue: the only question . . . is not *whether* but *how much*" (Rescher, "The Role of Rhetoric in Rational Argumentation," 315–16, 318).
43. Tindale, *Acts of Arguing*, 70.
44. See Johnson, *Manifest Rationality: A Pragmatic Theory of Argument*, and Johnson, "The Dialectical Tier Reconsidered."
45. See Weinstein, *On Alasdair MacIntyre*.
46. Ibid., chapter 5.
47. Ibid., chapter 6, esp. 83–86.
48. See Weinstein, "The Invisible Hand of Rationality: On the Intersection of Adam Smith and Alasdair MacIntyre."
49. Gregory, "Democracy and Care in the Community of Inquiry," 41.
50. Kennedy, "The Five Communities," 66.
51. Griswold, *Adam Smith and the Virtues of Enlightenment*, 50.
52. Johnson, *Manifest Rationality: A Pragmatic Theory of Argument*, 168. For a discussion of the plausibility of this definition, see Tindale, "A Concept Divided: Ralph Johnson's Definition of Argument," and Johnson "Manifest Rationality Reconsidered: Reply to My Fellow Symposiasts."

53. Van Rees, "Book Review: Manifest Rationality," 232.

54. There are, of course, questions regarding the plausibility of moving from factual premises to moral assertions, particularly in deductive arguments, which have a limited role in Smith's system. Mark Nelson argues that such a shift is possible, but even if it weren't, there would be little effect on moral argumentation: moral arguments require "evidential relations" between premises and not "logical relations" (Nelson, "Who Needs Valid Moral Arguments?").

55. Weinstein, "Some Foundational Problems with Informal Logic and Their Solutions," 27.

56. Weinstein, "Guest Editor's Introduction," 1. See also Weinstein, "Informal Logic and Applied Epistemology."

57. Smith, "Adam Smith on Progress and Knowledge," 300.

8. EDUCATION FOUNDATIONS

1. A prime example is Ryan Patrick Hanley's treatment of the subject. While he claims that education is a major theme in his book (the index lists nineteen mentions of the word, including two substantive discussions), the only actual and meaningful discussion is short and dismissive (Hanley, *Adam Smith and the Character of Virtue*, 60–61).

2. Weinstein, "Symposium: Adam Smith of Education."

3. Arrowood, *Theory of Education in the Political Philosophy of Adam Smith.*

4. Ibid., 10.

5. Ibid., 10, 13, 31.

6. MacIntyre, *Whose Justice? Which Rationality?*, 248. He continues this description in MacIntyre, "The Idea of an Educated Public."

7. Macintyre, *Whose Justice? Which Rationality?*, 248.

8. Herman, *How the Scots Invented the Modern World*, 190.

9. Richard Sher writes that Herman's work "has more to do with puffing the achievements" of the Scots than "elucidating the nature of Scottish thought" and argues that the book has a "tendency to carry its thesis beyond the point of credibility" (Sher, "Book Review: The Scottish Enlightenment: The Scots' Invention of the Modern World," 1397).

10. Rae, *The Life of Adam Smith*, 5.

11. Harrison, "Adam Smith, Natural Theology, and the Natural Sciences," 78.

12. Allan, *Virtue and Learning in the Scottish Enlightenment*, 9.

13. Ibid., 6, 12.

14. Ibid., 6.

15. Rae, *The Life of Adam Smith*, 5.

16. Ross, *The Life of Adam Smith*, 19.

17. Carlyle, "Recollections of a Student at Glasgow College," 228.

18. Muller, *Adam Smith in His Time and Ours*, 171.

19. Carlyle, "Recollections," 228.

20. As quoted in Allan, *Virtue and Learning in the Scottish Enlightenment*, 4.

21. According to the Belloughs' schema, the upper middle class "was made up of ministers (the most prestigious non-noble group in eighteenth-century Scotland), tackmen

(holders of leased land who did not farm but sublet the land to tenants), some of the untitled landowners (particularly the heritors, those liable for public assessment), professionals, such as lawyers and physicians, businessmen of wealth and success, military leaders (all officers), university teachers, and so forth" (Bellough and Bellough, "Intellectual Achievers: A Study of Eighteenth-Century Scotland," 1062, 1054).

22. At the time of his death the elder Smith had a library of eighty books, and all the people named in his will were from the "middling landed gentry, professional classes, and merchants" (Ross, *The Life of Adam Smith*, 11, 16, 19).

23. Ibid., 22.

24. West, *Adam Smith*, 64.

25. Leathers and Raines, "Adam Smith's [Weak] Case for Fee Incomes for University Faculty and Student-Consumer Sovereignty," 129.

26. *Fable* I, 317. See also Intro, lxxi–lx, xii.

27. Rothschild, "Condorcet and Adam Smith on Education and Instruction," 209, 219–20. See also Court, "Adam Smith and the Teaching of English Literature," 235–340.

28. Hyard, "Adam Smith and the French Ideas on Education," 89.

29. Ibid., 75.

30. Bonar, *A Catalogue of the Library of Adam Smith*; Hiroshi Mizuta. *Adam Smith's Library: A Catalogue*. The last volume does not appear in the Mizuta catalogue.

31. David Millar describes the structure of his lectures in Rae, *Life of Adam Smith*, 56.

32. Vivenza, "Adam Smith as a Teacher on Classical Subjects," 97–100.

33. Ibid., 96–97.

34. Scholars are uncertain when *ES* was written. Ross argues that the essay was most probably written before Smith read Hume and is thus quite early. However, as Ross acknowledges, Kevin Brown suggests a later date, 1758, immediately before the publication of *TMS*. See Brown, "Dating Adam Smith's Essay 'Of the External Senses,'" and Ross, *The Life of Adam Smith*, 104.

35. Land, "Adam Smith's 'Considerations Concerning the First Formation of Languages,'" 678.

36. Berry, "Adam Smith's 'Considerations on Languages,'" 136.

37. Stewart, *Smith's Works V*, 190, as quoted in Thomson, "Adam Smith's Philosophy of Science," 215–16.

38. I do not mean to suggest that the desire to learn is presocial. As discussed, Smith challenged the notion that humans could ever exist outside of society.

39. Peirce, "The Fixation of Belief."

40. Thomson, "Adam Smith's Philosophy of Science," 217.

41. Ibid., 223.

42. Ibid.

43. Griswold, *Adam Smith and the Virtues of Enlightenment*, 134.

44. For example, Smith writes, "The Language of Admiration and wonder is that in which we naturally speak of the Respectable virtues. Amplicatives and Superlatives are the terms we commonly make use of to express our admiration and respect. . . . Diminutives and such-like are the terms in which we speak of objects we love" (*LRBL* ii.104–5).

45. Vivenza, "Adam Smith as a Teacher on Classical Subjects," 103.

46. Recall that 'equality' does not denote identical characteristics and therefore allows for variation of natural talents.

47. Griswold, *Adam Smith and the Virtues of Enlightenment*, 131. Here, too, as throughout his book, Griswold uses the same ambiguous view of education that Smith does. He writes, "It is an inclination to be realized through moral education, such that the impartial spectator's practical reason becomes our own, becomes (as it were) our second nature."

48. This latter claim is, I would suggest, implicit throughout *TMS*. However, it is worth attending to the previous chapter in order to see how sympathy and imagination are unavoidable components of the human condition.

49. Fleischacker, *A Third Concept of Liberty*, 46.

50. Griswold, *Adam Smith and the Virtues of Enlightenment*, 191.

51. This is distinct from what Haakonssen calls 'system knowledge' or "the understanding of things, events, or persons in some sort of functional relationship to a greater 'whole' or system." See Haakonssen, *The Science of a Legislator*, 79.

52. See Weinstein, *On Alasdair MacIntyre*, chapters 4 and 5.

9. FORMAL EDUCATION

1. Rothschild, "Condorcet and Adam Smith on Education and Instruction," 212 (cf. 209, 211).

2. Ibid., 212.

3. Teixeira, "Dr. Smith and the Moderns—Adam Smith and the Development of Human Capital Theory," 140.

4. Ibid., 152.

5. Smith would probably not be guilty of this fault himself. Clyde E. Dankert makes a brief but convincing argument that Smith would have made the ideal modern faculty member, excelling in teaching, research, and service (Dankert, "Adam Smith, Educator," 17–19).

6. Teixeira. "Dr. Smith and the Moderns," 141.

7. Leathers and Raines, "Adam Smith's [Weak] Case for Fee Incomes for University Faculty and Student-Consumer Sovereignty." As the authors point out, they build on two other works offering related criticism: Mill, *Principles of Political Economy*, 953, and Rosen, "Some Economics of Teaching."

8. Ian Ross is more skeptical about Leathers's and Raines's conclusions and attempts to offer evidence from Balliol College that Smith is more focused on market-based reforms than they suggest. However, Ross does not connect the events of Smith's life to his argument but simply recounts Smith's experiences, and shortly after the initial reference backpedals, writing, "To some extent, an academic marketplace analogy holds here, not so much in terms of wages for the providers of higher education, perhaps, as in the competition among them for distinction in their fields." If this is the case, he is making a different argument altogether, and assuming that competition for distinction is analogous to market competition is question begging (Ross, "Adam Smith's Smile," 254–55).

9. Leathers and Raines, "Adam Smith's [Weak] Case for Fee Incomes for University Faculty and Student-Consumer Sovereignty," 137.

10. This is also a likely consequence of his accompanying the young Duke of Buccleuch on his postschool travels through Europe (1764–66). Smith would have observed a great deal about the effect of travel as education as the duke's private tutor. Scholars agree that this trip was essential to the development of WN.

11. This may be sarcasm or hyperbole on Smith's part, since one can assume a parent would react accordingly to prevent the child's ruination if they were at all capable of doing so.

12. As Campbell and Skinner write, "One of the main features of the *TMS* is the interest shown in the question of the way in which we form judgements concerning what is fit and proper to be done or to be avoided. Smith went on from this basis to argue that our ability to form judgements in particular cases enables us to form some notion of general rules of morality. Smith indicated that the content of general rules was a function of experience, and that they would be found in all societies" (WN p. 768fn). See *TMS* III, esp. 4 and 5.

13. The term 'indulgences' is mine. Leathers and Raines are referencing examples of bad behavior on the part of both students and faculty. See Leathers and Raines, "Adam Smith's [Weak] Case for Fee Incomes for University Faculty and Student-Consumer Sovereignty," 130–32.

14. See Weinstein, "Neutrality, Pluralism, and Education: Civic Education as Learning about the Other."

15. In addition to the textual arguments I have already made, I have in mind Smith's personal comments regarding the nationalist abuse the Scotts were subject to. Smith observes in his correspondences to Hume, "The church, the Whigs, the Jacobites, the whole wise English nation, who will love to mortify a Scotchman" (*Corr.* 93). And, "The hatred of Scotch men can subsist, even at present, among nobody but the stupidest of the People, and is such a piece of nonsense that it must fall even among them in a twelvemonth" (*Corr.* 88).

16. James E. Alvey argues that, according to Smith, "as the society increases in size and diversity, it becomes easier to achieve a vision of the ideal, impartial spectator. As the commercial society is the largest and most diverse, comparison with others is more likely to lead to a truly impartial standard" (Alvey, "Moral Education as a Means to Human Perfection and Social Order," 6). Obviously, I am sympathetic to this view. Nevertheless, one must remain cautious about attributing this argument to Smith himself. It is implicit in his work, as I have argued so far, but one might be safer to suggest that it is simply Smithian.

17. As Pedro Teixeira points out, "Smith frequently uses metaphors like 'instruments' or 'machines' to designate workers; the educated and trained ones in particular. His use of 'instrument of trade' to designate workers in the mercantile system is one such instance" (WN II.i.17, WN IV.viii.44). In the latter, he refers to individual workers as "the living instrument, the artificer" (Teixeira, "Dr. Smith and the Moderns," 140).

18. Wince, "Two Rival Conceptions of Vocational Education: Adam Smith and Friedrich List," 372.

19. Cropsey, *Polity and Economy*, 139.

20. See a conversation by E. G. West and Robert Lamb (West, "The Political Economy of Alienation: Karl Marx and Adam Smith"; Lamb, "Adam Smith's Concept of Alienation"; and West, "Adam Smith and Alienation: A Rejoinder").

21. Perfect liberty should also be understood as including religious liberty since, although Smith does have a heavily qualified discussion regarding the control of fanaticism, he does argue for freedom of conscience (WN V.i.g.18).

22. Viner, "Adam Smith and Laissez Faire," 231.

23. Cropsey, *Polity and Economy*, 12.

24. Young, *Economics as a Moral Science*, 133.

25. Ibid., 134.

26. I refer here to Hobbes's definition of liberty as "the absence of externall Impediments" (*Leviathan*, chap. xiv, p. 66, chap. xxi, p. 110), and his "Libertie of the Commonwealth," which is what "every man then should have, if there were no Civil Laws, nor Common-wealth at all" (*Leviathan* chap. xxi, p. 112). This has its most famous modern variation in the concept of "negative liberty" as articulated in Berlin "Two Concepts of Liberty."

27. Viner, "Adam Smith and Laissez Faire," 213–14.

28. Ibid., 223, 226, 227.

29. Ibid., 228. Viner points to another example of supposed inconsistency: Smith's approval of taxation as a disincentive for small "alehouses" and distilleries, motivated, at least partially, by health concerns (WN V.ii.k.50). He is joined by others in his concern about Smith's prescriptions. E. G. West, like Viner, suggests that Smith's economic prescriptions for education are inconsistent (West, *Education and the State*, 144–45), and James Stanfield argues that Smith's prescriptions "can only be described as a bit of muddle" (Stanfield, "Adam Smith on Education," 56).

30. These comments are linked to *TMS*'s earlier brief account of the sovereign's duties (*TMS* II.ii.1.8).

31. Skinner, "Adam Smith and the Role of the State: Education as a Public Service," 78.

32. Teixeira, "Dr. Smith and the Moderns," 142. See WN, I.x.c.42–43 and LJ(B) 306–7.

33. Teixeira, "Dr. Smith and the Moderns," 142.

34. This metaphor requires caution. As discussed in the previous chapter, Smith did not believe that society was formed by a social contract but was, rather, the product of evolution and political economic forces.

35. Martin, *Ancient Greece*, 84–85.

36. Viner, "Adam Smith and Laissez Faire," 226–27.

37. Ibid., 227.

38. Ibid., 218.

39. Evensky, *Adam Smith's Moral Philosophy*, 228.

40. Leathers and Raines, "Adam Smith's [Weak] Case for Fee Incomes for University Faculty and Student-Consumer Sovereignty," 125–26.

41. Vivienne Brown's text-only approach to reading Smith's books would have prohibited enlisting these pieces of evidence in trying to solve this particular interpretive puzzle.

42. Skinner, "Adam Smith and the Role of the State: Education as a Public Service," 87.

43. It is unclear how interested Smith was in the *content* of religion. Gary M. Anderson argues that "Smith tried to explain why rational self-interested individuals participated in religion, on both the demand and supply sides" (Anderson, "Mr. Smith and the Preachers: The Economics of Religion in the *Wealth of Nations*," 1067). As I show, Smith was interested in content at least insofar as religion supported fundamental moral principles that allow for a stable society. See also Minowitz, *Profits, Priests and Princes*, esp. chapters 8 and 11.

44. The term 'irrational' should not suggest 'immoral.' It only emphasizes the nature of the commitment and the influences that inspire it.

45. Mitchell, "Beautiful and Orderly Systems: Adam Smith on the Aesthetics of Political Improvement," 72.

46. In *letter philosophiques* 6, Voltaire wrote, "If there were only one religion in England, there might be a risk of despotism; if there were two, they would cut each other's throats; but there are thirty, and they live together in peace and happiness." While this attribution is speculation on my part, Smith and Voltaire were friends and traveled in many of the same circles; Smith visited Voltaire at his estate multiple times while he was researching *WN* (as quoted in Roger Pearson, *Voltaire Almighty* (New York: Bloomsbury Publishing, 2005, 103, 315).

47. Smith was writing before the advent of weapons of mass destruction. As recent years have shown, a small group of fanatics can do much more damage than he understood.

48. Haakonssen, *The Science of the Legislator*, 122.

49. Ross, *The Life of Adam Smith*, 13.

50. What Smith means by "the true" is uncertain. He also writes, "False notions of religion are almost the only causes which can occasion any very gross perversion of our natural sentiments in this way; and that principle which gives the greatest authority to the rules of duty, is alone capable of distorting our ideas of them in any considerable degree" (*TMS* III.6.12). By associating truth and falsity with religious belief, Smith is likely not referencing either a denominational or a general Christian belief; there just isn't the biographical evidence to suggest this. Many suggest that Smith, like many eighteenth-century thinkers, was, in fact, a deist since he articulated a conception of natural religion, "divinely ordained and harmoniously operating natural laws" (Ross, *The Life of Adam Smith*, xx). This is consistent with my argument regarding the connection between inquiry and nature in chapter 1. It also speaks to Smith's supposed realism. If there is a moral truth, anything that violates it would be pernicious, or so a realist could argue. In any case, this phrase is open to a great many interpretations. Both supportive and alternative views can be found in the varied and often contradictory essays contained in Oslington, *Adam Smith as Theologian*. See also Hanley, "Scepticism and Naturalism," esp. 207.

51. Griswold, *Adam Smith and the Virtues of Enlightenment*, 369.

52. Rothschild, "Condorcet and Adam Smith on Education and Instruction," 220–21.

53. Fleischacker, *A Third Concept of Liberty*, 174. For more on Smith's notion of philosophy, see Hanley, *Adam Smith and the Character of Virtue*, 206–8, and Schliesser, "Adam Smith's Benevolent and Self-Interested Conception of Philosophy."

54. Ross argues that "moral philosophy was at the core of the Scottish university education of Smith's time" (Ross, *The Life of Adam Smith*, 116). This, however, is a far cry from MacIntyre's claim of public deference to the faculty of moral philosophy.
55. Young, *Economics as Moral Science*,155.
56. Alvey, "Moral Education as a Means to Human Perfection and Social Order," 12.
57. Martha Nussbaum cites this aspect of *TMS* as her "central inspiration" (Nussbaum, *Poetic Justice*, xvi), as does Luc Boltanski in *Distant Suffering: Morality, Media, and Politics*.
58. Haldane, "Adam Smith, Theology, and Natural Law Ethics," 25.
59. Pabst, "From Civil to Political Economy," 109. Hanley helpfully refers to Smith as a "sceptical realist" (Hanley, "Scepticism and Naturalism," 208).
60. Glenn Morrow calls Smith "one of the least metaphysical persons of the century." He then defines the "chief concern of natural theology" to be "to furnish a foundation for morality independent of positive religion; with religion in the popular sense it had nothing to do" (Morrow, "Adam Smith: Moralist and Philosopher," 323, 334).
61. See Weinstein, "Overlapping Consensus or Marketplace of Religions," esp. section 2.
62. This does not run counter to my earlier claim that religious commitment is irrational. The criteria of choice are rationally adjudicated while commitment is a nonrational matter.
63. This should not suggest that either he or Hume were atheists, nor should it apply a universal skepticism to Smith, as Phillipson seems to do in his biography. It is simply unclear how much of a skeptic Smith is and, as a result, no radical skepticism should be postulated. See also Weinstein, "Review of Nicholas Phillipson's *Adam Smith: An Enlightened Life*."
64. Griswold, *Adam Smith and the Virtues of Enlightenment*, 376.
65. Frazer, *The Enlightenment of Sympathy*, 48.
66. This is not anachronistic. Great Britain did not have a true democracy until the reform acts of 1832.
67. Rawls, *A Theory of Justice*, 152–57.
68. Young, *Economics as Moral Science*, 140.

10. HISTORY AND NORMATIVITY

1. My use of the term 'history' may be ambiguous. As Smith does, I write of history both as a discipline and as historicity, the actual events the discipline tries to describe. Historiography bridges the discipline and the actual event, giving historians a constructed account of linked events that allows for explanation and, in Smith's case, for moral judgment. When I reference Smith's methodology I am discussing the discipline of history; when I describe his use of narrative I articulate his preferred historiographic method; and when I discuss the content of his discussions—the events he attempts to elucidate—I refer to history in the most literal sense.
2. Pocock, "Adam Smith and History," 271.
3. Eric Schliesser takes issue with Pocock's interpretation of Smith's view of history. His criticism, however, does not change Pocock's overall rejection of Smith as a historian (Schliesser, "The Philosophical Subtlety of Smith").

4. Rothschild and Sen, "Adam Smith's Economics."

5. Rothschild, "The *Theory of Moral Sentiments* and the Inner Life," 28–29.

6. See also Eric Schliesser's comments on the types of history in Smith: "The Philosophical Subtlety of Smith," 233.

7. Eric Schliesser, "Articulating Practices as Reasons: Adam Smith on the Social Conditions of Possibility of Property," 79.

8. Day, *The Philosophy of History*, 53.

9. Campbell and Skinner, "General Introduction," 56.

10. As Mark Salber Phillips explains, "Yet, if Smith limited history to what could be narrated, he also discovered new possibilities that extended the range of narrative in significant ways. In particular, he pointed to the technique he called 'indirect narrative,' by which history acquired a potential to explore dimensions of experience beyond the purview of conventional description" (Phillips, "Adam Smith, Belletrist," 73).

11. Schliesser, "Some Principles of Adam Smith's Newtonian Methods in the *Wealth of Nations*," 35.

12. Burrow, *A History of Histories*, xiii.

13. MacIntyre, *After Virtue*, chapter 15, and MacIntyre, *Whose Justice? Which Rationality?*, chapter 18. See also Weinstein, *On MacIntyre*, chapter 5.

14. Kett, *The Pursuit of Knowledge under Difficulties*, 1.

15. Rothschild, "The Theory of Moral Sentiments and the Inner Life," 32.

16. Newton, *Opticks*, 381.

17. Wood, "Science in the Scottish Enlightenment," 102.

18. Shapiro, *Reading 'Adam Smith,'* 46, 55.

19. Ibid., 46.

20. Campbell and Skinner, "General Introduction," 52.

21. Ibid., 53.

22. Ibid., 59–60.

23. Cf. WN I.xi.g.26, V.ii.k.29; Campbell and Skinner, "General Introduction," 52. In that they are editors of Smith's work, their introduction is intended to be critical advocacy, not condemnation.

24. Shapiro, *Reading 'Adam Smith,'* 53.

25. Ibid., 55.

26. Ibid., 56–57.

27. Campbell and Skinner, "General Introduction," 55.

28. Ibid., 56.

29. MacIntyre, *Whose Justice? Which Rationality?*, 332–33.

30. There are various theories as to whom, if anybody, Smith is referring. The most persuasive account is F. P. Locke's. He suggests that "the passage was intended to generalize Smith's views on the rivalry between Charles James Fox and William Pitt (the main theme of British politics in the 1780s), and on the character and reforms of Joseph II, Holy Roman Emperor and archetypal 'man of system.'" The article also has a compact overview of the competing positions (Locke, "Adam Smith and 'the Man of System,'" 37).

31. Smith is not alone in decrying the dangers of system. As Robert Mitchell shows, numerous eighteenth-century thinkers, ranging from Shaftesbury to Burke, were worried about its impact (Mitchell, "Beautiful and Orderly Systems," 63).

32. The editors of *TMS* suggest that this quote may refer to either the French Revolution or the rationalist philosopher Richard Price (*TMS*, 231n6).

33. Brown, "Adam Smith: Between Morals and Markets." Brown's paper was a work in progress, and some of my interpretation comes from lengthy personal discussion after its presentation.

34. I take the fact of injustice in capitalist societies as a given, despite Brubaker's request for evidence. See Brubaker, "Adam Smith's Enduring Relevance: Review of Jack Russell Weinstein's *On Adam Smith*," and Weinstein, "Author's Response."

35. Nozick, *Anarchy, State, and Utopia*.

36. Brown, "Adam Smith: Between Morals and Markets," 5.

37. Ibid.

38. Ibid., and Brown, "Agency and Discourse: Revisiting the Adam Smith Problem."

39. *HA* illustrates well the progression of astronomical theories and the way in which they collectively lead to knowledge in astronomy. In the essay, Smith offers an embryonic account of paradigm shifts that prefigures Kuhn, *The Structure of Scientific Revolutions*.

40. For an overview of this aspect of feminist writing, see Held, *The Ethics of Care*, and Held, *Justice and Care*.

41. Shapiro, *Reading 'Adam Smith,'* 57.

42. The introduction to Shapiro's text is explicit that "the theorist whose work he has found most instructive is Michel Foucault's" (Schoolman, "Series Editor's Introduction," x).

43. Day, *The Philosophy of History*, 179.

44. Griswold, *Adam Smith and the Virtues of Enlightenment*, 314–17.

45. Berlin, "The Concept of Scientific History," 10–11. Most scientists would reject Berlin's computational model of natural science. Judgment is pervasive in the hard sciences. Nevertheless, the comparison is helpful for our current purposes.

46. Day, *The Philosophy of History*, 62.

47. Aristotle, *NE* 1094b24.

48. Skinner, "Adam Smith: An Economic Interpretation of History," 155–56.

49. Wooton, "Narrative, Irony, and Faith in Gibbon's *Decline and Fall*," 81.

50. Ibid., 80.

51. MacIntyre, "Hume on 'is' and 'ought,'" 114. While I do not deal with the accuracy of MacIntyre's interpretation of Hume here, it is indeed a controversial perspective. For the opposing argument, see MacBeth "'Is' and 'Ought' in Context: MacIntyre's Mistake," and Hudson, *The Is–Ought Question*.

52. The normative use of 'natural' in these instances recalls Griswold's observation that nature is used to reference the perfect in comparison to the imperfect.

53. Hanley, "Scepticism and Naturalism," esp. 203, 205.

54. Grampp, "What Did Smith Mean by the Invisible Hand?," 450.

55. Ibid., 460.

56. Samuels, *Erasing the Invisible Hand*, 60–82.

57. Syed Ahmad argues that there are actually four uses of the invisible hand in Smith's corpus (Ahmed, "Adam Smith's Four Invisible Hands," 138–39).

58. Samuels argues against this, although he does so unpersuasively (as we shall see). The chapter on the invisible hand and knowledge is noticeably shorter than all the others (Samuels, *Erasing the Invisible Hand*, 164–78).

59. I am grateful to Vivienne Brown for this point.

60. Rothschild, "Adam Smith and the Invisible Hand," 319.

61. That he might be wrong about the natural division of goods does not change his intent. It only minimizes the persuasiveness of his overall argument.

62. Rothschild, *Economic Sentiments*, 118–21, and Rothschild, "Adam Smith and the Invisible Hand," 319–30.

63. Peter Harrison offers a shorter alternative history of the phrase, emphasizing its theological history (Harrison, "Adam Smith, Natural Theology, and the Natural Sciences," 86). Harrison's additions, however, do not change the rhetorical appeal; they only change the metaphysical assumptions.

64. Samuels, *Erasing the Invisible Hand*, 146.

65. Ibid., 146, cf. 155, 157.

66. Ibid., 166

67. Ibid., 168.

68. Ibid., 289.

69. Rorty, *Philosophy and the Mirror of Nature*.

70. Lakoff and Johnson, *Metaphors We Live By*. I find it odd that Samuels cites this book but seems to ignore its central and most influential point. This omission is the weakest element of an otherwise important and exhaustive study.

71. Lakoff and Johnson, *Metaphors We Live By*, 3.

72. Smith, for example, sees knowledge as the desire to resolve uncertainty and move from the sentiment of surprise to wonder to admiration (*HA* I.4).

73. Cropsey, *Polity and Economy*, 131.

74. Smith, "Adam Smith on Progress and Knowledge," 337.

75. Göçmen, *The Adam Smith Problem*, 119–55.

76. For a compelling but controversial recent attempt to compose an empirical account of progress, see Pinker, *The Better Angels of Our Nature*.

11. PROGRESS OR POSTMODERNISM?

1. Sen, *The Idea of Justice*, 15–18.

2. King, "How Long, Not Long."

3. Here I distinguish between attempts to actualize the vision of society as prescribed in the original position and progress as a forward-moving consequence of nature and the human condition. Rawls may allow for progressive realization of the principles of justice. However, the veil of ignorance, by design, rejects the possibility that the principles of justice can be discovered through historical or scientific inquiry (Rawls, *A Theory of Justice*, 136–49).

4. Foucault's critique of history is aimed at the nineteenth century rather than at Smith (see White, "Foucault Decoded: Notes from Underground"). Thus, Foucault's attack

of the a priori in history tends to attack idealist conceptions that Smith himself would not subscribe to. Nevertheless, his overall challenge to the philosophy of history applies to Smith.

5. I am not suggesting that a philosophy of history is all that is needed for normative discovery—an ethical theory is also required. A philosophy of history is likely necessary but not sufficient.

6. Even divine command or intuitionist ethics must have theories of interpretation.

7. I do not attempt to address Foucault's specifically political remarks about Smith or his cohorts. For a discussion of Foucault's response to the Scottish Enlightenment and political economy in general, see Burchell, "Peculiar Interests: Civil Society and Governing 'the System of Natural Liberty.'"

8. O'Brien argues that Foucault presents methods of study rather than theories. This point becomes relevant below (O'Brien, "Michel Foucault's History of Culture," 38–39).

9. Foucault, *The Birth of Biopolitics.*

10. De Lima, *Foucault's Archaeology of Political Economy*, 235.

11. Ibid., 86.

12. Foucault, *The Birth of Biopolitics*, 219–20.

13. Ibid., 62.

14. Ibid., 17.

15. De Lima, *Foucault's Archaeology of Political Economy*, 112. The term 'political economy' is ambiguous, according to Foucault, who claims that its meaning "oscillates between two semantic poles. Sometimes this expression aims at a particular strict and limited analysis of the production and circulation of wealth. But, in a broader and more practical sense, 'political economy' also refers to any method of government that can procure the nation's prosperity. And finally, political economy—the term employed by Rousseau in his famous article in the *Encyclopedia*—is a sort of general reflection on the organization, distribution, and limitation of powers in a society. I think that fundamentally it was political economy that made it possible to ensure the self-limitation of governmental reason" (Foucault, *The Birth of Biopolitics*, 13). The second definition is most consistent with Smith's own at the opening of WN IV.

16. Foucault, *The Birth of Biopolitics*, 102; see also 118, 133, 175.

17. Ibid., 15.

18. De Lima, *Foucault's Archaeology of Political Economy*, 210.

19. Again, de Lima writes, "Foucault used the term 'anthropology' not to refer specifically to the science of man, but literally as 'a logic of man': 'anthropologism' became the philosophical foundation of all human sciences. Anthropology or anthropologism is 'an ideology which privileges Man at the centre and source of the philosophical and human sciences' . . . Man replaced God (age of resemblance) and Logos (classical age). Foucault called the effect of philosophical anthropology on thought 'anthropological sleep'" (de Lima, *Foucault's Archaeology of Political Economy*, 106).

20. Hurtado-Prieto, "The Mercantalist Foundations of 'Dr. Mandeville's Licentious System,'" 225, 229.

21. O'Brien, "Michel Foucault's History of Culture," 30.

22. Foucault, *The Archaeology of Knowledge*, 15.
23. Ibid., 4.
24. Ibid., 5.
25. Foucault is explicit that his investigation is located within the disciplines despite the fact that they are "unsure of their frontiers, and so vague in content" (ibid., 21). He also states directly that his intention is "not to deny all value to these unities"—the term 'unities' references discourses—"or try to forbid their use" (71).
26. Foucault describes his project as follows: "Its problem is to define discourses in their specificity; to show in what way the set of rules that they put into operation is irreducible to any other; to follow them the whole length of their exterior ridges, in order to underline them the better" (ibid., 139). This is also related to what he terms "the historical a priori," or "group of rules that characterize a discursive practice: but these rules are not imposed from the outside on the elements that they relate together; they are caught up in the very things that they connect" (ibid., 127).
27. Ibid., 211.
28. Young, *White Mythologies: Writing History and the West*, 70, 74–75.
29. De Lima, *Foucault's Archaeology of Political Economy*, 7.
30. Robert Young sees the move away from the a priori in *Archeology of Knowledge* as a rebuttal to his earlier claim in *The Order of Things* that there is indeed an "a priori common to a (limited) number of knowledges" (Young, *White Mythologies*, 76).
31. "Impose" is Foucault's term; see *Archeology of Knowledge*, 15.
32. Ibid., 72.
33. Ibid., 74.
34. O'Brian, "Michel Foucault's History of Culture," 34–35.
35. For a discussion of Foucault as a philosopher of language, see White, "Foucault Decoded," 235.
36. Foucault, *The Archaeology of Knowledge*, 7.
37. Ibid., 190, 192.
38. Ibid., 195.
39. Ibid., 139–40.
40. Ibid., 191 (emphasis added). While there is no indication that Foucault intended to allude to Smith's language—the common phrasing may simply be a coincidence—given his attention to the invisible hand specifically, he must have seen the similarities and assented to them. However, common language should not be seen as an endorsement on Foucault's part of Smith's political economic theory (Foucault, *The Birth of Biopolitics*, esp. 286).
41. Harootunian, "Foucault, Genealogy, History," 113.
42. Ibid.
43. Ibid., 119.
44. Foucault, *The Archaeology of Knowledge*, 31–36.
45. Ibid., 37.
46. Ibid., 76.
47. Foucault argues that the desire to find order in the midst of anomalies is indicative of a holistically understood eighteenth-century project (ibid., 152).

48. Ibid., 206.
49. Ibid., 114.
50. In *Madness and Civilization* Foucault has a much lengthier discussion of the discovery and identification of rationality. See White, "Foucault Decoded," 38–39, and Foucault, *Madness and Civilization*.
51. MacIntyre, *Whose Justice? Which Rationality?*, 4.
52. Foucault, *The Archaeology of Knowledge*, 174.
53. Ibid., 86.
54. Ibid., 84.
55. Ibid., 86–87.
56. Ibid., 99.
57. Ibid., 102.
58. Ibid., 103.
59. Ibid., 113.
60. First, "humanity" should not be construed as a synonym for personhood; I am not making a moral claim. Rather, I seek to describe the activity of being human and the self-conscious asserting of existence (verbal or otherwise). Second, individuality, for Foucault, should not be confused with atomism. For Foucault, "there is nothing given or natural about our 'individuality,'" and "'subjectivity' is not an 'individuality,' an indivisible unit in which we locate our identity; and it is not 'particularity' or the exemplification of a common nature. It is not a single thing, and there are as many 'subjectivities' as there are accepted forms of self-relation" (Rajchman, *Truth and Eros*, 101).
61. I do not mean to suggest that Foucault is deterministic. For a discussion of freedom in Foucault's work, see Rajchman, *Truth and Eros*, 109–121.
62. "Statement" is the English translation of *énoncé*. The use of the English term 'enunciate' also helps emphasize a concern with clarity of language—of the complexities of articulation and the difference between what the speaker says and what the listener hears.
63. Foucault, *The Archaeology of Knowledge*, 144.
64. John Rajcham argues that by the end of Foucault's career, his "question was[,] . . . Outside the moral idealisms of our good, can we invent no other truths about ourselves, no other passion for truth, no other 'game of truth' than the psychoanalytic one?" (Rajchman, *Truth and Eros*, 87).
65. As Young points out, "The attempt to reject historicism absolutely results either in an utter particularism or in a surreptitious return of historicism in a different form" (Young, *White Mythologies*, 83). He then cites Foucault's own early recognition of the problem in *The Order of Things* (Foucault, *The Order of Things*, 371).
66. Hume too speaks positively of custom in his critique of cause and effect: it is only because of custom that we identify the contiguity of events and consider it as cause and effect, yet this identification is still central to human reason.
67. In the same paragraph he writes, "A linen shirt, for example, is, strictly speaking, not a necessary of life."
68. Foucault, *The Archaeology of Knowledge*, 15.

69. On the shift to genealogy, see Young, *White Mythologies*, 81, and de Lima, *Foucault's Archaeology of Political Economy*, 22.

70. White, "Foucault Decoded," 47–48.

71. While some argue that Foucault's histories are factually inaccurate, I make no such claim here. My investigation focuses solely on his philosophy of history inasmuch as it can be reconstructed as a coherent whole.

72. Foucault, *The Archaeology of Knowledge*, 27.

73. White, "Foucault Decoded," 31.

74. Foucault, *The Archaeology of Knowledge*, 29.

75. Ibid., 27.

76. Eric Schliesser also mentions that Smith may be able to avoid the Foucauldian critique, but he does so mostly in passing. See Schliesser, "Articulating Practices as Reasons: Adam Smith on the Social Conditions of Possibility of Property," 69, 87.

77. Rajchman, *Truth and Eros*, 138.

78. O'Brian, "Michel Foucault's History of Culture," 37.

79. Foucault, *The Archaeology of Knowledge*, 144, 200.

80. Ibid., 151.

81. Ibid., 148.

82. Cropsey writes, "Smith's vision of nature might be defective, but it does not differ from others in being a construction. No one has ever seen nature; what we see is the world, and from it we go on to arrive at nature, which is an explanation of the world" (Cropsey, *Polity and Economy*, 160). For an enlightening history of the idea of nature as distinct from artifact, see Oelschlaeger, *The Idea of Wilderness*.

83. I do not mean to disregard the famous anecdote of Smith reporting his approval of Burke's economics: "Mr. Smith, [Burke] said, told him, after they had conversed on subjects of political economy, that he was the only man, who, without communication, thought on these topics exactly as he did" (Bissett, *Life of Edmund Burke*, 429). The two theories do have common elements. See Dunn, "Adam Smith and Edmund Burke: Complementary Contemporaries," and Winch, "The Burke-Smith Problem and Late Eighteenth-Century Political and Economic Thought." For a discussion suggesting Burke plays a deeper role in contemporary liberalism than is usually acknowledged, see Cahoone, *Civil Society: The Conservative Meaning of Liberal Politics*. Second, there are those, Foucault included, who see Smith's work as preserving the political order rather than challenging it. While Smith was certainly concerned with protecting a certain way of life, this critique is overly simplistic and misrepresentative of the debates of which he was a part. Smith's economic, moral, and political theories represented a strong break from the past in many ways, even if he is not committed to either the twenty-first-century conservative or liberal viewpoints.

84. Fay, "The Idea of Progress," 231, 234.

85. Bossard, "The Concept of Progress," 5–6.

86. Again, the argument in Pinker, *The Better Angels of Our Nature*, offers empirical evidence for the possibility of progress.

87. Coates, "What Is Progress?" 69.

88. Ibid., 71.

89. Bossard, "The Concept of Progress," 8.
90. Fay, "The Idea of Progress," 235.
91. Ibid.
92. Here I abridge a much lengthier account of the history of progress that included attention to Bacon and Descartes as well as a longer discussion of Kant. See Weinstein, "On the Meaning of the Term Progressive."
93. See also Welter, "The Idea of Progress in America," 401–2.
94. Turgot, *Second discours en Sorbonne. Sur le progrès successif de l'esprit humain.*
95. Condorcet, *Sketch for a Historical Picture of the Progress of the Human Mind.*
96. For a full-length discussion of Smith and Condorcet, see Rothschild, *Economic Sentiments.*
97. By victims, I mean those whose cultures, economic or moral lives, or institutions did not survive the vast historical change, or who endured more suffering because of the successes of others. I do not claim that these tragedies are necessary for progress.
98. De Lima, *Foucault's Archaeology of Political Economy*, 44.
99. Harkin, "Natives and Nostalgia," 25.
100. Kipling, "The White Man's Burden."
101. I thank Lawrence Cahoone for this term.
102. One might suggest that a Foucauldian would never claim a narrative is wrong, per se, only that narratives need to be unmasked. But this misses the point. For Smith, the claim "history progresses" is true, and for a Foucauldian such a statement is either fictitious or nonsensical.
103. Gutting, *Foucault: A Very Short Introduction*, 2–4.
104. Gutting hints that Foucault may have actually been more interested in obfuscating the truth than I allow here. He writes, "Those who have struggled with the obscurities of Foucault's archly intense prose are vastly relieved by the easy lucidity with which he writes in his last two books. Had his final illness led to a peaceful reconciliation reflected in his writing? Or was it merely that, wanting to finish this project before he died, he didn't have time for baroque complexification" (Gutting, *Foucault: A Short Introduction*, 101).
105. MacIntyre acknowledges that the problem of relativism is "inescapable" (MacIntyre, "A Partial Response to My Critics," 296).
106. MacIntyre, *After Virtue*, chapter 9. MacIntyre sees Nietzsche as the inevitable consequence of enlightenment individualism but, as must be obvious from this discussion, I would argue that enlightenment commitments need not lead necessarily to Nietzsche or to any form of relativism.
107. Hayek, *The Constitution of Liberty*, 93.

WORKS CITED

For Smith's works, as well as those of Hume, Hutcheson, Mandeville, and Shaftesbury, see the list of abbreviations in the front matter.

Ahmed, Syed. "Adam Smith's Four Invisible Hands." *History of Political Economy* 22, no. 1 (1990): 137–44.

Akkerman, Tjitske, and Siep Stuurman, eds. *Perspectives on Feminist Political Thought in European History: From the Middle Ages to the Present*. London: Routledge, 1998.

Alderman, William E. "The Style of Shaftesbury." *Modern Language Notes* 38, no. 4 (April 1923): 209–15.

Aldridge, Alfred Owen. "Shaftesbury and the Test of Truth." *PMLA* 60, no. 1 (March 1945): 129–56.

Allan, David, ed. *Virtue and Learning in the Scottish Enlightenment*. Edinburgh: Edinburgh University Press, 1993.

———. "Moral Education as a Means to Human Perfection and Social Order: Adam Smith's View of Education in Commercial Society." *History of the Human Sciences* 14, no. 2 (2001): 1–18.

Alvey, James E. "Adam Smith on Gender." *History of Economics Review* 26 (1996): 167–71.

Anderson, Gary M. "Mr. Smith and the Preachers: The Economics of Religion in the *Wealth of Nations*." *Journal of Political Economy* 96, no. 5 (1988): 1066–88.

Aristotle. *Nicomachean Ethics*. Translated by Terrance Irwin. Indianapolis: Hackett, 1999.

———. *On Rhetoric: A Theory of Civic Discourse*. Translated by George A. Kennedy. Oxford: Oxford University Press, 1991.

Arrowood, Charles F. *Theory of Education in the Political Philosophy of Adam Smith*. Privately printed, 1945.

Ayer, A. J. *Hume*. Oxford: Oxford University Press, 1979.

Baroni, Chiara. "The Man of Credit: An Aristocratic Ethics of the Middle Class." Manuscript, 2002.

Bellough, Bonnie, and Vern Bellough. "Intellectual Achievers: A Study of Eighteenth-Century Scotland." *American Journal of Sociology* 76, no. 6 (May 1971): 1048–63.

Berlin, Isaiah. "The Concept of Scientific History." *History and Theory* 1, no. 1 (1960): 1–31.

———. "Two Concepts of Liberty." In *The Proper Study of Mankind*, 191–242. New York: Farrar, Straus and Giroux, 1998.

Bernstein, John Andrew. "Shaftesbury's Identification of the Good with the Beautiful." *Eighteenth-Century Studies* 10, no. 3 (1977): 304–25.

Berry, Christopher J. "Adam Smith's Considerations on Languages." *Journal of the History of Ideas* 38, no. 4 (January–March 1974): 130–38.

———. "Review of James R. Otteson, *Adam Smith's Marketplace of Morals*." *Journal of Scottish Philosophy* 1, no. 2 (2003): 184–87.

———. *The Social Theory of the Scottish Enlightenment*. Edinburgh: Edinburgh University Press 1997.

Bissett, Robert. *Life of Edmund Burke*. London: G. Cathorn, 1800.

Bitterman, Henry J. "Adam Smith's Empiricism and the Law of Nature I." *Journal of Political Economy* 48, no. 4 (1940): 487–520.

———. "Adam Smith's Empiricism and the Law of Nature." *Journal of Political Economy* 48, no. 5 (1940): 703–34.

Blair, J. Anthony. "Argument Management, Informal Logic, and Critical Thinking." *Inquiry: Critical Thinking Across the Disciplines* 15, no. 4 (Summer 1996): 80–93.

Bodkin, Ronald G. "Women's Agency in Classical Economic Thought: Adam Smith, Harriet Taylor Mill and J. S. Mill." *Feminist Economics* 5, no. 1 (1999): 45–60.

Boehmer, Elleke. *Colonial and Postcolonial Literature*. Oxford: Oxford University Press, 2005.

Boltanski, Luke. *Distant Suffering: Morality, Media, and Politics*. Cambridge: Cambridge University Press, 1999.

Bonar, James. *A Catalogue of the Library of Adam Smith*. New York: Augustus M. Kelley, 1966.

Bossard, James H. S. "The Concept of Progress." *Social Forces* 10, no. 1 (1931): 5–14.

Brearley, Margaret. "The Persecution of Gypsies in Europe." *American Behavioral Scientist* 45, no. 4 (December 2001): 588–99.

Broadie, Alexander, ed. *The Cambridge Companion to the Scottish Enlightenment*. Cambridge: Cambridge University Press, 2003.

Brown, Karin, and James E. McClellan. *Sophie de Grouchy: Letters on Sympathy*. Philadelphia: American Philosophical Society, 2008.

Brown, Kevin L. "Dating Adam Smith's Essay 'Of the External Senses.'" *Journal of the History of Ideas* 53 (1992): 333–37.

Brown, Vivienne. "Adam Smith: Between Morals and Markets." Presented at the International Conference of Political Economy, Adam Smith Today: Adam Smith's Significance for Our Century, Kopcaeli University, Turkey, October 1, 2009.

———. *Adam Smith's Discourse*. London: Routledge, 1994.

———. "Agency and Discourse: Revisiting the Adam Smith Problem." In *Elgar Companion to Adam Smith*, ed. Jeffrey T. Young, 52–72. Aldershot: Edward Elgar, 2009.

Brubaker, Lauren. "Adam Smith's Enduring Relevance: Review of Jack Russell Weinstein's *On Adam Smith*." *Adam Smith Review* 1 (2004): 188–94.

——. "Why Adam Smith Is Neither a Conservative nor a Libertarian." *Adam Smith Review* 2 (2006): 197–202.

Bryce, J. C. "Introduction." *Lectures on Rhetoric and Belles Lettres*. Indianapolis: Liberty Press, 1985.

——. "Lectures on Rhetoric and Belles Lettres." In *Adam Smith Reviewed*, ed. Peter Jones and Andrew S. Skinner, 1–20. Edinburgh: Edinburgh University Press, 1992.

Bryson, Bill. *At Home: A Short History of Private Life*. New York: Doubleday, 2010.

Burchell, Graham. "Peculiar Interests: Civil Society and Governing 'the System of Natural Liberty.'" In *The Foucault Effect: Studies in Governmentality*, ed. Graham Burchell, Colin Gordon, and Peter Miller, 119–50. Chicago: University of Chicago Press, 1991.

Burrow, John. *A History of Histories*. New York: Alfred A. Knopf, 2008.

Cahoone, Lawrence E. *Civil Society: The Conservative Meaning of Liberal Politics*. Malden: Blackwell, 2002.

Campbell, R. H., and A. S. Skinner. *General Introduction to* An Inquiry into the Nature and Causes of the Wealth of Nations. Indianapolis: Liberty Press, 1976.

Campbell, T. D. *Adam Smith's Science of Morals*. New Jersey: Rowman and Littlefield, 1971.

Carey, Daniel. "Hutcheson's Moral Sense and the Problem of Innateness." *Journal of the History of Philosophy* 38, no. 1 (2000): 103–10.

——. *Locke, Shaftesbury, and Hutcheson*. Cambridge: Cambridge University Press, 2006.

——. "Method, Moral Sense, and the Problem of Diversity." *British Journal of the History of Philosophy* 5, no. 2 (1997): 275–96.

Carlyle, Alexander. "Recollections of a Student at Glasgow College." In *Human Documents of Adam Smith's Time*, ed. E. Royston Pike, 228–29. London: George Allen and Unwin, 1974.

Carrasco, Maria Alejandra. "Adam Smith's Reconstruction of Practical Reason." *Review of Metaphysics* 58 (2004): 81–116.

Chichi, Graciela Marta. "The Greek Roots of the Ad Hominem Argument." *Argumentation* 16 (2002): 333–48.

Coates, Willson H. "What Is Progress?" *Journal of Philosophy* 45, no. 3 (1948): 66–77.

Cohen, Elliot C. "Reason and Experience in Locke's Epistemology." *Philosophy and Phenomenological Research* 45, no. 1 (September 1984): 71–85.

Court, Franklin E. "Adam Smith and the Teaching of English Literature." *History of Education Quarterly* 25, no. 3 (Autumn 1985): 235–340.

Crane, R. S. "Suggestions toward a Genealogy of the 'Man of Felling.'" *ELH* 1 (1934): 205–30.

Cropsey, Joseph. *Polity and Economy*. South Bend: St. Augustine's Press, 2001.

Danford, John W. "Adam Smith, Equality, and the Wealth of Sympathy." *American Journal of Political Science* 24, no. 4 (1980): 674–95.

Daniel, Stephen H. "Myth and Rationality in Mandeville." *Journal of the History of Ideas* 47, no. 4 (1986): 595–609.

Dankert, Clyde E. "Adam Smith, Educator." *Dalhousie Review* (Spring 1967): 13–27.

Day, Mark. *The Philosophy of History*. London: Continuum, 2007.

de Condorcet, Antoine-Nicolas. *Sketch for a Historical Picture of the Progress of the Human Mind*. London: Weidenfeld and Nicolson, 1955.

De Lima, Iara Vigo. *Foucault's Archaeology of Political Economy*. New York: Palgrave Macmillan, 2010.

Den Uyl, D. "Critical Notice: Samuel Fleischacker, *On Adam Smith's Wealth of Nations*." *Journal of Scottish Philosophy* 3, no. 2 (2005): 171–80.

Dewey, John. *Democracy and Education*. New York: Free Press, 1997.

Dickey, Laurence. "Historicizing the 'Adam Smith Problem': Conceptual, Historiographical, and Textual Issues." *Journal of Modern History* 58, no. 3 (September 1986): 579–609.

Douglass, Frederick. *Narrative of the Life of Frederick Douglass, an American Slave, Written by Himself*. Mineola: Dover Editions, 1995.

Dunn, William Clyde. "Adam Smith and Edmund Burke: Complementary Contemporaries." *Southern Economic Journal* 7, no. 3 (January 1941): 330–46.

Dworkin, Ronald. "Liberalisms." In *Liberalism and Its Critics*, ed. Michael Sandel, 60–70. New York: New York University Press, 1984.

Epps, Archie C., III. "The Christian Doctrine of Slavery: A Theological Analysis." *Journal of Negro History* 46, no. 4 (October 1961): 243–49.

Evensky, Jerry. *Adam Smith's Moral Philosophy*. Cambridge: Cambridge University Press, 2005.

Faust, Drew Gilpin. "A Southern Stewardship: The Intellectual and the Proslavery Argument." *American Quarterly* 31, no. 1 (Spring 1979): 63–80.

Fay, Sidney B. "The Idea of Progress." *American Historical Review* 52, no. 2 (1947): 231–46.

Feinberg, Walter. *Common Schools/Uncommon Identities: National Unity and Cultural Difference*. New Haven: Yale University Press, 2000.

Ferguson, Adam. "Of the Principle of Moral Estimation: A Discourse between David Hume, Robert Clerk, and Adam Smith." In *The Manuscripts of Adam Ferguson*, ed. Vincenzo Merolle, 207–16. London: Pickering and Chatto, 2006.

Ferguson, Adam. *An Essay on the History of Civil Society*. London: Transaction, 1991.

Firth, Roderick. "Ethical Absolutism and the Ideal Observer." *Philosophy and Phenomenological Research* 12, no. 3 (1952): 317–45.

Fleischacker, Samuel. *On Adam Smith's* Wealth of Nations. Princeton: Princeton University Press, 2004.

——. "Philosophy in Moral Practice: Kant and Adam Smith." *Kant Studien* 82, no. 249–69.

——. "Response to Den Uyl." *Journal of Scottish Philosophy* 4, no. 2 (2006): 173–76.

——. "Review of Jerry Evensky's *Adam Smith's Moral Philosophy*." *Adam Smith Review* 3 (2007): 194–98.

——. *A Third Concept of Liberty*. Princeton: Princeton University Press, 1999.

Fontaine, Phillippe. "Identification and Economic Behavior: Sympathy and Empathy in Historic Perspective." *Economics and Philosophy* 13 (1997): 261–80.

Force, Pierre. *Self-Interest before Adam Smith*. Cambridge: Cambridge University Press, 2003.

Forman-Barzilai, Fonna. *Adam Smith and the Circles of Sympathy*. Cambridge: Cambridge University Press, 2010.

——. "Sympathy in Space(s)." *Political Theory* 33, no. 2 (2005): 189–217.

Foucault, Michel. *The Archaeology of Knowledge*. New York: Vintage Books, 1971.

——. *The Birth of Biopolitics, Lectures at the Collège de France, 1978–1979*. Houndsmills: Palgrave Macmillan, 2008.

——. *Madness and Civilization: A History of Insanity in the Age of Reason*. New York: Vintage Books, 1988.

——. *The Order of Things*. New York: Vintage Books, 1994.

Frankena, William. "Hutcheson's Moral Sense Theory." *Journal of the History of Ideas* 16, no. 3 (1955): 356–75.

Frazer, Michael L. *The Enlightenment of Sympathy*. Oxford: Oxford University Press, 2010.

Gaus, Gerald F. *Justificatory Liberalism*. Oxford: Oxford University Press, 1996.

Göçmen, Dogan. *The Adam Smith Problem*. London: Taurus Academic Studies, 2007.

Goldsmith, M. M. *By a Society of Ladies: Essays in* The Female Tatler. Bristol: Thoemmes Press, 1999.

——. *Private Vices, Public Benefits: Bernard Mandeville's Social and Political Thought*. Christchurch: Cybereditions, 2001.

——. "Regarding Anew the Moral and Political Sentiments of Mankind: Bernard Mandeville and the Scottish Enlightenment." *Journal of the History of Ideas*, 49, no. 4 (October–December 1988): 587–606.

Gould, Stephen J. *The Mismeasure of Man*. New York, W. W. Norton, 1996.

Govier, Trudy. "Critical Thinking as Argument Analysis." *Argumentation* 3 (1989): 115–26.

——. *Problems in Argument Analysis and Evaluation*. Dordrecht: Foris, 1987.

Grampp, William D. "What Did Smith Mean by the Invisible Hand?" *Journal of Political Economy* 108, no. 3 (2000): 441–65.

Grean, Stanley. "Self-Interest and Public Interest in Shaftesbury's Philosophy." *Journal of the History of Philosophy* 2, no. 1 (1964): 37–45.

——. *Shaftesbury's Philosophy of Religion and Ethics*. New York: Ohio University Press, 1967.

Gregory, Maughn. "Democracy and Care in the Community of Inquiry." *Inquiry: Critical Thinking Across the Disciplines* 17, no. 1 (Autumn 1997): 40–50.

Griswold, Charles L., Jr. *Adam Smith and the Virtues of Enlightenment*. Cambridge: Cambridge University Press, 1999.

——. "Imagination." In *The Cambridge Companion to Adam Smith*, ed. Knud Haakonssen, 22–56. Cambridge: Cambridge University Press, 2006.

——. "Reply to My Critics." *Perspectives on Political Science* 30, no. 3 (2001): 163–67.

——. "Review of S. Justman, *The Autonomous Male of Adam Smith*." *Journal of the History of Philosophy* 35 (1997): 629–32.

Gutting, Gary. *Foucault: A Very Short Introduction*. Oxford: Oxford University Press, 2005.

Haakonssen, Knud, ed. *Adam Smith*. In *The International Library of Critical Essays in the History of Philosophy*. Aldershot: Ashgate/Dartmouth, 1998.

——, ed. *Index to the Works of Adam Smith*. Indianapolis: Liberty Fund, 2001.

———. "Introduction," *The Theory of Moral Sentiments*. Cambridge: Cambridge University Press, 2002.

———. *The Science of a Legislator*. Cambridge: Cambridge University Press, 1981.

Hadot, Pierre, and Arnold Davidson. *Philosophy as a Way of Life: Spiritual Exercises from Socrates to Foucault*. Oxford: Blackwell, 1995.

Haldane, John. "Adam Smith, Theology, and Natural Law Ethics." In *Adam Smith as Theologian*, ed. Paul Oslington, 24–32. London: Routledge, 2011.

Hall, Nor, and Warren R. Dawson. *Broodmales: A Psychological Essay on Men in Childbirth*. Putnam: Spring Journal, 1989.

Hanley, Ryan Patrick. *Adam Smith and the Character of Virtue*. Cambridge: Cambridge University Press, 2009.

———. "Scepticism and Naturalism." *The Philosophy of Adam Smith: Adam Smith Review* 5, ed. Emma Rothschild and Samuel Fleischacker, 198–212. London: Routledge, 2010.

Harkin, Maureen. "Natives and Nostalgia: The Problem of the 'North American Savage' in Adam Smith's Historiography." *Scottish Studies Review* 3, no. 1 (2002): 21–31.

Harman, Gilbert. *Moral Agent and Impartial Spectator*. Lawrence: University of Kansas Press, 1986.

Harootunian, H. D. "Foucault, Genealogy, History: The Pursuit of Otherness." In *After Foucault: Humanistic Knowledge, Postmodern Challenges*, ed. Jonathan Arac, 110–37. New Brunswick: Rutgers University Press, 1988.

Harpham, Edward J. "Enlightenment, Impartial Spectators, and Griswold's Smith." *Perspectives on Political Science* 30, no. 3 (2001): 130–45.

———. "Liberalism, Civic Humanism, and the Case of Adam Smith." *American Political Science Review* 78, no. 3 (September 1984): 764–74.

Harrison, Peter. "Adam Smith, Natural Theology, and the Natural Sciences." In *Adam Smith as Theologian*, ed. Paul Oslington, 77–91. London: Routledge, 2011.

Harth, Phillip. "The Satiric Purpose of the Fable of the Bees." *Eighteenth-Century Studies* 2, no. 4 (1969): 321–40.

Hayek, F. A. *The Constitution of Liberty*. Chicago: University of Chicago Press, 1978.

Held, Virginia. *The Ethics of Care: Personal, Political, Global*. Oxford: Oxford University Press, 2007.

———, ed. *Justice and Care: Essential Readings in Feminist Ethics*. Boulder: Westview Press, 1995.

Henderson, Willie. "A Very Cautious, or a Very Polite Dr. Smith? Hedging in the *Wealth of Nations*." *Adam Smith Review* 1 (2004): 60–81.

Herman, Arthur. *How the Scots Invented the Modern World*. New York: Three Rivers Press, 2001.

Hildebrand, Bruno. *Die Nationalökommie der Gegenwart und Zukunft*. Jenna: G. Fischer, 1848.

Hintikka, Jaako. "Is Logic the Key to All Good Reasoning?" *Argumentation* 15 (2001): 35–57.

———. "The Role of Logic in Argumentation." *Monist* 72 (1989): 1–24.

Hirst, E. W. "Moral Sense, Moral Reason, and Moral Sentiment." *Mind* 26, no. 102 (1917): 146–61.

Hobbes, Thomas. *Leviathan*. London: J. M. Dent and Sons, 1973.

Hohmann, Hanns. "Rhetoric and Dialectic: Some Historical and Legal Perspectives." *Argumentation* 14 (2000): 223–34.

Hope, V. M. *Virtue by Consensus: The Moral Philosophy of Hutcheson, Hume and Adam Smith*. Oxford: Oxford University Press, 1989.

Horne, Thomas A. "Envy and Commercial Society: Mandeville and Smith on 'Private Vices, Public Benefits.'" *Political Theory* 9, no. 4 (1981): 551–69.

———. *The Social Thought of Bernard Mandeville*. Cambridge: Cambridge University Press, 1978.

Howard, June. *Publishing the Family*. Durham: Duke University Press, 2001.

Howell, Wilbur Samuel. "Adam Smith's Lectures on Rhetoric: An Historical Assessment." In *Essays on Adam Smith*, ed. Andrew S. Skinner and Thomas Wilson, 11–43. Oxford: Clarendon Press, 1975.

Hudson, W. D., ed. *The Is–Ought Question*. London: Macmillan, 1969.

Hume, David. *An Enquiry Concerning the Principles of Morals*. Edited by Tom L. Beauchamp. Oxford: Oxford University Press, 2003.

———. *A Treatise of Human Nature*. Edited by David Fate Norton and Mary J. Hume. Oxford: Oxford University Press, 2000.

Hundert, E. J. "Bernard Mandeville and the Enlightenment's Maxims of Modernity." *Journal of the History of Ideas* 56, no. 4 (1995): 577–93.

Hurtado-Prieto, Jimena. "The Mercantalist Foundations of 'Dr. Mandeville's Licentious System': Adam Smith on Bernard Mandeville." In *New Voices on Adam Smith*, ed. Leonidas Montes and Eric Schliesser, 210–46. London: Routledge, 2006.

Hyard, Alexandra. "Adam Smith and the French Ideas on Education." *Adam Smith Review* 3 (2007): 75–95.

Hysee, Tim. "Why Logic Doesn't Matter in the (Philosophical) Study of Argumentation." *Argumentation* 11 (1997): 211–24.

Jacob, Henry. "To the High and mightie Prince, Iames by the grace of God, King of great Britannie, France, and Irelande: An Humble Supplication for Toleration and Libertie to Enjoy and Observe the Ordinances of Christ Jesus in th' administration of His Churches in Lieu of Human Constitutions." Middelburg: Richard Schilders, 1609.

Jevons, William Stanley. *The Theory of Political Economy*. London: Macmillan and Son, 1871.

Johnson, Ralph. "The Dialectical Tier Reconsidered." Keynote Address, International Society for the Study of Argumentation, Amsterdam, June 26, 2002.

———. *Manifest Rationality: A Pragmatic Theory of Argument*. Mahwah: Lawrence Erlbaum Associates, 2000.

———. "Manifest Rationality Reconsidered: Reply to My Fellow Symposiasts." *Argumentation* 16 (2002): 311–31.

———. "The Relation between Formal and Informal Logic." *Argumentation* 13 (1999): 265–74.

Justman, Stewart. *The Autonomous Male of Adam Smith*. Norman: University of Oklahoma Press, 1995.

Kail, P. J. E. "Hutcheson's Moral Sense: Skepticism, Realism, and Secondary Qualities." *History of Philosophy Quarterly* 18, no. 1 (2001): 57–77.

Kallen, Horace Meyer, and Stephen J. Whitfield. *Culture and Democracy in the United States*. New York: Boni and Liveright, 1924.

Kant, Immanuel. *Grounding of the Metaphysics of Morals*. Translated by James W. Ellington. Indianapolis: Hackett, 1980.

——. "The Idea of a Universal History with a Cosmopolitan Purpose." In *Kant's Political Writings*, ed. H. S. Reiss, 41–53. Cambridge: Cambridge University Press, 1991.

Kennedy, David. "The Five Communities." *Inquiry: Critical Thinking Across the Disciplines* 16, no. 4 (Summer 1997): 66–86.

Kett, Joseph F. *The Pursuit of Knowledge under Difficulties*. Stanford: Stanford University Press, 1994.

Khalil, Elias L. "Is Adam Smith Liberal?" *Journal of Institutional and Theoretical Economics* 158 (2002): 664–94.

——. "Is Justice the Primary Feature of the State? Adam Smith's Critique of Social Contract Theory." *European Journal of Law and Economics* 6 (1998): 215–30.

King, Edward. "From Logic to Rhetoric: Adam Smith's Dismissal of the Logic(s) of the Schools." *Journal of Scottish Philosophy* 2, no. 1 (2004): 45–68.

King, Martin Luther, Jr., "How Long, Not Long." Speech, Montgomery, Alabama, March 25, 1965.

Kipling, Rudyard. "The White Man's Burden." *McClure's Magazine* 12 (February 1899): 290–91.

Klein, Lawrence. "The Third Earl of Shaftesbury and the Progress of Politeness." *Eighteenth-Century Studies* 18, no. 2 (Winter 1984–85): 186–214.

Kneale, William, and Kneale, Martha. *The Development of Logic*. Oxford: Clarendon Press, 1962.

Knies, Carl G. *Die Politische Oekonomie vom Standpunkte der Geschichtlichen Methode*. Braumschweig: C. S. Schwetschke, 1883.

Kuhn, Thomas. *The Structure of Scientific Revolutions*. Chicago: University of Chicago Press, 1962.

Kuiper, Edith. "Adam Smith and His Feminist Contemporaries." In *New Voices on Adam Smith*, ed. Leonidas Montes and Eric Schliesser, 40–60. London: Routledge, 2006.

Lakoff, George, and Mark Johnson. *Metaphors We Live By*. Chicago: University of Chicago Press, 1980.

Lamb, Robert. "Adam Smith's Concept of Alienation." *Oxford Economic Papers* 25, no. 2 (1973): 275–85.

Lamprecht, Sterling P. "The Fable of the Bees." *Journal of Philosophy* 23, no. 21 (October 1926): 561–79.

Land, Stephen K. "Adam Smith's 'Considerations Concerning the First Formation of Languages.'" *Journal of the History of Ideas* 38, no. 4 (October–December 1977): 677–90.

Laski, Harold J. *Studies in Problems of Sovereignty*. New Haven: Yale University Press, 1917.

Leathers, Charles G., and J. Patrick Raines. "Adam Smith's [Weak] Case for Fee Incomes for University Faculty and Student-Consumer Sovereignty." *Adam Smith Review* 3 (2006): 119–38.

Leshen, Joel. "Reason and Perception in Hobbes: An Inconsistency." *Noûs* 19, no. 3 (September 1985): 429–37.

Letwin, William. "Was Adam Smith a Liberal?" In *Traditions of Liberalism*, ed. Knud Haakonssen, 65–80. Australia: Centre for Independent Studies, 1988.

Levy, David M. *How the Dismal Science Got Its Name*. Ann Arbor: University of Michigan Press, 2002.

———. "How the Dismal Science Got Its Name: Debating Racial Quackery." *Journal of the History of Economic Thought* 23, no. 1 (2001): 5–35.

Lindgren, J. Ralph. "Adam Smith's Theory of Inquiry." *Journal of Political Economy* 77 (1969): 897–915.

Lipman, Matthew. "Caring as Thinking." *Inquiry: Critical Thinking Across the Disciplines* 15, no. 1 (Autumn 1995): 1–13.

———. *Harry Stotlemeier's Discovery*. Montclair: Institute for the Advancement of Philosophy for Children, 1982.

Locke, F. P. "Adam Smith and 'The Man of System': Interpreting *The Theory of Moral Sentiments* VI.ii.12–18." *Adam Smith Review* 3, ed. Vivienne Brown, 37–48. London: Routledge, 2007.

Locke, John. *Essay Concerning Human Understanding*. Oxford: Oxford University Press, 1975.

Lux, Kenneth. *Adam Smith's Mistake: How a Moral Philosopher Invented Economics and Ended Morality*. Boston: Shambhala Publications, 1990.

MacBeth, Murray. "'Is' and 'Ought' in Context: MacIntyre's Mistake." *Hume Studies* 18, no. 1 (1992): 41–50.

Macfie, Alec. *The Individual in Society*. London: Routledge, 1967.

MacIntyre, Alasdair. *After Virtue*. 2d ed. Notre Dame: University of Notre Dame Press, 1984.

———. "The Idea of an Educated Public." In *Education and Values*, ed. Graham Haydon, 15–36. London: Institute of Education, University of London, 1995.

———. "Hume on 'is' and ought." In *Against the Self-Images of the Age*, 109–24. Notre Dame: University of Notre Dame Press, 1971.

———. "A Partial Response to My Critics." In *After MacIntyre*, ed. John Horton and Susan Mendus, 283–304. Cambridge: Polity Press, 1994.

———. *A Short History of Ethics*. 1966. Reprint, Notre Dame: University of Notre Dame Press, 1998.

———. *Whose Justice? Which Rationality?* Notre Dame: University of Notre Dame Press, 1988.

Mandeville, Bernard. *A Letter to Dion*. Edited by Bonamy Dobrée. Liverpool: University Press of Liverpool, 1954.

Marshall, David. *The Figure of Theater: Shaftesbury, Defoe, Adam Smith, and George Elliot*. New York: Columbia University Press, 1986.

Martin, Thomas R. *Ancient Greece*. New Haven: Yale University Press, 1996.

Martinich, A. P. *Hobbes: A Biography*. Cambridge: Cambridge University Press, 1999.

McKenna, Stephen J. *Adam Smith: The Rhetoric of Propriety*. Albany: State University of New York Press, 2006.

McPeck, John. *Critical Thinking and Education*. Oxford: Martin Robertson, 1981.

Mijuskovic, Ben. "Hume and Shaftesbury on the Self." *Philosophical Quarterly* 21, no. 85 (October 1971): 324–36.

Mill, J. S. *Principles of Political Economy*. New York: Augustus M. Kelley, 1961.

Minowitz, Peter. *Profits, Priests, and Princes*. Stanford: Stanford University Press, 1993.

Mitchell, Harvey. " 'The Mysterious Veil of Self-Delusion' in Adam Smith's *Theory of Moral Sentiments*." *Eighteenth-Century Studies* 20, no. 4 (1987): 405–41.

Mitchell, Robert. "Beautiful and Orderly Systems: Adam Smith on the Aesthetics of Political Improvement." In *New Voices on Adam Smith*, ed. Eric Schliesser and Leonidas Montes, 61–86. London: Routledge, 2009.

Mizuta, Hiroshi. *Adam Smith's Library: A Catalogue*. Oxford: Clarendon Press, 2000.

Montes, Leonidas. *Adam Smith in Context: A Critical Reassessment of Some Central Components of His Thought*. New York: Palgrave Macmillan, 2004.

Morrow, Glenn R. "Adam Smith: Moralist and Philosopher." *Journal of Political Economy* 35, no. 3 (1927): 321–42.

——. "The Significance of the Doctrine of Sympathy in Hume and Adam Smith." *Philosophical Review* 32, no. 1 (1923): 60–78.

Mossner, E. C. *Adam Smith: The Biographical Approach*. Glasgow: George Outram, 1969.

Muller, Jerry Z. *Adam Smith in His Time and Ours*. Princeton: Princeton University Press, 1993.

——. *The Mind and the Market*. New York: Anchor Books, 2002.

Nelson, Mark T. "Who Needs Valid Moral Arguments?" *Argumentation* 17 (2003): 35–42.

Newton, Isaac. *Opticks: or a Treastise of the Reflections, Refractions, Inflections and Colours of Light*. 4th ed. London: William Imnys, 1730.

Nieli, Russell. "Spheres of Intimacy and the Adam Smith Problem." *Journal of the History of Ideas* (1986): 611–24.

Nozick, Robert. *Anarchy, State, and Utopia*. New York: Basic Books, 1974.

Nussbaum, Martha. *Poetic Justice*. Boston: Beacon Press, 1995.

——. *Upheavals of Thought*. Cambridge: Cambridge University Press, 2001.

Nyland, Chris. "Adam Smith, Stage Theory, and the Status of Women." *History of Political Economy* 25, no. 4 (1993): 617–40.

O'Brian, Patricia. "Michel Foucault's History of Culture." In *The New Cultural History*, ed. Lynn Hunt, 25–46. Berkeley: University of California Press, 1980.

Oelschlaeger, Max. *The Idea of Wilderness*. New Haven: Yale University Press, 1991.

Oncken, August. "The Consistency of Adam Smith." *Economic Journal* 7, no. 27 (1897): 443–50.

Oslington, Paul, ed. *Adam Smith as Theologian*. London: Routledge, 2011.

Otteson, James. *Adam Smith's Marketplace of Life*. Cambridge: Cambridge University Press, 2002.

——. "How High Does the Impartial Spectator Go?" In *Adam Smith as Theologian*, ed. Paul Oslington, 92–97. London: Routledge, 2011.

———. "Review: Charles Griswold's *Adam Smith and the Virtues of Enlightenment*." *Philosophy and Phenomenological Research* 61, no. 3 (November 2000): 714–18.

———. "Shaftesbury's Evolutionary Morality and Its Influence on Adam Smith." *Adam Smith Review* 4, ed. Vivienne Brown, 106–31. London: Routledge, 2008.

Pabst, Adrian. "From Civil to Political Economy: Adam Smith's Theological Debt." In *Adam Smith as Theologian*, ed. Paul Oslington, 106–24. London: Routledge, 2011.

Paganelli, Maria Pia. "The Adam Smith Problem in Reverse: Self-Interest in *The Wealth of Nations* and *The Theory of Moral Sentiments*." *History of Political Economy* 40, no. 2 (2008): 365–82.

———. "Vanity and the Daedalian Wings of Paper Money in Adam Smith." In *New Voices on Adam Smith*, ed. Leonidas Montes and Eric Schliesser, 272–90. London: Routledge, 2006

Parsons, Terrance. "What Is an Argument?" *Journal of Philosophy* 93, no. 4 (April 1996): 164–85.

Paszkowski, Wilhelm. *Adam Smith als Moralphilosoph*. Halle a.S.: C. A. Kaemmerer, 1890.

Peach, Ceri. "The Mosaic versus the Melting Pot: Canada and the USA." *Scottish Geographical Journal* 121, no. 1 (2005): 3–27.

Pearson, Roger. *Voltaire Almighty*. New York: Bloomsbury, 2005.

Peirce, Charles Sanders. "The Fixation of Belief." In *Philosophical Writings of Peirce*, ed. Justus Buchler, 5–22. New York: Dover Publications, 1955.

Perkins, Howard C. "The Defense of Slavery in the Northern Press on the Eve of the Civil War." *Journal of Southern History* 9, no. 4 (November 1943): 501–31.

Phillips, Mark Salber. "Adam Smith, Belletrist" In *The Cambridge Companion to Adam Smith*, 57–78. Cambridge: Cambridge University Press, 2006.

Phillipson, Nicholas. *Adam Smith: An Enlightened Life*. New Haven: Yale University Press, 2010.

Pinker, Steven. *The Better Angels of Our Nature: Why Violence Has Declined*. New York: Viking Adult, 2011.

Pocock, J. G. A. "Adam Smith and History." In *The Cambridge Companion to Adam Smith*, 270–88. Cambridge: Cambridge University Press, 2006.

Prostko, Jack. "'Natural Conversation Set in View': Shaftesbury and Moral Speech." *Eighteenth-Century Studies* 23, no. 1 (1989): 42–61.

Rae, John. *The Life of Adam Smith*. New York: Macmillan, 1895.

Rajcham, John. *Truth and Eros: Foucault, Lacan, and the Question of Ethics*. London: Routledge, 2010.

Raphael, D. D. "The Impartial Spectator (Dawes Hicks Lecture on Philosophy)." *Proceedings of the British Academy* 58 (1972): 335–54.

———. *The Impartial Spectator*. Oxford: Oxford University Press, 2007.

———. *The Moral Sense*. London: Oxford University Press, 1947.

Rashid, Salim. "Mandeville's Fable: Laissez-faire or Libertinism?" *Eighteenth-Century Studies* 18, no. 3 (1985): 313–30.

Rauscher, Frederick. "Moral Realism and the Divine Essence in Hutcheson." *History of Philosophy Quarterly* 20, no. 2 (2003): 165–81.

Rawls, John. *Political Liberalism*. Cambridge: Harvard University Press, 1993.

——. "Reply to Habermas." *Journal of Philosophy* 92, no. 3 (1995): 132–80.

——. *A Theory of Justice*. Cambridge: Harvard University Press, 1971.

Rendall, Jane. "Virtue and Commerce: Women in the Making of Adam Smith's Political Economy." In *Women in Western Political Philosophy: Kant to Nietzsche*, ed. Ellen Kennedy and Susan Mendus, 44–77. New York: St. Martin's Press, 1987.

Rescher, Nicholas. "The Role of Rhetoric in Rational Argumentation." *Argumentation* 12 (1998): 315–23.

Richter, David H. *Falling into Theory*. Boston: Bedford/St. Martin's, 2000.

Robison, Lori. "An 'Imperceptible Infusion' of Blood: Iola Leroy, Racial Identity, and Sentimental Discourse." *Genre* 38, nos. 3–4 (2004): 255–82.

Rogers, A. K. "The Ethics of Mandeville." *International Journal of Ethics* 36, no. 1 (1925): 1–17.

Rorty, Richard. *Philosophy and Social Hope*. London: Penguin Books, 1999.

——. *Philosophy and the Mirror of Nature*. Princeton: Princeton University Press, 1979.

Rosen, Sherwin. "'Some Economics of Teaching.'" *Journal of Labor Economics* (October 1987): 561–75.

Ross, Ian Simpson. "Adam Smith's Smile: His Years at Balliol College, 1740–1746, in Retrospect." *Adam Smith Review* 5: *The Philosophy of Adam Smith*, ed. Vivienne Brown and Samuel Fleischacker, 253–63. London: Routledge, 2010.

——. *The Life of Adam Smith*. Oxford: Clarendon Press, 1995.

Rothschild, Emma. "Adam Smith and the Invisible Hand." *American Economic Review Papers and Proceedings* (May 1994): 319–22.

——. "Condorcet and Adam Smith on Education and Instruction." In *Philosophers on Education*, ed. Amelie Oksenberg Rorty, 209–26. London: Routledge, 1998.

——. *Economic Sentiments: Adam Smith, Condorcet, and the Enlightenment*. Cambridge: Harvard University Press, 2002.

——. "*The Theory of Moral Sentiments* and the Inner Life." *The Philosophy of Adam Smith: Adam Smith Review* 5, ed. Emma Rothschild and Samuel Fleischacker, 25–36. London: Routledge, 2010.

——, and Amartya Sen. "Adam Smith's Economics." In *The Cambridge Companion to Adam Smith*, 319–65. Cambridge: Cambridge University Press, 2006.

Ryle, Gilbert. *Dilemmas*. Cambridge: Cambridge University Press, 1954.

Said, Edward. *Culture and Imperialism*. New York: Vintage Books, 1993.

Samuels, Warren J. *Erasing the Invisible Hand*. Cambridge: Cambridge University Press, 2011.

Scazzieri, Robert. "A Smithian Theory of Choice." *Adam Smith Review* 2 (2006): 25–26.

Schliesser, Eric. "Adam Smith's Benevolent and Self-Interested Conception of Philosophy." In *New Voices on Adam Smith*, ed. Leonidas Montes and Eric Schliesser, 328–47. London: Routledge, 2006.

——. "Articulating Practices as Reasons: Adam Smith on the Social Conditions of Possibility of Property." *Adam Smith Review* 2, ed. Vivienne Brown, 79. London: Routledge, 2006.

——. "The Philosophical Subtlety of Smith." In *Adam Smith Review* 4, ed. Vivienne Brown, 231–37. London: Routledge, 2008.

——. "Review of *The Cambridge Companion to Adam Smith*, ed. Knud Haakonssen." *Notre Dame Philosophical Reviews* (2007), at http://ndpr.nd.edu/review.

——. "Some Principles of Adam Smith's Newtonian Methods in the *Wealth of Nations*." *Research in the History of Economic Thought and Methodology* 23-A (2005): 33–74.

Schmidt, James. "What Enlightenment Project?" *Political Theory* 28, no. 6 (December 2000): 734–57.

Schoolman, Morton. "Series Editor's Introduction." In *Reading "Adam Smith": Desire, History, and Value*, ix–xxiv. Newbury Park: Sage Publications, 1993.

Scott, William Robert. *Adam Smith as Student and Professor*. New York: Augustus M. Kelley, 1965.

Scott-Taggart, M. J. "Mandeville: Cynic or Fool?" *Philosophical Quarterly* 16, no. 64 (1966): 221–32.

Sen, Amartya. *The Idea of Justice*. Cambridge: Harvard University Press, 2009.

——. *Rationality and Freedom*. Cambridge: Harvard University Press, 2002.

Shanks, Caroline L. "The Biblical Anti-Slavery Argument of the Decade 1830–1840." *Journal of Negro History* 16, no. 2 (April 1931): 132–57.

Shapiro, Michael J. *Reading 'Adam Smith': Desire, History, and Value*. Newbury Park: Sage Publications, 1993.

Sher, Richard. "Book Review: The Scottish Enlightenment: The Scots' Invention of the Modern World." *English Historical Review* 118, no. 479 (November 2003): 1397–98.

Sherman, Sandra. "Adam Smith and the Poor: The Marker versus the Moral Economy." Presentation, annual meeting of the Northeast American Society for Eighteenth-Century Studies, New York, 2002.

Siegel, Harvey. *Educating Reason: Rationality, Critical Thinking and Education*. London: Routledge, 1988.

——. "On Some Recent Challenges to the Ideal of Reason." *Inquiry: Critical Thinking Across the Disciplines* 15, no. 4 (Summer 1996): 2–16.

Skinner, Andrew. S. "Adam Smith: An Economic Interpretation of History." In *Essays on Adam Smith*, ed. Andrew S. Skinner and Thomas Wilson, 154–78. Oxford: Oxford University Press, 1975.

——. "Adam Smith and the Role of the State: Education as a Public Service." In *Adam Smith's Wealth of Nations: New Interdisciplinary Essays*, ed. Stephen Copley and Kathryn Sutherland, 70–96. Manchester: Manchester University Press, 1995.

——. *A System of Social Science*. Oxford: Clarendon Press, 1979.

——, and Thomas Wilson, eds. *Essays on Adam Smith*. Oxford: Oxford University Press, 1975.

Skinner, Quentin. "Some Problems in the Analysis of Political Thought and Action." *Political Theory* 2, no. 3 (August 1974): 277–303.

Smith, Craig. "Adam Smith on Progress and Knowledge." In *New Voices on Adam Smith*, ed. Leonidas Montes and Eric Schliesser, 293–313. London: Routledge, 2006.

Snyder, David C. "Faith and Reason in Locke's *Essay*." *Journal of the History of Ideas* 47, no. 2 (April–June 1986): 197–213.

Sprague, Elmer. "Francis Hutcheson and the Moral Sense." *Journal of Philosophy* 51, no. 24 (1954): 794–800.

Stanfield, James. "Adam Smith on Education." *Economic Affairs* 25, no. 2 (June 2005): 56.

Stewart, Dugald. "Account of the Life and Writings of Adam Smith, LL.D." In *Essays on Philosophical Subjects*, ed. W. L. D. Wightman, 269–351. Indianapolis: Liberty Press, 1980.

———. *Smith's Works* V. London: Davies, 1811.

Stewart, M. A. "Religion and Rational Theology." In *The Cambridge Companion to the Scottish Enlightenment*, ed. Alexander Broadie 31–59. Cambridge: Cambridge University Press, 2003.

Sugden, Robert. "Beyond Sympathy and Empathy: Adam Smith's Concept of Fellow-Feeling." *Economics and Philosophy* 18 (2002): 63–87.

Sutherland, Kathryn. "Adam Smith's Master Narrative: Women and *The Wealth of Nations*." In *Adam Smith's* Wealth of Nations: *New Interdisciplinary Essays*, ed. Stephen Copley and Kathryn Sutherland, 97–121. Manchester, Manchester University Press, 1995.

Teixeira, Pedro Nuno. "Dr. Smith and the Moderns—Adam Smith and the Development of Human Capital Theory." *Adam Smith Review* 3 (2006): 139–57.

Tertullian. *Apology*. In *Apology and De Spectaculis*. Edited by R. Glover. London: Loeb Classical Library, 1931.

Thomson, Herbert F. "Adam Smith's Philosophy of Science." *Quarterly Journal of Economics* 79, no. 2 (May 1965): 212–33.

Tindale, Christopher. *Acts of Arguing*. New York: State University of New York Press, 1999.

———. "A Concept Divided: Ralph Johnson's Definition of Argument." *Argumentation* 16 (2002): 299–309.

Toulmin, Stephen. *The Uses of Argument*. Cambridge: Cambridge University Press, 1958.

Trianosky, Gregory W. "On the Obligation to Be Virtuous: Shaftesbury and the Question, Why Be Moral?" *Journal of the History of Philosophy* 16, no. 3 (1978): 289–300.

Tuck, Richard. *Hobbes*. Oxford: Oxford University Press, 1989.

Tufts, James H. "Note on the Idea of a 'Moral Sense' in British Thought Prior to Shaftesbury." *Journal of Philosophy, Psychology and Scientific Methods* 1, no. 4 (February 18, 1904): 97–98.

Turco, Luigi. "Moral Sense and the Foundation of Morals." In *The Cambridge Companion to the Scottish Enlightenment*, 136–56. Cambridge: Cambridge University Press, 2003.

———. "Sympathy and the Moral Sense: 1725–1740." *British Journal for the History of Philosophy* 7, no. 1 (1999): 79–101.

Turgot, A. R. J., *Second discours en Sorbonne: Sur le progrès successif de l'esprit humain* (1750). French edition from vol. 2 of *Oeuvres de Turgot*, ed. Eugène Daire (1844).

Tuveson, Ernest "The Importance of Shaftesbury." *ELH* 20, no. 4 (December 1953): 267–99.

Urquhart, Robert. "Adam Smith's Problems: Individuality and the Paradox of Sympathy." *The Philosophy of Adam Smith: Adam Smith Review* 5, ed. Emma Rothschild and Samuel Fleischacker, 181–97. London: Routledge, 2010.

van Eemeren, Franz H. *Advances in Pragma-Dialectics*. Amsterdam: Sic Sat, 2002.

——, Rob Grootendorst, Francisca Snoeck Henkemans. *Fundamentals of Argumentation Theory*. Mahwah: Lawrence Erlbaum Associates, 1996.

Van Rees, M. A. "Book Review: *Manifest Rationality*." *Argumentation* 15 (2001): 231–37.

Viner, Jacob. "Adam Smith and Laissez Faire." *Journal of Political Economy* 35, no. 2. (1927): 198–232.

Vivenza, Gloria. *Adam Smith and the Classics*. Oxford: Oxford University Press, 2001.

——. "Adam Smith as a Teacher on Classical Subjects." *Adam Smith Review* 3 (2006): 97–118.

von Skarzynski, Witold. *Moralphilosoph und Schoepfer der Nationaloekonomie*. Berlin: Theobold Grieben, 1878.

Wallech, Steven. "'Class versus Rank': The Transformation of Eighteenth-Century English Social Terms and Theories of Production." *Journal of the History of Ideas* 47, no. 3 (1986): 409–31.

Walton, Douglas N. "Argumentation Schemes and Historical Origins of the Circumstantial Ad Hominem Argument." *Argumentation* 18 (2004): 359–68.

——. "New Methods for Evaluating Arguments." *Inquiry: Critical Thinking Across the Disciplines* 15, no. 4 (Summer 1996): 44–65.

——. "Searching for the Roots of the Circumstantial Ad Hominem." *Argumentation* 15 (2001): 207–21.

——. "What Is Reasoning? What Is an Argument?" *Journal of Philosophy* 87, no. 8 (1990): 399–419.

Ward, Julie K., and Tommy L. Lott, eds. *Philosophers on Race: Critical Essays*. Oxford: Blackwell, 2002.

Weber, Todd Bernard. "The Moral Dilemmas Debate, Deontic Logic, and the Importance of Argument." *Argumentation* 16 (2002): 459–72.

Weinstein, Jack Russell. *Adam Smith and the Problem of Neutrality in Contemporary Liberal Theory*. Ann Arbor: UMI, 1997.

——. "Aliens, Traitors and Elitists: University Values and the Faculty." *Thought and Action* 19, no. 2 (Summer 2004): 95–106.

——. "Author's Response." *Adam Smith Review* 1 (2004): 194–96.

——. "The Invisible Hand of Rationality: On the Intersection of Adam Smith and Alasdair MacIntyre." Plenary Session, 31st Conference on Value Inquiry, University of North Dakota, Grand Forks, North Dakota, April 2003.

——. "Neutrality, Pluralism, and Education: Civic Education as Learning about the Other." *Studies in Philosophy and Education* 23, no. 4 (July 2004): 235–63.

——. *On Adam Smith*. Belmont: Wadsworth, 2001.

——. *On MacIntyre*. Belmont: Wadsworth, 2003.

——. "On the Meaning of the Term Progressive." *William Mitchell Law Review* 33, no. 1 (2006): 1–50.

——. "Overlapping Consensus or Marketplace of Religions? Rawls and Smith." *Philosophia* 40, no. 2 (June 2012): 223–36.

——. "Review Essay: *Adam Smith: The Rhetoric of Propriety* by Stephen J. McKenna; *Adam Smith's Moral Philosophy: A Historical and Contemporary Perspective on Markets, Law, Ethics, and Culture* by Jerry Evensky; and *The Adam Smith Problem: Reconciling*

Human Nature and Society in the Theory of Moral Sentiments *and* Wealth of Nations by Dogan Göçmen," *Journal for Eighteenth-Century studies* 34, no. 3 (September 2011): 403–8.

———. "Review of D. D. Raphael's *Impartial Spectator.*" *Economics and Philosophy* 245, no. 1 (March 2008): 129–37.

———. "Review: James W. Otteson's *Adam Smith's Marketplace of Life.*" *Mind* 113, no. 449 (January 2004): 202–7.

———. "Review: Leonidas Montes: *Adam Smith in Context: A Critical Reassessment of Some Central Components of His Thought.*" *British Journal of the History of Philosophy* 13, no. 1 (2005): 179–83.

———. "Review of Nicholas Phillipson, *Adam Smith: An Enlightened Life.*" *Journal of the History of Philosophy* 49, no. 4 (October 2011): 499–501.

———. "Symposium: Adam Smith on Education." *Adam Smith Review* 3, 49–157. London: Routledge, 2007.

———. "The Two Adams: Ferguson and Smith on Sympathy and Sentiment." In *Adam Ferguson: A Reassessment, Philosophy, Politics and Society,* ed. Eugene Heath and Vincenze Merolle, 89–106. London: Pickering and Chatto, 2009.

———. "*The Wealth of Nations* and the Morality of Opulence. Review Essay of Jerry Evensky's *Adam Smith's Moral Philosophy.*" *Research in the History of Economic Thought and Methodology* 25-A (2007): 61–69.

Weinstein, Mark. "Critical Thinking: Expanding the Paradigm." *Inquiry: Critical Thinking Across the Disciplines* 15, no. 1 (Autumn 1995): 23–39.

———. "Guest Editor's Introduction." *Inquiry: Critical Thinking Across the Disciplines* 17, no. 2 (Winter 1997): 1–3.

———. "Informal Logic and Applied Epistemology." In *New Essays in Informal Logic,* ed. J. Anthony Blair and Ralph Johnson 141–61. Windsor: Informal Logic Press, 1994.

———. "Some Foundational Problems with Informal Logic and Their Solutions." *Inquiry: Critical Thinking Across the Disciplines* 15, no. 4 (1996): 27–43.

Welter, Rush. "The Idea of Progress in America." *Journal of the History of Ideas* 17 (1955): 401–15.

Wesley, Charles H. "The Concept of Negro Inferiority in American Thought." *Journal of Negro History* 25, no. 4 (October 1940): 540–60.

West, E. G. *Adam Smith.* Indianapolis: Liberty Press, 1976.

———. "Adam Smith and Alienation: A Rejoinder." *Oxford Economic Papers* 27, no. 2 (1975): 295–301.

———. *Education and the State.* Indianapolis: Liberty Press, 1994.

———. "The Political Economy of Alienation: Karl Mark and Adam Smith." *Oxford Economic Papers* 21, no. 1 (1969): 1–23.

Whatley, Richard. "Review of *Uncle Tom's Cabin.*" *North British Review* 18 (1852): 235–58.

White, Hayden V. "Foucault Decoded: Notes from Underground." *History and Theory* 12, no. 1 (1973): 223–54.

Wightman, W. P. D., and J. C. Bryce. "Introduction." *Essays on Philosophical Subjects.* Indianapolis: Liberty Classics, 1980.

Wilde, Norman. "Mandeville's Place in English Thought." *Mind* 7, no. 26 (1898): 219–32.

Wilson, James Q. *The Moral Sense.* New York: Free Press, 1993.

Wince, Christopher. "Two Rival Conceptions of Vocational Education: Adam Smith and Friedrich List." *Oxford Review of Education* 24, no. 3 (1998): 365–78.

Winch, Donald. "Adam Smith and the Liberal Tradition." In *Traditions of Liberalism*, ed. Knud Haakonssen, 83–104. Australia: Centre for Independent Studies, 1988.

——. *Adam Smith's Politics.* Cambridge: Cambridge University Press, 1978.

——. "The Burke–Smith Problem and Late Eighteenth-Century Political and Economic Thought." *Historical Journal* 28, no. 1 (March 1985): 231–47.

Wollstoncraft, Mary. *A Vindication of the Rights of Woman.* London: J. Johnson, 1796.

Wood, Paul. "Science in the Scottish Enlightenment." In *The Cambridge Companion to the Scottish Enlightenment*, 94–116. Cambridge: Cambridge University Press, 2003.

Woods, John. "Fearful Symmetry." In *Fallacies: Classical and Contemporary Reading*, ed. H. Hansen and Robert Pinto, 181–93. University Park: University of Pennsylvania Press, 1995.

Woolhouse, R. S. *Locke.* Minneapolis: University of Minnesota Press, 1983.

Wootton, David. "Narrative, Irony, and Faith in Gibbon's *Decline and Fall*." *History and Theory* 33, no. 4 (1994): 77–105.

Yanaihara, Tadao. *Catalogue of Adam Smith's Library in the Possession of the University of Tokyo.* New York: Augustus M. Kelley, 1966.

Young, James Dean. "Mandeville: A Popularizer of Hobbes." *Modern Language Notes* 74, no. 1 (January 1959): 10–13.

Young, Jeffrey T. *Economics as a Moral Science: The Political Economy of Adam Smith.* Cheltenham: Edward Elgar, 1997.

Young, Robert. *White Mythologies: Writing History and the West.* London: Routledge, 1990.

INDEX

acculturation, 83–84, 180, 182, 281n16
active principles, 58–60
Adam Smith Problem, 3–7, 33, 40, 44–45, 49–67, 75–78, 279n67, 279n83
Adam Smith Review, 170
Adam Smith's Discourse (Brown), 4, 226
Adam Smith's Marketplace of Life (Otteson), 50
ad hominem argumentation, 42, 137–46, 155–56, 160, 290n6
admiration, 134, 177–78, 297n44
Aeschines, 137
aesthetics, 48, 76, 89–90, 100–101, 134–39, 145, 175–79, 211–13, 216, 230
Africans, 85
After Virtue (MacIntyre), 9, 261
agents, 15–16, 18, 72–73, 133, 151–53, 228–31, 264. *See also* diversity; economics; morality; rationality; self, the
alethea, 235
alienation, 194
Allan, David, 172
altruism, 3, 26, 45, 49–53, 58–59, 278n64
Alvey, James E., 284n23, 299n16
anachronism, 8–9, 14, 84
Analytics (Aristotle), 118, 120
Anarchy, State, Utopia (Nozick), 225
anthropology, 26–27, 36, 146, 221, 241
apprenticeships, 186, 199–200, 216

approbation, 56–58, 62, 70–71, 111, 126, 142, 144
The Archaeology of Knowledge (Foucault), 240, 247, 250, 252–53, 255, 260
archeology, 241–52
architecture, 130–31
argumentation: ad hominem strategy and, 42, 137–46, 155–56, 160, 290n6; contemporary theory and, 154–66; definitions of, 109, 154; historical writing and, 222; logic and, 154–64; MacIntyre and, 161–63; prices and, 147–54; rhetoric and, 110, 114–15, 120–21, 131–36, 154, 249, 265, 295n42
Aristotle, 16, 69, 118–28, 130, 136–38, 146, 150–51, 156–61, 170, 228–29, 261
Armstrong, Louis, 167
Arrowood, Charles Flinn, 170
authenticity, 82, 136, 159–60, 257

Bacon, Francis, 222
Barry, Brian, 265–66
Becker, Gary, 54
Bellough, Bonnie and Vern, 173
Berlin, Isaiah, 228
bettering one's condition. *See* judgment; progress; rationality; self-interest
The Birth of the Clinic (Foucault), 250
Black, Charlie, 167